The
MAGIC
HOURS

The MAGIC HOURS

THE FILMS *and* HIDDEN LIFE *of* TERRENCE MALICK

JOHN BLEASDALE

UNIVERSITY PRESS OF KENTUCKY

Copyright © 2024 by The University Press of Kentucky

Scholarly publisher for the Commonwealth, serving Bellarmine University, Berea College, Centre College of Kentucky, Eastern Kentucky University, The Filson Historical Society, Georgetown College, Kentucky Historical Society, Kentucky State University, Morehead State University, Murray State University, Northern Kentucky University, Spalding University, Transylvania University, University of Kentucky, University of Louisville, University of Pikeville, and Western Kentucky University.
All rights reserved.

Editorial and Sales Offices: The University Press of Kentucky
663 South Limestone Street, Lexington, Kentucky 40508-4008
www.kentuckypress.com

Library of Congress Cataloging-in-Publication Data

Names: Bleasdale, John (Film critic), author.
Title: The magic hours : the films and hidden life of Terrence Malick / John Bleasdale.
Description: Lexington : The University Press of Kentucky, 2024. | Series: Screen classics | Includes bibliographical references and index.
Identifiers: LCCN 2024028937 | ISBN 9781985901186 (hardcover) | ISBN 9781985901193 (paperback) | ISBN 9781985901216 (pdf) | ISBN 9781985901223 (epub)
Subjects: LCSH: Malick, Terrence, 1943- | Motion picture producers and directors—United States—Biography.
Classification: LCC PN1998.3.M3388 B44 2024 | DDC 791.43023/3092 [B]—dc23/eng/20240702
LC record available at https://lccn.loc.gov/2024028937

This book is printed on acid-free paper meeting
the requirements of the American National Standard
for Permanence in Paper for Printed Library Materials.

Manufactured in the United States of America.

Member of the Association
of University Presses

To
Lidia, Alice, and Rosaleen
(In order of appearance)

The evening mist clothes the riverside with poetry, as with a veil, and the poor buildings lose themselves in the dim sky, and the tall chimneys become campanili, and the warehouses are palaces in the night, and the whole city hangs in the heavens, and fairy-land is before us.

—James McNeill Whistler,
"Mr Whistler's Ten O'Clock," 1885

Contents

Preface   xi

1. Beginnings (1943–1955)   1
2. Schooling (1955–1968)   14
3. Hollywood (1969–1971)   32
4. *Badlands* (1971–1973)   45
5. *Days of Heaven* (1973–1978)   70
6. Paris–Texas (1979–1995)   95
7. *The Thin Red Line* (1995–1998)   116
8. *The New World* (1999–2005)   137
9. *The Tree of Life* (2005–2011)   157
10. *To the Wonder* (2010–2011)   178
11. The "Weightless Trilogy" and *The Voyage of Time* (2010–2016)   192
12. *A Hidden Life* and *The Way of the Wind* (2015–2023)   212

Acknowledgments   233
Notes   235
Index   259

Illustrations follow page 94

Preface

"You've reached your destination," my phone assured me. I parked in the shade of a tree and double-checked my notes. Was this the right house? Smaller than others on the street, the bungalow with a tree in the front yard sat back from the road. A couple of movers were filling the back of a flatbed truck with furniture. A dusty Oldsmobile Delta 88 occupied the drive. I introduced myself to the men working, told them I was writing a book about a man who had grown up in the house. I mentioned his films, and they both recognized *The Thin Red Line*. They were pleasantly surprised by this bit of history. Could I take some pictures? They phoned the landlord, and I spoke with the owner. He told me that the house had not changed since Terrence Malick lived there in the 1950s. He said that the inside was a state but insisted that I go into the yard.

"Why?" I asked. "What's in the yard?"

"The Tree of Life," he said.

Sure enough, in the backyard, the garden was dominated by a huge oak. Near the trunk, one root stretched up into a head-level arch. A child's swing hung from the branch.

An ancient bloodhound plodded wearily toward me from the house, sniffed, and then returned. I took photographs and made a short video, with Lubezki-esque forward movement, then turned the camera upward to catch the glints of sunlight through the branches. It was the clichéd moment a biographer dreams of. Was this Rosebud? The key to everything? The tree was urging me to crane my neck and look up at the sky, but the sun was hot and I had no hat.

The removal men suggested good places for breakfast, and I sat on a metal chair on the porch, waiting for them to leave so I could photograph the house from the front without their truck in the way.

Preface

Terrence Malick lived in this house in Waco from 1952 until he left for St. Stephen's boarding school in 1955. Here he grew up, went to church, played out in the street, and argued with his father so frequently it partly motivated his move to St. Stephen's. At the time of this writing, Malick lives a fifteen-minute drive from St. Stephen's and is married to Alexandra Wallace-Brown, a woman he met at the school. It's his spiritual home, near Austin on the Colorado River, rather than the one-and-a-half-hour drive north on the I-35 to Waco.

And yet Waco is a special place, representing a move from innocence to experience that is reenacted in all his films and providing the setting for his most overtly autobiographical work, *The Tree of Life*. To this day, Malick's memories of the town are so intense and valuable to him that if he has to pass through it, he has someone else drive and covers his eyes with his hands so the changes won't spoil his memories.

A beginning is a precious thing.

A Note on the Text

To honor the privacy treasured by Terrence Malick, some of my sources would only speak on condition of anonymity, which I have respected throughout the following text.

1

Beginnings (1943-1955)

Terrence Malick is a filmmaker obsessed with beginnings. If we trace a life to the point when it all began, will we get the answer to why things are the way they are? In our origins, will we find the solution? A lost Eden, an original sin? It's an impulse that also drives biographers. How much do our own beginnings explain where we go? Who we are? Who we become?

Despite his refusal to talk about his life, Malick's films arc to the past with a consistency bordering on obsession. He might not want critics tapping his biographical roots to interpret his films, but his life provides a constant source of inspiration for most of them. In some—*Lanton Mills, Badlands*, and *Days of Heaven*—he appears on camera. In others—*The Tree of Life, To the Wonder, Knight of Cups*, and *Song to Song*—he appears as a character, via a proxy. In all of them, he leaves traces: in names, events, relationships, places, allusions, pets, themes, ideas, and private jokes.

But this goes further than biography. Malick's debut feature, *Badlands*, glances back to his small-town upbringing in the 1950s but also represents a generational beginning: the cultural birth of the American teenager. On a more political level, *Days of Heaven, The Thin Red Line*, and *The New World* portray formative events from American history: the Depression, entry into the Second World War, and the first colonial settlements in Jamestown. *The Tree of Life* is the most explicit melding of autobiography and the broader questions of origin. The film delves into the intimacies of a remembered childhood and lunges back to the big bang, inspired by the pain of grief.

Returning to beginnings: there's no simple route, no certain destination. We can't go home again, we are told; you can't step into the same river twice. The onion doesn't just have layers; it *is* layers. The family tree branches upward; its roots dig like fingers deep into the soil.

So where to begin?

THE MAGIC HOURS

Roughly 13.8 billion years ago, the entire universe was contained in a tiny dense point, which exploded—creating time and space. About 4.6 billion years ago, a shock wave from a nebula in a neighboring galaxy caused a star to form. A disk of orbiting material began to coalesce into planets. One hundred million years later, the earth formed a rocky crust encompassing a liquid magma core. At an early stage, a large planet-sized object struck the earth, and debris from the impact formed the moon. Volcanoes vented into the poisonous skies while acidic seas boiled below. The first signs of life flickered into being 3.5 billion years ago. It began in the seas, then on land. Dinosaurs reigned for 165 million years until a meteorite strike in the Gulf of Mexico caused the extinction of non-avian dinosaurs. Their disappearance allowed for the evolution of mammals. Two million years back, hominins began to appear in Africa, and about three hundred thousand years ago, the first *Homo sapiens* arrived. Five thousand years ago, the first writing systems were developed in Egypt, China, Mesopotamia, and Anatolia.[1]

Just beyond the eastern borders of Anatolia, around 2000 BCE, a small group of villages were settled. These grew together into the city of Urmia, Persia, in what is now Iran. The city occupies the high plains in the North near the Turkish border, close to what was once one of the largest saltwater lakes in the world (today catastrophically depleted because of climate change). Here, Terrence Malick's paternal grandfather, Abimelech Malick, was born on May 15, 1882, to Asmar (née John) and Jacob Malick. His family name derives from the title of Malik, which was used for the chiefs of the Assyrian tribes who lived in the mountains northwest of Urmia. The use of family names wasn't native to the Assyrians but became more common with the influence of missionaries. The Assyrian community in Urmia were Christians who spoke Syriac, a dialect of Aramaic, the language Jesus the Nazarene spoke.

In the early part of the nineteenth century, the city became a focus of missionaries from the United States and France ministering to a sizable Christian minority in an otherwise Muslim area. By the start of the First World War and due in part to forced migrations from the Ottoman Empire, just under a third of Urmia's population of thirty thousand was Assyrian. American Presbyterian, Russian Orthodox, and French Catholic Lazarist missions were established, preaching to the Assyrian and Armenian populations. Despite the support they gave to Assyrians, this also provoked hostility, marking the Assyrian Christian community as outsiders. As war approached, they were seen with suspicion as agents of Christian imperialism by the

Beginnings (1943–1955)

Muslims of the Ottoman Empire and Persia itself. In the tension preceding the First World War, many Assyrians moved to Urmia seeking escape from the violence of the authorities and their militias.

Before the violence reached genocidal proportions and led to a flood of Assyrian refugees, many young men were already leaving the region. The first Assyrians to arrive in the United States were sent by the missionaries to study before returning to Urmia to spread the gospel. But these pioneers also spread word about the wealth and opportunity to be had in the New World, prompting a flow of migrants hoping to make their fortune. Some returned to Urmia wealthy enough to buy land; others settled in the industrial heartlands of the US—New Jersey and Chicago, among others—and formed communities. Levels of immigration were such that the weekly newspaper *Kokhva*, published in Urmia between 1906 and 1917, had a regular column "The Rueful Emigrant" that regularly complained about the downside of émigré life: "The young Assyrians in U.S.A. have been very unlucky in using their talents and the skills they had in the old country, or developing them in America," a typical column reads, complaining that "trained teachers and priests" were making more money working in factories "as low-grade laborers."[2] But what else was there to do? One irate reader responded: "We're tired of reading about the ills of emigration. What is a college graduate in Urmia to do if he does not want to be a priest or a teacher?"[3]

Abimelech Malick was among the first wave of emigrants. At seventeen, he left Urmia, sailing on the *Daria* from Hamburg on July 20, 1899. Existing records present a dizzying number of variations on his name. Avimaly, Ayimelk, Armenag, and Abimelick are used, and Malick becomes Melick, Melech, or Malech. (For the sake of clarity, Abimelech will be used throughout this book.) Having worked and saved money, he soon applied for citizenship. A passport application dated May 11, 1905, states that he was living in New Jersey, gives his occupation as merchant, and describes him as short (five feet, three inches) with a low forehead and dark eyes, a straight nose, a regular mouth, a square chin, an oval face, and black hair. Settled in the US, Abimelech needed the passport to see to unfinished business at home.

Nanajohn Sargis was born on November 9, 1879. Her parents had come from Georgia, then part of the Russian Empire, and she spoke Georgian until the end of her life. Her father was killed when she was young. Family legend held that he was an outlaw or revolutionary, executed in the town square while his wife and children hid in the woodpile. Abimelech returned to Urmia in 1906 to marry Nanajohn. In 1908, Freydon Malick, their first son,

3

was born in Urmia. It is unlikely that Abimelech was there to witness this because in 1907 he returned to New Jersey with Nanajohn's fourteen-year-old brother, John Absalon Sargis.[4] Abimelech worked at the Singer sewing machine factory and rented rooms at First Street, Elizabethport, New Jersey, a ten-minute walk from his workplace.

In 1913, Nanajohn, Freydon, and Nanajohn's brother, John, sailed to the US and joined Abimelech in his new lodgings at 313 South Park, Elizabeth, Union, New Jersey. Nanajohn stayed home, and Abimelech now worked as a foreman at Singer, as a relatively skilled and well-paid worker. His 1917 draft card describes him as having a medium build, with hair now graying. Social gatherings with the small Assyrian community in Elizabeth provided an opportunity to speak their own language and share news from home.

And that news was grim. The family had escaped Urmia in the nick of time. On October 26, 1914, the eve of Turkey's entry into the brewing world conflict, Ottoman interior minister Talaat Pasha ordered Djevdet Bey, governor of Van Vilayet, to deport any Assyrians who lived near the Persian border to the west, limiting the number allowed in any given settlement to twenty, in an attempt to further suppress and destroy their culture, language, and traditional way of life. This was the start of what became known as Sayfo (literally translated as "sword"): the Assyrian genocide, a smaller-scale series of massacres than the better-known Armenian genocide.

With the beginning of the First World War, as the Ottomans attacked Assyrian villages near the border, many refugees fled to Urmia, where they were easily persuaded to support the Entente and the Russians in the growing conflict. However, in January 1915, with scant regard to the vulnerability of their recently recruited allies, the Russians pulled out of the area, leaving the Assyrian Christians to fend for themselves. Thousands sought refuge in the American Presbyterian and French Lazarist missions at Urmia, only to die of disease in cramped, filthy conditions. In the following months, the Assyrians of Urmia and occupied territories were subject to kidnapping, extortion, and mass killings. Hundreds were taken from the Lazarist mission, women were raped, and dozens of men were executed.[5] In May, the Ottomans retreated and abandoned the city. Those refugees who had managed to escape with the Russian forces returned to find family members injured or dead and, in some cases, entire villages wiped off the map.[6] With ethnic divisions systematically aroused and violence endemic, many fled the region entirely, and further arrivals in Elizabethtown and Chicago swelled the Assyrian diaspora.

Beginnings (1943–1955)

In America, news of the genocide was widespread. In England, the "Blue Book"—officially titled *The Treatment of Armenians in the Ottoman Empire*, by Viscount Bryce and Arnold J. Toynbee—devotes 100 of its 742 pages to the treatment of the Assyrians. Dr. Abraham Yohannan, part of the diaspora to land in the United States, wrote *The Death of a Nation* in 1916 to document the massacres suffered by the Assyrian community.[7] Relief organizations staged rescue operations and funneled money to missionaries on the ground.

In the community in Elizabeth, relief at having escaped was mixed with worry for those left behind. For the Malicks, attitudes toward their new country solidified. If a life were to be had, it was to be made here as Americans. This feeling of citizenship and belonging was compounded by the birth, on January 17, 1917, of another son, Emil Avimalg Malick, whose middle name was borrowed from one of the many spellings of his father's name. He was baptized ten days later at Elmora Street Presbyterian Church.

The 1920 census found them still in Elizabethtown, but Abimelech and his family were soon on the move, halfway across the country, to Chicago, another enclave of the Assyrian diaspora. Here, Abimelech got a job as an insurance salesman. They rented a house at 64 West Elm, in downtown. They also invested in the Liberty Lumber Company, a construction firm. A storm in 1927 destroyed a garage and truck shed belonging to the company, but two years later, a bigger storm ripped the heart out of the US economy as the financial crash on Wall Street sent shock waves across the country. Banks closed, businesses failed, and by 1930, both Abimelech and Nanajohn were named in legal proceedings against the Liberty Lumber Company, which finally forced it, like hundreds of businesses across the country, to declare bankruptcy.

They were back where they started, but now they had growing boys to feed and clothe. At this point, Emil was attending the Lake View High School, an imposing redbrick edifice with faux medieval gatehouses for porticoes. Here he flourished, captaining the fencing team and the rifle company and becoming chess club vice president and an ROTC (Reserve Officers' Training Corps) first lieutenant. An accomplished pianist and organist, he found an outlet for his love of music in the school orchestra. He was a high achiever, winning a gold pin from the Honor Society. His 1934 yearbook photograph shows a young man of calm self-assurance, with a dark complexion, long hair swept back, and a gaze of placid appraising confidence.

Another beginning. Irene Thompson was born on April 6, 1912. Her family hailed from Ireland via Canada. Her mother, Katherine "Kettie" (or

THE MAGIC HOURS

"Kitty") O'Brien, was born in 1889 in Tipperary, Ireland. Irene's father, John Thompson, eighteen years Katherine's senior, was born in Canada in 1871. Also with Irish parents, John was one of ten children, living on the family farm in Wallace Township, La Salle, Illinois. Irene was the second of four children born over a ten-year period from 1910 to 1920. These were big, close families, united by their Irish ancestry, farmwork, and the Catholic faith brought over from the old country. When her elder brother, John, married, Irene served as a witness.

Farms and farming appear again and again in Malick's films. In *Badlands*, the main character Kit (Martin Sheen) works briefly in a stockyard. *Days of Heaven* is set on a large farm in the midst of the wide-open prairies of the Panhandle. In *The Thin Red Line*, Private Witt recalls the haymaking of his youth as a moment of innocence. In *The New World*, Pocahontas (Q'orianka Kilcher) teaches her second husband, John Wolfe (Christian Bale), how to fertilize the soil using fish. Rachel McAdams's character in *To the Wonder* owns a ranch. In *A Hidden Life*, the Jägerstätter family (August Diehl and Valerie Pachner) live a bucolic existence on their farm in the Austrian Alps.

The Thompson farm couldn't be further away from the Jägerstätters' in terms of surroundings. As portrayed in *A Hidden Life*, the Jägerstätters' farm has a backdrop of sublimely dramatic Alpine mountains. (In reality, Sankt Radegund in Austria is in the midst of a fairly uncinematic countryside.) But the Thompson farm sat in the midst of flat fields stretching as far as the eye could see. Freezing winters gave way to scorching summers, and the rituals of farm life, the early mornings and hard work, were a reality from earliest childhood. The Irish farmers were relative newcomers, standing apart from the older generations of Scandinavian settlers. In *The Tree of Life* script, Mr. O'Brien tells his sons: "Your mother's from a farm family. Irish. They had people down from Chicago every weekend. That's why they never got the weeds out of their fields. The Norwegians would drive by and laugh!"[8] The Irish preferred playing dominoes and drinking to working the fields.

Irene attended the St. Xavier School for Girls, an imposing five-story building where she received instruction from the Sisters of Mercy nuns. "The nuns taught us there are two ways through life: the way of nature and the way of grace," says Mrs. O'Brien. "You have to choose which one you'll follow. Grace doesn't try to please itself. Accepts being slighted, forgotten, disliked. Accepts insults and injuries." The passive aggression of the Catholic faith shines through, funneled via the Thomas Aquinas–inspired dualism.

6

Beginnings (1943–1955)

Emil and Irene first met in Chicago, though when exactly is unclear. She was five years his senior. For both of them, the differences of their backgrounds were exciting. Irene's northern European descent contrasted to Emil's Middle Eastern roots. Hers was a pastoral upbringing, compared with his urban childhood in New Jersey and Chicago. She was settled on the land her family had farmed for a generation, whereas his father's geographical and social mobility, his striving toward greater respectability and financial security, hinted at a second-generation ambition to assimilate and succeed. But they also had a lot in common, not least an attachment to a religion that linked them to the countries of their immigrant parents. The family history also carried its weight of remembered suffering. Emil heard stories of the Assyrians and the genocide his family escaped. Likewise, the voyage from Ireland to Canada and from there to the United States included a fair share of hardship. Racial prejudice was also a factor, stronger against the more ethnically marked Emil, although the Irish were still an ethnicity barraged by crude stereotypes and negative press. Recall the local Norwegian farmers criticizing the Irish for the state of their fields and branding them as lazy.

Or maybe this next generation shucked it all off. Perhaps they were integrated to the point of "all-Americanism." Financially, as well as owning the farm, John was comfortable enough to employ a servant, and both the O'Briens and the Malicks could afford higher education for their offspring, although neither completed their degrees. Irene's mother, Kitty, had been a schoolteacher and imbued in her daughter the value of education, as well as the twin virtue of hard work. Though she never graduated, Irene studied at the University of Chicago, after which she worked as a stenographer for the Auto Supply Company. She lived on Blackstone Avenue in Chicago with a slightly older woman—Gladys Nuttall—as her roommate. The 1940 census finds Irene single at twenty-eight, working as a secretary. In *The Tree of Life*, Mrs. O'Brien boasts of knowing shorthand and typing two hundred words a minute.[9] She had ambitions to be a doctor, just as Mr. O'Brien longed to be a professional musician.

On leaving school, Emil enrolled in the Massachusetts Institute of Technology, appearing in the 1936 yearbook.[10] This was a remarkable achievement for a young man coming from a relatively impoverished background. If he had any sense of impostor syndrome, he did well to hide it: he competed on the varsity fencing team and was elected captain in 1938, specializing in the saber.[11] Although Emil was projected to graduate in 1939, he never did. He had to leave college to earn money to help his family, which was struggling. His brother wasn't much help, and his father had lost his job. At one point, the electricity company turned the lights out. Massachusetts Institute of Technology (MIT) was a luxury they couldn't afford, so Emil joined the US Army Air Force and studied at the Wright Aeronautical University before going to the Air Force Flying School at Randolph Field, Texas. He trained on a Consolidated Model 21—a biplane that was the standard trainer. Early in *The Tree of Life*, we see Mrs. O'Brien going up in a biplane, a ride given as a graduation present. Planes sweep from the sky in *Days of Heaven* as well, in the form of a flying circus that carries away the hopelessly adrift Bill.

Leaving the army air force, Emil went through different jobs, working at the Precision Scientific Company and then the Bendix Aviation Company, a corporation formed by Vincent Bendix in 1929, which specialized in motor parts for airplanes. He worked as a research and development engineer, but with the bombing of Pearl Harbor and the US entry into the war in 1941, Emil's life changed direction once more. He entered the navy as an officer, an ensign, serving initially in the Pacific theater, where he was an aviator, test-flying advanced airplanes. But it was soon apparent that his talents were better applied elsewhere. By 1942, Emil was working in the Power Plant Division of the Bureau of Aeronautics in Washington, DC. He won a personal commendation from the secretary of the navy, James Forrestal. This important wartime research was recognized by the highest authorities.

On June 26, 1942, Emil, aged twenty-five, and Irene, thirty, were married. In this unsettled period, Emil and Irene moved to Alexandria, Virginia, to be close to Emil's job. Despite his work and marital responsibilities, Emil continued to pursue his passion for music. By 1942, he was giving regular recitals, featuring a range of music from "the Londonderry Air to J.S. Bach," as one notice announces, the first choice a nod to his new wife's Irish roots. Emil's character—as shown by his yearbook entry—was that of a clubbable fellow, a joiner who quickly rose to a leadership position in any organization. He had a lifelong taste for publicity and, in stark contrast to his famous son, self-promotion. He liked to be part of the community, a model citizen, a leader.

On March 13, 1943, in San Francisco, Emil's father, Abimelech Malick, was struck by a car late one evening in a hit-and-run. He was left in the street to die, only to be discovered the next morning. He had been away for work, and his body was returned to Chicago for burial in the Elmwood Cemetery in Cook County. It was a terrible shock. Nanajohn felt alone, a widow with an

Beginnings (1943–1955)

imperfect grasp of English, and her sons were away. But with Emil's war work deemed essential, and with his own wife at home, he had barely enough time to console his mother and see to the formalities. On Abimelech's headstone, a photograph of him stares out over the word "Husband." He was fifty-nine years old.

But a new life was coming into the world. Irene was pregnant. As she came close to term, she returned home to Ottawa, Illinois, to have her baby. "She had no family there, so she came home to have Terry with her parents," Irene's sister-in-law Josephine Thompson recalls. On Tuesday, November 30, 1943, at the Ryburn-King Hospital in Ottawa, Illinois, Terrence Frederick Malick was born. The child's middle name came from his uncle Freydon, but mother and child didn't stay long with her family. Once able to travel, she returned to Alexandria.[12]

Emil wasn't present at the birth of his son. Mr. O'Brien claims that the navy forbade it, telling him "an officer had to be present at the laying of the keel of the ship but not at the launch"—a rather crude metaphor to express that a father's job is done at conception and that he doesn't need to be present at the birth. In *The Tree of Life*, Malick imagines the birth of Jack, and obliquely his own conception, "the laying of the keel." We also see the newborn baby, cleaned and pink, in the hands of his uniformed father, who gazes with wonder, suspended between adoration and scientific curiosity. It is a gaze mirrored by the camera's own. Has a baby ever been filmed with such focused adoration? Such fierce concentration? Malick looking at himself as a baby is a moment of sublime cinematic narcissism. Malick/Jack's childhood is one of a sunlit house, attention and affection from his mother, and a visit from his grandmother, Kitty (the name of Malick's own grandmother), played by Irish actor Fiona Shaw. From the child's point of view, we see the underside of tables, a leaf stirring in the yard, his first book. "Two alligators," he mutters as he plays with the wooden toy animals. A new cradle appears as if by magic. Lawrence Raymond Malick, Terrence's brother, was born in Washington, DC, on May 18, 1946. In the film, he is named RL, a mirror image of LR.

The war had ended triumphantly for the Allies, and postwar optimism reigned. After his release from the navy, Emil's engineering skills and scientific knowledge could be used to forge a peacetime career. It kept him traveling. Soon after Lawrence's birth, Emil got a job with Phillips Petroleum Company, and the family settled in Bartlesville, Oklahoma, where the company had its headquarters. The Malicks lived first on Nowata Road, near the

THE MAGIC HOURS

town cemetery, and then at 1533 Hillcrest Drive, Bartlesville. The home was spacious, with plenty of room for guests. Though Emil was busy with work, the young family made full use of their relatives, returning to Wallace County to spend time with Irene's parents on the farm and particularly Terry's beloved grandmother Kitty, who made Terry her favorite.[13] Christmas with his grandparents gave Terry his first experience of snow. A few miles away in Chicago, Emil's family also provided support and a presence in the lives of Terry and his brother. On June 6, 1948, the Malicks' last son, Christopher Barry Malick, was born. The local newspaper reports the Malicks' return home from Chicago, where they had introduced the newest member of the family to relatives.[14]

The Malicks were prominent citizens in Bartlesville, eagerly engaged in all sorts of activities. Irene joined the Child Guidance Club, and Emil resumed his organ recitals and gave regular educational talks on jet engines and their fuels. Irene hosted book clubs in her home. The family regularly attended St. Luke's Episcopal Church, where Emil was choirmaster and organist. Terry grew particularly close to his brother Larry.

In 1952, Emil earned a promotion to assistant manager of the Bluebonnet plant in McGregor, Texas. Here JATO—jet-assisted takeoff—was developed and refined. JATO comprised supplementary booster rockets that were fired during takeoff to assist heavily loaded aircraft. The new job meant a move to Waco, Texas. Terry was nine years old, and the move had a huge effect on his life. Texas is the state Malick most closely associates himself with, to the point that it is often given as his birthplace. He is regularly referred to as a Texan, and his accent has a distinctive Texan twang. This is also reflected in his films. Though *Badlands* is set in South Dakota and was filmed in Colorado, Holly Sargis (Sissy Spacek) has moved from Texas, and her Texan-accented voice-over narrates the story. *Days of Heaven*, *The Tree of Life*, and *Song to Song* are all set in Texas. In *The Tree of Life*, the central childhood section takes place in Waco. In the screenplay, a scene titled "Simpler Times" describes Malick's childhood environment: "The neighbors' yards are shaded by oak trees and surrounded by low hedges that the children have cut gaps through. The O'Brien house stands with five or six others on the last street in a subdivision. Its front is turned towards the other houses. Behind it lie the open woods: rolling hills of juniper, broken here and there by cow pastures."[15]

At this point, it's worth briefly considering Malick's later treatment of his upbringing. *The Tree of Life* portrays the coming-of-age of the eldest boy in a middle-class family, Jack. Growing from an innocent baby, Jack accrues

Beginnings (1943–1955)

layers of complexity and loss of innocence: "They stamp on snails, burn up wasps. They make a glory of their infamy and lies."[16] His arguments with his father deepen to an understanding of the man. If Mr. and Mrs. O'Brien are read as Emil and Irene, Irene as the embodiment of grace wins hands down. She can literally tempt the butterflies into her hands or fly around the garden in an image that merges Andrei Tarkovsky and Mary Poppins. Mrs. O'Brien reads Beatrix Potter and *The Jungle Book* to her boys and makes their lives rich and exciting. She is generous to others, giving water to prisoners they meet on the main street of town. She is full of hope and happiness—patient toward the boys, even indulging their rambunctiousness when their father is away, as if she is one of them: an older sister, a Wendy to their Lost Boys. However, as he grows older, Jack resents her passivity and the way it facilitates her husband's authoritarianism.

Mr. O'Brien, on the other hand, coincides closely with Emil. Like Emil, he served in the war as an officer; he has the same job, and his career is on the same upward trajectory, despite some frustrations. He applies for patents. He's frequently absent, a strict figure, coming between the boys and their mother, as well as insisting on rules at odds with their own free spirits. No door slamming, he orders, and he insists on being addressed as "sir." In this, he conforms absolutely to the norms of the time: the "father-knows-best" Eisenhower years. But Jack grows to dislike his father, not only for his bossiness, partly epitomized by his short back-and-sides haircut, but also for his endless pontification, his hypocrisy, his glad-handing of and rudeness toward strangers, and his flirtation with waitresses. His key gesture is the shoulder grip, at once affectionate and paternal but also controlling, only a squeeze away from violence.

Even his love of classical music—which drenches the movie so thoroughly it leaves only a few minutes for Alexandre Desplat's original score—is initially rejected by Jack, who vandalizes and scratches his records once his father is absent. Mr. O'Brien is a mass of contradictions, needy for physical affection and respect, financially unorthodox (gambling and attempting to skip on his taxes), cruel and full of rage, vulnerable and full of enthusiasms. Family meals are particularly trying: "Dinner is a nervous time. A symphony is playing on the record player. From time to time, Mr. O'Brien leaps up from the table to conduct a passage that has inspired him." In *Badlands*, when Kit burns Holly's family home, it's the piano he first douses with gasoline.

Terry's brothers (especially LR/RL in *The Tree of Life*) shared their father's affinity for and proficiency with music. Larry and Chris both became members of musical bands, and Larry went on to study music seriously, specifically the guitar, which is featured in a particularly moving scene in *The Tree of Life* when one afternoon the father and son casually improvise a piece for guitar and piano. Music becomes a language through which they truly communicate with each other. As Malick writes: "Their home is never more friendly and at peace than when [Mr. O'Brien] sits at the piano, playing Bach or Chopin."[17] Jack, by contrast, turns the pages of the music score for his father or listens but doesn't play. One major difference between Emil and Mr. O'Brien is their ethnicity. In photographs, Emil has a darker complexion, but rebaptized with his grandmother's Irish surname and played by Brad Pitt, Mr. O'Brien has nothing Middle Eastern about him and is solidly in the Anglo-American bracket, WASPish even.

In Waco as in Bartlesville, the Malicks quickly engaged once more in community activities, taking part in Episcopalian church socials. Their new house on 3814 MacArthur Drive, in a quiet affluent neighborhood, came with a large yard where the children could play and where the family Studebaker sedan could be parked. Today the house is virtually unchanged, as is the neighborhood. In the yard, a huge oak tree dominates. This idyllic scene was disrupted one day in May 1953. The morning was muggy and humid. The wind began to pick up, and a storm touched down that afternoon. Nine-year-old Terry and his mother and brothers crouched in the house, listening to the rain pounding outside, as a few miles away in downtown Waco a tornado a third of a mile wide tore through the downtown area, destroying buildings and killing people in its path. It was the deadliest tornado in Texas history, killing 114 people.[18]

In the wake of the tragic event, Emil, along with other local worthies, lent his support to a community outreach program designed to develop ideas for improving the city as it rebuilt. Emil was soon in charge of the section devoted to public works. His star continued to rise at work, and he secured a number of patents in his name. He gave speeches and recitals. He was soon the choirmaster at his church.

For his part, on his ninth birthday, the precocious Terry also got a mention in the *Waco Tribune-Herald*, revealing an early fascination with the universe. "Terry surprised his classmates at Lake Waco Elementary School by presenting a 43-page paper on the planets."[19] In *The Tree of Life* script, Jack says good night to his rock collection: "Apatite, chalcedony, azurite, obsidian."[20] This has the exactness of a real memory. Another mention in the newspaper came early the following year, when Terry told his classmates about a trip over the holiday season to Monterey, Mexico, with his family. But were these stories volunteered by young Terry, or was Emil supplying them to the local paper? Emil won the photography competition that October, placing first with a picture of a sleeping girl using her mother's purse as a pillow. Another of Emil's photographs, a group of boys climbing on a military display, earned him an additional fourth-place prize. Arming the turret with the seriousness of any eleven-year-old handling a piece of serious military hardware: Terry Malick.[21] Was Malick's later privacy a reaction to his father's oversharing? Even as a senior citizen, Emil occasionally telephoned the local newspaper, suggesting stories and sharing gossip, including news about his famous film director son. The Golden Bear, the top prize from the Berlin Film Festival, stood in pride of place on the family mantelpiece.[22]

The photography, the record player and classical music collection, the guitars and piano, the rock collection and the science projects, the mementos from his father's travels and the artwork, and the fully stocked library—the Malick house was full of exciting, interesting things. Culture and art mixed with science and civic duty, alongside his mother's Catholic and his father's Episcopalian faith. But there were to be further upheavals. In the theatrical version of *The Tree of Life*, the end of childhood comes with the closing of the plant and the family's transferal away from Waco, the house, and the neighborhood. The film is a portrait of a home and community, "a simpler time." At that age, our immediate surroundings slowly expand—until at some point they become the adult world and beyond.

In the extended edition, these moments are preceded by another imminent move. Jack has been failing at school. He is disruptive, and his behavior toward his father becomes increasingly aggressive and rebellious. At one point, the boy even contemplates killing his father by knocking out the jack holding the car under which his dad is working. Mr. and Mrs. O'Brien sit the boy down and explain that he is to be sent away to a boarding school—"only a hundred miles away." This is framed as an educational opportunity, but given what we have seen in the film, it is obviously motivated by Jack's problems with his father.

Terrence Malick was separated from his family at the age of twelve. He would never fully return.

2

Schooling (1955-1968)

In the fall of 1955, Terrence Malick left home for St. Stephen's Episcopal High School, a boarding school 110 miles from the family home in Waco. Part of the reason for sending Terry away was aspirational. He was a clever child with a keen curiosity and a love of reading and science. But the arguments between Terry and Emil had become too much. Here was an opportunity for him to learn about self-reliance and get out from under the shadow of his parents' influence into a structured environment. In contrast, Larry and Chris stayed at home and attended a local school. From the start, Terry was exceptional.

From twelve, Terry was separated from his family for most of the year. He lived in a new community that emphasized rules and encouraged intellectual curiosity. Lights-out at St. Stephen's was ten o'clock. Boys shared communal showers and rooms with swing doors that didn't lock. A proctor, a young man named Samuel Todd in Terry's case, slept in a neighboring room, enforcing discipline. Every evening, students attended chapel, and Sunday church was compulsory. Terry's class had thirty-two students. A canteen served lunch, but for dinner, students dressed in jacket and tie and sat at long tables, where food was brought by other students assigned to the task. The conversation was serious, and the food good.[1] The discipline and the hardship of the Texan heat led the students to nickname themselves the "Spartans," but St. Stephen's was also a liberal institution, the first coeducational boarding school in the United States. In 1960, the year before Terry graduated, it became the first boarding school in the South to integrate. Its founder, Bishop John E. Hines, was a leading crusader against racism and an active member of the civil rights movement whose work fighting apartheid in South Africa was later recognized by Archbishop Desmond Tutu. St. Stephen's reflected Hines's religiously inspired social activism.

Schooling (1955–1968)

Geographically, the school stands on an elevation, overlooking the wide bend in the Colorado River known to locals as Lake Austin. At the time Terry was there, Austin itself was a long car ride away down narrow winding lanes with names like Hill Billy Lane and Bunny Run. The sandstone buildings blended into the environment; none stood taller than the chapel, which was built from limestone quarried on campus.[2] When students wanted to get away from supervision, they hiked up to the Gulch, a deep canyon over which sycamores and cypress trees arched. The Hill—as students called the school—provided inspiration: "It was in Austin that I had the idea for *Days of Heaven*," Terry later said. "I found myself alone for a summer in the town I had left as a high school student. There were those green, undulating hills, and this very beautiful river, the Colorado. The place is inspired and inspiring."[3] A fellow student, Bill Krohn, agrees: "St. Stephen's was out in the middle of fucking nowhere, like the farm in that film."[4]

Terry took courses in performance arts and musical theater. In his freshman year, with something of his father's bravado, he took on the role of Malvolio, the would-be lover and arrogant fool, in *Twelfth Night*. Faculty members were willing to engage students in debate. Terry had a particular affinity for Ann Dewey Guerin, his drama teacher, whose tastes included Jean-Paul Sartre and who was married to the painter John Guerin. She was a serious taskmaster, not above adding her own blank verse to Shakespeare when she felt the bard lacking. Drama wasn't for time wasters, and Terry took to acting with enthusiasm. She also encouraged an interest in European cinema, as well as the work of Satyajit Ray.[5] Jim Melcherd, an English teacher, also had long conversations with the promising student.

Terry found academic demands relatively easy. Away from home, his delinquency was cured. The proctor found him an easy charge, but he was not above a prank. One day Terry caught an armadillo and walked it around the school grounds on a leash as his pet.[6] His classmates remember him as a hard worker who was happy to poke fun at himself, as can be seen from his yearbook picture, where he poses as Rodin's *Thinker*. He was nicknamed the Russian Bear because of his dark, bulky appearance.

In his first two years at the school, Terry played varsity football, excelling as both offensive lineman and defensive linebacker. Football camp started a week before school, and although St. Stephen's had a smaller pool to draw from than its competitors, they trained hard with a seriousness that saw them punching above their weight, led by the much-feared coach Mr. Glidewell, nicknamed Fat Dog. As a sixty-minute man, Terry was at the heart of the

THE MAGIC HOURS

game. He was even hospitalized with heat exhaustion after the opening game of the 1957 season.[7] His career progressed as a tackler, and he broke the school record for the most quarterback sacks. He was even nominated for Texas Football Player of the Year, no mean feat. By the end of his school football career, he featured regularly in the games as the heaviest (183 pounds) and most experienced player, an achievement he takes great pride in to this day.[8]

By 1956, the family home in Waco had been vacated. Following Emil's work, his parents and brothers had returned to the old house in Bartlesville, Oklahoma: 530 miles away from St. Stephen's. The separation between Terry and his family had gone beyond any distance that would allow for frequent weekend visits. But Terry was thriving at school. An English teacher, Bob Pickett, took students off campus, to the University of Texas or the old Varsity Theater in Austin, for screenings of Ingmar Bergman and François Truffaut films. After the screenings, back at Pickett's house, Malick was an eager participant in the discussions. Away from Emil's stifling enthusiasm, Terry's love of classical music flourished.

Malick also wrote for the school newspaper. An article penned in early 1961—"The Negro in Faulkner's Works"—survives; it is an intelligent and far-reaching study of Faulkner, citing a slew of his novels and short stories to describe his view of the Black man as "the victim and savior of Southern society." The extent to which eighteen-year-old Malick's own views can be discerned is limited as he restricts himself to describing rather than commenting on Faulkner, but his uncritical presentation shows a point of view that aligns with a progressive but white and southern view of race, entirely objectifying the suffering of Black people as a symbol from which white society can learn. The short story "Dry September," about a lynching, leads Terry to suggest that "one can hardly avoid comparing" the victim of the lynching "to Christ, for here in him is the noble acceptance of suffering for a greater purpose, that purpose being the salvation of human society." This is not uninterrogated: "The question that inevitably arises in the reader's mind is why the Negro alone has this capacity for sacrifice and endurance."[9] Faulkner's answer is that whites are too busy in "the whirl of commercialism," whereas the Black person's suffering "immerses him in the sublime emotion of the human spirit; it lays open to him the breadth and meaning of all existence." We shouldn't read too much into what is essentially juvenilia, to say nothing of Faulkner's racial politics, which have not aged well, to say the least. (James Baldwin wrote a damning analysis of the response to desegregation that Faulkner typified in

Schooling (1955–1968)

his essay "Faulkner and Desegregation," published in the *Partisan Review* in 1956.)[10] And yet the idea of suffering opening someone up to the "breadth and meaning" of existence emerges throughout Malick's work.

In 1957, Alexandra "Ecky" Wyatt-Brown arrived as an eighth-grade boarder at St. Stephen's. She was beautiful, glamorous, and full of life. She was born on March 7, 1942, in Sewanee, Tennessee, to Charles Wyatt-Brown, the son of an Episcopalian bishop in Harrisburg, Pennsylvania, who himself became a priest, and Mary Shepherd Quintard, the daughter of a colonel in the US Army, stationed at the time of Alexandra's birth in the Philippines.[11] Ecky was from storied, wealthy stock. Her great-grandfather, Alexander "Boss" Shepherd, the governor of the District of Columbia was nicknamed the "father of Washington." He was considered a progressive, even radical force. After a downturn in his political fortunes, Shepherd moved to Mexico and remade his fortune with a silver mine. After his death, his ashes were returned to Washington, DC, for internment.

Ecky was a year and a half older than Terry, but they started dating. In some ways, they were unlikely companions. His bulky good humor contrasted with her refinement and wit: he was gauche; she was gregarious. How long or how serious the relationship was is uncertain. Dating at St. Stephen's had a musical-chairs quality.[12] But the relationship would make a permanent impression on Terry.

The impact of St. Stephen's on Malick's life is impossible to overstate. Here, he first developed his passion for cinema. Here, he read of the Starkweather murders, which inspired his first film, *Badlands*. And the school's rural location and isolation directly inspired his second, *Days of Heaven*. Many of his fellow Spartans remained close friends for the rest of his life. Occasional references to Malick in the alumni newspaper, *Spartans*, don't mention his career as a film director; he is a Spartan first and foremost, going on vacation and attending reunions.[13]

However, St. Stephen's had a dark side, or, as one former pupil put it, "a split personality." There was the liberal curriculum and the mind-broadening embrace of culture, as well as the twice-daily visits to chapel and the strict discipline that led to a high number of expulsions. No doubt the emphasis on discipline was part of the appeal for Emil and Irene in choosing the school for their wayward son. And then there was the isolation. Friendships between students were intense, and relationships with the faculty were likewise focused. Along with Ann Guerin, Samuel Todd, and Jim Melcherd, another influential teacher was Chaplain James Lydell Tucker, a popular priest and

THE MAGIC HOURS

teacher who arrived in 1958 and served as a confidant for many students. Tucker ran the student lounge with its canteen and invited students to his house, where he lived with his wife and five children. A charismatic and popular teacher, "Friar Tuck" organized a boycott of local businesses to protest segregation and taught sex education in Senior Ethics.

There was, however, another side to the priest. In 1993, a former student informed the school that Tucker had sexually abused him. Rather than acting on the accusation, the school declined to investigate and shortly thereafter set up a scholarship in the chaplain's name. Other former students present at St. Stephen's between 1962 and 1968 also came forward with accusations. In 1968, Tucker had been moved to another parish, where again he worked with children, some of whom made similar accusations.[14] The allegations were not contested, and in February 2008, Tucker was finally defrocked.

Malick knew and liked Tucker, continuing a friendship with him well into adulthood.[15] There is no suggestion that Malick himself was a victim of abuse or had any knowledge of it, but it does reveal a darker aspect to school life. St. Stephen's provided a progressive approach to knowledge, but it was also a place where children living apart from their families vied for the attention of the friendly adults who made up the staff.

In Bartlesville, Malick's family continued their lives without Terry. His brothers progressed in school and played in bands. Larry was the most talented musically, excelling in classical guitar and dreaming of a career as a concert musician. Chris also played guitar, as well as piano and organ, in local bands. Irene volunteered at the hospital, and Emil claimed more patents for his inventions. Every Sunday, he conducted the choir and played the organ at St. Luke's Episcopal Church. They occasionally visited Terry, sometimes taking him out of school for a weekend. He rarely spoke of his family with classmates, though he confided that his upbringing had been strict.[16]

Far from missing home, Terry was increasingly happy to minimize the time he spent in Oklahoma. During the summer before his final year at St. Stephen's, Terry and a school friend decided to go up to the Panhandle of Texas and follow the wheat harvest, working in the fields as hired farmhands, driving trucks and operating farm machinery. The experience fed into the idea for *Days of Heaven*: "I had not liked working for harvest time, I have memories of the severe heat on those days, and the wheat, of the comings and goings in the fields, and of all the people I met that were mostly petty criminals on their way to Phoenix, Arizona or Las Vegas for the rest of the year."[17] During work breaks, he read Jack Kerouac's *The Subterraneans*, which he

18

Schooling (1955–1968)

found opaque.[18] Reality was a lot less romantic. On one occasion, Terry lost control of a combine harvester and tore through a barbed wire fence.[19]

In 1961, Malick graduated from high school as valedictorian. A Bartlesville newspaper relayed his achievements—no doubt proudly communicated by Emil. "Terrence had won first place scholastic standing in his class each year for the past four years and is senior class representative on the student council," the newspaper reports, adding that he had won eight varsity letters in basketball, football, and baseball.[20] In the school yearbook, he features throughout, as an active member of the sports teams, a proctor, and a member of the drama society, sporting a precocious but unembarrassed goatee. He delivered the senior address on June 1. But despite his pride, Emil wasn't happy with Terry's plans. Emil had in mind MIT and a career in oil that would follow in his footsteps. But Terry was his own man and wanted to major in philosophy at Harvard. Emil was furious. If Terry wanted to go to Harvard, he'd have to do it on his own dime. Emil wouldn't pay.[21]

Terry had broken away from his father and, to some extent, was also at a distance from his idealized mother. By that point, he had been living his own life for several years. His parents had primed him for a big world of ideas and beauty, books and movies, but St. Stephens had extended the possibilities, and now there was also a yearning for freedom and experience. Science and classical music were part of that, but there were other experiences to be had: adventures.

Throughout his life, Terry made fiercely loyal friends willing to support and sustain him. According to Todd, Kenneth Wagner, an older classmate, had come into an inheritance and decided to help pay for Terry's first year in Harvard.[22] If this was the case, it was a generous offer. There was rumored to be some money from a football scholarship, though Malick ended up not playing at Harvard.[23] It was a courageous step for him. MIT was a prestigious school, and science lay within the scope of Terry's many fascinations: he had won a chemistry prize as one of his many academic achievements. But going his own way was to be a defining characteristic of Terrence Malick's life. He knew what he wanted, and he pursued it regardless of family pressure.

Others close to the family dispute this narrative, insisting that Malick received financial support from his family throughout his academic career and supplemented it with his own hard work in the summer and part-time during the academic year. Regardless of the dispute with his father, the prospect of returning home was unappealing, so the summer after high school, Malick stayed in Texas and, once more, followed the harvests. He slept in

THE MAGIC HOURS

Greyhound stations and ate in cheap diners. There was work in a lumber-yard. Out in the world, among drifters, petty criminals, cowboys, and ranch-ers, Malick listened to the talk, the turns of phrase that hosted an unsuspected poetry, so different from the arid conformity of a middle-class household of church socials and school dances.[24]

Malick enrolled at Harvard in the fall of 1961. For the first year, he lived at Matthews Hall, a redbrick building built in 1872 in Harvard Yard. His first graded paper came back with a top mark and effusive praise from the profes-sor: "I've never seen such a good treatment of a difficult topic."[25] The momen-tum he had built up at St. Stephen's showed no sign of flagging, but small-town insecurities lingered. Keen to catch up intellectually, Malick read anything he'd missed, not only the classics but also children's books like *Winnie the Pooh*.[26] The main focus of his study—or his "concentration," in Harvard lingo—was philosophy, and in his professor Stanley L. Cavell, he found a sympathetic tutor whose interests aligned with his own and with whom he established a close relationship. At the time he met Malick, Cavell, though twenty years Malick's senior, was a relatively young professor. Cavell had been brought up in a Jewish family in Georgia, which in itself made for a cul-tural clash. Similar to Malick, Cavell had a musical family. His mother, an accomplished pianist, taught him music from an early age, and he was soon playing jazz saxophone in a band. Cavell held an eclectic range of interests, which included cinema, and he eventually published widely and influentially on the subject in books such as *The World Viewed* (1971) and *The Pursuits of Happiness* (1981). As well as being a hugely influential philosopher, Cavell also broke ground in applying philosophical ideas to art and film and used his own life experience in his work: "In philosophizing, I have to bring my own language and life into imagination."[27] In his later books, Cavell appraised his former student's work highly, thanking him in the acknowledgments.[28]

In the early 1960s, American philosophy was still in the throes of prag-matism and harbored a strong anti-European bias, resisting the more Euro-pean existentialism. Cavell rowed against this current with his interest in Ludwig Wittgenstein and, later, the high priest of postmodernism, Jacques Derrida. In American philosophy, he tended toward transcendentalists such as Henry David Thoreau and Ralph Waldo Emerson, reassessing them as serious thinkers rather than mere essayists. Malick's interest in Martin Hei-degger was especially encouraged by Cavell, even though the German phi-losopher was not a popular choice on most American campuses. Not only an existentialist, from 1933 Heidegger had also been a member of the Nazi

Party. A political anathema to most, he also had a nasty personal aspect. When his former patron and father figure, Edmund Husserl, was vilified by the Nazis as a Jew and banned from publishing in Germany, Heidegger stood by and himself benefited. Malick also read and was fascinated by Husserl, but he devoted his thesis to Heidegger, specifically his conflict with Husserl, siding with the student against the surrogate father.

In his most influential work, *Being and Time*, Heidegger rejects the Cartesian view of the human being as a subjective spectator of objects. Rather, subject and object are inseparable to Heidegger. He reformulated the German word for existence, "Dasein," to mean an entity (e.g., a person) who can exist in the world, "being open" or "being in the world," engaging in the world, through perceptions and concepts. Throughout Malick's cinema, characters find themselves fully apprehending themselves as part of the world and sometimes attempting to create their own worlds: Kit and Holly in their tree house retreat in *Badlands* or Private Witt in his Polynesian village in *The Thin Red Line*. But for Heidegger, this individualized perception of the world can also be a perception of nothingness, provoking an angst, a sense of alienation and solitude. Some of Malick's more recent films explore characters losing their grip on what they took to be defining notions of their world: love, faith, art.

Cavell encouraged Malick in his pursuit of Heidegger, later acknowledging that at the time of their meeting, Malick "had read and studied more Heidegger than I had."[29] Malick learned German and French specifically to read the original texts of philosophers who interested him, some of whose work had not yet been translated. His dedication paid off handsomely when he was named in the dean's list in the spring of 1962, allowing him to maintain his financial independence. A parental entente had been reached, as the news of Malick's academic achievements was reported in the Bartlesville *Examiner-Enterprise*. The *Chicago Tribune* the following year reported: "Proud grandmothers" received the news that Terrence Frederick Malick had once more won a John Harvard Scholarship, reserved for the top 5 percent of the year "in recognition of the highest distinction."[30] The newspaper notices continued to proudly proclaim Malick's high-flying academic career, fed by Emil's phone calls to the local news desk.

In his freshman year, Malick attended a class taught by Paul Tillich called the Self-Interpretation of Man in Western Thought. Tillich was a German professor of theology and an ordained Lutheran minister who had known and worked with Heidegger. One of the few non-Jewish academics to lose his

THE MAGIC HOURS

position as a direct result of the Nazis, Tillich emigrated with his family to the US in the 1930s to escape the increasingly hostile environment. In 1951, he published the first volume of his major work *Systematic Theology*, before following it the next year with *The Courage to Be*, which gained a wide readership. For Tillich, God is posited not as a higher being but as being itself, "the ground of being," as he calls it. Thus, simple existence is a participation in the divine. Politically, Tillich was a Christian socialist—hence the antipathy toward the Nazis—a position Malick was already familiar with from his conversations with Father Tucker at St. Stephen's. Father Quintana, played by Javier Bardem in *To the Wonder*, represents a clergyman attempting to play a social role among the marginalized of society. As it would be shown also in *A Hidden Life*, Christianity was an ethical and therefore political inspiration as well as a way of addressing the mystery of being.

It was in Tillich's class that Malick first met Jacob Brackman, a New Yorker who shared many of Malick's passions. At first the two were passing acquaintances, though they had mutual friends, including Cavell and Paul Tillich's assistant Paul Lee. It wasn't until the following year that Brackman and Malick became close, after a screening of Alain Resnais's masterpiece of cinematic surrealism *Last Year at Marienbad*. Brackman aspired to be a writer, working at the Harvard newspaper, the *Crimson*, as a critic and editor, and was already keyed into the counterculture, taking psychedelics and following the changes in the world of popular music.[31] Meanwhile, Paul Lee had started teaching at MIT and introduced Malick to the likes of Timothy Leary, Richard Alpert (later known as Ram Dass), Rolf von Eckartsberg, and Ralph Metzner, with whom Lee cofounded the *Psychedelic Review*.

In 1962, Malick moved from Matthews Hall to Adams House, a dormitory with a wild reputation. Stephen Most, a classmate who roomed next door, took immediately to Malick, sharing with him a sense of alienation from their families. When Most burned a painting his grandfather had given him in the fireplace, Malick delighted in the act of "adolescent rebelliousness."[32] When not studying, Malick saw films at the Brattle Theatre in Cambridge, where the French nouvelle vague was having an impact. When Most directed *The Exception and the Rule*, by Bertolt Brecht, Malick took a role along with his friend Rand Rosenblatt. Rosenblatt later became a prominent legal scholar. The play was performed at the Loeb Experimental Theater in February 1964. When one performance clashed with the Sonny Liston–Cassius Clay fight, Malick rushed backstage whenever he could to catch the fight's progress on the radio. One critic enjoyed his comic acting, though

Schooling (1955–1968)

expressing some doubt as to how intentional it was: "And Terry Malick inadvertently adds much-needed 'ah-so' humor as a kimono-clad, Ernie Kovacs–like innkeeper."[33]

For Malick, the 1960s counterculture was fascinating, but in the words of fellow student William Weld: "Terry spent most of his time drinking coffee and talking about Wittgenstein and Husserl."[34] Weld later became the governor of Massachusetts, and the two remained friends for life, as was the case with many of the friends Malick made throughout his academic years. Weld even appears briefly in *Badlands* and was one of many tapped to raise money for the film. Along with Brackman, Lee, and Weld, Malick also saw a lot of Cavell socially. It helped that the recently divorced professor was living in the same building as Malick, Adams House. Brackman joined them to shoot pool. Conversations were wide-ranging—from existentialism to classical music, art, and cinema—as they chatted for hours to the crack of pool balls and music on the radio in the background. In 1963, Malick's horizons were further broadened by the arrival and friendship of William Alfred, a teacher as well as a playwright and novelist. Alfred was a lifelong Catholic and a friend of the poets Elizabeth Bishop and Robert Lowell. Along with fascinating conversations, these friends provided a model for Malick's ambitions. Everyone seemed one friend away.

Malick spent some of his senior year in Europe, staying in Paris to improve his French and attending classes at the Sorbonne. During this stay, he met the philosopher Hannah Arendt. Sympathetic to Malick's work on Heidegger's philosophy, she gave him a letter of introduction to the philosopher, and so armed, Malick traveled to the Black Forest. Heidegger, living in the suburbs of Freiburg, struck Malick as kind and patient, despite the young American's limited grasp of German. They spoke about Heidegger's work and the possibility of translating his writing into English. There's an admirable headlong simplicity to Malick's approach. He was twenty-one years old and sitting in a room with the philosopher he most admired, discussing the philosopher's work in a language he'd expressly learned for the purpose.

After his graduation in 1965, Malick competed for and won a prestigious Rhodes scholarship. "He was unbelievably intelligent," fellow Rhodes scholar Curtis Hessler said. "He was renowned as probably the most brilliant student of philosophy at that time."[35] The scholarship gave Americans the opportunity for two years of study at Oxford University in England and came with an annuity of $2,500. Before leaving for England, Malick was introduced to John Womack Jr., a prior Rhodes scholar. The Oklahoma native, who had just

THE MAGIC HOURS

embarked on his own career as an assistant professor at Harvard, gave Terry advice about England and the English. He'd later become a respected historian of Latin America, publishing his dissertation and his book *Zapata and the Mexican Revolution*.[36] Womack met Malick at lunch in the dining hall at Harvard in the spring of 1966. "It was a New England spring, when everybody is happy that it's warm again," Womack recalls. Malick "was a wonderfully open and good-humored young man, kindly, modest, cheerful, eager to learn, and gentle. And as far as I could tell, being no philosopher, he was learned, very smart, and sharp on philosophical questions."[37] Jacob Brackman suggested that Malick write journalism to earn money while in England. At twenty-three, Malick was already well traveled and had proved himself—in meeting Heidegger via Arendt—adept at the alert hustle a journalist needs.

Along with his fellow Rhodes scholars, Malick crossed the Atlantic by ship and was soon installed at Magdalen College in Oxford to begin his master's degree in philosophy under the supervision of Gilbert Ryle. It was supposed to be a two-year course, but if the pragmatism of American philosophy was stifling, Ryle's brand of "ordinary language philosophy" was the complete opposite of Malick's own approach. Ryle was old school, strident, and dogmatic, far removed from the collegial friendship Malick enjoyed with Stanley Cavell. Fortunately, Malick's knack for making friends didn't fail him. American philosophy student and actor Andreas Teuber was also studying at Oxford. Teuber and Malick were soon close friends. Teuber had just appeared opposite Richard Burton and Elizabeth Taylor in the film version of *Doctor Faustus* (1967). The adaptation of Christopher Marlowe's most famous play was critically trashed and flopped commercially, but as Mephistopheles, Teuber received the best notices of a bad lot.[38] Influenced by Cavell, Teuber was coming to cinema from philosophy. He also knew about the intricacies and practicalities of making a film. For Malick, it was a glancing contact with someone who had actually made a film.

But Malick wasn't enjoying Oxford. Magdalen College was on beautiful grounds close to the river and the deer park, but having grown up in the heat of Texas, he found the cold and damp of England unpleasant, and his room didn't have central heating. He fed shillings into an electric bar heater and learned to type while wearing mittens.[39] Talking to the Brits was like talking underwater, Malick confided.[40] He took every opportunity to escape. In the winter, a heavily subsidized ski trip was organized to Switzerland, and Malick tagged along more for the opportunities to meet girls than to ski. Curtis Hessler says, "Terry was disinclined to ski and so we spent a lot of time in the bar,

Schooling (1955–1968)

doing après ski and hatching plots." One of Malick's plots involved a trip to Paris to meet up with the North Vietnamese peace envoys and try to get a story to sell to the magazines. "There were all kinds of rumors about pending negotiations with the Americans over the war. Terry had thought it through and he had contacts."[41]

Meanwhile in Oxford, Ryle had rejected his proposed thesis on the concept of "world in Kierkegaard, Heidegger, and Wittgenstein" as not philosophical enough. Malick was twenty-three years old. He could have changed his thesis or requested a more amenable tutor. But he was tiring of philosophy as a discipline. With no grounding in Plato and Aristotle, he felt as if he was coming in halfway through a conversation. And wasn't the whole point of Heidegger's thought "to be in the world" and not just stuck in a library?

And the world was calling. Following Jacob Brackman's suggestion, Malick began earning money as a stringer for *Newsweek*. He worked at New Zealand House in London and from there was sent all over the country on assignments. He went up to Glasgow to cover the Rangers-Celtic football match, the historical "Old Firm" game, the locus for bitter sectarian rivalry between Protestants and Catholics. An American with little knowledge of "soccer," Malick picked up what he could quickly and without fully comprehending it. Likewise, he immersed himself in the ritual and history of the British Parliament when sent to cover a debate in the House of Commons. He interviewed the pop singer Donovan and the new Miss World, Reita Faria. Faria was from Goa but had taken the crown as a representative of India. Eager for adventure, Malick asked her for a date and panicked when she agreed to dinner that evening. Malick booked a table at a restaurant, worried about what to talk about. Highly accomplished, Faria led the conversation. Many years later, the encounter served as inspiration for the character of a supermodel played by Freida Pinto in *Knight of Cups*.

Malick wrote up his stories and sent them to New York. He enjoyed the company of journalists. The bureau chief Kevin Buckley was only a few years older than Malick and was about to embark on a legendary stint as a war reporter in Vietnam. Malick stayed in Buckley's apartment while in London. As an academic, Malick had achieved a degree of success—the scholarship, his growing academic reputation. He had the support of a powerful and important philosopher in Cavell. But at Oxford and Harvard, he also encountered the narrow-mindedness of academia: its limits. His work at *Newsweek* whetted his appetite for adventure, and so, on returning to the US, he got a job in Miami working for *Life*. Although primarily a photo magazine, it

25

THE MAGIC HOURS

required copy to give the images context. For one assignment, Malick was sent with a photographer to Haiti, where he sat with François "Papa Doc" Duvalier, the bloody dictator who came to power in the later 1950s and ruled from Port-au-Prince with murderous violence. The dictator was aging, but this was a dangerous mission. From a drawer that also contained a revolver, he pulled some poetry he had written and handed it to Malick to ask his opinion.

In the fall of 1967, while on assignment for the *New Yorker*, Malick hitched a ride to Bolivia with female journalist Michèle Ray to cover the trial of Régis Debray, a French philosopher and associate of Ernesto "Che" Guevara who had traveled to Bolivia with the Cuban revolutionary. Debray had been taught in Paris by Louis Althusser before taking a teaching post at the University of Havana in postrevolutionary Cuba. Here he wrote an influential study of the tactics and strategies of revolutionary movements, titled *Revolution in the Revolution? Armed Struggle and Political Struggle in Latin America*, and became one of the most important European intellectuals of 1960s politics. He had been captured in Bolivia that April and was accused of being part of Guevara's guerrilla army, which was attempting to foment an uprising in the jungle. The Frenchman seemed a romantic figure to Malick: a philosopher who was literally a thousand miles from Gilbert Ryle.

Likewise, his traveling companion was an inspiration. Ray had modeled for Chanel before reinventing herself as a freelance journalist at the age of twenty-four. In 1966, she embedded herself in US forces and traveled throughout South Vietnam. With remarkable bravery, she pursued the story to the North, where she was captured by the Vietcong. She became sick, but she was liberated after a number of weeks. This ordeal and her reporting became the basis of her book *The Two Shores of Hell*. Her footage was included in the documentary *Far from Vietnam*, directed by, among others, Jean-Luc Godard and Agnès Varda. She later married Costa-Gavras, the director responsible for *Z* (1969) and *Missing* (1982). Malick was the neophyte beside this courageous veteran war journalist. She was intent on finding Che Guevara for an interview.

All this changed on their arrival on October 10, 1967, when news broke of Che's killing the day before. Che's group had been surrounded by Bolivian special forces at their encampment in the Yuro ravine. In the ensuing battle, Guevara had been shot twice before surrendering his pistol. He refused to be interrogated but spoke with the Bolivian soldiers. A Cuban-born Central Intelligence Agency (CIA) agent was on hand to photograph the captured

Schooling (1955–1968)

revolutionary and his diaries. Orders came from the Bolivian high command that "Senor" Guevara was to be "eliminated," and the radio broadcast that the Cuban-Argentinian revolutionary had already died in battle. Mario Terán had been in a fight with Guevara's unit several days earlier and was eager to avenge his fallen comrades. He volunteered to pull the trigger. Instructed not to shoot him in the face, Terán hit Guevara with two bursts of automatic fire. Guevara was thirty-nine years old.[42]

Undeterred, Malick and Ray tried to get as close as they could to where Guevara had died and to discover the circumstances surrounding his death. Near the village, they met a priest who had torn a comic strip from a newspaper and dipped it in Guevara's blood, offering it to the journalists like a relic. From the *New Yorker* came instructions to write up a long feature on the death of Guevara. The task of plumbing the complexities of Bolivian politics, guerrilla warfare, the charismatic figure of Che himself, and the murky circumstances surrounding his final days was daunting to the relatively inexperienced journalist, but it was also a plum of an assignment: an internationally important story to be written for one of the most prestigious magazines in America. It was a remarkable position to be in for a young man. He wanted to be in the world. Well, here he was.

Malick threw himself into the research energetically but soon found himself at a loss. His Spanish wasn't up to the task. He interviewed the people around Che, his sister and some of his comrades.[43] Pages piled up as Malick attempted to turn the assignment into something more personal, his own subjective impressions of the country. Deadlines passed, and still Malick hadn't filed anything. He began to suspect he wasn't suited to journalism. During interviews, he failed to take notes, believing it to be bad manners and trusting to his memory, but back in his hotel room, his recollection of the conversation "evaporated like a phantom in daylight," as he mused to a friend. The article unfinished, Malick returned to the United States in the spring and continued to write draft after draft. With Jacob Brackman, he coauthored a *New Yorker* "Notes and Comments" piece on the death of Martin Luther King Jr.[44] William Shawn, the editor of the *New Yorker*, had taken to Malick, who had been friends with Shawn's son Wallace at Harvard. For his part, Malick absorbed Shawn's gentlemanly manner. Brackman recalls: "It kind of smoothed Terry's own temperament, which, at the time, was a kind of 'hail-fellow-well-met' from Texas."[45]

Through Brackman, Malick also met a young woman, a singer-songwriter, called Carly Simon. Malick was smitten, and between him and Brackman,

27

Simon reports "a mild rivalry for my attention, though I suspect neither Jake nor Terry was as interested in me as they were in each other's company." Simon and Malick began dating, and Simon began to believe they were having an affair. The situation was complicated by Simon's relationship with Brackman, which was confused, even though Brackman had a girlfriend at the time. Simon was obviously very attracted to Malick, but it was an uneasy fit: "I listened attentively as he talked with the kind of fervid enthusiasm about Che that I secretly hoped he might have an iota of for me, too."[46]

Despite this enthusiasm, the Che article was abandoned, and Malick's career in journalism was over. Perhaps it's not surprising that the discipline of deadlines, word counts, and fact-checking—not to mention note-taking during interviews—was inimical to Malick, but this failure, on top of his abandonment of his academic career, meant another bust. A series of opportunities had somehow slipped by. The abandonment of his Oxford MPhil was justifiable, but his failure at journalism, with its opportunity for adventure, was more depressing.

In the fall of 1968, a tragedy sideswiped Terrence Malick. While he had been out in the world—at St. Stephen's, at Harvard, and now abroad—his brothers had grown up largely without him around. The brother closest to him, temperamentally and in age, had always been Larry. Inheriting his father's love of music, Larry was a successful guitarist. In high school, he played bass in groups in Bartlesville and performed classical guitar at public events. A popular student, he was dark and handsome, playing the Cary Grant role for the school production of *Arsenic and Old Lace*.[47] Larry and young Chris both completed their high school education in Bartlesville before heading to college. Larry studied at the University of Texas in Austin but, determined to master flamenco guitar, moved to Spain and enrolled at the Música en Compostela in the town of Santiago de Compostela in northern Spain, home of the shrine to Saint James and the destination of pilgrims. Here also, the maestro Andrés Segovia taught. Segovia was one of the greatest proponents of the classical guitar and the man chiefly responsible for promoting the instrument as worthy of concert halls and classical music programs. With a mission to spread his own particular technique, his teaching approach was rigid, and he could be a snob to other types of music, wary of anything he saw as bringing the instrument into disrepute. Accusations of bullying were rife. His most famous pupil, the Australian guitarist John Williams—who crossed over into popular fame with "Cavatina," as heard on the soundtrack to *The Deer Hunter* (1978)—complained

Schooling (1955–1968)

of his former teacher's stifling of creativity.[48] Segovia had a reputation for publicly dressing down students. While studying under him, Larry became depressed. During the summer of 1968, he intentionally injured his playing hand, breaking his own fingers. Rumor was he'd broken his hand with a hammer.

On September 8, 1968, he took his own life in a room in the Hotel Carlton, Alicante. It was on the opposite coast of Spain, over six hundred miles away from Compostela. Two days later, Emil and Irene received the telegram giving them the news of the death of their middle child.

The family's devastation is movingly portrayed in *The Tree of Life*. For Terrence Malick, the subject was too painful to broach among friends and even within the family. Emil flew to Spain to claim his son's body. The death certificate recorded the cause of Larry's death as "cardiac collapse caused by an embolism." This was discretion trumping accuracy. Larry's personal effects were given to his father. But Emil did not bring the body home. Instead, Larry was buried in the Almudena Cemetery in Madrid. The coroner's verdict allowed for burial in a Catholic graveyard.

The death came as a wake-up call to Malick. It was a trauma that affected him for the rest of his life. There was pain and guilt. Something irreversibly bad had happened. An innocence was lost. Life was not endless: the future not limitless. From then on, death stained the lens through which he saw life; the possibility of loss haunted every moment. In *The Tree of Life*—which begins with the anniversary of his brother's death—Jack tells his father on the phone: "I think about him every day." At home, behind closed doors, what comfort could the family give each other? Did Malick see that his remaining brother, Chris, was drinking too much? Did Emil blame himself for inspiring his son to enter the high-pressure world of concert music? They all wondered what more they could've done, what danger signs they could've seen. Was there an alternative world in which Larry survived?

As a stopgap, Malick returned to teaching, but without a graduate degree, this was never going to be a realistic career path. His reluctance to return to academia was to some extent mitigated by another consideration. The Vietnam War had been a background noise throughout his youth, but successive presidents had begun an apparently unstoppable escalation, and in 1965, the American ground war saw the deployment of thousands of young Americans to the conflict. By 1968, Malick felt the draft beginning to breathe down his neck.[49] While in England, he joined fellow Rhodes scholars in signing an open letter to former Rhodes scholar and now secretary of state Dean Rusk,

THE MAGIC HOURS

demanding the immediate cessation of bombing and the opening of negotiations with Ho Chi Minh. The war was everywhere, especially "on television," as Muhammad Ali pointedly quipped. It soaked into the culture, and audiences, despite their initial overwhelming support for military action, were beginning to see footage of violence and body bags on the nightly news. Malick's own political opposition was a matter of public record—the letter from London had been covered by newspapers in the US.

Malick accepted a temporary job at MIT—his father's alma mater—teaching a course on Heidegger to replace Professor Hubert Dreyfus, who was on sabbatical. Dreyfus—incidentally the inspiration for *Futurama*'s Professor Hubert Farnsworth—reports how at one point Malick stalled in the middle of a lecture on Heidegger. Malick "got to the part on anxiety and discovered he wasn't experiencing anxiety, so he couldn't talk about anything. He just stared off into space for about ten minutes, making the class and me as his auditor at that point very nervous. So, he gave up teaching that day and became a movie director."[50]

Whether the transition was really that immediate is debatable. It smacks too cleanly of the anecdote. Malick didn't regard himself as a good teacher, feeling that his students were smarter than he was.[51] But he had completed his translation of Heidegger's 1929 lecture "The Essence of Reasons" and submitted it to the Northwestern University Press, which agreed to publish it as a dual-language edition in 1969. It remains at the time of writing the only English translation of the work available. In the translator's introduction, Malick outlines the conflict between the elder Husserl and his junior Heidegger, as the teacher becomes aware that his former student's ideas are detaching themselves from his own worldview: a quite literal worldview, as the question concerns how the world's existence and being in the world relate to one another. Turning to his own understanding of Heidegger, Malick argues that because of the totalizing nature of Heidegger's philosophy, it is impossible to agree with him only in part: "One cannot agree with Heidegger 'on certain points' any more than one can, even in a manner of speaking, be insane or revolutionary on certain points."[52] The translator's task is doubly difficult not only in translating from the original German but also in understanding when Heidegger's concepts find German an inadequate language and newly modified terms—notably "Dasein"—are required. With an interesting twist, Malick valorizes this difficulty, asking, What is it to be wrong about Heidegger? "Our confusion," he writes, "is not anarchic; it has its own discipline."[53] It is also telling that Malick's approach to Heidegger was to

Schooling (1955–1968)

outline the conflict between generations, the student defying his mentor, the young man defying his father figure.

This introduction and English translation was to be Malick's only published contribution to academic philosophy. Could Malick have become an authority and popularizer of Heidegger in America? Or a philosopher in his own right? Malick doesn't think so. "I was a total failure as an academic," he told the journalist Joseph Gelmis in 1974. "I wasn't a philosophy teacher and I certainly wasn't a philosopher. I felt I was doing my students a disservice, which is a worse failure than being a career failure."[54] More importantly, he didn't enjoy it. Academia was narrow and didn't appreciate the kind of philosophy that was his main area of expertise. A token existentialist sat in each department, with little prospect of advancement. At the same time, the colleges were exploding with dissent and disruption. At MIT in March 1969, the Strike for Peace exploded, with Nobel laureate George Wald and then professor Noam Chomsky giving speeches on the dangers of militarism, of the war in Vietnam, and of the very existence of nuclear weapons. Classes were canceled and buildings occupied. But while at MIT, Malick was also thinking about something else. Fellow faculty member Ed Pincus had founded the film program, along with Richard Leacock, a legend in documentary filmmaking. Malick audited his course and began to write ideas for films. Jacob Brackman telephoned about a new school opening up in Los Angeles under the aegis of the American Film Institute. It was looking for candidates to teach how to make films.

Was Terry interested?

3

Hollywood (1969–1971)

Malick borrowed a tripod and a 16mm Canon Scoopic camera. Originally, he had two helpers: Andreas Teuber, a fellow Rhodes scholar who had once played opposite Richard Burton and Elizabeth Taylor, and Harvard friend John Womack Jr. The story was rudimentary: two deaf people try to rob a gas station. Malick and Teuber played the deaf people, and Womack was the gas station attendant. After a morning of filming, Womack decided he'd wasted enough time and returned to his office. Malick ushered Teuber into the car with a new story in mind. They needed a tall building. Driving toward Boston, Malick spotted the gasholder rising on the horizon. A stair spiraled around the outside to the top—easy enough to climb.

The film, *Loose Change*, told the story of an office worker who climbed tall buildings during his lunch break. "You climb the buildings, I'll do the filming," Malick told Teuber. He checked the light meter and set up the camera while Teuber began climbing. When Teuber looked down, his friend waved him higher and began filming.[1] The next day, they drove to the New England Telephone Tower.

Reviewing the footage, Malick realized there was no ending. He wrote a scene where the main character runs across an airport tarmac while change falls from his pockets. Hence the title *Loose Change*. They grabbed the equipment and drove to Logan Airport, where a security guard stopped them from getting onto the runway. Teuber ran down the highway close to the airport, spilling coins and desperately avoiding traffic. The film was a black-and-white 16mm short with postsynced sound. It was his application film for the first competition of the American Film Institute (AFI) for fellowships.

With aborted careers in academia and journalism, Malick needed a new direction. Jacob Brackman had written and published a long piece in the *New Yorker* on *The Graduate*.[2] It caught the eye of George Stevens Jr., the son of celebrated Hollywood director George Stevens, who had made such classics

Hollywood (1969–1971)

as *Shane* and *Giant*. As well as a powerful Hollywood presence, Stevens Jr. was a player in Washington, and he was in the process of setting up AFI, a body devoted to preserving America's film heritage and promoting artists of the future. As part of the Admission Committee, Brackman advised Malick to make a short film. Stevens was keen to recruit people from diverse walks of life, with experience outside the usual Hollywood mill. Malick fit the criteria perfectly. But was Malick interested in cinema?

His Harvard tutor Stanley Cavell took cinema seriously as a form of philosophical inquiry, both in its creation by filmmakers and in its reception by the audience. Since St. Stephen's, Malick had watched and talked about cinema sporadically. He had a taste for European cinema but was not a cinephile.[3] He liked James Dean. Elia Kazan's *America America* (1963) profoundly moved him, and he connected the story of immigration to that of his own grandparents' plight. It was at this point that he began to understand the role of the director, realizing Kazan had also directed *East of Eden* (1955).[4] To be a film director "seemed no less improbable a career than anything."[5]

The AFI Conservatory was settling into its Los Angeles home. In the heart of Beverly Hills, the sprawling fifty-five-room Greystone Mansion was built by Edward L. Doheny, the oil tycoon on whom Upton Sinclair based his character Daniel Plainview in the novel *Oil!* (1926). When Paul Thomas Anderson filmed an adaptation of the novel as *There Will Be Blood* (2007), he shot the climactic violence in the mansion's bowling alley. This fictional murder echoed the mansion's violent history. Doheny's son, Edward Doheny Jr., was killed in a murder-suicide that left Hugh Plunkett, his secretary, also dead. From the 1950s on, the mansion was regularly rented to movie studios. *Death Becomes Her* (1992), *The Last Tycoon* (1976), *The Big Lebowski* (1998), and *The Muppets* (2011) all shot scenes there.

Now Greystone housed the AFI Conservatory. By 1967, supported by the National Endowment for the Arts, the Motion Picture Association of America, and the Ford Foundation, AFI was fully established, with George Stevens Jr. in charge and Gregory Peck chairing the twenty-two-member Board of Trustees, which included Sidney Poitier, as vice-chairman, and the wunderkind Francis Ford Coppola. A new organization first announced by President Lyndon B. Johnson in 1965, AFI had a threefold task: to preserve film, to award and honor artists for outstanding achievement in cinema, and to train and educate the next generation of filmmakers. The conservatory was to realize that ultimate goal, joining established cinema courses provided by the likes of the University of Southern California, New York University, and the University of California, Los Angeles (UCLA).

Malick arrived for his interview at the mansion in a tie. Stevens was impressed. "Most of the fellows had a passing resemblance to 'Che' Guevara," Stevens remembers. Physically imposing—"built more like a linebacker than a professor of existential philosophy at MIT"—Malick had a wry sense of humor and was the most impressive candidate Stevens had seen.[6] Frank Daniel, the Czech screenwriter and the first dean of the conservatory, remembered Malick having a version of the screenplay for *Badlands* already written. On glancing through it, Daniel asked Malick, given that he'd already written his screenplay, what he hoped to learn at AFI. After a moment of contemplative silence, Malick smashed the flat of his hand down on the desk in front of him. "Karate!" he told the astonished dean. Despite the suit, this was still the Malick who had taken armadillos for a walk around the grounds of St. Stephen's. The Russian Bear. The "Thinker."

Malick was joining an eighteen-strong class that inaugural year. It was full of talented individuals, among them Paul Schrader—the future writer of *Taxi Driver* (1976) and *Raging Bull* (1980) and director of *Blue Collar* (1978) and *American Gigolo* (1980)—and cinematographer Caleb Deschanel, whose credits include *The Black Stallion* (1979) and *The Right Stuff* (1983). David Lynch joined in the second year and spent the following years filming his debut movie *Eraserhead* (1977) in the stables of Greystone, where he also slept. Yet in this pack of talented individuals, Malick stood out. "Terry was perhaps the most self-assured of the first class and was less preoccupied by sixties politics," Stevens recalls. "He had nothing to prove."[7]

Malick wasn't moving to LA alone. During his time in New York, he'd met and started dating Jill Jakes. Jill Bowman Jakes was born in Nashville on February 22, 1935. Her father was the owner of a foundry; her mother, a glamorous golf player. Having grown up in the South, she was keen to escape. "I left as soon as I could," she says.[8] After attending Vassar, Jakes worked as a production assistant for film director Arthur Penn. Her duties were largely administrative, but she enjoyed mixing with filmmakers. She went to Chicago with Penn and Warren Beatty to film *Mickey One* (1965), one of the first American films to strive for the energy of the French nouvelle vague. As Jakes told Penn's biographer Nat Segaloff: "Truffaut was there, Godard was there, and Leslie Caron, the actress having an affair with Warren at the time, was there. . . . She later became a very good friend of mine, and when I was living in Hollywoodland with Terry, she was living there with one of her husbands

Hollywood (1969–1971)

at the time [Michael Laughlin, the producer of *Two-Lane Blacktop*], and she had a little salon of talented people like Terry that she took up with."[9]

Jakes was clever, assertive and Malick's senior by eight years, and she was not pleased with his decision to move to California. In fact, she was furious. She referred to Hollywood as "Hollyweird": "I wasn't particularly drawn to going out with famous people." Despite her continuing friendship with Penn, she "couldn't stand to hear the word 'movies' anymore."[10] She had been studying law at New York University—generously paid for by the Penns—but she transferred to UCLA to be with Malick and complete her studies. They stayed for a while at George Segal's home, a big Spanish-style villa in Beverly Hills.

AFI courses combined practical experience with theoretical approaches. Malick enjoyed the practical aspects of filmmaking: the cameras, Moviolas, film processing, and sound.[11] He liked getting his hands dirty, as his inventor father did. Later in his career, Malick operated the camera himself and had no fear of studying the technology required to bring his vision to the screen, whether it was lenses, practical effects, or computer-generated imagery (CGI). He also paid close attention to the state of theatrical presentation, the quality of the screens and the projectors.

In addition to the practical instruction, legendary filmmakers as diverse as Harold Lloyd, Ingmar Bergman, Federico Fellini, and Billy Wilder came in to give seminars. A legend like John Ford might visit to offer ornery advice about filming westerns, while an American independent cinema guru, John Cassavetes, had an office in the building as filmmaker in residence. Screenings of films prompted debates that could be political, aesthetic, or technical. "Terry came in with probably the greatest sort of reputation and cachet because he had written a script and everybody recognized that he was a little bit above everybody else in terms of the experience that he had," Caleb Deschanel recalls.[12] The fellows ordered films to screen from the studio, organizing impromptu seasons of Howard Hawks and Alfred Hitchcock, three or four films a day, followed by discussions and hot chocolate.

Vitally, the conservatory created an informal network penetrating an industry where connections were everything. Malick interned with French composer Maurice Jarre, who was scoring *The Only Game in Town* (1970), George Stevens's final film, starring Elizabeth Taylor and Warren Beatty. He saw firsthand the recording and use of music in film. Malick recalled AFI in its inaugural year as a chaotic environment. The improvisational spirit was partly born of necessity and partly inspired by the revolution going on in society. Lecturers from the industry taught part of a course and then dropped out as their films were suddenly green-lit. There was no order. Malick sat in his first class on sensitometry, the study of light-sensitive film, its processing, and exposure's effect on contrast. He assiduously took notes, aware that others in the class seemed ahead of him. He learned to operate a Moviola: "You pick it up the way a child does. You hear words you don't know, and gradually you learn to imitate people."[13]

The legend of Terrence Malick as a recluse living and working outside the Hollywood mainstream doesn't match the man who arrived in California in the summer of 1969. As at St. Stephen's, Harvard, Oxford, *Newsweek*, and the *New Yorker*, Malick made powerful friends: his quiet intelligence and reserve belied a powerful charisma. His knack of inspiring lifelong devotion never faltered. George Stevens Jr. was so impressed by Malick that they became friends, and Stevens intervened at key moments throughout Malick's career. Stanley Cavell, William Shawn, and now Stevens provided inspiration and support intrinsic to Malick's success.

Stevens invited Malick and Jill Jakes to his house for dinner along with Arthur Penn on the evening of July 20, 1969. They spent the meal talking about the recent Chappaquiddick incident engulfing Teddy Kennedy. Stevens was a Kennedy loyalist and friend of the family. After dinner, the couples sat down in front of the television and watched Neil Armstrong step off the lunar landing craft and onto the surface of the moon.[14] Malick, the boy who once brought a forty-three-page presentation on the planets into school, felt like he was dreaming. What possibilities were opening up before him? A mere eight years since Kennedy had promised to put a man on the moon, Neil Armstrong was walking on the lunar surface.

A few weeks later, news of a different tenor spread through Hollywood when Sharon Tate and a group of her friends were murdered in a bungalow only a few miles away from where Malick was living in the Hollywood hills. Weeks of paranoia followed. Gun sales rocketed, and the open world of the 1960s began to creak shut. A man could land on the moon, or people could be murdered in their own homes in a grotesque act of violence. The possibilities were endless, and some of them were horrific.

This simmered in the background as Malick began working on a new film. There was a queue for the limited supply of equipment. Malick put his name down to get some kit early to make a short film. He wanted to work as soon as possible. His script—provisionally entitled "Lanton Mills: Cincinnatus Heiner of the West"—was ready, the subtitle referring to the pen name of the American poet Joaquin Miller. Classmate Caleb Deschanel was

Hollywood (1969–1971)

recruited as cinematographer: "It was a tongue-in-cheek film, and I liked that."[15] Malick recruited an impressive cast for what was essentially a student film. Clu Gulager and Harry Dean Stanton were to play Tilman and Lanton Mills, two cowboys lost in time, traveling from the prairies of the Wild West to contemporary Los Angeles to rob a bank. Lash LaRue also had a role. LaRue was a former western star of the 1940s and 1950s who had fallen on hard times and was living in his Cadillac and making money from public appearances. His luck worsened when his whips—the use of which gave him his name—were stolen from his trunk during the shoot. Gulager was an established TV star. Later, he'd sell a copy of Thomas Hardy's *Tess of the D'Urbervilles* to Sharon Tate (Margot Robbie) in Quentin Tarantino's *Once Upon a Time in Hollywood* (2019). Harry Dean Stanton, in an early stage of his career, was still being credited as Dean Stanton but had appeared in small speaking roles in a slew of big pictures, including *Cool Hand Luke* (1967), and his reputation as a character actor was growing. Warren Oates was following a similar path, and his latest film, Sam Peckinpah's *The Wild Bunch*, was a major release that summer. With its depiction of slow-motion violence and its nihilistic politics, Peckinpah's film represented part of the revolution sweeping the big screen and revitalizing old genres. It was an evolution of the revolution Arthur Penn had sparked with *Bonnie and Clyde.*

The day before filming began, Clu Gulager dropped out. Without a main actor, the film was in danger of being canceled altogether. Aware that it might be months before the equipment was again available, Malick decided to substitute Gulager himself in the role of Tilman. "Terry liked being in front of the camera too," Deschanel remembers. "There are a couple of scenes where he's really running about."[16]

A twelve-minute short, *Lanton Mills* is currently stored in the AFI archives in Los Angeles, and Malick refuses to allow anyone to see it beyond the faculty and fellows, citing technical inadequacies and general embarrassment. This reticence has the paradoxical effect of amplifying its importance. He's not the first director to wish his juvenilia hidden from sight. Stanley Kubrick disowned his first film, *Fear and Desire* (1952), and suppressed copies. Despite multiple requests, I was unable to see the film, but Theresa Schwartzman did have that opportunity and wrote a detailed account of it. She describes it as "marked by a goofy, sprawling, messy humor" that resided in "Malick's own touching performance as a slow-witted cowboy buffoon."[17] She notes that it's beautifully photographed, with an immediate importance given to the quality of the light. The offbeat dialogue anticipates the voice-overs of Holly in *Badlands* and Linda Manz in *Days of Heaven*. The eponymous lead, Lanton Mills, has the desert-dry deadpan Stanton excels at, whereas Malick's Tilman is an amiable buffoon. "You like a particular kinda joke?" he asks his partner at one point. "What kind?" "Well, you hear the one about the rabbit? This rabbit, see . . ." "Oh, yeah, yeah, yeah, I did hear that one." It's the banter Malick might have heard after the harvest between semesters.

Lanton and Tilman go to collect their boss, an older man with whom they intend to rob a bank. At his place, they meet a young man (Tony Bill, an actor turned producer), who appears wearing a sign with "deaf" written on it. Oates "sidles into his entrance" as John Sparks and confesses to having killed their boss.[18] He claims to be the slowest draw in the West: "slow on the draw and fast on the trigger." Lanton Mills shoots him, and there's a protracted death scene. After Sparks's death, Tilman suggests burying their things, including the picture of a Victorian lady; the burying of time capsules appears again in *Badlands* and *The Tree of Life*: "Somebody'll dig this up 100 years from now, they won't know any more about this lady than you or me. And we'll come back some day maybe and they won't be any different, but we will." Lanton refuses, and so Tilman does what he calls his Big Bird dance, arms pumping like a chicken as he jigs down a hill before wandering away, only to resume his jig.[19] This dance could be the reason Malick doesn't want the film seen.

Shifting to present-day Beverly Hills, the two bandits enter a bank, though Lanton is too quiet to announce the robbery. Tilman begins to scoop up the glossy brochures, believing them to be valuable. They finally manage to get a bag of petty cash from a teller, only for the alarm to be rung and the police to arrive, shooting Lanton and arresting Tilman. Lanton reveals he's from Texas as he lies dying. Asked why he tried to rob the bank, he says, "I always wanted to be a criminal, I guess, just not this big of one." It was a line that could easily have been spoken by Kit in *Badlands*. In fact, it was spoken by Charles Starkweather—the real-life murderer Kit was based on—upon his arrest, further proof that the Starkweather story was already on Malick's mind.[20] For this part of the film, streets were closed to allow filming, and one has to wonder at the pull of the student filmmaker. Warren Oates's biographer Susan Compo writes that the film is "a fevered dream filled with inscrutable lyricism, lovely camera work from Caleb Deschanel, and an appealing soundtrack credited to The Weasel Brothers. Oates who acted here with his

Hollywood (1969–1971)

entire being, might not have thought too much about what it all meant—'surprise me' is one of his lines—but he knew for certain he would work with the wunderkind Malick again in a heartbeat."[21]

The English director Alex Cox of *Repo Man* (1984) and *Sid and Nancy* (1986) also caught a glimpse of *Lanton Mills*: "I have a recollection of seeing it in Hollywood, back in the seventies. Harry Dean and Warren Oates stood around and improvised dialogue against a fence rail. There were trees in the background, and it was mostly a head-to-foot master shot. . . . Yet it inspired me! For if this film student could get Warren Oates and Harry Dean Stanton to act in his project, so could I! Oates had moved to Montana, so it was poor Harry whom I persecuted."[22] (Cox cast Stanton in his 1984 film *Repo Man*.)

Malick had made his first proper film, but he was also beginning to look outside AFI. Tony Bill, who played the deaf boy in *Lanton Mills*, and his partner, Vernon Zimmerman, had set themselves up as independent producers. Though by no means a star, Bill had a decent career as an actor, featuring in films such as *Come Blow Your Horn* (1963) with Frank Sinatra and *Ice Station Zebra* (1968) with Rock Hudson. Bill and his wife, Toni Gray, and Malick and Jill socialized frequently. Bill says: "It was love at first sight. One of the reasons we hit it off was that we were both pretty well-educated young men. It was rare to meet a kindred soul in the film world because it was such an old timers' world and it was also a pretty closed-off world. The idea of someone coming from the outside and becoming a writer, director, actor, functioning in the movie world was rare."[23] Bill and Malick talked movies, music, and literature.[24]

Bill introduced Malick to John Calley, the head of production at Warner Brothers, as a potential scriptwriter for an idea Bill pitched about big rig truckers. The low-budget biker movie *Easy Rider* (1969) was a surprise sensation, and the studios were on the lookout for new young voices. Warner Brothers paid Malick $5,000 to write the script. Malick found inspiration at the Palomino, the North Hollywood center for country music, also known as the Pal. Inspired by its own subculture in country music, truck drivers later had a brief vogue in cinema, with films like *Smokey and the Bandit* (1977) and *Convoy* (1978). Malick's script was called *Deadhead Miles*. Although fronting the money, Warner Brothers backed out of the project and allowed Bill to take it across the street to Paramount, who green-lit the film. For a first-time screenwriter, this kind of success would normally be undreamed of, but Malick had a tendency to start at the top—as a stringer for *Newsweek*,

THE MAGIC HOURS

then a writer for the *New Yorker*, a teacher at the Massachusetts Institute of Technology (MIT), and now a screenwriter for a studio picture.

Malick enjoyed scriptwriting. He was a quick writer with a good memory and a sensitive ear for dialogue. Plus, the pay was good: very good. Michael Laughlin, who was married to Jill's friend Leslie Caron, was producing a film called *Two-Lane Blacktop*. Director Monte Hellman was impressed with Rudy Wurlitzer's 1968 psychedelic novel, *Nog*, and asked him for a draft of the screenplay. Wurlitzer—whose family had introduced the jukebox to America— agreed but found himself stumped. He asked Malick to help out, and Malick provided a treatment, which Wurlitzer handed on to Hellman, before taking up the project again on his own. Along with *Two-Lane Blacktop*, which starred Warren Oates, Dennis Wilson, Laurie Bird, and James Taylor, Wurlitzer went on to write *Pat Garrett and Billy the Kid* (1973) for Sam Peckinpah and *Walker* (1987) for Alex Cox. Everybody knows everybody.

A few days after submitting his treatment for *Two-Lane Blacktop*, Malick received a phone call from a man named Mike Medavoy, asking if he had representation. Malick said no. Medavoy had read Malick's treatment upside down as the agent sat across the desk from Hellman (also Medavoy's client) and had been impressed by the originality of his approach, even upside down. "I thought, wow this was really good," says Medavoy.[25] And Medavoy had an eye for talent. Having started in the mail room of Universal Studios, he had become a powerful agent, currently at Creative Management Associates, where his client list included George Lucas, Steven Spielberg, Francis Ford Coppola, Robert Aldrich, and Hal Ashby. Actors such as Jane Fonda, Gene Wilder, and Donald Sutherland trusted him with their careers. Born into a Jewish family who had fled their native Ukraine, Medavoy grew up in Shanghai before he moved with his family for a time to Chile, learning how to be a survivor and an outsider as he gained his life skills. At twenty-three, he was living in Los Angeles and working at Universal. Medavoy spoke Russian and Spanish fluently. He was an eclectic, vital intellectual force, gifted with the cutthroat moxie that would propel him to the heights of the business. He was at the heart of what became known as New Hollywood, as well as counting filmmakers such as Michelangelo Antonioni and François Truffaut as personal friends.

But Malick was cautious at first, calling around to check Medavoy's credentials. He phoned Sandy Whitelaw, who was the number two guy at United Artists on the West Coast. Medavoy recalls: "I was actually staying at Sandy Whitelaw's house, so it was kind of a gas when I found out that Terry had

40

Hollywood (1969–1971)

called Sandy to find out about me." It is interesting to note that Malick, a neophyte filmmaker who had barely arrived in Los Angeles, was friends with Sandy Whitelaw, a senior studio executive. Medavoy signed Malick, and the two became friends, meeting to drink coffee and talk movies.[26] Most importantly, Medavoy was able to funnel high-paying rewrite work to Malick as well as representing original screenplays, which Malick was beginning to write on spec, hoping to use the leverage to get himself a directing job. The money helped support Malick and Jill as they continued their studies. Jill was deep into the process of becoming a lawyer, and Malick was at AFI in the morning, before heading to the studio in the afternoon to work on scripts. Sometimes, when he needed to concentrate, he'd drive to Death Valley, rent a room at a hotel, and spend days writing. In *Knight of Cups*, a screenwriter is introduced, wandering in the desert alone, a wilderness in which the sudden appearance of a car feels like a baffling apparition.[27]

Among his first jobs was a rewrite of *Drive, He Said* (1971), an adaptation of Jeremy Larner's novel, which was slated to be directed by Jack Nicholson. Malick worked a couple of days on a few pages and received no credit.[28] It's all but impossible to see if any of his work made it on-screen. The film premiered at the Cannes Film Festival in 1971, where it met with a virulently hostile reception, proving that the *Easy Rider* phenomenon wouldn't be easy to repeat.

The most intriguing rewrite job came via friend and mentor, film director Irvin Kershner. Kershner had made several films, including *The Luck of Ginger Coffey* (1964), starring Robert Shaw, and *A Fine Madness* (1966), a dated comedy with Sean Connery as a misogynistic writer.[29] The new script Kershner handed Malick was owned by Warner Brothers and written by Harry Julian and Rita Fink. It had received some rewrite work from John Milius, and now Warner Brothers wanted Kershner to take it on as his next directorial project. Kershner called in Malick. The film had originally been named "Deadly Target" but was now called *Dirty Harry*.

Malick's version differs significantly from the film eventually released, starring Clint Eastwood and directed by Don Seigel, though there are some through lines.[30] Harry Callaghan, a teacher, is introduced lecturing to a class of police officers about firearms, where he displays a meticulous knowledge of weaponry while at the same time demonstrating the destructive potential of the various guns by blasting holes in milk cartons, watermelons, and paint cans. This has more Milius to it in its salivating over firepower, but there's also a surreal element to the extremity of the demonstration that hints at Malick.

THE MAGIC HOURS

The choice of the iconic .44 Magnum handgun was Kershner's. A sniper is terrorizing the city, a vigilante shooting suspected criminals. Callaghan is getting something to eat from a food truck when the first murder is committed, which explains—rather incredibly—why he becomes attached to the case. He's given a partner, Bresser, a more conventional cop but as white bread as Callaghan, downplaying the racial angle that permeates the Eastwood/Siegel version. The rooftop vigil, the prevention of the suicide, and the cat-and-mouse phone chase are all present. The chase is scripted for an older actor: John Wayne was considered at one point. The dialogue also has an old-worldliness to it. Callaghan swears "Judas Priest" and calls someone a "pepperbelly," and one tough accuses the cop of "having the willies," to which Callaghan snaps back: "I don't want any trouble, but I don't have the willies." This is more *Lanton Mills* silliness than the terse delivery of Clint Eastwood's "Do you feel lucky, punk?" The killer Travis—who later became Scorpio—hires someone to beat him up, but the final confrontation is located in an abattoir, with Travis dying and falling onto a pile of bones while Harry is surrounded by sheep.

Although it's difficult to unpick Malick's contribution, his fingerprints can be detected. Harry's politics are casually racist, sexist, and as violently right-wing as they appear in the final film.[31] The prison system is "a revolving door," he says. But his backstory is whimsical: "I used to sell stolen melons on the crosstown highway, was fifteen before I found out the city paid the cops too." Harry Callaghan, melon thief. A bum tells Harry: "Give me a dollar and I'll give you a smile." These odd moments of dialogue and Harry's observation that the moon is 250,000 miles away sound like Malick. If the guns feel like Milius, the moon belongs to Malick.

Terry Malick, as the credit reads on the title page, also leaves a smattering of in-jokes throughout the screenplay. Medavoy gets name-checked as a cop, as does St. Stephen's classmate James Romberg, as one of the men shot in Harry's opening lecture. Throughout the script draft, names are penned in as casting ideas for the smaller roles, presumably by Kershner. *Jaws* screenwriter Carl Gottlieb and future *Big* director Penny Marshall both are allotted walk-on parts. Gottlieb was to play a detective interrogating a man working on his boat in the back garden surrounded by animals, like some latter-day Noah preparing for the flood. The name scribbled as a casting suggestion beside the man's first line is Terry Malick.

It's tempting to think this was how Malick was living in those months. Jill and Malick had bought a dog, a large hound named Abimelech after his grandfather, and their house had filled with assorted pets over the years. That old

Hollywood (1969–1971)

school friend name-checked as a dead cop in the *Dirty Harry* script, Jim Romberg, attending a ceramics course up the coast, came down to visit. Romberg found his old Spartan schoolfriend relaxed, playing on a touch football team. They went out to get hamburgers and talked about the old days, Malick driving his Volkswagen Bus, a vehicle that looks like the 1960s in vehicular form.[32] Fellow Rhodes scholar Curt Hessler also arrived to attend law school, and Malick offered to squire him around the Hollywood party scene and get him a screenwriting job. Remarkably, Hessler was hired by Christian Marquand, the director of the rightly maligned *Candy* (1968), to write a screenplay.[33]

By the fall, *Deadhead Miles* was moving into production. Alan Arkin was cast to play Cooper, the truck driver, and Peter Bart at Paramount had green-lit the film despite some reservations about the script, which he found "fuzzy." Bart called Malick in and asked him to explain the plot. Malick talked for ten minutes, but by the end of it, Bart was even more confused than he had been to begin with: "Not only did I not understand his script, I didn't even understand his understanding of his script. It wasn't just that he talked in abstractions: Terry Malick, I realized, was a living abstraction."[34]

Meanwhile, Irvin Kershner was in the full throes of preproduction on *Dirty Harry*. Locations were scouted in San Francisco, and both Marlon Brando and Steve McQueen were separately sounded out to play the lead after John Wayne had turned down the original draft as too violent, a move he later regretted and tried to rectify with his own tough-guy cop in *McQ* (1974). Malick, a great admirer of Brando's 1961 western, *One-Eyed Jacks*, was sent to see the actor and talk through the screenplay. He found the actor easily distracted and so got his attention with a card trick. Both Brando and McQueen were ready to go forward, leaving Kershner embarrassed at having to choose between the two, but just then Kershner was horrified to learn that the studio had made the deal with Clint Eastwood after a chance meeting at a barbecue. Eastwood preferred the earlier draft of the screenplay. Kershner was off the picture as director, as was Malick, though the financial compensation proved significant.[35] Milius maintained that both he and Malick should have received full credit on the finished film: "You know who else did a draft after me and probably should have gotten credit? Terry Malick."[36] When John Milius was hired once more to write the sequel *Magnum Force*, he took the concept of the vigilante killer from Malick's version of the script and turned it into a group of rogue police officers.

As Christmas approached, Jill Jakes and Malick flew to New York for a special occasion. They were married on December 29, 1970, at the Chapel of the Good Shepherd in the General Theological Seminary on Ninth Avenue. Malick had befriended the Penns as well, and they showed their support of Jill by providing the couple with a venue for their reception in the Penns' apartment.[37] In a photograph of the wedding, Malick is wearing a formal tailcoat and Jill is in a loose white gown. The reception was held at the Sign of the Duck restaurant on the Upper East Side. Guests included old school and university friends. Harvard friend Tony Hiss attended with his father, Alger Hiss, the Harvard-educated diplomat who had been accused of espionage and served a prison sentence for perjury. Even at his wedding, Malick was brushing with controversial historical figures.

As 1970 gave way to 1971, Malick was newly wed and secure on the West Coast, where he had successfully carved out a niche for himself. He had a wide circle of friends in Los Angeles and was making money writing, and more frequently rewriting, scripts. He was more than halfway through his master's at AFI. He'd made a short film with *Lanton Mills*, and *Deadhead Miles* was about to go into production from a screenplay for which he was receiving sole credit. He had a powerful agent in Mike Medavoy and patrons in Arthur Penn, George Stevens Jr., and Irvin Kershner. In the second year at AFI, a new classmate, David Lynch, had arrived and begun his marathon seven-year shoot of *Eraserhead*. But if Malick was making friends, he was also making some enemies. Pauline Kael was a skeptic of the conservatory's mission. Was filmmaking really something teachable? Stevens asked his two most promising students, Malick and Lynch, to meet Kael, hoping to make a favorable impression for the AFI. According to Stevens, Kael seemed like a woman on a mission. Her questions were challenging, and she showed impatience, pushing back on the answers Stevens and his students gave. Malick spoke of the experience in positive terms, but Kael expressed skepticism and questioned him. When Kael reviewed Malick's first film negatively—in comparison to the untutored Steven Spielberg—Stevens wondered: "Perhaps Terry had fallen on his sword that afternoon with Pauline Kael."[38]

Malick had also seen how precarious a position the writer in Hollywood occupied. All your hard work could be thrown out at the whim of a star or a studio executive because of one barbecue you didn't attend. The money was good, but when had that ever been the motivating factor for Malick? In his conversations with Medavoy and Kershner, he began to understand that if he wanted to take film seriously as an artistic endeavor, then he would have to take control.

And the only way of doing that was to be in charge. To be a director.

4

Badlands (1971-1973)

Thirteen-year-old Caril Ann Fugate had been dating Charlie Starkweather for two years, but she was done. Five years her senior, he was too old for her, her mother, Velda, said. Worse still, the boy was Trouble, with a capital *T*. Born in the large-for-Nebraska city of Lincoln, Charlie dropped out of school and worked a line of dead-end jobs, quitting or getting fired as the prairie wind blew. He finally ended up as a garbageman. His penchant for mischief wore his charm thin. But as bad as Charlie's reputation seemed, reality was much worse than anyone suspected. Charlie Starkweather wasn't just no good: Charlie was a psychopathic murderer.

He first drew blood on Christmas in 1957 when he got into an argument with a twenty-one-year-old gas station attendant, Robert Colvert. Charlie wanted to buy a cuddly toy on credit, and Colvert said no. Charlie went back a couple of times to see Colvert, fuming over the altercation. He had entertained the notion of robbing the gas station for some time. Finally, he went back with his shotgun, robbed the station, and got his cuddly toy. Afterward, he drove Colvert out to the countryside, where he shot him. Charlie reloaded the shotgun and shot him in the head.

Local police were stumped. No witnesses. No clues. No trail. Charlie had gotten away with murder.

If Charlie wasn't going to take no for an answer when it came to a cuddly toy, he was hardly going to do so when it came to his girlfriend. He decided the problem lay with Velda and Caril's stepfather, Marion. On January 21, with the paint on 1958 still wet and Robert Colvert barely a month dead, Charlie went to her house in the suburbs of Lincoln to have it out with her people. Caril was at school. Charlie's version of events had him arguing with Velda and Marion, who then physically attacked him, forcing him to kill them in self-defense. This was a line he gave with almost all his murders. There'd be an argument; the victims would attack Charlie, and

THE MAGIC HOURS

Charlie would defend himself. It always ended with the victims dead, so there was no one to contradict his version of events. However, we do know that midway through this argument, Charlie left the house, went to the local store, and used a pay phone to tell Marion's employers that she was sick and wouldn't be at work for a few days. Then Charlie returned to the house, and the killings took place. Charlie shot and stabbed Caril's mother and stepfather dead and then stabbed her two-year-old sister, Betty, before beating her to death with the butt of his rifle. He hid the bodies of Velda and Marion in the chicken hutch out back and slung Betty into the outhouse.

When Caril came home from school, she found Charlie alone. He told her that her family was being held hostage by a friend and that she had to do what he said or he would have them killed. (Later, Charlie claimed that she had participated in the murders.) For six days, Charlie and Caril lived in the house, turning visitors away with a lie about the family having the flu. Caril wanted to alert the visitors, but Charlie was standing beside her, just out of sight, with a gun ready. They watched *The Thin Man* (1934), with William Powell and Myrna Loy, and an Abbott and Costello movie on television. Eventually, neighbors and friends grew suspicious and called the police. Caril and Charlie fled Lincoln to the small town of Bennet, about thirty minutes away by car. Here an acquaintance of Charlie's, August Meyer, owned a farm. The farm was down an unpaved road, and their car got stuck in the mud. August saw them and was taking them to get horses to help pull it out when Charlie suddenly shot the seventy-year-old man in the back with the shotgun. To Caril's horror, he then beat August's dog to death with the rifle, just as he had beaten Betty a week earlier.

Charlie somehow managed to extricate the car from the mud and returned with Caril to Lincoln to get the car serviced and find something to eat. Having witnessed August's murder, Caril was too frightened to make any attempt to alert people or escape. She still believed her family was alive somewhere but now knew for sure that Charlie was a stone-cold killer. As they were returning to Bennet, the car once more got stuck in the mud. A couple of teenagers—Robert Jensen and Carol King—stopped to give them a lift, and Charlie kidnapped them at gunpoint and drove them back to a storm cellar near Meyer's farm. Here Charlie murdered Jensen and tried to rape King before becoming frustrated and murdering her also. (He later claimed that Caril had shot King.) Having stolen King's car, Caril and Charlie slept in it before returning once more to Lincoln. There, they broke into a house, and

Badlands (1971–1973)

Charlie stabbed the maid Lillian Fencl to death. Charlie also killed the family dog. When Mrs. Clara Ward, the homeowner, returned, she was stabbed to death. (Later, Charlie claimed that Caril killed her.) Lauer Ward returned home that evening, and Charlie shot and killed him. Charlie then looted valuables and stole the family Packard.

A manhunt was launched, with Governor Victor Emanuel Anderson calling in the Nebraska National Guard. Houses were searched block by block. But Caril and Charlie had fled.

Merle Collison, a salesman, was taking a nap in his Buick just outside Douglas, Wyoming. He awoke to see Charlie peering in at him. As he began to get out of the car, Charlie shot him. (Once more according to Charlie at his trial, Caril put a gun to the man's head and pulled the trigger.) "She's the most trigger-happy person I've ever met," he told the court. But Charlie stalled the car, and when a passing motorist stopped to offer assistance, Charlie began to shout, brandishing the gun. Natrona County sheriff's deputy William Romer witnessed the scene as he drove past. When he stopped to investigate, Caril made a dash for it, running toward him, yelling: "It's Starkweather! He's going to kill me!"

Charlie jumped back in the car and sped off as fast as the car would go, with the police tearing after him. It was only when a bullet shattered Charlie's windscreen, cutting his face, that he stopped and surrendered. Both he and Caril were arrested and separately extradited back to Lincoln to face trial. Charlie admitted to most of the killings but also declared that Caril was a willing participant and committed some of the murders. Caril assumed she was being treated as a victim. She was kidnapped, and her family murdered, a fact she only now discovered. But the police charged her as an accomplice. It didn't help that she admitted holding a shotgun on Robert Jensen but denied any further involvement. The jury was unconvinced by her protestations and believed the prosecutor's argument that, had she wanted to, she had had ample opportunity to escape.

Charlie was found guilty of the murder of Robert Jensen—the only murder he was charged with—and sentenced to death. On June 25, 1959, at the Nebraska State Penitentiary, only a few miles from where the murders had been committed, four minutes after midnight without last words or remorse, Charles Starkweather died in the electric chair. About his murders, he had told a psychologist: "If you pull the chain on a toilet, you can't blame it for flushing, can you?"

Caril Ann Fugate was sentenced to life imprisonment.[1]

THE MAGIC HOURS

The killing spree, the manhunt and arrest, and the trial and execution created a media frenzy. At the time, Terrence Malick was a student at St. Stephen's. "As a kid, I was fascinated by the case," Malick said. "I grew up in Texas and Oklahoma, and you couldn't get away from the story."[2] Brought up in a small town, he was the same age as Caril Ann Fugate, younger by just a few months. Here was a radical image of escape from family. It was appalling and horrific, certainly, but wasn't there also a frisson of excitement in the idea of lighting out for the territories in a rich man's stolen Packard? The stifling conformity of family life and school rules in 1950s America pitted against outlaw freedom and those wide-open spaces. Freedom to go where you will. Freedom from any sense of moral constraint. Later, would he come to recognize Charlie as a corrupted version of Heidegger's "Dasein"?

In 1970, as Malick was working on the violent thriller *Dirty Harry*, the Manson trial was also unfolding, laying out an altogether different but no less brutal expression of murderous nihilistic freedom. The Tate-LaBianca murders the previous summer were met with horror by America and particularly by the Angelino film community of which Malick and Jill Jakes were a part. Model and actor Sharon Tate epitomized the beautiful people of the 1960s and the Summer of Love. Married to Roman Polanski and eight months pregnant with his child, Tate was also intrinsically linked to the New Hollywood and the influx of European influences on the aesthetics and storytelling of American cinema. John Cassavetes—whom Malick knew from AFI—starred in Polanski's *Rosemary's Baby* (1968), which with its plot of Satanism foreshadowed the "witchiness" of the killings.

Along with Tate, the victims included heiress Abigail Folger and her lover, Voytek Frykowski, as well as celebrity hairstylist Jay Sebring. If such rich and successful people could be killed, anybody could. The night after the murders on Cielo Drive, Manson and his crew—Tex Watson, Patricia Krenwinkel, Leslie Van Houten, Susan Atkins, Clem Grogan, and Linda Kasabian—drove to 3301 Waverly Drive, the home of Leno and Rosemary LaBianca. The middle-aged couple were tied up and murdered. The word "war" was carved on their bodies, and the words "Rise" and "Helter Skelter" were written on the walls and icebox in their blood. The paranoia and media frenzy were reminiscent of the Starkweather-Fugate case of Malick's youth. Here was a story waiting to be told, about a loss of innocence, young women caught in the whirlpool of an older man's psychotic charisma. As Starkweather's murders darkened the end of the 1950s, so Manson's would cast a shadow over the 1960s. It was a violence that Malick recognized from his childhood, as he

48

Badlands (1971–1973)

told Michel Ciment: "I was raised in a violent environment in Texas. What struck me was how violence erupted and ended before you really had time to understand what was happening. Take, for instance, Lee Harvey Oswald's murder by Ruby: it took place in a flash."[3]

Meanwhile, scriptwriting was proving lucrative. *Deadhead Miles* filmed in January 1971. The director, Vernon Zimmerman, used a lot of improvisation, and the fuzziness of the plot—which had already been noted by Paramount executive Peter Bart—was becoming a problem for the production. There was a listlessness to the rushes that pushed Paramount to agitate for a change of personnel at the helm, but Tony Bill resisted taking over himself: "I made the two biggest mistakes a producer can make on my first film. One, I hired the wrong director, and two, I didn't fire him."[4] He regretted not giving Malick the director's chair. And yet the film has its charms, with its focus on a blue-collar oddball, played with charisma by Alan Arkin, and the story has its own cussed vision. It glories in a regional Americana of folktales, outlaws, and eccentrics. But Paramount buried it before granting it a release a year later, in January 1972. Malick has only talked about the film in terms of how long he worked on the script and how he used the money, but the actions of the studio and the director were a lesson for him to consider.[5]

Another script heading into production was an adaptation of J. P. S. Brown's 1970 novel *Jim Kane*. A laconic tale in Malick's comfort zone of rural eccentrics and working stiffs, it tells of Jim Kane, a cattleman hired to buy a head of cattle in Mexico and transport them back to the US for use in the rodeo. He recruits his friend Leonard, and the two find themselves in a variety of sticky situations. As with *Lanton Mills*, it's a quirky comedy featuring a double act whose dialogue runs like a routine. Paul Newman and Lee Marvin play Kane and Leonard, respectively. The title was changed to *Pocket Money* to de-emphasize Kane's leading role, balancing the star quality of the leads. Malick was on set, available for rewrites. He took on a small role opposite Paul Newman as a worker repairing a tipped-over cement truck, drilling through the solidified cement, but the scene ultimately ended up on the cutting room floor. Still with the acting bug, Malick enjoyed playing opposite one of the biggest stars of the day.

Having overseen one of Paul Newman's most iconic roles in *Cool Hand Luke* (1967), director Stuart Rosenberg reunited Newman with Strother Martin and Wayne Rogers from the earlier hit, but Marvin and Newman didn't gel, and their on-screen friendship never sparked into life. Malick got on with both men but found heavy-drinking Marvin the more amenable. He stayed up until dawn, listening to the actor's war stories. In Marvin's case, these were literal war stories, as he'd seen combat in numerous battles in the Pacific theater. Malick admired Marvin's appetite for life.

Dirty Harry was released in late 1971, directed by Don Seigel and starring Clint Eastwood in a role that successfully transferred his nihilistic western persona into the contemporary urban setting of San Francisco. *Deadhead Miles* and *Pocket Money* were both released in early 1972. Malick now had money and firsthand experience of the limited power of the director and the utter powerlessness of the screenwriter. Eager to direct his own film, Malick decided to finance his *Badlands* script independently of the studios. He had been working on the script for some time, with a draft already prepared in 1969, though the earliest available draft is dated December 1973. As his own producer, he took complete control.

Supported by his agent, Mike Medavoy, his friend Arthur Penn, and actor Warren Oates, Malick began to raise money. Max Palevsky, a wealthy computer pioneer and venture capitalist, met with Malick and was persuaded to the tune of $50,000. Shares were sold to investors, and family members were tapped for cash, with Emil putting up $7,000 and Jill's mother $13,000. Crucially, Malick himself staked $25,000 of his own money from his scriptwriting. There was a lot of rejection along the way; Malick estimated he had a success rate of one in twenty. He approached people from outside the film industry—dentists and lawyers. He prepared a package of photographs, outlines, and a film script to show potential investors but found they were less interested in the plot than in their potential return. The numbers, not the vision, were the important thing. Malick's willingness to sink his own savings was more impressive than the slides.[6]

By early 1972, Malick had formed T. F. Malick Productions and opened an office on Wilshire Boulevard in Los Angeles. Among his allies were a pair of independent producers. Writer-director Paul Williams had produced and directed *Out of It* (1969) and *The Revolutionary* (1970), starring actors in formative roles, such as Jon Voight, Tommy Lee Jones, and Robert Duvall. Socially outgoing and driven, Williams was a fellow Harvard man with a wide social circle. His producing partner Ed Pressman was socially awkward, quiet, and reticent but no less ambitious. The son of a famous toy maker—the "king of marbles"—who died when Pressman was only sixteen, Pressman was inspired by the New Wave cinema coming out of France. Once more, Jacob Brackman served as the facilitator, introducing Malick to Williams and, through Williams, to Pressman. Though Williams and Pressman were

Badlands (1971–1973)

already producing Brian De Palma's *Sisters* (1972), they were impressed by Malick's network of contacts. They raised financing, with Pressman contributing some of his mother's money, without her knowledge. When she found out, she fortunately was persuaded to continue the investment.[7]

Malick also approached Larry Reger, a lawyer who headed the National Endowment for the Arts. He had unsuccessfully pitched to Reger for an earlier project, but this time Reger responded positively. Part of the reason was that Reger knew Caril Ann Fugate's attorneys—brothers John and James McArthur—and he put Malick in contact with them. Malick traveled to Lincoln, Nebraska, accompanied by another friend, Wallace Wolf. Wolf made for a fascinating traveling companion. He'd worked for 20th Century Fox as a lawyer for twenty years, representing some of the most powerful names in Hollywood, gaining particular fame when he filed a suit against CBS after the cancellation of *The Smothers Brothers Comedy Hour*. The comedy duo of folk singers fought with the network about their platforming of political comedy, including antiwar material, on their show. The suit became a landmark case in censorship and the role of popular entertainment in political debate. Wolf was also Roman Polanski's lawyer and so had an insider's perspective on the Tate-LaBianca murders and subsequent trials. Polanski himself had been a suspect in the early stages of the investigation but was cleared after passing a lie detector test.

Malick and Wallace met the McArthurs at the Village Inn in Lincoln for dinner, and the two lawyers were soon taken with the director. Malick insisted that the film he wanted to make wasn't exploitative, nor would it be presented as a "true story." Elements of the case would be used as inspiration. Won over, James McArthur asked if he wanted to meet Caril. A visit was arranged immediately, with the McArthurs careful not to reveal Malick's role as a filmmaker. As far as the prison authorities knew, the two visitors were out-of-town lawyers curious to meet the infamous prisoner.

Malick made it clear to the lawyers that he'd only make the movie with Caril Ann Fugate's permission. Because of the widespread publicity, the story was in the public domain, so Malick had no legal reason to request authorization, just as David Newman and Robert Benton didn't need any from the Barrow and Parker families before they wrote *Bonnie and Clyde*. However, Caril was different from Bonnie Parker. She insisted she wasn't an accomplice of Starkweather but a victim whose family had been murdered by her embittered ex-boyfriend: a child who had been kidnapped, threatened, and coerced into staying with Starkweather. "Why didn't she escape?" everyone asked. It

THE MAGIC HOURS

was the dead of winter with flat stretches of frozen ground surrounding her for miles. Where was she to run? A fifteen-year-old girl with an armed man she soon realized was a murderous psychopath? When she was captured, she asked repeatedly about her parents, to the amazement of the various law enforcement officers and their wives who were charged with her detention. She had no idea they were dead. Instead of an immoral outlaw, they saw a traumatized child. A photograph of her drinking a Coca-Cola and smiling, which appeared in the *Lincoln Evening Journal* on February 4, 1958, however, convinced the public she was a remorseless accomplice, the embodiment of all that was wrong with the youth of the day. James Landis's B-movie treatment *The Sadist* (1963) featured a pair of teenage killers, modeled on Starkweather and Fugate, who drink soda pop while gloating over their victims.

Understandably, Caril didn't want another film made. She wanted to forget and, more importantly, to be forgotten. But she listened to this large, softly spoken man in the visitor's room as he explained his film. "I see the look in your eyes," she said. "And I think you're honest, and I trust you." And with that, Malick had permission to make his movie.[8]

Arthur Penn agreed to serve as an executive producer, giving the project the imprimatur of a successful filmmaker, opening doors, and encouraging investment. Penn's acceptance also offered Malick a primary source of inspiration. Penn's *Bonnie and Clyde* (1967) ushered in a new form of filmmaking that broke with conventional storytelling and squeamishness about portraying sex and violence. Its lovers-on-the-lam story has a passing resemblance to *Badlands* as well, but Malick's film would distance itself from generic antecedents, including Penn's. *Lanton Mills* actor Warren Oates accepted the small but significant role of Mr. Sargis, the father of the girl. Malick and Jill scouted locations, and AFI provided equipment to tape casting sessions. A friend at AFI also provided an introduction to a young painter called Jack Fisk, who arrived in LA along with his childhood friend David Lynch. He'd collaborated with Lynch on his early shorts. Like Malick, Fisk was born in Illinois, and they established an immediate rapport. They spoke the same language in their understanding of film, and both had a focus on their art, which consumed them completely. It helped also that Fisk had experience working at the low-budget end of filmmaking. Fisk was the art director of *Angels Hard as They Come*, written and produced by Jonathan Demme for Roger Corman's company in 1971, as well as working on the blaxploitation heist film *Cool Breeze* and cult horror *Messiah of Evil*, both of which came out in 1972. Educated by the Corman method of inventiveness, cost cutting, and commercial exploitation, Fisk was a one-man band who could design, build, and decorate anything from scratch. He had an artist's eye for what would photograph well, as well as what would add an eloquent detail to a character, but biker and horror flicks only went so far. Fisk wanted to work with artists, and in Malick he believed he'd found one. At their first meeting, Malick asked if he could have everything ready for the shoot in ten weeks. Being young and brave, Fisk agreed.[9]

In his script, Malick changed the names of the characters: Charlie Starkweather becomes Kit Carruthers—"sounds a little too much like Druthers," he complains in the film—and Caril is Holly Sargis, named after Malick's grandmother Nanajohn Sargis. Like Starkweather, Kit is a garbageman with a James Dean obsession, but Holly's family has been pared down to a single lone father, played by Oates. The violence is also toned down. Starkweather confessed to murdering a gas station attendant before the killing spree, but this isn't referred to in the film, and the sexual violence has been eliminated as well. The murder of two-year-old Betty has also been eliminated, and the rich man and his maid survive their encounter with Kit and Holly. The only dog killed is shot by Holly's father. A scene in which Kit ambushes a posse bent on capturing them makes Kit's violence almost heroic, falling into line with his dreams of boyhood adventure. Viewed today, with Kit's bandanna and homemade hides and traps, the scene anticipates such childish fantasies of vengeful violence as *Rambo: First Blood* (1982).

As he was writing, to make the cadence of Kit's conversation accurate, Malick listened to tapes of Charlie Starkweather talking from prison. Some of Starkweather's words, he repurposed for Holly's voice-over, so the two characters were blended.[10] The $250,000 budget was small, and Malick decided to shoot with a nonunion crew to keep costs down. Some worked for free, whereas actors such as Warren Oates deferred their pay. Dianne Crittenden was appalled to hear that her cousin Dona Baldwin, who appears in the film as the rich man's maid, was working unpaid as Malick's assistant. Crittenden confronted Malick, but he quickly charmed her to the extent that she ended up being hired as his casting director, for the time being, without pay.

The first of the two leads was easy to cast. Mary Elizabeth Spacek was born on Christmas Day in 1949 in Quitman, Texas. Her family called her Sissy, and the name stuck. Initially, Spacek tried for a career in pop music, recording the single "John, You Went Too Far This Time," which chides John Lennon for the cover of *Two Virgins*, before being dropped by her record label. She studied briefly in New York under Lee Strasberg and appeared in

THE MAGIC HOURS

Andy Warhol's Factory production *Flesh* (1968). Her first major role was as a girl sold into sex slavery in *Prime Cut*, an odd Lee Marvin–Gene Hackman thriller set in the meat industry, which didn't make much of a splash on its release in 1972. She met Malick in an old Spanish house with no furniture in the middle of Hollywood and, in lieu of a script, was handed scraps of paper. "I'd roll out this little, tiny piece of paper and read the line and he would just dissolve in hysterics and laughter."[11] When Malick discovered that Spacek could twirl a baton, they went to a music shop on Hollywood Boulevard and bought a Star Line baton, which was incorporated into Holly's character. He grilled Spacek about the character, asking her questions that he then fed back into the script.[12]

For the role of Kit Carruthers, the search lasted into 1972. Malick was fascinated by the charm of evil: "I really felt that one of them was evil, but he was evil in a way [like] most of the people I've known who are evil, who gave no tipoff to their character. It's really true—not just with the people I grew up with." Malick auditioned many young actors for the role, including Robert De Niro, Don Johnson, and Peter Fonda, often pairing them with Spacek to see if the chemistry worked. Malick was gripped by indecision. He liked all the actors he saw. Crittenden devised video auditions to put distance between the actors and the director. Dianne Crittenden was auditioning actors in a hotel when she spotted Martin Sheen leaving. She'd seen him in a production of Tennessee Williams's *Rose Tattoo* in New York and called him in. Sheen was reluctant to audition for a no-name director, but after he saw some pages from the script, his interest was piqued. Malick later phoned, asking to meet, though he was worried that Sheen, at thirty-one, was too old to play Starkweather. For a long time, Don Johnson was a leading candidate, but producer Paul Williams advised that, as a first-time director, Malick needed an experienced actor, someone who could be relied upon to give a performance without too much direction and allow Malick to concentrate elsewhere.[13]

Malick talked to Sheen on the phone and had Sheen and Spacek improvise together. In the process, Sheen was falling in love with the part and the young director. When he was finally given the full script, Sheen's heart sank. It was one of the best scripts he'd ever read, but his part was for a nineteen-year-old. When he voiced his reservations to Malick, Sheen was told it wouldn't be a problem. The character could be aged up to twenty-five. In the end, the decision was between Sheen and Peter Fonda.

Sheen tried to concentrate on the job at hand: a lead role in "To Kill a Memory," an episode of *Mannix*. He was playing a young army ranger who

54

Badlands (1971–1973)

has lost his memory and needs Mannix's help to find out what happened to him. During a break on the Paramount lot, he phoned home and got a message from his wife, Janet, that Malick had called. He wanted Sheen to pick up the new script later that evening. Malick promised him a decision soon. When he got home, Janet greeted him with the news that the part was his. The next morning, on the drive to work on the Pacific Coast Highway while listening to Bob Dylan's "Desolation Row," Sheen pulled over to the side of the road and wept. He'd landed the role of a lifetime.[14]

La Junta is in the southeastern part of Colorado. Off to the west, the mountains shimmer in the distance, and for 360 degrees, short grass prairie and sagebrush stretch away. The Arkansas River runs close by the town. Jack Fisk arrived ten weeks before the shoot to secure locations and build and dress the sets. Having already scouted, Malick gave Fisk a list of addresses to check out. Malick flew out a couple of weeks before the shoot to start rehearsals. Martin Sheen, Janet, and their sons, Ramon, Charlie, and Emilio, drove their station wagon to the location. It was over a thousand miles and took two full days. Jill took their eight cats and their hound Abimelech in their Volkswagen Bus. Likewise, Warren Oates and his wife used the opportunity to do some driving, stopping to enjoy the sunsets at the end of the day.

The small town was tiny and isolated. "You could scream, and no one would notice," Fisk says.[15] Fisk's preparations involved building and dressing sets in such a way as to suggest the background for many of the characters. Holly's house would actually be three separate houses. Her room was full of things Fisk had acquired, the cupboards and drawers filled with the clothes sent from the costume designer in Los Angeles, a doll's house, ornaments, and hairbrushes. Spacek balked at having her hair cut but eventually, if tearfully, acquiesced.

Kit's look took some adjustment. Malick envisioned him wearing a cowboy hat and took Sheen to a store to try on different styles: felt, straw, and cotton. Finally, Malick gave up. "It seems your IQ drops considerably when you put on a hat," he told him. Sheen's first day of shooting was the scene in which he confronts Holly's father about dating his daughter. Unhappy with the way Sheen looked, Malick rubbed some earth into his hair to take the freshly shampooed shine off. For the same scene, Fisk had put up a billboard with a painted advertisement by Joan Mocine to stand in for the work of Mr. Sargis. On seeing it, Malick asked Fisk to remove a panel. It gave a sudden depth to the shot. Fisk was impressed with Malick's eye and ability to improvise and find something interesting.

THE MAGIC HOURS

The film launched many careers—those of Fisk, Spacek, Sheen, cinematographer Tak Fujimoto, whose credits include *Ferris Bueller's Day Off* (1986) and *The Silence of the Lambs* (1991), and of course Malick himself—and many memories are bathed in the light of nostalgia. But at the time, for the thirty-five strong nonunion crew, a handful of hired locals, and a cast of relative unknowns, there were discomforts, disagreements, and dangers galore. Large rattlesnakes were common on location, forcing Fisk to use a long-handled shovel to pick things up from the ground. The bugs bit, the sun burned, and once filming began, grave doubts about Malick's competence as a director crept into the group. This film school graduate and screenwriter, this ex-teacher and ex-journalist—did he really have what it took to pull together a production and make an actual film? Malick himself was prey to insecurity. He felt the crew's skepticism keenly mixed with his own uncertainty but did his best to bluff his way through it: "When you have to maintain a lot of conviction, have absolute conviction, and show it, and you're not feeling it inside, then the worm can get in."[16]

Early scenes of Holly and Kit talking as they walk down the street near her house had to be reshot when the rushes revealed that a technical fault on the camera was causing the image to judder. The small budget meant that such costly mistakes were an existential threat to the film. Experienced crew members began to rebel when they felt that Malick was making rookie errors. Shots were planned that the script supervisor argued wouldn't match previous footage. She insisted that the clapboard be filmed upside down to register her protest. The cameraman Brian Probyn supported her in this and began to insist on the same process, arguing that his reputation would be compromised by the inferior camerawork. Probyn was an English cinematographer who had filmed some of Ken Loach's early work and had particularly impressed Malick with *Downhill Racer* (1969), starring Robert Redford. The film boasted documentary-like, seemingly unlit footage, which Malick was drawn to. Probyn previously worked on a Paul Williams film, but the fifty-two-year-old veteran was underwhelmed by Malick's approach and furthermore started to develop bad ulcers. He called Williams to tell him that his health was deteriorating and that he needed to quit the film. Hoping to placate the crew, Malick found himself shooting material he knew he had no intention of using: "They knew that the scene was rotten, and I was just making it worse by doing the coverage on this rotten scene."[17]

The actors were more enthusiastic. Martin Sheen was especially happy to lend a hand coiling cable or lifting flats. At thirty-one and with a family, he

Badlands (1971–1973)

was at a stage in his career when he wondered if he'd ever get further than guest spots on *Columbo*. Here was a role he loved and a director with whom he connected. In one scene, after shooting his friend Cato, Kit ran to open the door for him. Malick loved the touch.[18] Takes were done of the script, followed by improvised takes, or even takes without dialogue, with the actors thinking their lines in their heads as they hit their marks. Some of the crew looked askance at such methodology, but others were converted. What many saw as inexperience or ineptness, Fisk recognized as artistry and inventiveness.[19] Shots were stolen on the way back to town when the light was beautiful. Malick was driving Sheen back to the hotel after a day's shooting. He pulled the car over to a vacant lot beside the Capri Motel, leaped out, and started filming. Fisk had some stuffed animals—a bird and a large reptile—and he positioned them on the prairie. A living owl was also filmed, seeming very still before turning its head: a moment that sold the stillness of the other animals as natural to the audience. Thus was captured the most iconic image from the film: Kit standing in the fading light, the moon rising behind him, the rifle yoked over his shoulders like the crossbeam of a crucifix, a cross between James Dean in *Giant* (1956) and Jesus in the Gospels.

A favorite scene for Malick summed up the film and the peculiar empathy it has for its killer. While looking at stereopticon slides of different parts of the world, Holly speaks about how she wishes she could fall asleep and be transported to a magical land. Meanwhile, Kit has been fishing with a primitive net, and, frustrated by not catching anything, he takes out his pistol and starts shooting at the fish. "That was the only place where my heart went out to him in the whole picture," Malick recalls. "When he's trying to shoot the fish. I feel like some people are just born to this, to a bad life."[20]

With such different visions on set and money increasingly short, some of the crew began to leave, including Probyn, who hated the heat of the Oklahoma summer. According to his son, Robin Probyn, the split wasn't as acrimonious as previously thought—the cause was purely medical. Probyn's ulcer burst, and he was hospitalized. When he recovered, Malick gave him a beat-up Cadillac they'd been using, to drive home.[21] Tak Fujimoto was promoted from camera operator to director of photography. Whereas he had argued with the experienced Probyn, Malick found Fujimoto opaque, offering no feedback whatsoever. Later, when Fujimoto left for another job, Stevan Larner came in to finish the shoot. Larner was an experienced cameraman who had been working on films since the mid-1960s and whose credits included *Symbiopsychotaxiplasm: Take One* (1968). He had studied in Paris

THE MAGIC HOURS

and apprenticed with the legendary French cinematographer Ghislain Cloquet. He was also Malick's instructor at AFI, and Malick credited him with the best cinematography on the film.[22]

Everyone was working hard, taking up the slack. Jill pitched in as a producer, hiring and firing, paying extras five dollars in cash, making food, soothing egos, and acting as intermediary between her husband and the production. Everyone was invited to view dailies in the evening, but it did little to alleviate tensions. A single bar at the motel in town became a gathering spot. Other than that, there was nothing to do but go to bed early as summer dragged on.

Sheen recalls the filming as one of the best times of his life and his professional career. His sons—future actors Charlie Sheen and Emilio Estevez— appear in the film as children playing beneath the streetlight, unaware that in the house overlooking them a murder has just taken place. Their long hair was pinned back and greased down to conform to the period. Spacek found herself more and more in the company of Jack Fisk, and the pair were soon an item, something the crew realized when Fisk angrily interrupted a take after Sheen—in character—slapped Spacek's behind.

There were seeds of marriage but also of divorce. Warren Oates had arrived early in his RV with his wife, English actress Vickery Turner. Turner sought Malick's advice on accepting the role of Célimène in *The Misanthrope* back in Oxford. Malick was encouraging, but the separation from Oates the part entailed contributed to the dissolution of their marriage.[23]

Janit Baldwin, Spacek's friend and costar from *Prime Cut*, had a small role in the film as Holly's high school friend. Her character helps the naive Holly practice kissing. Baldwin felt uncomfortable, and Malick telling her to loosen up didn't help. The small part of the state trooper who escorts Kit on the B-26 plane flying him to trial went to John Womack, Malick's old Harvard friend who had walked away from *Loose Change*. He'd interrupted a camping vacation in Colorado with his wife to see his friend. Sheen stayed on the ground, but Womack was aloft in the plane when an engine cut out. The two-man crew had flown up from Amarillo, Texas, but had neglected to reset the carburetors for La Junta's higher altitude. The pilot manually choked the gas and landed it safely.[24] Disaster averted.

Economy forced some creative solutions. The real National Guard served as extras. A cherry picker was borrowed to create a crane shot. Jack Fisk was constantly engaged in the creative process, literally world-building. When Holly and Kit hide out in the woods, the script describes them as living in a

Badlands (1971–1973)

wickiup, and Fisk suggested he build them a tree fort instead. "I was so fortunate and happy it didn't fall apart, because I hadn't thought about holding up the weight of all these actors and cameras, stuff like that. But it worked out and he made it look much more exciting than it probably really was." The wickiup in the script was inspired by research he was doing for another script about John Smith and Pocahontas, called "The Mother of Us All."[25]

As the shoot went on, emotions reached the boiling point, and for all his soft-spoken patience, Malick also had moments when he found it difficult to control his temper. While they were shooting the tree house scene, an argument broke out between Malick and production manager Lou Stroller. Stroller was on the set as Pressman's and Williams's eyes and ears. He saw his role as that of the professional reining in the inexperienced artist. In some cases, he had a point. Malick didn't know basics of film vocabulary such as "coverage," or more embarrassingly "honey wagon," thinking it was the catering truck rather than the portable toilets. Setting up a series of shots, Malick didn't realize the lighting needed to be reset, and the crew found themselves resetting the same scene multiple times. But Malick had a stubbornness his gentlemanly manner belied. If there wasn't enough light, he didn't care; he insisted the shoot continue. Two interior shots—the very first shot of the film, with Sissy Spacek on her bed playing with Malick's own dog, Abimelech, and another with Martin Sheen lying on his bed at night—were so dim that they had to be pushed in postproduction, a costly process that produced a grainy image on the big screen.

But that stubbornness arose because Malick knew what he wanted, and what he wanted wasn't to shoot a conventional picture. Dianne Crittenden says: "Terry Malick is a great, great writer, but he's not really the best communicator."[26] Some felt his inexperience was being exploited by the crew to make him do things their way, and, sensing this, he became more stubborn. Jack Fisk recognized that Malick "thought more like an artist. He'd change his mind or make decisions or go here when it was scheduled to go there. And it frustrated the production manager who had sent all the trucks to the left, and Terry wanted to go to the right. But he was working to get everything better for the film. Terry taught me in that short time that film could also be an art form."[27] Fisk believed that, far from being lost, Malick arrived with his own aesthetic, specifically a love for natural light, especially when softened by dusk or dawn. Fisk credits Malick's amateur photographer father, Emil, with informing Malick's passion for light and his knowledge of lenses and lighting effects.

THE MAGIC HOURS

One of the most experienced people on set was actually the person closest to Malick, Jill Jakes. Jakes had been part of Arthur Penn's team that made *Mickey One* and *Bonnie and Clyde*. She and Malick had visited Penn on set for *Little Big Man* (1970) a few summers earlier. As a freshly minted lawyer—she'd just passed the California bar—she was an expert in confrontation and argument, acting as Malick's intermediary with the crew and gaining a reputation, with a whiff of misogyny, of being "a little bossy."[28] Tensions exploded when Lou Stroller directed a disparaging comment at her. Malick jumped on him and started swinging. "He didn't even hesitate," Martin Sheen says. "Terry just whupped him."[29] The new director might have once been a philosophy teacher, but he had also been a linebacker, and he had weight to throw. Stroller flew back to New York and informed Edward Pressman's mother—one of the investors in the film—that chaos reigned on set and that Malick was out of his depth. Pressman, never comfortable even in normal social situations let alone confrontational ones, called on Paul Williams to visit the set and ease tensions. Williams assured everyone they were working for an artist on a great film that would outlast all of them. Work proceeded, but the atmosphere wasn't good.[30]

Worse was to come.

In a vital scene, Kit burns down Holly's house. Effects veteran Roger George and a locally hired assistant were positioning the pyrotechnics and rubber cement around the rooms of an old house. Sheen felt hinky and abruptly sent his wife and kids back to the motel. Two cameras were being operated. The windows and doors were closed. When George's assistant lit the torch prematurely, the unventilated air caught fire, and flames roared through the house. Tak Fujimoto dived out the window, followed by other members of the crew. But Roger George was at the center of the flames, covered in the flammable glue he'd been spreading around. Somehow, he got outside and rolled on the ground as the crew beat his flaming body with blankets. The fire department arrived but gaped at the fire, and George was in a bad way, burned over a large part of his body. The nearest hospital didn't have the facilities to treat him. He was flown by helicopter to the nearest airport, where a plane was chartered to take him back to California and Sherman Oaks Hospital for treatment. George recovered and continued in his career but was scarred for life.

The emergency led to another blowup between Stroller and Jill Jakes. Stroller claimed that Jakes didn't want to pay for the charter flight to evacuate George. According to Peter Biskind, Stroller told Jakes: "If you were a man,

Badlands (1971–1973)

I'd put you right through that plate glass window."[31] Jakes denied she ever refused to pay for the plane. The accusation was a complete fabrication, according to the Malicks. Leaving aside the sexism, the seriousness of the accusation showed how bad the blood was between the couple and Stroller. He became a source for Peter Biskind's influential version of Malick's early career.[32] Williams once more arrived to calm things down and get the film moving again.

Accusations and recriminations swirled. To save money, Malick had hired a nonunion crew, and the locals had no experience. The accident was blamed on this inexperience. Ironically, George himself was an expensive hire, an expert special effects coordinator flown in especially for the fire shot. But money was at a premium, and it had been his idea to burn a real house rather than build expensive sets out in the open air, where the fumes could dissipate. That penny-pinching had cost the production expensive camera equipment, the house they were supposed to be using, and the price of the emergency evacuation and, most importantly, had almost cost a man his life. Fisk rebuilt the sets on flats in a parking lot, and the fire was filmed in carefully controlled stages, with Fisk thinning out the rubber cement with gasoline to avoid any repetition of the accident.[33]

Jill Jakes was now getting up at five o'clock in the morning to make meals for the cast and crew. The money was gone. Much of the crew was gone. Fujimoto left, to be replaced by Steve Larner. For the car chase that ended in Kit's arrest, the Corvair's hood was removed along with the spare tire (the motor was in the rear), and Malick was strapped to the floor of the trunk, holding a 35mm Arri camera as the car sped across the prairie. For protection, he wore his old football helmet.[34]

Favors were called in. George Stevens Jr. was tapped for extra cash. Stevens wired the money from Washington, DC.[35] Jill Jakes's father, Hays Jakes, was another source of emergency funds. Charlotte Jakes, Jill's mother, says: "I'll never forget the day Jill called her Daddy and said they had run completely out of money, and they had to have $10,000. Hays asked her how soon they had to have it and she said, 'This afternoon.' Bless his heart, he arranged it and the money was in her hands within two hours."[36] The IRS was not so accommodating when it learned that Malick was dipping into the withholding taxes.

Another cost-cutting move saw Malick himself appearing in the film as a visitor to the rich man's house where Kit and Holly have taken refuge. Malick is a big man in a light suit. His voice is high-pitched and soft, the southern accent discernible. He wears a straw hat—his IQ apparently intact. He has a roll of architectural plans under his arm. And he towers over Kit, who despite being on a step is still shorter by a head or two. In an earlier scene, Malick can be glimpsed in a montage of media coverage: a man in a raincoat pointing at a clue, "a famous detective from Chicago" stumped by the case. It's a playful Hitchcockian cameo.

Malick was over budget and out of time. They arrived in the scorching heat and were leaving as snow began to fall. For some shots, the leaves were painted green to match the earlier shots from the summer. Malick was the last to leave. Jack Fisk noticed Malick looked his happiest when left alone with a camera. But by December, Malick had also returned to LA with thousands of feet of film and a mountain of debt. The IRS was threatening to repossess Malick's car, and Jakes and Malick stayed at friends' houses to avoid the repo men. Malick's connections came through. Mike Medavoy got Malick a high-paying rewrite rush job on a script for Steve McQueen.[37] The Volkswagen Bus was traded in for an orange Volkswagen Thing. Jill Jakes went to work as a lawyer as Malick tried to finish his film.

The editor Robert Estrin made the first cut, but Malick was dissatisfied. Estrin was out, and, with assistant editor Billy Weber, Malick began to cut the film himself. Weber was a friend of Jack Fisk, having also worked on *Messiah of Evil*, the cult horror film in which Weber both served as assistant editor and appeared as a "supermarket zombie." He'd met Malick during preproduction and, once filming had begun, he'd driven to the airport every night to pick up the footage coming in from Colorado and deliver it to the lab. Weber viewed the dailies with increasing admiration.[38]

A routine was established. Malick arrived at the editing suite early and, with Weber, watched the unfolding drama of the Watergate hearings on a small television until noon. Then they worked on the film until midnight. "It was really fun. That's how we became friends," Weber says. Weber and Malick went out socializing as well and went to see movies together, including the new Edward Pressman Jr.–Paul Williams production, Brian De Palma's *Sisters* (1972). *Pocket Money* was also released while Malick was editing. Although the film boasted Paul Newman and Lee Marvin, Stuart Rosenberg was unable to reproduce the success of his previous Newman collaboration. Roger Ebert called it "a real curiosity, all style and no movie."[39] Malick's script is criticized in several reviews as the source of the film's disappointing performance: "Terry Malick's script seems like it was left over from an Elvis Presley movie that was never made, minus the spaces for Presley's songs."[40]

Badlands (1971–1973)

According to John M. McInery, the script "just strung together a series of medium funny episodes."[41] A lot rests on Newman's lead role as Jim Kane, a dopey, good-hearted cowboy who has a knack for taking things literally. When an old friend asks in greeting, "Where you been hiding?" he responds indignantly, "I ain't been hiding." Dialogue between Kane and his friend and partner Leonard (Lee Marvin) plays out elliptically and with whimsy. In its humor, its setting, and the otherworldly nature of its characters, *Pocket Money* is identifiably a Terrence Malick story, but it lacks the poetry.

With no distribution deal in place or studio to please, Malick took his time getting *Badlands* right. Billy Weber and Malick regularly spent twelve to fourteen hours a day working on the picture. In Los Angeles, pickups were filmed of the rich man's house, with Steve Larner acting once more as cinematographer. Much of the soundtrack was made unusable by the noise of the camera. Seventy percent of the dialogue needed to be rerecorded. For the music, Malick chose a piece by Carl Orff that Irvin Kershner had played for him. Orff wrote it as a didactic tool to teach children about music, and the recording featured child musicians. For the choral pieces, another choir was recorded singing over the original German lyrics to obscure them. Carl Orff, like Martin Heidegger, had a Nazi-stained past, and Malick wanted to remove any hint of the politics of having clearly audible German on the soundtrack. George Tipton was hired to write additional music and did a remarkable job adapting the existing music to the scenes, in some cases extending or shortening it to fit.

Malick asked Kershner to watch his cut. Before seeing a frame, Kershner told him the two-and-a-half-hour length wouldn't fly. He sat bent over the Moviola with Malick at his side with a pad and pencil. As the film unwound before him, Kershner gave him notes in real time. "That's good. That's redundant. You're repeating yourself," he said as Malick scribbled. There was a film in there, but Malick was too enamored of his own shots: "He wasn't a filmmaker at the time, he was someone who loved film, and saw a metaphor in everything."[42]

According to Jacob Brackman, a voice-over was necessary: "It was like patching the holes in the road."[43] However, both Sissy Spacek and Billy Weber insist that the voice-over was always part of the film, and indeed, it is present throughout the 1972 draft script, where it functions as more than exposition. Holly speaks in a language of teen-magazine cliché—"Little did I realize that what began in the alleys and back ways of this quiet town would end in the Badlands of Montana"—and provides an affectless poetry to the journey she undertakes with her sociopathic partner.

THE MAGIC HOURS

Despite the tens of thousands of feet of film, other pickup shots were added. The lights of Cheyenne Holly and Kit see shimmering in the distance were actually the lights of Malibu. The point of view sequence taken from the plane carrying Kit to his fate, depicting the clouds passing and the sun dipping between them, was bought from a cache of plate shots from *Ice Station Zebra* (1968), a film Malick's friend Tony Bill had starred in.

With the film print still wet from the lab, Malick flew to New York with Sissy Spacek to screen the movie for the Selection Committee of the New York Film Festival. Malick recalls: "The sweat ran down my back. I wasn't allowed in the theatre; I had to stay in the projection room with the projectionist. We had a screaming battle throughout. Everything went wrong—the sound, the focus, the reel broke."[44] Despite this, the film was chosen as the closing picture of the festival. It showed twice at the Alice Tully Hall on Saturday, October 13, 1973. The festival had opened with François Truffaut's *Night for Day* and featured Andrei Tarkovsky's *Andrei Rublev*, Werner Herzog's *Land of Silence and Darkness*, and Rainer Werner Fassbinder's *The Bitter Tears of Petra von Kant*, as well as premiered Martin Scorsese's *Mean Streets*. Warner Brothers was impressed with both Scorsese's and Malick's films and bought them on the same day, paying a $950,000 nonreturnable advance for *Badlands*. This allowed Malick to pay his debts, taxes, and deferments for the cast and crew and realize a small profit.

The audience reaction and critical reception were positive. The *New York Times* critic Vincent Canby wrote a glowing review, concluding: "One may legitimately debate the validity of Malick's vision, but not, I think, his immense talent. *Badlands* is a most important and exciting film."[45] Malick undertook press for the film, attending and participating in press conferences as well as giving interviews to journalists. Michel Ciment from the *Cahiers* rival *Postif* describes his first impressions of Malick: "Like most great directors, he was rather simple and Kubrick was the same. He was friendly, talkative, did not shun the questions, just a decent person, which you can see in his cinema. He's a humanist."[46] Malick used the opportunity to express gratitude to his collaborators and especially his wife, Jill. The importance of her contribution was underlined by the film's billing as "A Jill Jakes Production." "My wife Jill held the picture together," Malick said. "She was tremendous, taking care of all the details that I didn't have time for. When we could no longer afford a caterer, she got up at 5 a.m. and made fantastic lunches. Not just sandwiches but beef stroganoff."[47]

Badlands (1971–1973)

The interviews revealed the proximity Malick felt to the film's protagonists: "I wanted to do a film on what it meant to be fourteen in the Midwest in 1958. I think there are things you're open to as an adolescent that close up forever afterward. I wanted to show a kind of openness, a vulnerability that disappears later, when you get a little savvier."[48] Far from feeling superior about Holly and Kit, Malick said, "I see no gulf between them and myself." Kit is a closed book, an example of how suffering doesn't necessarily give a character depth but actually can make a person shallower. Malick links him to his own background: "There's something about growing up in the Midwest. There's no check on you. People imagine it's the kind of place where your behavior is under constant observation, where you really have to toe the line . . . people can get really ignored there and fall into bad soil. Kit did, and he grew up like a big poisonous weed."[49]

In Starkweather, Malick recognized elements of himself, which he transposed to Kit and also to Holly. Holly's voice-over, in its cadence and phrasing, sounds close to Starkweather's pronouncements as recorded by the psychiatrist James Reinhardt, who would publish the first account of the murders. Take this account Starkweather gave of his feelings on being ostracized by schoolmates when he was in elementary school: "My heart became a grimace of hatred, crimson . . . and it seemed as though I could see my heart before my eyes, turning dark black with hate and rage."[50] In prison, Starkweather handwrote an autobiography. Its self-mythologizing and wistfulness closely resemble Holly's narration. Starkweather writes: "When I was younger, I always said to myself that I was going to have the knowledge of what life was good for in this world, but as I grew older, the more I didn't care to find out, and that's the reason why I didn't have time. . . . By this time my head was spinning, and whirling, the remembrance of happy times and unpleasant events that happen throughout my life came crowding through a foggy mist of recollection. This recollection of events were coming back to me like a[n] after vision of my past life."[51] In some ways, Holly and Kit can be seen as a split version of Starkweather and by extension Malick himself. As Malick identified as Texan throughout his life, so Starkweather claimed—with far less justification—to be from Texas. As noted, Holly's identity is also informed by Spacek's Texan identity.

When talking about Holly, Malick describes himself, a closeness underlined by the fact that he gives her his grandmother's maiden name. "Holly's Southernness is essential to taking her right. She isn't indifferent to her father's death. She might have cried buckets of tears, but she wouldn't think

THE MAGIC HOURS

of telling you about it. It would not be proper. You should always feel there are large parts of her experience she's not including because she has a strong if misplaced sense of propriety. You might well wonder how anyone going through what she does could be at all concerned with proprieties. But she is."[52] There can also be heard the beginnings of Malick's own retreat, his sense of discretion and privateness, which will see him shun the public eye later in life. Holly's father has traces of Emil. Both men are artists, one a painter and the other a musician, but both are to some extent disappointed and strict with their offspring. Mr. Sargis shoots Holly's dog when she defies her father's ban on seeing Kit, a sudden and cruel eruption of violence that foreshadows Kit's.

Holly's final summary of the events includes a nod to the help Malick received from John McArthur and his son James in gaining access to Caril Ann Fugate: "Later I married the son of the lawyer who defended me." It also further binds Holly to Malick. Hadn't he just married the lawyer, Jill Jakes? Malick hadn't forgotten Caril. In fact, he'd been in telephone contact with her throughout the production and afterward, while he was editing. He also promised the film wouldn't be promoted as being "based on a true story," so as not to compromise her attempts at an appeal. He respected this, insisting that Warner Brothers monitor the publicity used by the cinemas.

And yet the film differs quite markedly from Caril's version of events. Holly is more of a willing protagonist than Caril claimed to be. In the film, Holly witnesses her father's murder, for instance, and so doesn't have Caril's ignorance as a justification for not escaping. Holly also considers running away from Kit when he takes her to the school to collect her textbooks, but she decides that her fate is entwined with Kit's. By the end of the film, Holly refuses to go any further with him, and instead of threatening her, he accepts her decision. As well as being more culpable than Caril claimed, Holly also receives less in terms of punishment: "Myself, I got off with probation and a lot of nasty looks." Caril—serving a life sentence—might have smarted on hearing that line when a theater in Lincoln was hired for a private viewing of the film and permission was granted for Caril to attend. Malick, Jill, the lawyers, the warden, and some other friends were also there. Malick watched Caril's reaction carefully. She watched the film with a stern expression, showing no emotion except for the scene where Kit, having shot Cato, goes into a field and starts punching the air. Caril turned to Martin Sheen, who was sitting next to her, and hit him. After the film, he asked her why she hit him. "Because at that moment, you were exactly like Charlie," she told him. Caril

Badlands (1971–1973)

told Malick she hadn't liked the film. She wasn't able to see the lyricism he could in a traumatic and violent event that had killed her family, left her in jail, and branded her as complicit in their murders. She'd be justified as well in feeling betrayed. The film was obviously her and Starkweather's story, but Holly was not an innocent victim. When Holly refers to Kit as "the most trigger-happy person I ever met," she's actually quoting Charlie Starkweather's description of Caril.

Remarkably, though, she accepted the film as it was. There are photographs of the star and director with Caril and the McArthurs after the screening. Malick wears a plaid sports coat and holds a small home movie camera. He is large in comparison to the tiny Caril, who wears a purple trouser suit and smiles guardedly.

Sheen and Spacek felt that their trust in Malick had been fully redeemed, and their careers were significantly boosted. Janit Baldwin turned up at the cinema only to discover that her role as Holly's high school friend had been completely cut from the film. She would not be the last actor to end up cut from a Terrence Malick film.

The distribution of the film was problematic. Having bought the film, Warner Brothers was soon distracted by the mega-success of *The Exorcist* (1973), so Pressman decided to invest in the distribution of the film himself, opening *Badlands* in three cities: Little Rock, Arkansas; Memphis, Tennessee; and Dallas, Texas. With a small advertising budget, it attracted sizable audiences, and word of mouth spread. Warner Brothers rereleased the film with a more concerted campaign. The film's critical reputation grew, despite a Pauline Kael drubbing in the *New Yorker* that compared it unfavorably to Steven Spielberg's *Sugarland Express*, also released that year.[53] Kael argued that Spielberg appealed to the heart while Malick appealed to the head. She preferred the heart. *Badlands* "is a succession of art touches," she writes. "Malick is a gifted student, and 'Badlands' is an art thing, all right, but I didn't admire it, I didn't enjoy it, and I don't like it." When the *New Yorker* editor and Malick's old boss William Shawn read Kael's review, he called her into the office. "I guess you didn't know that Terry is like a son to me," he told her. "Tough shit" was her immediate response.[54] Kael also might have been predisposed to dislike the film. After all, she had met the director several years previously when she visited the AFI Conservatory and had impatiently heard his defense of the school. This was the kind of pretentious stuff—an "art thing"—film schools created, unlike Spielberg, who had come up through television and had a more direct relationship to the audience.

THE MAGIC HOURS

Despite Kael's dismissal, *Badlands* is now widely considered a masterpiece, even by those who don't rate the rest of its director's career. David Thomson in *The New Biographical Dictionary of Film*, for one, writes that the film "may be the most assured first film by an American since *Citizen Kane*," which only lends more bitterness to his conclusion that "Malick's decline is one of the most alarming tales in the death of film."[55]

Badlands is an act of alchemy. It turns a tale of savage, vicious killing in the midst of winter into a summery tale of freedom and youth: a romance that ironizes its own cliché of teenage rebellion with the sociopathy of its protagonists. Garbage trucks and abattoirs are shown in a magic-hour light with a soundtrack of wistful music. Kit and Holly burn the house down but rescue a lamp. They are children who hide in the woods and murder the grown-ups who pursue them. They dance to rockabilly and Nat King Cole, kill their elders, and advise their peers to listen to their parents. They play house and dress up, and they read articles from magazines. They run away until they don't want to anymore. Kit sleeps like a baby during his trial and is sentenced to die in the electric chair. For Malick, the film was also an examination of the past: his own childhood and upbringing, as well as a violent fantasy of escape and freedom. Kit pours fuel on the piano and sets it alight, a beautiful act of vandalism that creates its own music.

On the one hand, the film sits in a readily recognizable genre—killers on the run—which stretches from *They Live by Night* (1948) through *Bonnie and Clyde* (1963) to *Wild at Heart* (1990), *True Romance* (1993), *Natural Born Killers* (1994), and *Ain't Them Bodies Saints* (2013). However, it's also entirely its own thing. In retrospect, *Badlands* is obviously a Terrence Malick film. The music, the sound, the voice-over, the cinematography, the intelligence, the wit, and the attention to light and the natural world are already established here, a fully formed aesthetic, a coherent confident vision. The influence goes beyond genre. The film frequently turns up on "Best of . . ." lists of influential filmmakers and critics and retains today a sway over generations of directors. Malick had established himself as a transcendent filmmaker with a unique vision. He might be compared to Spielberg by the reviewers or Scorsese by the Warner Brothers acquisitions team, but the filmmakers with whom he shared the New York film festival—Herzog, Tarkovsky, Fassbinder, and Jean Eustache, whose *The Mother and the Whore* was also shown—were comparable figures also.

Terrence Malick was thirty years old and had finally settled on a career that would define him. He was a film director. In Washington, a special

Badlands (1971–1973)

screening was organized at the Kennedy Center to celebrate the most successful protégé of the AFI. Malick attended with his parents and Jill. *Tulsa World* reported that Malick "has had a varied career and appears headed for a brighter future. He and his wife live in Hollywood Hills, Los Angeles, where they are pursuing their professional interests, separately and together."[56] Jill began her work at the American Civil Liberties Union (ACLU), though she had requested that she be allowed leave when her husband began his next film. But what was the next film? Malick didn't want to be too precise: "If I seem vague about my plans it's only because I'm going to have to be very careful what I do next. I'm no longer an underdog in this business. I miss that feeling. I love the feeling of fighting from below. *Badlands* has established my name, good or bad. From this point I'm being watched."[57]

5

Days of Heaven (1973-1978)

The morning after *Badlands* premiered, Malick talked to the *AFI Newsletter* about his next picture. A western, perhaps, but no cowboys: just set in the West. The western was in fact one of several completed scripts.[1] He told Joseph Gelmis he had ideas for four pictures: "if I can get that far."[2] But first he had to pay off debts and then take a break. He and Jill might go to Latin America.[3] Jill was increasingly busy in high-profile cases for the ACLU, involving politically progressive causes: the defense of a whistleblower, a push to legalize marijuana, and a case against the police for wrongful arrest.

Despite the difficulty of making *Badlands*, Malick wanted to maintain his independence. He recognized the risk—"like betting on a single number at roulette"—but the reward was freedom. Malick's agent, Mike Medavoy, secured him a rewrite job on a film called "The Third Truth," about an attempted assassination of Charles de Gaulle, in the vein of *The Day of the Jackal* (1973). He later claimed: "I made more on this one rewrite than I did on the two years of work on *Badlands*."[4] It was a good payday, but the film was never made: an empty form of creation revisited in *Knight of Cups*.

Badlands was released in 1974. Malick's friends and colleagues were impressed with the picture. Stanley Kubrick sent a note offering his congratulations. He was being compared with the most exciting contemporaries in film, Martin Scorsese and Steven Spielberg among them. Hollywood friends felt vindicated. Deferrals were actually coming in. George Stevens Jr. had joked that he was handing over his son Michael's college fund when asked for $10,000. Malick wrote on the check repaying his debt: "Go, Michael! Go!"[5] Producer and friend Tony Bill—now a millionaire riding high on the success of his production of *The Sting*, released the year before—attended a preview in Westwood, Los Angeles, and found the film "one hundred percent Terry Malick's vision and sensibility and sense of humor and sense of life. It is like an autobiography. It's totally Terry."[6] The fact that the preview screened to an

Days of Heaven (1973–1978)

audience who had just watched Mel Brooks's *Blazing Saddles* (1974) created a mixed reaction. From the start, Malick's films proved divisive, never quite fitting into the ostensible genre the studio's marketing tried to put them in. The tagline read: "In 1959, a lot of people were killing time. Kit and Holly were killing people." It was the glib exploitation Malick strove to avoid. Weirdly, it also provoked a letter to the *San Francisco Chronicle* that read: "Sirs—I would like to expression my consternation concerning your poor taste & lack of sympathy for the public, as evidenced by your running of the ads for the movie 'Badlands,' featuring the blurb—'In 1959 most people were killing time. Kit & Holly were killing people.' In light of recent events, this kind of murder-glorification can only be deplorable at best (not that glorification of violence was ever justifiable) why don't you show some concern for public sensibilities & cut the ad? A citizen."[7] The handwriting and the addressee led many to believe it was from the Zodiac killer, a serial killer who inspired Scorpio in *Dirty Harry*.

Even as he worked on his western, more writing work came his way. *The Dion Brothers* (1974)—released in some territories as *The Gravy Train*—was well inside Malick's area of interest, exploring territory similar to that of *Badlands* and *Lanton Mills* but in a goofy grindhouse key. Calvin (Stacy Keach) works on an assembly line, while his brother Russell (Frederick Forrest) spends his days down the West Virginia mines. When Calvin decides he's bored with wage slavery, the two brothers head for Washington, DC, to become armed robbers with the dream of opening a lobster restaurant. Fortunately, Keach and Forrest spark off each other in a way Lee Marvin and Paul Newman hadn't in *Pocket Money*. There's a real anarchic energy to their performance—"I'm Kirk fucking Douglas," a bare-chested Keach yells in the opening scene—a verve that is infectious and a charisma that makes their outlaw behavior likable. It helps that the film is directed by Jack Starrett, an actor who cut his teeth on biker movies and gave the film a healthy chunk of irreverent fun. Starrett had the blaxploitation cult classic *Cleopatra Jones* (1973) under his belt and went on to direct *Race with the Devil* (1975), with Forrest and Peter Fonda, entertainingly combining RV vacationers with a devil-worshipping cult. Malick's love of the outlaw and his skill at producing colloquial, witty dialogue is in evidence. Protective of his freshly earned reputation as a director, he's credited as David Whitney, perhaps unhappy at not getting the director's chair.[8] In recent years, *The Dion Brothers* has been championed as a lost gem, a view promoted by directors David Gordon Green—a future collaborator of Malick's—and Quentin Tarantino, who

THE MAGIC HOURS

would write the script for the *Badlands*-inspired *True Romance* (1993), complete with Hans Zimmer's Orff-like score.

There was also an acting job in a short film on emigration by a Cuban cameraman named Felipe Herba. The short is called "Victor's Notebook," and there is barely a trace of the film, beside a few stills of Malick wearing a purple shirt. When there was the possibility to program the film as part of the Rome Film Festival in October of 2010, Malick himself requested it be withdrawn, motivated perhaps by the embarrassment he felt about "Lanton Mills."

For his next project, Malick had several ideas running parallel. Alongside the western, he was keen to develop another script, titled "The Mother of Us All": the story of Pocahontas and Captain John Smith and the early Jamestown settlement, which had already influenced the wickiup in the *Badlands* script. Billy Weber stayed on the payroll to help with research while Malick polished the script. But financing proved elusive. Another project was a new version of "Sanshō the Bailiff," the Japanese short story adapted for the screen in 1954 by Kenji Mizoguchi. Weber contends that a script about Eleanor Roosevelt was one of the best things Malick had done. Malick was stalled, and Weber went off to work on Martin Scorsese's *Taxi Driver* (1976). A few months later, Weber got a phone call to come back. Malick "had a green light on the farming movie."

The "farming movie" was called *Days of Heaven*. The title is from Deuteronomy 11:21: "That your days may be multiplied, and the days of your children, in the land which the Lord swore unto your fathers to give them, as the days of heaven upon the Earth." Malick recruited his friend Jacob Brackman to be his producer. As well as writing songs for Carly Simon, Brackman had written for *Badlands* as well as scripting Bob Rafelson's *The King of Marvin Gardens* (1972), starring Jack Nicholson and Bruce Dern.

Malick kept in touch with the music world via Brackman. Carly Simon and Malick were still friends, having briefly dated in 1969, and on her sixth studio album, *Another Passenger*, he agreed to appear on the sleeve. Photographed by photojournalist and portrait photographer Mary Ellen Mark, Malick is dressed in period garb, sitting at a table and dealing a card, as the singer sits on the table in front of him. He is the riverboat gambler from one of the songs Brackman wrote for the album: "Riverboat gambler, / Hiding that ace up your sleeve / I can see through all that debonaire style / The irony bending your smile." Malick's camera shyness was not yet evident. In 1976, he was willing to have his photograph published on an album sleeve of one of the biggest pop singers of the day.

Days of Heaven (1973–1978)

Days of Heaven was to be a bigger film than *Badlands* with more moving parts. It was set further in the past, which made the period more expensive to effectively reproduce, and with the kudos from *Badlands*, Malick hoped to attract a star. Dustin Hoffman and Al Pacino were both approached for the lead, but both said no. Mike Medavoy was no longer Malick's agent, having left his company to become the head of production at United Artists. Medavoy's protégé Paula Weinstein now represented Malick. Despite their history, Medavoy's new studio turned down *Days of Heaven*: "It was, I think, in part because of its sparsity. It was also more expensive than the first film and the cast was unknown. There were a number of reasons."[9] TV actor John Travolta quickly became Malick's preferred choice, but Travolta's commitment to *Welcome Back, Kotter* made it impossible. This was a blow for Malick, who had written the script with Travolta in mind.[10] According to Travolta, Malick wept when Travolta told him he couldn't be in the film. In several interviews, Travolta has returned to the idea that not only was Malick emotionally devastated by the news but it contributed to the twenty-year hiatus in the director's career, which is contradicted by pretty much all the evidence.[11] Of course, it's possible Malick gave Travolta this impression, without it necessarily being true. Then relatively unknown, Sylvester Stallone was also considered, and he liked the script but ultimately chose to concentrate on *Rocky* (1976), which he was writing as a prime role for himself.

With no recognizable stars, Malick at least had powerful allies behind the camera. Enter Bert Schneider.

No one was more New Hollywood than Bert Schneider. Malick knew him from his script-doctoring days when Malick worked briefly on Jack Nicholson's *Drive, He Said* (1971). Schneider came from a wealthy New York Jewish family with deep connections in the motion picture industry. His father, Abe Schneider, was a high-ranking studio executive who took over Columbia when Harry Cohn died, and Bert and his brother Harold set themselves up as independent producers. Despite, or perhaps because of, their privilege, Bert had a rebellious streak, which saw him expelled from college and endeared him to the radical politics of the day, helping him forge ties to the Black Panther Party. He initially made his name with the TV show *The Monkees*, but it was *Easy Rider* in 1969 that ushered in a new era of bold experimentation. Blowing away the stuffy clichés, the film revealed a youth market waiting to be tapped with a relatively low investment. A new generation of young acting and directing talent inspired by James Dean—*Easy Rider* star and director Dennis Hopper was a close friend of Dean—and Marlon

Brando were creating fresh models of naturalism, but now accompanied by a heady atmosphere drifting in from the counterculture.

Malick considered himself on the periphery of the counterculture and Hollywood generally, but his friends and colleagues were very much part of it. In 1975, Malick accompanied Schneider, along with Jacob Brackman, Candice Bergen, Francis Ford Coppola, and *Badlands* producer Paul Williams, on a trip to Havana, Cuba. Here they played baseball and talked movies and politics. Schneider possibly introduced the film people to Huey Newton, the Black Panther leader, who was then a fugitive in Cuba. With his fascination for revolutionary leaders, Malick surely jumped at the chance. Schneider had funded and masterminded Newton's escape from charges that he had murdered a seventeen-year-old sex worker and beaten his tailor with a pistol.

After attending one of Fidel Castro's speeches, Williams was approached by Castro, and the two talked. The conversation ended up with an arrangement for an Americans-versus-Cubans basketball game the next morning. And so it came to be that Terrence Malick, Paul Williams, and Francis Ford Coppola faced off against Fidel Castro and two of his bodyguards on the basketball court. The game was not fair, with Castro taking a home advantage, fouling with impunity, and calling fouls where none existed. The Americans didn't stand a chance.[12] Malick once more saw the sublime pettiness of power up close. Duvalier with his poetry and revolver; Castro with his body checks and stolen points. Considering his search for Guevara, his signature on the Rhodes scholars' antiwar letter, the feelers he sent to the North Vietnamese peace envoys in Paris, and now this trip to Cuba, Malick's FBI file must have made for interesting reading at this point. They were almost certainly monitoring Schneider's activities, and so Malick would be on their radar as an associate.

But this was being in the world. Aside from his brush with figures of international fame, Malick was positioned at the heart of the most influential and creative circles of the New Hollywood. While he was hanging with Malick in Cuba, Schneider's mood was triumphant. He'd just won an Oscar for his documentary *Hearts and Minds*. Resplendent in his white tuxedo, he accepted his award, expressing his hope for "the liberation of Vietnam." He read a wire from the North Vietnamese Peace Delegation to the people of America. A furious battle broke out backstage, and Frank Sinatra read out a hastily written disavowal of Schneider's speech later in the ceremony, which in turn caused the ire of Shirley MacLaine. The

Days of Heaven (1973–1978)

fractures were generational and political: the old guard against the young revolutionaries.

Schneider liked Malick, impressed by his mind, and wanted to produce *Days of Heaven*. He took it to Paramount and Barry Diller, who yearned to work with the influential producer. Guaranteeing any overages personally, Schneider promised to deliver the film for $3.5 million. This way he minimized studio interference, but he was putting a huge amount of trust in his director to work in a timely and efficient manner. Otherwise, Schneider's own fortune would be forfeit. With financing secured, his brother Harold took on the role of line producer, managing the day-to-day running of the picture and keeping an eye on the schedule, costs, and Malick.

The shooting script dated June 2, 1976, is "set in Texas just before the First World War" and headed by a quotation from Hamlin Garland's *Boy Life on the Prairie* (1899). After the death of his brother, Steve, during a robbery (the first dead brother to haunt Malick's writing), Bill escapes Chicago with his girlfriend, Abby, and her fourteen-year-old sister, Ursula. Bill "looks fallen on hard times, without ever having known any better—like Chaplin, an immigrant lost in the heartless city, with dim hopes for a better way of life." The trio find work on a large Bonanza ranch. Here they pretend to be brother and sister, and Abby catches the eye of the farmer Chuck, the wealthiest man in the Panhandle, who lives alone in a large house overlooking the vast expanse of his land. Learning of Chuck's imminent death, Bill persuades Abby to marry the farmer so they can inherit his money when he dies. Unfortunately, Chuck begins to suspect Bill and is killed when a jealous fight breaks out. Bill flees with Abby and Ursula but is hunted and killed by the police.

Some changes occurred before production. Bill's brother was eliminated. Other changes took place later—Ursula became Linda and is now Bill's sister—and still others during postproduction, most importantly the addition of a voice-over. The script is dense with precise historical detail about farming equipment and techniques but also about the immigrant communities and their rituals, showing Malick's usual depth of research and a wish to connect the farmer's background to that of his own immigrant grandparents. There's an anthropological fascination in the detail. Chuck, the farmer, is explicitly an immigrant too, with a Russian heritage, a father who appears in a dream in an Astrakhan hat, and a Russian children's book. In one flashback, Chuck's father catches smallpox and drowns himself in the river so as not to be a burden to his family. Incidentally, the ruse of the lovers pretending to be brother and sister comes from the Bible. Abraham twice pretends he and his wife Sarah are brother and sister, the second time causing a local king to take Sarah into his harem. The name of the king is Abimelech, the namesake of Malick's grandfather.

With Hoffman, Pacino, Travolta, and Stallone out of the picture, Dianne Crittenden advocated for Richard Gere to play Bill. He had the right urban air, she argued, for a grown-up street kid. As with Sheen on *Badlands*, Malick dithered over his choice, calling Gere for further auditions and putting him opposite different actresses. Many actors auditioned, including young newcomers like Jeff Goldblum, Dennis Quaid, and John Lithgow. Malick viewed the Betamax videotapes, unable to get Travolta out of his head. Gere became exasperated. "Terry can't make a decision anyhow. This went on and on, on both coasts, forever. I finally went to Terry and said, 'Look, Terry, I can't do this anymore. You've got to make a decision.' And I remember very clearly in LA he called me up and said, 'Look, I really want you to do this.' And I felt, very clearly, that my life was taking a certain direction at that point."[13] Born in Pennsylvania in 1949, Gere appeared in theater, including some plays by Sam Shepard, before breaking out in the London production of *Grease*. He was cast in a leading role in *The Lords of Flatbush* alongside Sylvester Stallone and Henry Winkler, but after getting into a fight with Stallone over a fried chicken sandwich, Gere was fired, and so *Days of Heaven* was going to be his second chance at a major film.[14] For Malick, Gere was the third or fourth choice, with his first—Travolta—still occupying his mind.

For the part of the farmer, Malick originally wanted Warren Oates, but during a dinner with an old Harvard college friend, Wallace Shawn (playwright, actor, and son of Malick's old boss at the *New Yorker*) argued that the farmer should be a younger man. That way, Abby would fall in love with him and form a genuine love triangle, rather than a simple tale of exploitation. Crittenden began considering actors like Robert De Niro and Tommy Lee Jones. Rudy Wurlitzer, screenwriter of *Two-Lane Blacktop* and *Pat Garrett and Billy the Kid*, suggested Sam Shepard to Jacob Brackman during a lunch. Brackman didn't get far with Shepard, who was nervous about acting and wary of being compromised as a playwright. Brackman struck him as too Hollywood. Malick, however, liked the idea and visited Shepard on his Mill Valley Ranch in Northern California. Shepard and his friends got stoned, and Malick rode with them while they toured the ranch, feeding livestock. Shepard recalled Malick being so shy he didn't want to talk about the film directly. This shyness endeared Malick to him.[15]

Days of Heaven (1973–1978)

Carrie Fisher, Meryl Streep, and Geneviève Bujold all auditioned to play Abby. Brooke Adams also caught Malick's attention. Initially, she recorded an improvisation on a videotape, which the casting director rejected, but Malick came across it by accident and called her. It took fifteen more taped auditions, some opposite John Travolta, and finally she heard that Geneviève Bujold had been cast opposite Richard Gere. The Canadian actress made her international breakthrough as Ann Boleyn opposite Richard Burton's Henry VIII in *Anne of a Thousand Days* (1969). However, a meeting with Bujold, Gere, and Malick in Malibu went badly, and Bujold was out: Adams was in. Adams met her director for the first time in Canada, rehearsing. She described the original script as "very literary: it had the feeling of a Thomas Hardy novel."[16] Adams was born in New York in 1949 into a show business family: her father was a vice president at CBS, her mother was an actress, and her sister, Lynne, starred in a long-running soap opera. Trained with Lee Strasberg and at the Institute of American Ballet, she got TV roles in *Kojak* and *The Bob Newhart Show* and a small part in *Car Wash* (1976). The character was eighteen years old, but Adams looked younger than her actual late twenties. With her raven hair, she could credibly pass for Richard Gere's sister in the film's central ruse.

Malick's indecisiveness had a positive conclusion in the casting of Abby's sister, named in the script as Ursula. Crittenden posted the casting call to schools across New York City. Two of the girls auditioning seemed perfect for the role: Linda Manz and Jackie Schultz. To avoid having to decide, Malick changed the role of Ursula's boyfriend into a girlfriend and cast them both. Manz got the role of Ursula. She lacked many of the conventional skills of the actor; she couldn't remember lines or other characters' names. But she possessed an immediacy and naturalness Malick was drawn to. She walked up to him during their first meeting and said: "I liked your script."[17] Malick was taken with her streetwise moxie. The way she talked in real life instantly became a narrative. In an interview with Bobbie Wygant from Dallas–Fort Worth's Channel 5, she said: "I was born in the streets, I grew up in the streets, and I know everything that's going on in the streets." Asked if she was ever "busted," she responds: "Uh-uh. No. Never. I always chicken out of those things. Like if the kids are going to rob something, I say, see you later."[18] Born on August 20, 1961, in Upper Manhattan, Manz never knew her father. Her mother was a cleaner in the Twin Towers. "I was raised by my mother and my grandmother," Manz said. "My mother used to take me to the Metropolitan Museum of Art, she took me to Central Park, she took me ice skating at

Rockefeller Center, she took me to Radio City Music Hall for the Christmas shows and the Easter shows, and we probably had some of that good New York Chinese food!"[19] For the part of Benson, the farm manager, Crittenden chose Robert J. Wilke, a veteran actor of TV westerns who resembled the crinkly features of Charles Bukowski.

With the cast in place, it was almost time to start filming. The problem was that the fields of wheat required by the script were already being harvested in Texas. As the year progressed and the harvest moved, the location of the tall grass moved north until Harold Schneider finally found a location in Alberta, Canada. The wheat there was cultivated by a Hutterite community, an Anabaptist sect similar to the Amish, who retained their old farming ways. Production designer Jack Fisk recruited a number of Hutterites to help his crew build the farmhouse, which would dominate the skyline for miles. It was built in four weeks because the wheat was due to be harvested within six weeks and the house needed to be filmed while the wheat was still high in the fields around it. Fisk thought it was doable. He told Malick he could have the exteriors ready. But Malick insisted that he also needed the interior of the house camera-ready so he could shoot through the windows to the wheat outside. It was an absurd schedule, but Fisk found himself sketching the plans for the house—the Belvedere, as it's called in the script—on his flight up to Canada.[20]

Arriving in Lethbridge, Alberta, Fisk found that the location didn't have a road. He borrowed some equipment from a farmer and built an access road, bringing the lumber to build the house, the barn, and large gates through which the farmworkers would arrive. The house was anchored to the ground by four telephone poles driven deep into the earth. The wallpaper and furnishings, chosen to show the farmer's aspirations to culture and education, were trucked in by a friend of Fisk's from Los Angeles. Howard Schneider went ballistic at Fisk because the driver was nonunion and the film, unlike *Badlands*, was a union shoot. Schneider wasn't happy with the look of the house either. He'd envisioned something more traditionally western looking. Inspired by Rock Hudson's mansion in *Giant* (1956) and Edward Hopper's painting *The House by the Railroad* (1925), Fisk based the house on homes built by the sea, with a widow's walk where you could climb to the roof and look for the ships coming in. It stood surveying an ocean of wheat, and from the turret-like roof, the farmer would witness what he believed to be proof of his wife's infidelity.[21]

By the summer of 1976, Malick was staying at the Holiday Inn in Lethbridge, overseeing progress as production geared up. Here, he signed the

Days of Heaven (1973–1978)

divorce papers that ended his marriage to Jill Jakes. The divorce was relatively amicable. If there was any fault, Malick believed it was his. Their lives were simply heading in different directions. An old school friend was surprised to telephone Malick's house to talk to him, only to be told by Jill: "That marriage didn't work out." He had no idea they were even separated.[22] They were both ambitious and on diverging career paths. Jakes set her sights on being a judge and was busy with her legal career, and Malick was throwing himself into his film. Jakes was at the forefront of a number of political campaigns, and by 1978, she had become a judge. In the 1980s, she regularly appeared on television as the judge in the show *Superior Court*. She and Malick remain friends to this day.

Despite the lack of rancor, it was a dispiriting way for Malick to begin his second film. Whatever *Days of Heaven* turned out to be, it wouldn't be a Jill Jakes production. Rehearsals started with Shepard, Adams, and Gere in Canada. Whenever there was difficulty, Malick cut the line from the script. Adams recalls: "He just kept saying to each of us, 'Oh God, no, cut it.' And we'd say, 'Well, maybe we can do it better.' 'No, no, no, cut. It's not necessary.' So by the time we started shooting, there was practically no dialogue."[23] By the beginning of the fall, shooting began in Whiskey Gap, Alberta, which was fifty miles north of the motel where the cast and crew were staying. Malick hadn't been on set as a director for three years; his personal life was in flux, and he was about to begin shooting a film with actors who weren't his first choice. The familiar presence of Jacob Brackman, Jack Fisk, and costume designer Patricia Norris provided some comfort.

A new addition to the crew was the celebrated cinematographer Néstor Almendros. Born in Barcelona in 1930, at eighteen Almendros moved to Cuba with his father, who had been exiled by the Franco regime. Here he made several documentary shorts, but when he came up against Castro's censors, he returned to Europe, settling in Paris, where he quickly established himself as Éric Rohmer's preferred cameraman, shooting such classics as *My Night at Maud's* (1969) and *Claire's Knee* (1970). While editing *Badlands*, Malick had referenced *The Wild Child*, François Truffaut's 1970 film. Almendros, as Truffaut's cinematographer, had managed to retain a contemporary New Wave feel though it was a period piece. Malick sought out the cameraman for a potential collaboration, and they held long telephone conversations before the shoot. It was a chance to work with a more European New Wave aesthetic. But Almendros was in demand and was already booked for Truffaut's next film: *The Story of Adèle H.* (1975). The schedule was tight, but

79

THE MAGIC HOURS

Malick hoped that, with the experience earned from *Badlands*, the shoot would go smoothly. There was also the chance that Truffaut's film might be delayed, giving them more time. Neither supposition would prove to be true.

On arriving on location, Almendros and Malick immediately established a rapport. Almendros writes in his memoir:

> When I got to Alberta I realized that Malick knew a lot about photography, which is oddly enough unusual for a film director. He has exceptional visual sense and an equally exceptional knowledge of painting. Communication between a director and a cinematographer is sometimes ambiguous and confused, because many directors know nothing about the technical and visual aspects. With Terry, however, it was easy to establish a dialogue. He immediately went to the heart of each problem, and not only allowed me to do what I wanted—which was to use hardly any studio lighting, in this period film—but encouraged me.[24]

If Almendros understood Malick, it became clear his crew did not. "They were accustomed to a glossy style of photography: faces never in shade, blue skies etc. They felt frustrated because I gave them so little work."[25] Almendros offered to shoot the same scene using both the Hollywood style of artificial light and his own and Malick's preferred use of natural or available light. The crew either didn't show up to view the dailies or, if they did, preferred the conventional version. The electricity department soon found itself redundant, with no lights to set up. They slung hammocks in the workers' cabins to nap until they were called on to light some interiors. "Terry would not allow a generator on set," Billy Weber recalls. A shot would be set up, only for Malick to decide he didn't like the light. The crew would then move to another location. If the light wasn't right, they'd move again. "The crew didn't like that. It made it harder. Because he was always waiting for late light or light that looked like that, and that was hard to do."[26] The script itself specifically calls for the "magic hour" or dusk in many of the scene headings, so the practice can't have been a surprise to the producers or the camera department.

The weather was cold, with the wind whipping through the period costumes. For a scene where Adams and Gere wade through a river, they wore wet-suit bottoms under their clothes to keep out the chill. Once shooting was underway, Malick became enthusiastic, especially with the technical

Days of Heaven (1973–1978)

possibilities. As well as shooting on the Panaflex, Almendros had brought along a Panaglide, which was Panavision's answer to the Steadicam, the camera Stanley Kubrick would utilize so effectively in *The Shining* (1980). It allowed the operator to film with the mobility and flexibility of a handheld camera but retain a smoothness of motion. Almendros remembered: "At first Terry was so taken with the new device that he wanted to shoot the whole film with the Panaglide."[27] However, Almendros protested that this would be distracting for the audience.

Unbeknownst to Almendros, another cameraman, Paul Ryan, was shooting with a second unit in Montana, picking up footage of specific wildlife shots Malick had listed: birds in flight, wind rippling across a pond. Much of Ryan's footage ended up in the finished film. The parallel second unit was a working practice for every Malick film thereafter. The secrecy was necessary partly because Malick wanted to save Almendros's feelings and partly because Ryan was nonunion.

Some experienced the shoot as a literal nightmare. Rick Drew, a production assistant on the set, says that the shoot was renamed "Nights of Hell."[28] The "magic hour" became the "tragic hour," or the "magic fifteen minutes," in reaction to the intense importance of this short period of filming. Camera operator John Bailey disputes this though, arguing that Alberta had long twilights that actually allowed for a forty-minute period. He also remembers Malick shooting past when the light meter indicated zero usable light and some of these shots making it into the final film.[29] The crew judged Malick indecisive at best, incompetent at worst, but his creative team was finding the experience invigorating. Almendros writes:

> In every film there is a small group of leaders whom the others follow. In *Days of Heaven* seven people formed this group around Malick: Jack Fisk, who designed and built the mansion among the wheatfields and also the smaller houses where the workers were supposed to live; Patricia Norris, who with extraordinary care and taste designed and made the period costumes; Jacob Brackman, a personal friend of Malick, who was assistant director; and naturally the producers, Bert and Harold Schneider. This close little unit would drive for an hour each day in a van from the motel where we were living to the wheatfields. On the way we would invariably talk about the film, so each day the trip turned into a spontaneous production meeting.[30]

THE MAGIC HOURS

Unable to acclimatize to Malick's method, some of the crew quit. Others were converted. Almendros and Malick set up and rehearsed several scenes during the day and then rushed to film them when the light was right, running between setups. For Almendros, shooting in this time frame made narrative sense: "The decision to shoot these scenes at the 'magic hour' was not gratuitous or aestheticist; it was completely justifiable. Everyone knows that country people get up very early to do their chores (we shot at twilight to get the feeling of dawn). . . . At that time people worked from sunrise to sunset."[31]

In support of his love of the magic hour, Malick paraphrased "Mr Whistler's Ten O'Clock," saying, "It is the time when warehouses become palaces." The full quote reads: "The evening mist clothes the riverside with poetry, as with a veil, and the poor buildings lose themselves in the dim sky, and the tall chimneys become campanili, and the warehouses are palaces in the night, and the whole city hangs in the heavens, and fairy-land is before us."[32] Malick insists that the claim the film was shot in the magic hour is overstated, contending that the diffuse light of northern latitudes, even at normal times of day, was often mistaken for the magic hour.

Painstaking preparation could be disrupted if something else, like a flock of geese flying close by, caught Malick's attention. A vintage train was hired and a spur of track sectioned off for the scene where President Woodrow Wilson passes the farm. The shot was set up, but Malick decided the camera needed to be moved to the other side of the track to make better use of the light. The only problem was that the train had only been "greeked" on one side: the side supposed to face the camera was painted and dressed to fit the period. Hurriedly, the crew had to slap fresh paint on the other side so it matched. As it appears in the film, the shot is so dark, any markings are completely invisible.[33]

Between scenes, the actors hung out in the trailer that stored the costumes. "Linda was a trip," Adams recalls. "She was always driving everybody crazy. She was singing at the top of her lungs: 'I'm a star in New York, a star in LA!' constantly. The guys would just pick her up and throw her out the door, yelling, 'Don't come back.'"[34] Manz's mother accompanied her, but Linda didn't want her on the set. The two had shouting matches in the hotel. "The first thing Linda said to me when we met was to ask if I had any weed," Adams says. "Luckily I did."[35]

Malick was happy to hang out at the hotel, but he didn't enjoy the close relationship he'd had with Sissy Spacek and Martin Sheen on *Badlands*. With some theater experience behind him, Gere was young and cocky and could

Days of Heaven (1973–1978)

prove a disruptive presence. Despite having been fired from one film set already, he hadn't moderated his mischievous, playful attitude at all. When he showed up on set, Gere point-blank refused to cut his hair, which Malick wanted short to fit the period. It was a battle Gere won, sporting his 1970s locks throughout 1916. But in other aspects he proved game, falling into a cold river fifteen times without complaint.[36]

Never a great communicator with actors, Malick didn't know how to make them feel valued. "I don't think any of us felt that Terry was really pleased with our performances, to be honest, and that's never fun," Adams says.[37] One direction he gave Adams revealed something important about the attitude of the whole film: "You are a woman of mystery. The way to get the breath of life into your performance is not by making things clear to the audience." Adams explained: "The idea is that I'm not in control of myself, that people weren't into psychology in 1916."[38] Of the cast, Shepard was the closest to Malick, fascinated by him, and willing also to write his own dialogue when the director requested it. But this was Shepard's first film role as an actor, and Malick sought to keep his lines to a minimum, not trusting him to deliver a performance. Shepard struggled on: "It was very frustrating for me to work in those circumstances, but slowly I got the impression that I was involved in something really extraordinary and the more I worked with Terry, the more I got that impression that he wasn't just trying to make a movie. He was trying to make something that would last."[39]

Manz found it difficult not only to memorize her lines but to remember the name of her character. Ursula was renamed Linda. "Terry really didn't know about actors," Gere says. "So it was really a question of not knowing quite how they work, not knowing how to communicate with them. He knows when it's right; he knows when it's wrong, but he doesn't know quite how to make it work or why it's wrong . . . he wanted a very special thing, a breath of life, something very difficult to communicate."[40]

Far from home with nothing to do, the actors formed an ongoing love triangle. Adams remembers: "I, of course, fell in love with both Richard and Sam, which was difficult, and they were both very fascinating and introspective. I'd read Sam's plays, so I was already in awe of him." The two male leads were completely different: "Basically, Richard was a motorcycle guy. And Sam was on horseback. They never really had that much in common. So I was just kind of bouncing between the two of them." Sex and drugs alleviated the boredom, but Adams to this day doesn't know whether Malick liked her performance.[41]

THE MAGIC HOURS

Malick shot the scenes as written and then without dialogue, or with modified dialogue. He returned to scenes already done and reshot them. The phrase "the breath of life," which both Gere and Adams recall, might be lovely as a phrase, but it is wispy as a direction. Did he know what he wanted? He was looking for the lightning to strike: something unexpected, a moment of authenticity. Watching the ninety-four minutes of the film today, one can see the sense of this. The film is packed with moments, glances, vignettes, details, and accidents, rich with authentic life, but as the seven-week shoot doubled in length, it was easy to assume that Malick was lost. Actors like Armand Assante flew up from New York, had dinner with Malick, shot scenes for a week, and then flew out, unsure how their parts fit into the film as a whole or if they'd even be in the finished film. (They wouldn't be.) Paul Jabara, songwriter of disco hits such as "It's Raining Men," came out to play Linda's music teacher, who turns out to be a pedophile.[42] Fiddler extraordinaire Doug Kershaw provided both the music and the role of the wild-eyed yodeling musician. Extras were hired from the local Hutterite community, many of whom didn't need costumes because their ordinary clothes were close enough to the period. Between takes, some of the Hutterite men showed Malick where they hid the stills where they made rhubarb wine to drink in the fields away from their womenfolk. Sadly, the youngsters passed notes to the cast and crew, asking for help running away.

The cast and crew weren't the only ones feeling frustrated. Malick hated the rushes. His answer was to take more dialogue out of the picture, occasionally shooting whole scenes as a silent movie. Sam Shepard says: "Terry told me very early on that he wanted to make a silent movie. He didn't want dialogue. . . . Dialogue somehow engages the audience too much. He almost wanted a voyeuristic thing from the audience, to witness the image."[43] A freak summer snowstorm fell, but instead of canceling the day's shooting, Malick filmed, and the scene remains in the picture, fundamental in showing the hardship the city dwellers faced: Abby and Bill, huddled in the snow, talk about where to go after the harvest. It contrasts as well with a later scene when, once a part of the farmer's household, they can enjoy the snow as a plaything rather than a dangerous calamity, going for a sleighride. Almendros showed Malick the "French reverse shot." To save time, instead of turning the cameras and lighting rigs around to shoot a reverse shot of a dialogue scene, the characters swap out, and the camera continues to shoot from the same direction. This meant that the natural light was consistent though it made no logical sense. How could both characters be facing the sun when they were talking face to face?

Days of Heaven (1973–1978)

For the scenes of plague and fury—first the locusts and then the inferno—inventiveness and preparation were called on. For the locusts, some live creatures were delivered and filmed in close-up: some were glued to stalks of grass to allow the camera enough time to capture them. For a particularly wide shot, helicopters dropped peanut shells from the sky while the actors and tractors moved backward, so that when the film was reversed, it looked like the insects were rising from the ground in a huge swarm. This technique was borrowed from Sidney Franklin's *The Good Earth* (1937).

Another technique solved a persistent problem: how to film an actor's face in firelight. The fire itself didn't give enough light, but when artificial light was added, it overpowered the natural light source. Almendros happened on a solution when he realized that he could control the kerosene burners used to light the fire. A burner held off camera but close to the actor's face provided enough light and flickered naturally.[44]

Fire brought a solution but also presented a dangerous problem. After the *Badlands* experience, Malick was not taking the use of fire lightly, but his script called for a large fire with many people running and trying to douse the blaze. Weeks before the scenes were filmed, an expert on prairie fires from the Agricultural Office was brought on set to advise how best to organize the shoot. He instructed the crew on how to light the fires and create a fifty-lane firebreak alternated with fifty lanes of wheat to be burned. Five acres of wheat were bought, and the Hutterites were asked to harvest at fifty-lane intervals, leaving the untouched wheat in between, earmarked to be burned. The equipment and actors could be positioned in the cleared safety lanes while a field was set on fire with diesel. Actors played their scenes in these safety lanes, and the camera crew ran to catch the best shots as the flames leaped in the background. Malick drove one of the land locomotives, the heavy tractors, through the fire. The fire was shot over six nights.[45] According to Rick Drew, the shot of the coyote shows an actual wild animal that was caught in the midst of the flames.[46]

Almendros describes the filming: "Each night we set fire to a new wheat-field. Several times we were alarmed because the fire spread too rapidly. On one occasion we were suddenly surrounded by huge flames and the air became suffocating. But our grips reacted quickly, evacuating the trucks with all the equipment—and ourselves as well—through the flames. No one wore special clothing, and we had only goggles to protect us from the smoke. It was a dangerous adventure, but this was a blessed film."[47] The blessedness of the film is open to argument, and Almendros's rosy view of the production is in part influenced by the fact that *Days of Heaven* won him an Oscar and paved the way for the extensive and successful Hollywood phase of his career. Almendros's failing eyesight is often quoted as one of the almost comical litany of things going wrong on the shoot—the blind cameraman, the deaf piano player—but he managed to see well enough to find his way up the steps to pick up his Oscar.

Harold Schneider, painfully aware any extra expenditure went out of his brother Bert's pocket, balked at the lengthening delay. Also, Almendros's next film, Truffaut's *The Man Who Loved Women* (1977), hadn't been delayed, so—again—Malick needed another cinematographer. Haskell Wexler came in to finish the shoot. Almendros recalls that he selected Wexler and that Wexler arrived for a week of overlap so the new cinematographer could familiarize himself with Almendros's technique, hoping to match it consistently. Wexler shortens the time of the overlap to a day and suggests that he was brought in by Bert Schneider: "I knew Bert Schneider, and they were way behind schedule, and I think they thought there was a need for someone who could push Terry a little bit. Bert wanted me to keep things going."[48] With a new impetus, Wexler completed principal photography in three weeks, moving down to Calgary to shoot the final scenes of Linda and Abby's parting after Bill's death. Linda's escape from school was the last shot filmed in Canada.

The production was over budget and over schedule. Worse still, Malick wasn't sure he even had a film. A huge amount of footage had been shot, but when he watched the assembly cut back in LA, the performances seemed flat; the story stale. It bored him. With Billy Weber beside him, he started work. "Richard was quite good," Weber says. "But Sam was not an actor. He's a great, wonderful playwright, and a pleasant person. Brooke was fine. But Terry wasn't happy with what he'd written for Brooke and Sam."[49] Dialogue already cut to a minimum was cut even further, creating an almost silent movie. Without dialogue, the film became beautiful but opaque. The audience wouldn't be able to follow what was happening.

One solution was to use voice-over, but Malick resisted. He'd used it once already, and wasn't it evidence of poor storytelling? He'd conceived of *Badlands* with Holly's narration as a crucial element, but there was no narration in the *Days of Heaven* script. Who'd tell the story? Abby? Malick wrote diary entries and had Adams read them but wasn't pleased. The other options were Linda Manz and Jackie Schultz, and Malick wrote a voice-over with them conversing to lay over the action of the film. Manz flew out to Los Angeles

Days of Heaven (1973–1978)

from New York, but with no more money for hotels, she stayed at the house of Billy Weber's assistant, whose wife, Colleen, was very religious. Weber says: "Colleen used to read from the Bible every night to her kids when Linda was staying there." The recording sessions took place at Malick's house. On the night of the last session, with Malick using a Nagra recorder, Manz said to him: "Oh, you should hear what Colleen read to us last night." Malick wanted to finish the session and have her simply read the script he'd prepared. But she insisted. At eleven o'clock that night, Weber got an excited phone call from Malick: "He said, 'You're not going to believe what's going on here. I've run out of quarter-inch tape. I've recorded on all of it.'"[50]

Manz was retelling Colleen's story of the end of the world and the apocalypse but using her own language, and Malick was enraptured. Manz recalls: "They took me into a voice recording studio. No script, nothing, I just watched the movie and rambled on. . . . I dunno, they took whatever they liked."[51] The apocalypse became a full story:

> I met this guy named Ding-Dong. He tell me the whole earth is
> going up in flames. Flames will come out of here and there, and it'll
> just rise up. The mountains are going to go up in big flames. The
> water's going to rise in flames. There's going to be creatures running
> every which way, some of them burnt, half their wings burnin'.
> People are going to be screaming and howling for help. They—The
> people that's been good, they're going to go to heaven and escape
> all that fire. But if you've been bad, God don't even hear you. He
> don't even hear you talking.

The film clicked: the missing element in place. Weber says: "We kept Linda in LA. We'd show Linda a scene in the movie and then turn off the picture and say, 'What just happened there?' She'd give her version of what happened: 'He didn't get any sicker. He didn't get any better. He just stayed the same.' That was Linda telling her version of what happened. When Terry realized, he started to write voice-over for her like that. In her case, we recorded maybe sixty hours of voice-over. There's fifteen minutes in the movie."[52] Jacob Brackman contributed to the writing.

Linda Manz's narration had a relationship with what was being seen on the screen, but it wasn't a straightforward expository voice-over. Instead, it added another layer of meaning, a poetry. "Give him a flower he'd keep it forever," Malick wrote, but he was careful to keep her voice consistent. Placing the voice-over was fluid. Billy Weber says: "We'll take one line of voice-over, make a loop of it, and play it against an entire reel of the picture to see where it works."[53]

The studio was antsy, and Bert Schneider was panicking. Weber prepared a reel and screened it for Paramount. The cinematography was impressive; the execs liked what they saw and agreed to foot the bill, even covering some extra shooting and Bert Schneider's exposure. Malick, Wexler, and Paul Ryan shot some more material in California. The opening of the film in the Chicago steel mill was shot on location in Los Angeles with Wexler using the handheld camera to immerse the audience in the noisy industrial environment. Malick is in the background of a shot as Brooke Adams sorts through the scrap heap outside the mill. The fluid movement and the violent fire rhymes with the fires of the tractors as well as the locusts and fire scene later on. The mill foreman was played by Stuart Margolin, a regular on the TV show *The Rockford Files*.

Sam Shepard was shot from a low angle against the sky to hide the change of location. According to Richard Gere, this almost constituted another film's worth of footage.[54] One shot of a dropped wineglass in a river was filmed in Sissy Spacek and Jack Fisk's house in Topanga Canyon, using their fish tank. The same was used for the scene in which Bill is gunned down on the river. In one of the most surprising and moving shots of the whole film, Bill falls into the water, and there is a quick cut to an underwater shot looking up as Bill's face splashes into view, the bubbles forming an instant death mask. As Bill's face passes from one element to another, he passes from this life into the next. That such a sublime and poetic image was achieved by repeatedly dunking Richard Gere's head in Sissy Spacek's aquarium is an almost perfect summation of the mystery and magic of filmmaking combined with the mundane trickery Malick enjoyed using.

The film had already paid off for Gere before it was even released. Harold Schneider showed director Richard Brooks some early scenes, and Brooks was impressed, casting Gere in *Looking for Mr. Goodbar* in the eye-catching role of the street punk Tony, opposite Diane Keaton. The film was shot, edited, and released in 1977, a year before *Days of Heaven*. This fact did nothing to dispel Malick's growing reputation for meticulous slowness.

For the music, Italian soundtrack maestro Ennio Morricone was hired. Guitarist Leo Kottke had provided some music already, but Weber and Malick had been using Morricone's score to Bernardo Bertolucci's *1900* (1976) as a temp track while editing. Malick flew to Rome to watch as

Days of Heaven (1973–1978)

Morricone recorded the score. Morricone says: "In some cases, not always, he suggested some musical solutions, which annoyed me. I remember he asked me to orchestrate a piece for three flutes, something impossible which of course was finally excluded. But exactly this way of working made me appreciate him, for the attention and devotion with which he worked on the film."[55] Malick spent a month in Italy with the composer, eating with his family and becoming close friends. Morricone enjoyed chess and challenged Malick constantly while they were working. Understandably reluctant— Morricone was an expert chess player—Malick tried to decline, only for the composer to lure him by giving up pieces in advance: "I'll give you a rook and a bishop." Nevertheless, Morricone always won.

To Morricone's frustration, Malick used Camille Saint-Saëns's 1886 composition "The Aquarium" from *The Carnival of the Animals* as the title music. The suite was mostly written for the musician's own amusement as he recovered from a particularly harsh critical mauling. Played on a string quartet with an additional two pianos, a flute, and a glass harmonica, the piece is a haunting, magical theme with the glissandi and arpeggios suggesting a downward trickling. The music was adopted by the Cannes Film Festival in the official introduction played before all competition films. Although irritated, Morricone used it as a model for the score, mirroring its scales and instrumentation. Leo Kottke's guitar piece "The Train and the Gate" accompanies the migrant workers as they arrive on the train and later is replayed as Bill, Abby, and Linda escape by boat. On his 1978 album *Burnt Lips*, Kottke included the track, along with more music he had composed specifically for the film, in "The Credits: Outtakes from Terry's Movie."

The final cut of the film was blown up from 35mm to 70mm to maximize its visual beauty. Malick supervised the Dolby mix. "Dolby purifies sound and is able to record multiple audio tracks (the wind, the rustle of corn stalks, the pulse of crickets)," he explained. "I wanted to remove any distance from the public."[56] The sound at the beginning of the picture is particularly immersive, with the pounding of machinery in the steel mill drowning out the dialogue—oddly reminiscent of a David Lynch–style industrial soundscape used in *Eraserhead*—and proving that the environment has an immediate impact on the characters and audience. The pounding industrial sound returns as the tractors harvest the wheat fields: the countryside is no escape from industrial progress.

The film has frequently been reported as another example of an "out of control" New Hollywood director, as popularized by Peter Biskind's 1998 book *Easy Riders, Raging Bulls: How the Sex-Drugs-and-Rock-'n-Roll Generation Saved Hollywood*. But these claims are exaggerated. The *Days of Heaven* shoot began on August 31, 1976, and finished in November of the same year. It was roughly fourteen weeks—long but by no means extraordinary. Another frequently quoted number is the two years the film took to edit. This number is also inflated. The film was previewed in Los Angeles in early August 1978. In comparison, Michael Cimino's *Heaven's Gate* (1980) took almost an entire year in principal photography and cost $44 million. William Friedkin's *Sorcerer* (1977) also took a year to shoot and cost $22 million. Francis Ford Coppola's *Apocalypse Now* (1979) had so many delays that it provoked the headline "Apocalypse When?," taking over a year to complete photography and costing $35 million with a further two years in postproduction. *Days of Heaven* cost $3 million, taking fourteen weeks to shoot and a year and a half to edit: the time between the start of filming and the first screening was less than two years in total. Paramount, which had a much worse headache brewing in South America with *Sorcerer*, was worried but not panicked. Malick was indulged but not out of control.

The preview in August included guests such as John Milius, Candice Bergen, and François Truffaut. John Travolta also attended, feeling a twinge watching Gere in his role. The applause was "strong and sustained."[57] On September 13, it had its New York premiere, before going on general release. As with *Badlands*, the film was not universally acclaimed. Many of the reviews struggled with the elliptical storytelling despite the undeniable beauty of the visuals. In fact, was the film too beautiful? For the *New York Times*, Harold C. Schonberg wrote: "*Days of Heaven* never really makes up its mind what it wants to be. It ends up something between a Texas pastoral and Cavalleria Rusticana. Back of what basically is a conventional plot is all kinds of fancy, self-conscious cineaste techniques."[58] The *Chicago Tribune's* Monica Eng expressed a common reaction, lamenting that "the story becomes secondary to the visuals."[59] Perhaps the most piercing expression of this criticism came from a critic who had been a voice of dissent in the original appraisal of *Badlands*, Pauline Kael. In a capsule review written for a book in 1985, she writes: "The film is an empty Christmas tree: you can hang all your dumb metaphors on it."[60] As with much of Kael's criticism, it takes aim at the audience rather than the film.

The film had its champions. Dave Kehr of the *Chicago Reader* wrote: "Nestor Almendros's cinematography is as sharp and vivid as Malick's narration is elliptical and enigmatic. The result is a film that hovers just beyond our grasp—mysterious, beautiful, and, very possibly, a masterpiece."[61]

Days of Heaven (1973–1978)

Variety called the film "one of the great cinematic achievements of the 1970s." Gene Siskel of the *Chicago Tribune* responded to some of his colleagues' doubts: "Some critics have complained that the *Days of Heaven* story is too slight. I suppose it is, but, frankly, you don't think about it while the movie is playing."[62] Frank Rich wrote in *Time*: "There is enough beauty here for a dozen movies; yet the total effect is far from pretty."[63]

The film received four nominations for the Academy Awards: Ennio Morricone for his music; John Wilkinson, Robert W. Glass Jr., John T. Reitz, and Barry Thomas for sound editing; Patricia Norris for costume design; and Néstor Almendros for cinematography. Retrospectively, it's astounding that the film didn't receive other nominations—not least of all one for Malick himself as best director. It is equally baffling that Giorgio Moroder's score for Alan Parker's Turkish jail movie *Midnight Express* beat out Ennio Morricone's score to win best soundtrack. The only award granted *Days of Heaven* was picked up by Almendros, encapsulating the consensus that this was a beautifully photographed film. In his speech, he thanked his camera operators and Haskell Wexler by name for finishing off his work but gave his most heartfelt thanks to Terrence Malick: "These images belong entirely to him. This Oscar should be for him."

The Oscar win served as an affirmation of Malick's approach, but Wexler was upset that his credit was reduced to "additional photography." He wrote a letter to Roger Ebert, describing how he sat in a theater with a stopwatch as he watched the film and timed his contributions.[64] Later he changed his mind: "I thought, 'Well, God damn it. I should get credit with Néstor on it.' And then I had talks with the producer, Bert Schneider, and he said, 'Look, you've won Oscars already. What the hell, Néstor should have it.' So then I said to myself, 'Well, Haskell, you're being a little selfish.'" Almendros, he realized, had set the tone of the film, so he resigned himself to Almendros taking the trophy.[65]

However, as with *Badlands*, *Days of Heaven* actually had three cinematographers. Along with Almendros and Wexler, Paul Ryan contributed significantly to the film with his second unit and their extensive photography in Montana. Ryan also filmed some of the steel mill scene. Ryan says Malick hired him when he first arrived in LA: "Over lunch, we went through the whole script and he articulated descriptions that made it come alive. I took a small crew to Montana and spent seven weeks shooting wheat fields in the wind, people floating down the river, fires at night, grasshoppers and curious-looking birds." In postproduction, Wexler had left the steel mill footage incomplete, and so Ryan was asked to complete the scenes. Ryan shot for another week with the actors in Ojai and Piru, two Californian towns doubling for Texas.

In 1979, Malick traveled to the Côte d'Azur to attend the Cannes Film Festival, where his work was applauded and he himself was awarded the Palme for Best Director, the first time an American director had won the award since 1955. In France, he also gave his final interview to date. Other contemporary American directors—Steven Spielberg, George Lucas, Francis Ford Coppola, Brian De Palma, and Martin Scorsese—were becoming celebrities in their own right, appearing on Dick Cavett and looking like rock stars. Malick wanted the two parts of his life to be completely separate. He wanted privacy and began to insist that his image not be used as promotional material.

The final interview with Yvonne Baby was published in *Le Monde* on May 17, 1979. It begins with a rare glimpse of Malick outside the editing suite or a film location: "It is a May afternoon. I join Terrence Malick on a familiar terrace of a Parisian café. His goodness is visible in his short beard and black eyes. Terrence Malick, as I see and will see in each ensuing encounter, is fully present yet fully absent. He leads the double life of the artist: resolute, constant, and acrobatic in a way that maintains and strengthens his internal balance. My eldest son believes Terrence Malick is a wise man and my son is right." In the article, Malick talks about his upbringing and his education, as well as the making of *Badlands* and *Days of Heaven*. As ever, he is generous with his praise for his collaborators: "Linda [Manz], the teenage girl, is the heart of the film." Néstor Almendros is "courageous."

Malick is aware of how the film exists outside of audience expectations: "For the audience, I am tempted to say, to experience it like a walk in the countryside. You'll probably be bored or have other things in mind but perhaps you'll be struck, suddenly by a feeling, by an act, by a unique portrait of nature." He describes his reason for working on period films: "It would be difficult for me to make a film about contemporary America today. We live in such dark times and we have gradually lost our open spaces." However, there is hope, rooted in cinema: "These films can enable small changes of heart . . . to live better and to love more."[66]

Despite the difficult production, *Days of Heaven* stands as one of the best American films ever made. Unlike *Sorcerer* (1977), which Friedkin himself disowned for many years, or Cimino's tinkered-with *Heaven's Gate* (1980), it didn't need to be rediscovered or go through a series of alternative cuts. The

Days of Heaven (1973–1978)

theatrical cut is the only cut. And it's as near to perfect as a film can be. Whatever had gone into its making clearly worked. What others viewed as Malick's chaotic and unconventional approach had produced two of the most startling and impressive films of the 1970s. The film to some degree was found in the edit. The original script offered roughly the same story, but scenes of dialogue were reduced to single shots in montages, speeches became glances—everything was pared down and overlayered with Linda Manz's remarkable voice-over. Its claim to being poetic has as much to do with its economy as its beauty.

There's some continuity with *Badlands*. Both films center on an unorthodox couple of outlaws; both feature beautiful photography, naturalistic performances, and a gorgeous use of music. Both take place in a distinctly American past and out of doors in a sharply realized natural world. Both boast female voices that tell and comment on the story with a wry humor. Both conclude with their male leads dead and their women unmoored and out in the world. But *Days of Heaven* has a breadth and depth and ambition. The story earns its biblical allusion. The characters learn and change, even as they are trapped by their own misunderstandings. There's an empathy that makes their ending genuinely tragic. The farmer spies what he thinks is an ongoing betrayal when what he is seeing is, in fact, the end of Bill and Abby's relationship. The conclusion of Bill and Abby's love is remarkably without rancor. Bill blames himself entirely and absolves her of guilt. In the context of grinding poverty and the injustice of inequality, Abby and Bill are justified in their subterfuge, but despite his riches, the farmer too is from immigrant stock. It's a tragedy in which everyone is right and no one is happy.

And the beauty of the film is not just decorous: a Christmas tree. The light in which warehouses become cathedrals and farmland looks like fields of heaven can console or mock the poor and the lovelorn, elevate or belittle them, and is as fickle as a cloud passing over the sun. That's the thing about the magic hour: the light is always dying. Linda, as the "mud doctor"—someone with dirt under her fingernails who could keep a flower forever—is the most connected to the natural world. She notices the locusts, listens to the earth:

> At first it was a bit frustrating to work with her. She couldn't remember her lines, couldn't be interrupted, and was difficult to photograph—she couldn't help but stare at the camera lens. Despite this, I started to love her and I believed in her more than anything else. She transformed the role. I am glad that she's the narrator. Her

personality shines through the film's objectivity. Every time I gave her new lines, she interpreted it in her own way. . . . I feel like I have not been able to grasp a fraction of who she really is.[67]

The prize from Cannes was a remarkable accomplishment for the young director. More importantly, Charles Bluhdorn, the president of Gulf and Western, the parent company of Paramount, was so impressed, he offered Malick a sweetheart deal. Bluhdorn told Malick: "I want you to make movies for me. I don't care if your movies never make a nickel." Malick was given an office on the Paramount lot, and key collaborators, like Weber, were put on the studio payroll.[68] Paramount already made money with its "high-concept" movies such as *Saturday Night Fever* (1977) and *Grease* (1978). It wanted prestige pictures, which Robert Evans had once been fundamental in bringing to the studio: films like *Rosemary's Baby* (1968), *The Godfather* (1972), and *Chinatown* (1974)—films that did well at the box office, picked up Oscars, and dominated the conversation. Bluhdorn believed Malick to be this kind of filmmaker, and so he offered him carte blanche. It was a surprise. When Malick finished filming *Days of Heaven*, he told Fisk: "Now, we have to do one for uncle," meaning the studio. No more hunting up finances from a mixture of friends and associates, no more independent producers and penny-pinching budgets.

So the question was: What film would he direct next?

The answer was not immediately apparent. And after a while, the silence lengthened. In fact, Terrence Malick would not release another film for twenty years. This gap in his filmography has shaped his reputation arguably more than any one of his films. Linked to his refusal to give interviews, it has led journalists to characterize him as cinema's equivalent of J. D. Salinger or Thomas Pynchon, or "Hollywood's Big Foot," as *TMZ* tagged him.[69] It's created a mystique around him unlike that of any other living film director, albeit not without a cost. As early as 1985, David Handelman wrote an article for *California Magazine* titled "The Absence of Malick," wondering at the mystery of the director's disappearance and cold-calling him to no avail.[70] Peter Biskind wrote a profile for *Vanity Fair* titled "The Runaway Genius."[71] Gossip and legends filled the vacuum left by the director: Malick was walking across the country, observing birds, teaching philosophy at the Sorbonne. He had become a hairdresser. He had retired from filmmaking entirely. He was a drug addict, or a hermit, or both.

The truth, however, is at once more prosaic and more interesting.

The Tree of Life, Waco. (Photograph by author.)

Terrence Malick. (Photograph by Emil Malick.)

Malick attending a screening at the Greystone/AFI Theater. (©1969 courtesy of American Film Institute.)

Terrence Malick performing in a school play. (Courtesy of St. Stephen's Episcopal School.)

Filming *Lanton Mills*, Caleb Deschanel kneels in front of Harry Dean Stanton. Malick, in costume, directs with a gun in his belt. (*Lanton Mills* ©1970, courtesy of American Film Institute.)

Pocket Money, First Artists/National General Pictures, 1972.

Malick as "a famous detective." *Badlands*, Pressman-Williams Productions/Warner Brothers, 1973.

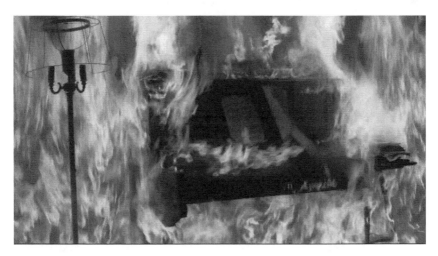

The piano burns. *Badlands*, Pressman-Williams Productions/Warner Brothers, 1973.

Malick's other cameo as the visitor. *Badlands*, Pressman-Williams Productions/Warner Brothers, 1973.

From left to right: Malick, Patsy McArthur, Caril Ann Fugate, Martin Sheen, James McArthur, and John McArthur after a screening of *Badlands* in York, Nebraska. (Courtesy of Jeff McArthur.)

Paul Williams and Terrence Malick in Cuba. (Courtesy of Paul Williams.)

Drawing for the Belvedere, by Jack Fisk. (Courtesy of Jack Fisk.)

Painting *Days of Heaven*, by Brooke Adams. (Courtesy of Brooke Adams.)

Bill (Richard Gere) dies. *Days of Heaven*, Paramount, 1978.

Rue Jacob, Malick's home when he first arrived in Paris. (Courtesy of Uwe Meyer.)

Col. Tall (Nick Nolte) with a digitally inserted "rosy-fingered dawn." *The Thin Red Line*, Geisler-Roberdeau, Phoenix Pictures, Fox 2000/20th Century Fox, 1998.

The O'Briens' house today. (Photograph by author.)

Terrence Malick. (Photograph by Emil Malick.)

Marina/Michelle (Olga Kurylenko) sees the Wonder. *To the Wonder*, Brothers K Productions/Magnolia Pictures, 2012.

6

Paris-Texas (1979-1995)

Cinema's great recluses are almost never actual recluses. Greta Garbo famously "wanted to be alone" but was also referred to as "the recluse about town" for how often she was spotted being alone.[1] Stanley Kubrick didn't grant many interviews, but he had a wide circle of friends, spoke with people frequently on the phone, and was a common figure in his neighborhood, to the extent that a friend of mine once bumped into him by the pick-and-mix at the Woolworths in St. Albans. Up until 1978, Terrence Malick was available for interviews, though not particularly in demand. He'd made two films, neither of which had garnered more than moderate success. But for the next twenty years—until the release of *The Thin Red Line* in 1998— his reputation as one of cinema's most mysterious figures grew among cinephiles.

Many have speculated about exactly why Malick chose to withdraw from the spotlight. *Variety*'s Peter Bart gave three reasons: "1. He thinks auteurs sound fatuous and defensive when they try to explain themselves and their work. 2. He has an exaggerated sense of privacy. He doesn't want to be asked questions like 'Why haven't you made a movie for 20 years?' because, to his way of thinking, that's nobody's business. Besides, he doesn't know the answer. 3. He's not a very good talker. Sure, like any Harvard man and Rhodes Scholar, Terry uses the language masterfully, but his ideas are so abstract that they tend to get lost in an epistemological fog."[2]

A disastrous interview has been posited, although of the few interviews he gave, none match that description. Crippling shyness is perhaps plausible, except for the evidence of so many friendships, many of which were initiated by a phone call out of the blue from Malick himself. Whatever the cause, the silence remains to the time of writing—begetting the paradoxical but predictable effect of being louder than the interviews, commentary tracks, and verbiage of his more conventional colleagues.

THE MAGIC HOURS

But despite not talking to the media, Malick—like Kubrick—has a wide collection of friends and acquaintances with whom he communicates on a regular basis. He's even prepared to talk to journalists, on condition that those conversations remain off the record. David Thomson met him in the 1990s: "It turned out that there was nothing reclusive about him. He was friendly, every bit as intelligent as you expected, and informed and experienced in many subjects—but disinclined to talk about movies. After the self-preoccupation of some other directors, he was refreshing and endearing."[3] He was generous with other filmmakers. He typed letters congratulating them on their work. An early example is dated July 8, 1974, and addressed to Mike Hodges, the director of *Get Carter* (1971): "I have just come from seeing 'The Terminal Man' and want you to know what a magnificent, overwhelming picture it is. You achieve moods that I've never experienced in the movies before, though it's only in hope of finding them that I keep going."[4]

By the end of the 1970s, Malick was well connected with the film industry and the counterculture. He had many offers of work, and not only from the powerful studio head of Paramount, Charlie Bluhdorn. Tommy Chong, half of the stoner comedy duo Cheech and Chong, phoned Malick to ask him to direct the follow-up to *Up in Smoke*. Malick told Chong he should direct it himself: "If it's your vision then you have to see it through yourself."[5] Former agent Mike Medavoy felt that Malick always intended to take a break, "just not that long," a line reminiscent of Lanton Mills wanting to be criminal, "just not this big a one."[6] The work on *Badlands* and *Days of Heaven* had been exhausting, but Malick had future projects in mind.

Part of the mystery was strategic. Often collaborators wouldn't know that other projects were being developed in parallel with their own, each compartmentalized in case one fell through (which it should be noted is standard industry practice). An independent producer, Bobby Geisler, approached Malick to film David Rabe's play *In the Boom Boom Room*. Geisler told Peter Biskind he was stunned to receive an invitation to a screening of *Days of Heaven*. Malick hadn't mentioned that the film was finished. "I thought Terry was a genius, an artist, and I was completely mesmerized by him," Geisler says. "I felt better when I was with him, and more than anything I wanted to learn from him, swore that I would produce a play or a movie of Terry's if it was the last thing that I did."[7]

But *In the Boom Boom Room* wasn't going to be that production. Perhaps a revival was premature. First performed in 1972, the play reached Broadway in late 1973, with Madeline Kahn in the lead, as a dancer in the eponymous nightclub. Malick's counterproposal was a theatrical version of the story of Joseph Merrick, the Elephant Man. Rather than aiming for Broadway, Malick saw the production as playing through the Midwest, envisioning an experimental, interactive experience. Malick's proposal read: "It will be organized roughly like a Victorian carnival," mixing theater, film, vaudeville, and the Chautauqua, "an electronic circus, with sound and projection techniques beyond the capability of any movie theatre or concert hall."[8] Douglas Trumbull, *2001: A Space Odyssey* special effects ace, was recruited. The costume and set designers Frances and Eugene Lee and the magician Ricky Jay all met with Malick to discuss the project.

Merrick was another of Malick's outsiders, able to maintain nobility in the face of brutal treatment. The story had inspired a play by Bernard Pomerance, first performed in London in 1977 and Broadway in 1979. News of a film under the supervision of Mel Brooks began to filter into the trades, effectively voiding Malick's idea. Malick's AFI classmate David Lynch directed *The Elephant Man* in 1980.

The setback was temporary. Boosted by Charles Bluhdorn's confidence, Malick was thinking big. With Paramount's backing, Malick began to assemble his ideas before *Days of Heaven* was released. By the spring of 1979, he had a bulging folder of notes under the title "The Cosmogony." Billy Weber read it: "There was about a hundred pages written for the natural history part of it," but there was no story.[9] Another title for the project was "Q," short for "Qasida," an Arabic word for a type of ode. In the future, Malick often used letters as placeholders for titles: *To the Wonder* was Project D, for instance. "A great rose window of light, lasting only five or six seconds, so you can't testify to what you've seen," his notes read. A blend of astrophysics and mythic imagination follows: galaxies whirling in the void, primordial chaos, Dante's angels, a new god. All with the express purpose to "create a sense of the glory of the universe, its fathomless harmony, its deeply tonic character, even as we look at ancient scenes of violence." The film flows "like a river." According to Jacob Brackman, this Genesis/prehistoric sequence was to be a prologue to a conventional story but kept growing, "like the monster who ate Chicago!"[10]

Malick's preproduction team included Billy Weber, Paul Ryan who had photographed some of *Days of Heaven*, Peter Broderick, his assistant, and sound technician Jim Cox. Having finished production on *Star Trek: The Motion Picture* (1979), visual effects specialist Richard Taylor received a call from Malick. "It was night and day," Taylor recalls: "Working for Terry Malick was entirely one hundred and eighty degrees to anything—he's secretive, he's a decision-maker. Just his demeanor and everything about him was entirely different."[11] The hours were long and the work intense, but the challenges were inspiring, and the welfare of the team was not neglected. "Terry was one of the coolest guys I ever worked with," says Taylor. To foster group spirit, activities were organized, including playing Peruvian whistles in a circle, engaging in meditation exercises, and playing some good old-fashioned baseball on the back lot. When he needed money, Malick called Paramount exec Jeff Katzenberg. If there was any reluctance, Malick went over his head to Bluhdorn.[12]

Malick directly contacted nature documentarians and quizzed them on frost photography, cymatics (the study of fluids), and microphotographic techniques. A hint of this was already present in *Days of Heaven*, in which Malick included a short time-lapse sequence of a seedling sprouting through the earth. Malick sent Paul Ryan and a crew to record natural phenomena around the world: volcanic eruptions at Mount Etna and solar and lunar eclipses. Micro-jellyfish at the Great Barrier Reef were filmed for three months by photographer Peter Parks, who also worked at Oxford Scientific Films in England to produce what Malick referred to as "primeval images." Footage was made at the Pentecost Mines in Utah, where molten slag from the copper mine was poured at night, creating brilliant images that resembled an early stage in Earth's history. In the search for compelling footage, emissaries were sent to the two polar regions: Alaska and Antarctica.

As material was collected, the script morphed. In one version, the central narrative section was occupied with a multicharacter drama set in the Middle East during the First World War. A prologue was set in prehistoric times. But though he had scouts looking for locations in the Middle East, the section was abandoned, and the prehistoric sequence became the whole script.[13] The Middle Eastern section connected to Malick's own background, with the lives of his grandparents Nanajohn and Abimelech in Urmia, in northern Iran, as part of the source material. Malick had written a script based on his Armenian great-grandfather, whose life as a bandit was a source of constant fascination.[14] Despite the lack of a conventional story, a structure emerged. A first section tentatively referred to as Apsu, an ancient Akkadian/Sumerian word that denotes a primeval sea. For the film, Apsu was a sleeping god, dreaming the creation of the universe. The next sequence featured a light breaking through the chaotic soup and structure beginning to coalesce. Malick tasked pioneer computer animator John Whitney with creating a sequence showing the creation of galaxies and stars. Malick traveled to New York to meet light designer Richard Sandhaus, who later designed laser shows for Pink Floyd concerts. Malick was intrigued by a laser show used in Xenon, a new nightclub in New York. According to Sandhaus, Malick wanted the laser to shoot out of the screen and above the heads of the audience. Sections were set in the Precambrian and Devonian periods, and the Jurassic age was to include dinosaurs shot by Terry Carr and special effects legend Rick Baker, who would later win an Oscar for *An American Werewolf in London* (1981).

The longest section was devoted to the post-asteroid world with the extinction of the dinosaurs. For music, Malick hired Francesco Lupica, a street musician he'd met while walking with Billy Weber on the Venice boardwalk. He'd bought Lupica's cassette of the *Cosmic Beam Experience* and written him a letter of admiration asking him to come over to the offices where the Malick team was working. Lupica's unique sound was created by a long iron girder—his cosmic beam—which he rigged with wires and electrified. It had been used on *Star Trek: The Motion Picture*, but Malick saw it as having a role in his new film. It would feature in several Malick films.

Time, however, was an issue. A year and money had been spent and a team hired. Footage had been shot, but the film itself had no recognizable shape. With the chance to do everything, it was impossible to settle on one thing. Paramount wanted some return. With Bluhdorn's attention drifting, Malick's status began to shift in the studio, and with no conventional script, the film couldn't be budgeted or green-lit. For Billy Weber, the problem was simple. Malick just didn't have a story to tell. He told Weber he was closing the office, "and he moved to France."[15]

The cosmic ambitions of "Q" fizzled. Both *Badlands* and *Days of Heaven* were difficult shoots, rife with conflict—something Malick despised—and moments of intense self-doubt. Now in the heart of Hollywood and no longer a newcomer, he felt the weight of expectations. Both his films garnered praise, but they were divisive. The unconventional narratives split audiences, and although neither flopped, neither film was a significant commercial success. Perhaps he needed a break from Hollywood. It was like an army town, he thought. Everyone talking about the business. Constant pressure. Constant awareness he might miss a telephone call or an important meeting. That was the push factor.

The pull factor was his relationship with Michie Gleason, his assistant on *Days of Heaven*, who he had begun dating. Gleason was a UCLA film school graduate who had directed a documentary about women prisoners called *We're Alive* (1974) along with fellow graduates Kathy Levitt and Christine

THE MAGIC HOURS

Mohanna. A writer and activist, Gleason was preparing her first feature film, produced by Bert Schneider. *Broken English* told the story of Sarah (Beverly Ross), an American woman working for a Paris photo agency who falls in love with Maas (Jacques Martial), a young Senegalese intellectual she later learns is involved in anti-apartheid politics as part of an underground group. Malick moved to Paris with Gleason for the duration of the shoot. It was a city he loved. He could improve his French, recharge his batteries, read some Balzac, and do some writing. Then he decided to stay.

For Malick's team, the abandonment came as a shock. Richard Taylor got a call with instructions to pack everything up: Malick was in Paris with Michie and had no plans to return. Taylor says: "I had never put my heart into a project as much as I did that one."[16] Malick and Gleason shared an apartment on the Rue Jacob in the heart of Paris, but Malick soon rented another space to write, banging away at his typewriter. Néstor Almendros lent Malick his Paris apartment when he was out of town.

The filming was fraught. Bert Schneider pressured Michie to write more scenes for his wife, Greta Ronningen, and to include more sex scenes. Gleason had in mind a serious meditation on race, politics, and an engagement with the world, but Schneider sold the financiers a European sex film. Pressures mounted, and as filming finished, Malick and Gleason's relationship also came to an end. *Broken English* played at the San Francisco International Film Festival in 1981 but was not distributed, and it disappeared. It's now unavailable, except for some clips viewable via Gleason's own website. Over the next decades, Gleason's filmmaking was sporadic, with *Summer Heat* in 1987 and *The Island of the Mapmaker's Wife* in 2001.

Malick stayed in the Rue Jacob apartment, where he met another tenant of his building: Michèle Marie Morette. Michèle was born on April 19, 1947, in a Parisian suburb, Neuilly, a half-hour's drive from the Eiffel Tower. She was thirty and had a young daughter from a previous relationship, Alexandra. The three formed the beginnings of a family. Michèle told Peter Biskind: "He takes you places where you never go with regular people. He's interested in everything from ants and plants and flowers and grass to philosophy. And it's not superficial. He reads all the time and remembers everything. He's got this incredible charm . . . something interior."[17] According to Biskind, "She thought of herself as average, unglamorous. She cooked and did dishes while Malick played father to Alex. Occasionally, they attended Mass."[18] The relationship is depicted in *To the Wonder*, a film as intensely personal and autobiographical as *The Tree of Life*.

100

Paris–Texas (1979–1995)

Malick's Parisian sojourn was briefer and more intermittent than is usually thought. For the first year, he was flying to Los Angeles to keep tabs on his cosmology project, "Q." After shutting it down, Malick spent more time in Paris but still communicated with family and friends in the United States and regularly received visitors. One meeting was particularly significant. In the spring of 1981, Martin Sheen bumped into Malick on the street in Paris. Sheen was shooting *Enigma* (1982), an espionage thriller. He'd last seen Malick five years earlier during a break in the filming of *Apocalypse Now* (1979). He writes in his autobiography that Malick had "moved to Paris and married a Frenchwoman named Michèle. They were living on Rue Jacob, close to [Sheen's] hotel."[19]

Michèle and Malick weren't yet married, but the relationship must have struck Sheen as serious. He took to seeing Malick every evening after filming. Sheen reports: "He spoke four languages, and I couldn't mention a book he hadn't read. Conversations with him were like a tutorial."[20] For the duration of the shoot, Sheen says, he became Malick's "informal education project." As well as showing him how to get around on the metro, Malick took the actor further afield on tours of Île Saint-Louis and Île de la Cité. They spent an evening at the Saint-Germain-des-Prés, the oldest church in Paris, where local musicians played and others prayed. Sheen observes: "Terry loved hearing their beautiful voices fill that space and sometimes we would sit listening for long periods, in rapture." Sheen opened up to Malick about the doubts and fears he'd been experiencing since his near-fatal heart attack in the Philippines while filming *Apocalypse Now*. From playing the tourist guide, Malick became something far more significant to the actor: "Deeply spiritual, Terry was a devout Anglican and he recognized that I was going through a personal transition. Slowly, without either of us realizing it at first, he became my spiritual director. We talked about the need to live an authentic life and that the individual is the only one who truly knows when he or she is being honest or dishonest. 'Our opinions of ourselves are the only ones that matter,' Terry told me."[21]

One day, during a visit to the Shakespeare & Company bookshop, Malick gave Sheen a copy of *The Brothers Karamazov*, telling him: "Read this book. I think it'll have an effect on you."[22] Later, he gave Olga Kurylenko the same book as part of her preparation to play Marina/Michèle in *To the Wonder*. Soon after, Sheen visited Saint Joseph's Catholic Church near the Arc de Triomphe, and there he returned to the Catholic Church, affirming a faith he'd lost: a life-changing moment he ascribes to his friendship with Malick.

THE MAGIC HOURS

Other friends visited while in Europe. His St. Stephen's roommate Jim Romberg and his wife met up with Malick and Michèle.[23] John Womack's daughter Liza came over to stay in Paris: "Terry was there, and he brought me to all sorts of dinner parties and introduced me to counts and countesses, which I thought was pretty cool."[24] Charlie Bluhdorn was dead, and Malick's deal with Paramount expired in 1983. His ex-agent and friend Mike Medavoy dined with Malick in Paris and regularly phoned, always on the lookout for writing projects that might interest Malick and on which they could work together. The 1970s had been good to Medavoy. As West Coast head of production at United Artists, he was instrumental in the revival of the studio's fortunes, with a series of hits, including three straight Best Picture Oscars: *One Flew Over the Cuckoo's Nest* (1975), *Rocky* (1976), and *Annie Hall* (1977). Just before United Artists floundered into the money pit of *Heaven's Gate* (1980), Medavoy left and founded Orion Films, which produced 1980s hits like *The Terminator* (1984), *Amadeus* (1984), and *Platoon* (1986).

Orion optioned Myra Lewis and Murray Silver's 1982 book *Great Balls of Fire: The Uncensored Story of Jerry Lee Lewis*, and Medavoy hired Malick to write a script. The *Los Angeles Times* announced: "Terrence Malick—absent from the screen for nine years, since writing and directing the acclaimed 'Days of Heaven'—is coming back."[25] The deal was already packaged with Malick writing, Jim McBride directing, and Dennis Quaid cast to star as the pioneering rock and roll singer and hell-raising piano player. It was the first glimpse of Malick active in the world, and his agent, Paula Weinstein, was keen to impress on the *LA Times* readership how active Malick was: "Malick's rep seemed relieved that he's back at work ('The phone sure rings a lot for him'), but couldn't say why he opted to return with this project ('I guess it's just something he's interested in'). She added that he's just getting started on the script and that 'he'll probably do most of the writing from Europe.'"[26]

Malick spent his time reading, listening to music, and bird-watching. He enjoyed walking in the mountains in France, Germany, and Italy, staying in hostels along the way. Meanwhile, he was writing, working, and reworking the "Q" script throughout this period, as well as redrafting and writing other original screenplays. Any journey he and Michèle took could double as a location scout for "Q" or any other project he hoped eventually to make. He kept files for all his projects.

As he had at AFI, Malick was earning good money as a script doctor, a secretive and uncredited role involving nondisclosure agreements. Most of the scripts did not make it to production, but the money was good. Ned

Paris–Texas (1979–1995)

Tanen at Universal hired Malick to rework a Robert Dillon script for a film called *Countryman*, to be produced by Edward Lewis and Robert Cortes in 1984. It never got made. He also worked on a project for Louis Malle. During the summer, he would stay with Michèle at Malle's country home in France, where Malle appeared at breakfast wearing a shirt with the inscription "I survived a Catholic childhood." Malle was now married to Candice Bergen, who knew Malick from their trip to Cuba with Bert Schneider, with whom she had been involved. The film was based on Tracy Kidder's nonfiction work *Among Schoolchildren*, which offered a profile of a teacher working in a deprived area. Malick shifted the location from Massachusetts to El Paso, Texas.

The many projects pursued in this period show that Malick's interests were wide-ranging, and he was willing to work in a number of different genres and on other people's material. *Countryman* had been described as a *Grapes of Wrath*–style story, and so the writer of *Days of Heaven* was eminently suitable. On the other hand, the musical biopic of Jerry Lee Lewis was a departure although it took him to a period only slightly later than the setting of *Badlands* and keyed into his intense interest in music and musicians. According to Medavoy, Malick's script was too dark. And yet when the film was finally made, from a screenplay by Jack Baran and Jim McBride, it was criticized for overly sanitizing its subject.[27] Malick's fascination with the story remained, and he continued to pitch it as the years went on. Many of his ideas found their way into *Song to Song*.

By 1985, Malick was back in the United States with Michèle and Alexandra, moving among several addresses in Austin, Texas. He and Michèle got married on July 5 in Williamsburg, just north of Austin, Texas. Malick had come full circle, though his homing instincts returned him to the proximity of St. Stephen's rather than Waco or Bartlesville, Oklahoma, where his family lived. Most of the information about this period and Michèle Morette can be gleaned from Peter Biskind's *Vanity Fair* article "The Runaway Genius," but it was written after the breakup of the marriage and partly at the behest of two producers who were alienated from Malick. With Malick refusing to comment for the piece, the recriminations paint an inevitably one-sided picture. It isn't to be discounted, but should be treated with caution.[28]

Malick, Alexandra, and Michèle visited his family in Bartlesville frequently, according to Biskind. Malick got on well with his mother but still argued bitterly with his father over trivial things like whether to wear a tie to church. In *The Tree of Life*, we overhear a phone conversation as adult Jack apologizes for arguing with his father the previous day. Emil's unstinted fondness for taking photographs also irritated his famous son. Malick had developed a genuine dislike of being photographed. Michèle reports that her first real fight with Malick was over the buying of a television, which she thought would help Alexandra to adapt better to American life and improve her English, but Malick regarded television as trash. In Biskind's article, Malick emerges as a domestic tyrant, a paranoid defender of his own privacy: he hides the covers of the books he's reading. (Another source told me that the spines of all the books on Malick's shelves face the wall.) The article describes Malick as "compulsively neat and possessive of things." He doesn't like to talk to Michèle about his work. Biskind describes Michèle as an isolated figure trying to fit into Malick's world but discovering on a trip to LA that none of his friends knew they were married. This sounds similar to the compartmentalization that had friends learning about his divorce from Jill Jakes only indirectly and once it was completed.

Though Biskind's article portrays Malick as the kind of eccentric who fits neatly into the gallery of New Hollywood obsessives populating *Easy Riders, Raging Bulls*, Michèle's perspective deserves heeding, and her unhappiness feels palpable: "She felt she had ceased to exist." With no friends in the country, she felt increasingly distant from her husband. One reason for taking the article seriously is how closely it matches the portrait of Marina in *To the Wonder*. She marvels at the supermarkets and Americana but is quickly stymied and depressed by the anonymous spaces of the suburbs and her lover's emotional froideur. Michèle's daughter, Alexandra, also began to rebel against Malick's austere discipline (replaying his own conflicts with his father but with Malick now taking on the martinet role). Eventually, Alexandra asked her father to send her money so she could return to Paris to stay with him. She left without telling anyone. "Michèle was not strong enough to protect her," Biskind writes.

In 1986, Taft-Barish Productions' head Rob Cohen—who later launched the *Fast and Furious* and *xXx* franchises—hired Malick to adapt Larry McMurtry's *Desert Rose*. McMurtry's books had been successfully adapted before, as in Peter Bogdanovich's *The Last Picture Show* (1971) and James L. Brooks's *Terms of Endearment* (1983). Barry Levinson—coming off *Diner* (1982) and *The Natural* (1984)—was to direct. "Malick was someone who was listening to a high whine in his head," Cohen told Biskind. "He was very tense and fragile, the least likely person to be a director. I once had to have a meeting with him in Westwood. He was getting up every five

104

Paris–Texas (1979–1995)

minutes and hiding behind pillars; he kept thinking he saw somebody he knew. He would call me, and I'd hear trucks rolling by on the highway, and I'd say, 'Where are you?' and he'd answer, 'I'm walking to Oklahoma!' 'What do you mean, you're walking to Oklahoma? From Texas?' 'Yeah, I'm looking at birds.'"[29]

Cohen's account should also be handled carefully. Malick was a keen walker and ornithologist. A hiking holiday is turned into a quixotic quest. Likewise, Malick's discomfort sitting with Rob Cohen might have something to do with Rob Cohen as much as it has to do with Malick. For those in the center of the industry, portraying Malick as some out-there hermit served to make Hollywood feel more normal. It has the bitterness of the jilted. Not to mention, it's simply a better story. But Malick was in a position to do what he wanted to do, so he did what he wanted to do.

It's tantalizing to think of the unrealized Malick projects, but not making films is normal industry practice in Hollywood. The process of pitching, adapting, writing, and rewriting only rarely ends up producing an actual film. *Knight of Cups* features Rick (Christian Bale) as a screenwriter who supports an affluent lifestyle, with a Venice Beach apartment and a vintage Lincoln Continental convertible he drives from party to party, while producing very little. The often-tortuous route wending from conception to theaters is fittingly described as "Development Hell," but it's a well-paid hell with valet parking and a free bar. *The New World*, *The Tree of Life*, and *Voyage of Time* were all conceived decades before they were realized. Malick tenaciously kept working: researching, scouting, considering casting possibilities, sounding out collaborators, and rewriting. After *Great Balls of Fire*, Malick continued to work on a Jerry Lee Lewis project, which is to this day listed on Malick's IMDb page as "in development."

Another project mooted was *The Moviegoer*, based on the 1961 novel by Walker Percy. The novel takes place in New Orleans in the early 1950s. Stockbroker Jack "Binx" Bolling is attempting to negotiate his life via movies. He engages in what he calls the "Search": an existential practice heightening awareness of his own existence outside the everydayness of life. Bolling is an outsider, a middle-aged Holden Caulfield, who, despite being a stockbroker and war veteran, has yet to find his role in the world. A loner who likes being in a crowd, Bolling finds comfort in the movie theater: not as a cinephile but in order to continue his "Search." In his wish to systematically repeat some moments in his life, he echoes Malick's thoughts on Heidegger: "Our confusion is not anarchic."

THE MAGIC HOURS

Sometimes an engagement with a book is so close it takes on an autobiographical value. The proximity Malick felt to Percy's novel and his affinity for Bolling were long-lasting. In the 1970s, he was already recommending the book to interviewer Joseph Gelmis: "It will change your life. It will just define a whole month for you. It is fantastic. I was sort of an avid moviegoer, like the character in this book, but I had no idea who Hitchcock was, or Fellini or Antonioni. I never looked at the credits and didn't know what a producer was or a director, anything like that."[30] Like Bolling, Malick is a seeker, yet one who feels a detachment from the world around him. His relationship with cinema is willfully naive. He wrote a script, but nothing came of it. As with other projects, it was revived several times throughout the next decade, with Tim Robbins and Julia Roberts attached at one point. But the influence of the novel runs throughout his later films. The trio of male protagonists played by Ben Affleck, Christian Bale, and Ryan Gosling throughout the "Weightless Trilogy" embody the first-person affectless narrator of *The Moviegoer*: bemused and detached, they seek a deeper meaning, a transcendent, unreachable insight.

In 1988, producer Bobby Geisler returned to Malick's orbit, this time with his partner John Roberdeau. Roberdeau was younger than Malick by a few years, born on August 17, 1953, in Fort Belvoir, Virginia. The son of a US Air Force colonel, he partnered with Geisler both in business and romantically in life. Roberdeau was as devoted to the idea of working with the director as Geisler, and his southern upbringing provided him with a direct link to Malick. Geisler and Roberdeau had managed to gain one production credit since the aborted "Elephant Man" project on Robert Altman's Vietnam-era film *Streamers* (1983), starring Matthew Modine and written by *In the Boom Boom Room*'s David Rabe. In the process, however, they alienated Altman with their interference. Not a promising sign.

Geisler and Roberdeau suggested that Malick adapt D. M. Thomas's novel *The White Hotel* (1981), which features a fictional correspondence between a female opera singer and concentration camp victim and Sigmund Freud. The powerful erotic book had been a subject of several attempts to turn it into a movie, including one by Barbra Streisand. The producers offered Malick an eye-watering $2 million to write and direct. They'd bought the rights to the book. D. M. Thomas described meeting the relatively young producers in a Paddington hotel in London: "Bobby Geisler was stout, with a round, soft face that looked at me quizzically and respectfully through small metal-framed glasses. In his sales pitch for the film rights he was

Paris–Texas (1979–1995)

shining-eyed, idealistic, rapturous about their determination to do the novel justice. John Roberdeau was neat, trim, quieter, more businesslike, but equally enthusiastic and with an infectious chortle."[31]

Although interested, Malick rejected the idea and countered with two alternative projects. One was an adaptation of *Tartuffe*—a classic Molière farce, filmed by F. W. Murnau in 1926 with Emil Jannings in the lead role and widely considered a classic of silent cinema. The other option was a new version of James Jones's World War II novel *The Thin Red Line*. Combat veteran turned journalist turned novelist, Jones made his name as the author of *From Here to Eternity* (1953). Fred Zimmerman's adaptation won five Oscars and offered the iconic scene of Burt Lancaster and Deborah Kerr clinching in the foaming Hawaiian surf. In 1964, *The Thin Red Line* got a low-budget, black-and-white treatment with Keir Dullea as Private Doll and Jack Warden as Sergeant Welsh. Joan Didion judged the film "a quite mediocre war movie," though it had "some of the best battle scenes—fast, lucid, beautiful—that [she'd] ever seen."[32]

The producers agreed on *The Thin Red Line*, and Malick set to writing. He contacted James Jones's widow, Gloria Jones, and sought permission when making changes. By the end of May 1989, Malick delivered the script. The following month, Geisler and Roberdeau flew to Paris to meet Malick and Michèle. They dined at Jones's favorite restaurant, the Brasserie de L'Île Saint-Louis, and visited the house where the author lived: no. 10 Quai d'Orléans. They also gave Malick a silver flask from Tiffany's, inscribed with a line from the novel: "Billions of hard, bright stars shone with relentless glitter across the tropic night sky." As he had with Martin Sheen years earlier, Malick gave the producers his tour of Paris.

The next month, they met again at the Avignon Theater Festival, where they talked over the copious notes Geisler and Roberdeau had given Malick. Geisler insists their involvement was instrumental in keeping Malick on board, but others viewed their reputation as shaky at best. According to Geisler, Malick was the fickle, otherworldly genius—the runaway—who required constant corralling by the worldly-wise producers. In reality, Malick was the more experienced producer: he had raised the financing of his own films and controlled every aspect of them. He had also seen his scripts adapted into films by other directors. As heartening as their enthusiasm might be, Malick was also a keen judge of character, and it's unlikely that he didn't sense the distance between the men's aspirations and their capabilities. It's also unlikely that the same Malick who phoned a studio exec to check

THE MAGIC HOURS

Mike Medavoy's credentials before accepting him as an agent had failed to similarly vet Geisler and Roberdeau and take their full measure.

This legitimate wariness created a hesitancy to commit. Guarding his independence, Malick remained open to other projects, some of which he offered Geisler and Roberdeau; others he kept to himself. The first was a stage adaptation of "Sanshō the Bailiff," which he'd once considered as a film. Here—as with *Tartuffe*—Kenji Mizoguchi's film was already considered a classic of world cinema. Eager to keep Malick onside, the pair reportedly paid him $200,000 for the script, with a $50,000 bonus promised as payable the night the play opened. He spent much of the year working on the play and on the script for *The Thin Red Line*. He was also writing an original screenplay called "The English Speaker," of which Geisler and Roberdeau knew nothing.

In December 1989, the producers dined in Austin with Malick, Michèle, Lukas Haas—the actor who had broken out as a child performer in Peter Weir's *Witness* in 1989—and his parents, who were friends of Malick's. The focus shifted between *The Thin Red Line* and "Sanshō the Bailiff." Research trips took Malick and Michèle to San Francisco to hear Kodo drummers performing and to Quebec to see Japanese director Yukio Ninagawa's *Macbeth*; Malick walked out of the latter after a few minutes. By the summer of 1990, Malick had handed over his completed draft of "Sanshō the Bailiff." Based on a folktale retold in a 1915 short story by Mori Ōgai, it tells of an honest governor who is exiled and whose wife, Tamaki, and their children, Zushiō and Anju, travel to join him. On the way, they are tricked by a priestess, and the children are kidnapped and sold into slavery, where they grow up under the brutal treatment of the eponymous Sanshō. Malick described it as the "Hansel and Gretel of Japan," and his script reimagines the story on a stage setting, with long speeches and direct addresses to the audience. In one of these, the exiled father soliloquizes: "Are you thoughtful and kind? Are you righteous? Does your confidence lie in this? Are you loved by all? So was I! Do you trust in virtue? Do you imagine your sufferings will be lighter because you praised her name? So did I!" This speech returns in *The Thin Red Line* as a voice-over paired with the image of a dead Japanese soldier whose face barely breaks free of the soil. Consistent with Malick's other work, the "Sanshō" script also revealed a dialectic: the search to find humanity in the most inhumane behavior and to find a space of moral choice even when circumstances ensnare the individual. These options are illustrated by Zushiō's and Anju's different reactions to captivity and their attempts to survive a brutal regime.

Paris–Texas (1979–1995)

On March 12, 1991, Malick signed an agreement with Geisler, Roberdeau, and financier Gerry Rubin for *The Thin Red Line*, and he finished a second draft of the script. But as Malick moved back toward cinema, his relationship with Michèle was becoming increasingly estranged. Geisler and Roberdeau saw her as an important intermediary when they couldn't talk to Malick directly. The couple spent more time apart, with Michèle staying in Paris with Alexandra. They remained friends, and she was even willing to go to London to see a few plays Malick was curious about and report back. Another draft of "The English Speaker" was also completed, and "Sanshō" was sent out to a number of top theater directors. Peter Brook, Peter Stein, and Ingmar Bergman all received copies. Malick had no experience writing for the theater. The producers needed a top director to guide the ambitious production. However, each director rejected it. Bergman refused to even read it and was badgered to return the script.

In the summer of 1992, Malick and Michèle visited the celebrated music festival in Salzburg, Austria. There they met up with the producers and saw a performance of Stanisław Wyspiański's play *Wesele* (*The Wedding*) directed by Andrzej Wajda, the film director who made his name as part of the Polish New Wave with such masterpieces as *Kanal* (1957) and *Ashes and Diamonds* (1958). He had also filmed *The Wedding* in 1972, but the Salzburg version was the premiere of a German-language version of this key nineteenth-century Polish drama. Malick saw Wajda as the perfect fit for "Sanshō the Bailiff." The producers flew Wajda to New York to screen Malick's pictures. During a meal, he agreed a deal with Geisler and Roberdeau, and they phoned Austin with the good news.

The lives of the Malicks and their producers were entangled. When the Malicks decided to purchase a house in Paris, Bobby Geisler arranged a mortgage broker to close the deal. Michèle flew from Paris and Malick came down from Boston to meet her in Miami, where they signed the papers together. Geisler and Roberdeau were also in Miami, having helped arrange the logistics of the meeting. Here, Malick presented Geisler with "The English Speaker," which Malick insisted Geisler read immediately with Malick in the room.[33] It was similar territory to *The White Hotel* with its Freud-adjacent story of a female psychiatric patient and a Viennese setting. It adapted Josef Breuer's case study of Anna O. Peter Biskind describes it as "*The Exorcist* as written by Dostoyevsky."[34]

Set in late nineteenth-century Vienna, the script boasts firsthand knowledge of the city and establishes its milieu effortlessly. Anna lives with her family, including her stern patriarchal father, who exhibits traces of Emil Malick and whom Anna must care for. Anna's psychopathology is illustrated partly from her point of view, and there are hints that her hallucinations constitute a visionary aspect of Anna's character, an apprehension of a larger metaphysical universe. She also displays symptoms of dissociative identity disorder, appearing possessed—hence Biskind's *The Exorcist* comparison—by another Anna who speaks exclusively English. Dr. Breuer, a contemporary and friend of Sigmund Freud, is inspired by Anna's case to develop his own theory. In taking the case, Breuer risks his reputation and marriage to the conventional Mathilde. He is compassionate but also obsessive, similarly to Dr. Treves in the abandoned version of "The Elephant Man," but with the added complication of a growing intimacy, which veers into a frustrated romance. It also resembles John Huston's *Freud: The Secret Passion* (1962), starring Montgomery Clift and Susannah York. Breuer begins to meet Anna's metaphysical visions later in the story.

Malick's protectiveness of the screenplay might also have been motivated by the fact that it clearly relates to his own terminally compromised marriage and his new feelings for another woman. Malick describes Breuer's marriage to Mathilde: "Once their love was passionate. Now they do not know how to put things back in place. Each seems to hope they will resolve themselves naturally, of their own accord. Until then, they keep their talk as light and practical as possible"—a strategy Malick and Michèle were perhaps employing. Mathilde is the good wife, while Anna is a femme fatale—not in the conventional sense of the manipulative and devious angel of destruction but rather in the sense of someone who, with her demonic possession or multiple personality states, is literally two-faced, representing suffering and saintly victimhood on the one side and powerful transgressive forces on the other. Malick's Breuer is racked with guilt. "It seems that you can't live without causing pain or turning your back on it," Breuer confides to Freud. None of the men can properly explain Anna. Her priest expresses something that sounds very like motivation for Malick's reluctance to have his utterances publicized: "What is true to me as long as I keep it to myself becomes untrue the moment I say it to someone else."

"The English Speaker" anticipates *To the Wonder* as Malick's first artistic attempt to work out his failing relationship with Michèle through film. But whereas *To the Wonder* is a straightforward autobiographical account of his second marriage, "The English Speaker" breaks up Malick's point of view and scatters it among different characters. The pain Malick felt and believed he

Paris–Texas (1979–1995)

was inflicting is at the script's core. This can drift into misogyny, as expressed in a scene in which Breuer's brother-in-law, Paul, rails against the sacrifice men make to help unhappy women: "They act as if they had a right to happiness. If they aren't happy, they suspect that they have been cheated and avenge themselves on whomever is close by. They have no peace in themselves and allow others to have none." Paul's despair is rooted in his own failing marriage, and the raw emotion of the speech is clear. It is worth quoting in full: "She is a tyrant. She sulks. She rules me with her moods. Weakly, I give in— for fear of disturbing the peace of our hope. It is so—precarious. With her everything is blackmail. She calls her hunger—love. . . . I've thought of getting a divorce, but I've never felt I had quite enough of a reason. It's as though I were—waiting for one. And then I brought it all on myself, didn't I? I ought to see through it."

Paul, however, only represents one-half of the dialectic, and the script spends as much time with Anna and her family as they deal with the consequences of her pain, caused significantly by her dominating father. Frau O, Anna's mother, gives a counterpoint to Paul's self-pity: "Pain can be very calm, child. After a while you don't feel it. . . . You wake up, you find you've no other life. There is what there was. Your life has passed away like an afternoon." This contrasts with Freud's dismissal of the moral aspect of suffering: "People think that suffering ennobles, that it builds character, makes you deeper. No, you have to bear it patiently, but it is an evil. It doesn't make men noble but bitter, shallow, envious." This echoes a line in the voice-over of *The Thin Red Line*: "War don't ennoble men. It turns them into dogs . . . poisons the soul." One of the visions anticipates a striking shot from *The Tree of Life*: "Before Anna stands a door. It opens out into a desert."

On reading "The English Speaker," Geisler was impressed, offering $400,000 for it. In Biskind's 1998 article, the producers portray Malick as someone receiving large sums but endlessly delaying the actual work. This fits in with profiles of the director, who spent much time over his films, which in turn fit with Biskind's broader *Easy Riders, Raging Bulls* thesis of how New Hollywood imploded with self-indulgence and hubris. But this narrative is off. Geisler and Roberdeau were promising sums of money they didn't have, taking most of it from their investment partner Gerry Rubin. Geisler was briefly imprisoned because of a bad debt with caterers, and the sums the producers proposed didn't always materialize. Their reputation in the business was not good. As already seen, their one production, *Streamers*, resulted in a falling-out with Robert Altman. *The White Hotel* debacle went on so long, it

THE MAGIC HOURS

was chronicled in D. M. Thomas's book *Bleak Hotel: The Hollywood Saga of the White Hotel*.[35] The novelist feels a great deal of affection for the pair of producers but proves that their modus operandi was one of overpromising and underdelivering. Even their passion for Malick, to the point of idolatry, could be off-putting. Geisler and Roberdeau were paying almost half a million dollars for a screenplay of over three hundred pages (over twice as long as a conventional screenplay), which was a period piece (expensive), featured hallucinatory sequences requiring major special effects (expensive), and was almost entirely in German. It had to be in German because Anna's alter ego was the only character to speak English. Hence the title. What American studio was going to green-light this? Geisler and Roberdeau genuinely believed they were the only ones capable of bringing Malick to Hollywood, but their knowledge of the business seemed limited. Geisler—with a jaw-dropping lack of perspicacity—didn't even know Malick was finishing *Days of Heaven* when they first met, despite it being reported in the trades.

Malick—now fully aware of Geisler's and Roberdeau's limits—hedged his bets with other projects of his own. Malick briefly attached himself, as a producer, to an adaptation of *Brighton Rock*, Graham Greene's classic novel of disaffected juvenile criminals on the British south coast, which had already been filmed in what is considered the definitive British crime film of the period by John Boulting in 1948. In 1994, Malick's adaptation of his beloved novel *The Moviegoer* was still in development, with Julia Roberts and Tim Robbins. A far more commercial prospect, it had possible stars, an American setting, and a conventional narrative novel and was in English. By the spring of 1993, Malick was once more appearing in the press, mostly framed with quotes from Geisler. In a piece for the *Los Angeles Times* headlined "Re-enter the Reluctant Dragon, Terrence Malick," Mary Williams Walsh declares the mystery of the "Hollywood dropout" solved and goes on to outline a number of projects, including "Sanshō the Bailiff," "The English Speaker," and *The Thin Red Line*. Geisler is credited as Malick's "fifteen-year colleague." Malick is described having lunch with *Badlands* producer Ed Pressman and dinner with Mike Medavoy, who says: "We've skirted around the idea of doing something. I'm sure when Terry's ready, it'll happen."[36] Explaining his absence, an anonymous friend reports Malick describing his life as "standing up in a rowboat . . . making phone calls, missing phone calls and wondering about the phone calls I didn't get." Geisler, obviously the motivating source behind the story, aims to build Malick up in the eyes of potential investors. "What Hollywood types fail to grasp about Malick," Geisler adds, is that movies "are not,

Paris–Texas (1979–1995)

for him, something to be urgently involved with around the clock. He's perfectly satisfied to take his time and live the life he's living."

The article reads like a puff piece intended to drum up business by putting Malick in front of the public and potential investors. Geisler aligns himself closely with Malick, but the lunches with Pressman and Medavoy show Malick's deeper relationships with other more established and experienced Hollywood players. His old, trusted friends and colleagues no doubt gave Malick the benefit of their advice and their assessment of his producing partners. Medavoy and Pressman are undoubtedly "Hollywood types," but they are impressive producers with résumés to match. Geisler and Roberdeau are also "Hollywood types," and of a much more common genus: that of the producers endlessly packaging deals that rarely result in actual films.

In June 1993, Malick traveled to New York to meet with Andrzej Wajda to talk about "Sanshō." Here, Malick also spent a few days with Michèle, who had flown in from Paris. Geisler and Roberdeau hired the Lepercq Space for a month in November from the Brooklyn Academy of Music. As well as a $74,000 fee, they also pledged $50,000. When the workshops began in New York, Malick attended, but this time he was accompanied by Alexandra "Ecky" Wallace, his old sweetheart from St. Stephens. This new relationship signaled that his marriage to Michèle was effectively over. It also further weakened his bond with Geisler and Roberdeau. To make matters worse, Wajda and Malick didn't click. They were two powerful egos. A legend in his own country and a significant filmmaker, Wajda saw no need to defer to Malick or treat him differently from any other writer. Wajda demanded rewrites, and Malick reluctantly complied. Though he could speak English, Wajda refused to do so with Malick, further alienating him. The workshop hadn't advanced the play toward production or provoked significant interest from investors. Malick rewrote the play again, but disaster loomed for his overextended financial partners. The checks to the Brooklyn Academy of Music for the rental of the performance space in November bounced, and with a new workshop scheduled for the spring and yet more outlay, Geisler and Roberdeau had bottomed out. Their main backer, Gerry Rubin, pulled the financing, leading Roberdeau to pen a desperate letter: "Gerry, the stupidity of this situation is rivaled only by my disgust of what seems to be your desertion under fire."[37] Hardly a message designed to inspire confidence. The producers were distraught. They tried to buy out Rubin's interest in *The Thin Red Line*, "The English Speaker," and "Sanshō the Bailiff" for ten dollars per title. Unsurprisingly, Rubin didn't dignify the offer with a response, and he

THE MAGIC HOURS

sued the producers, claiming they had systematically drained him of money with constant requests for cash. He received nothing in return and would later sue Malick.[38]

By May 1994, in an unpromising reversal, Malick provided $25,000 to the producers so they could make the payroll for the second "Sanshō" workshop in Los Angeles. Geisler and Roberdeau recruited a talented team of collaborators, from Wajda and Malick to lighting designer Jennifer Tipton and costumer Eiko Ishioka. However, their enthusiasm only carried them so far, and their financial mismanagement meant the chances of the play ever appearing on Broadway were zero. From Malick's scripts and from the whole saga, it is apparent that, as with "The English Speaker," Geisler and Roberdeau hadn't considered the commercial viability of the project. Malick's script called for expensive effects and a large-scale Broadway production, but it was also a wordy take on a Japanese film without any real popular appeal to sustain a long run. Would audiences have flocked to see it? It's unlikely, and investors stayed away. By the fall of 1994, the project was dead. Money was owed all over town, and Geisler and Roberdeau hovered on the precipice of bankruptcy.

Perhaps inspired by the mess Geisler and Roberdeau had wrought, Malick returned to his first producer, Ed Pressman, with whom he formed a production company, Sunflower Productions. Malick decided to serve as a producer for new talents and became involved in the graduate screenwriting program at the University of Texas, based in Austin. Sabina Murray, a Michener scholar and novelist from New York, elected to take the screenwriting course. A group of graduates were introduced to Malick as part of the program, and, along with Pressman, he pitched a series of stories that Sunflower was looking to develop into screenplays. Suggestions included a new version of *Jane Eyre* and an adaptation of Anton Chekhov's short story "The Duel." Sabina was pitched a story of the *Golden Venture*, a cargo ship that, while packed with hundreds of undocumented Chinese immigrants, ran aground at Rockaway, New York. Malick was attracted to the story but also thought it could be linked to the bụi đời, the Amerasian offspring left behind by American personnel in the aftermath of the Vietnam War. "He's a reader of the news and very much, deeply involved with what happens to people who other people might think are random, but in Terry's mind these were individuals whose stories needed to be told," Sabina says.[39] They met on and off for the next ten years, usually on a Tuesday at Luby's in Austin or at the cafeteria of a local Whole Foods near Malick's house.

114

Malick showed Sabina the screenplay of *The Thin Red Line*, which at that point was five hundred pages long. He immediately told her not to write a five-hundred-page screenplay. "All the things that he relied on in scriptwriting, he taught me not to do," Sabina says. He forbade voice-over and said dialogue for a character should be restricted to two lines maximum unless it is a speech. Actors from the University of Texas participated in read-throughs, and Malick directed them, kneeling in front of them and whispering his instructions so only the actor could hear. Malick pushed for the screenplay to have more emotion, and when Sabina objected, using her research into the Vietnamese community and her own Filipino heritage, he told her: "If it wasn't an anomaly, we wouldn't be making a film about it. We film the anomaly."

Together they wrote dialogue, and "[they] would read it back and forth, which was always a bit awkward sitting in a public place having Terry saying lines in a bad Vietnamese accent very loudly with tremendous passion." Sabina was struck by Malick's lack of pretention and the fact that he treated her completely as a creative equal, asking for her suggestions on actors and potential directors. They argued over points, and he was candid and frank. He cared deeply about the script: "It's never just a script, it's his way of coming to terms with an injustice."[40]

Early on in their collaboration, Malick asked Sabina to pick him up. She freaked out. Her pickup truck had no air-conditioning, and her dog shed hair: "I just went nuts, trying to clean my car and make it into something worthy of one of the world's best directors. Then when we picked up his car, his car was so much worse than mine. It was a twenty-year-old Toyota that was rusting. No air-conditioning. Oh my God, I cleaned my car out for this?"

At the same time Malick was mentoring and cowriting the screenplay with Sabina Murray, he was also working with Joe Conway on another screenplay, as well as playing basketball with him at St. Stephen's. Both *The Beautiful Country* and *Undertow* would eventually be released in 2004, with Malick's contributions credited under the pseudonym Lingard Jervey, which combines the names of Ecky's aunt and sister.

But by then Malick was ready to return as a director in his own right.

7

The Thin Red Line (1995-1998)

On January 2, 1942, a part of the 25th Division of the US Army arrived on Guadalcanal, the largest of the Solomon Islands, tasked with clearing Mount Austen of Japanese defenders and securing the hilltops and ridges located around the inland forks of the Matanikau River. Identifying the Japanese defensive positions in the sea of grass covering the hills was impossible. Approaching the hills, the Americans came under intense fire from machine guns, which pinned them down. The US soldiers found themselves stuck. Poisonous snakes, malaria, dehydration, and exhaustion began to take their toll. A twenty-one-year-old infantry corporal, James Jones, was among the troops.

Born and raised in Robinson, Illinois, Jones joined the US Army at seventeen. While serving in Hawaii, he witnessed the attack on Pearl Harbor, an experience that inspired his first novel, *From Here to Eternity* (1951). Jones was shipped to Guadalcanal, where he fought, was wounded, and eventually was evacuated. "My own part in all of this was relatively undistinguished," he writes. "I went where I was told to go, and did what I was told to do, but no more. I was scared shitless just about all of the time."[1]

Published in 1962, Jones's fourth novel, *The Thin Red Line*, was a fictionalized account of this experience. The protagonist is not any single character but rather "C for Charlie Company." The narrative slides through the perspectives of different members of the company: Privates Doll, Bell, and Witt; Corporal Fife; Sergeants Welsh and Keck; and Captain Stein, among many others. We witness the war through the eyes of the soldiers as they grouse, joke, and confess. The book explores sexuality, masculinity, bravery, cowardice, morality, and politics with remarkable frankness. Racism and anti-Semitism divide the company just as the comradeship of coming under fire

The Thin Red Line (1995–1998)

unites the men. Behind the lines, an incompetently run army intervenes arbitrarily, driven by the personal ambition and petty rivalry of the top brass rather than any notion of defeating the enemy. Jones's dedication reads: "This book is cheerfully dedicated to those greatest and most heroic of all human endeavors, WAR and WARFARE; may they never cease to give us the pleasure, excitement and adrenal stimulation that we need, or provide us with the heroes, the presidents and leaders, the monuments and museums which we erect to them in the name of PEACE."[2] The universe is indifferent. The quotation on Malick's flask reads: "Billions of hard, bright stars shone with relentless glitter across the tropic night sky." The difference between life and death, madness and sanity is a matter of chance. On another level, the novel is also a closely observed study of the minutiae of battle: the landscape, the weather, the effects of weapons and munitions on men's bodies and minds, and the natural world all play into the men's psychological and physical experiences.

Jones's own experiences appear throughout the book. During a break in the fighting, Jones left the trenches to relieve himself in the jungle, only to be surprised in the act by a Japanese soldier who attacked him with a bayonet. After a vicious fight, Jones killed the man with his bare hands. This episode appears in the novel. Jones's decision to return to the battle after being wounded mirrors Corporal Fife's and Private Witt's choices to return to Charlie Company. When wounded and ordered to clear out, Jones gave away his water canister, just as Sergeant Keck does after being fatally wounded. Fife has an old ankle injury that sees him evacuated; the same wound ended Jones's campaign.[3] Jones had found many terrible things in the war, but he was also alert to the specialness that war bestowed on experience: "When you think, when you know, you are going off to die somewhere soon, every day has a special, bright, delicious, poignant taste to it that normal days in normal times do not have."[4]

Terrence Malick was never a soldier. He opposed the war in Vietnam and feared being drafted. Unlike Steven Spielberg, whose *Saving Private Ryan* was released only months before *The Thin Red Line*, Malick never discussed his father's war record publicly, and the film's advertising avoided paeans to the "Greatest Generation" and the recent promotion of the "good war," typified by historian Stephen Ambrose's popular history books. It was an attitude Jones himself resisted: "The truth is, thirty-five years has glossed it all over and given World War II a polish and a glow that it did not have at the time."[5]

Although Bobby Geisler and John Roberdeau credited themselves on Malick's return to filmmaking, the possibility of a new Terrence Malick film increased as their influence waned. They had overextended themselves in their generous but self-aggrandizing largesse. Unpaid bills and angry creditors were accumulating in their wake. A day of reckoning approached. Desperate, the beleaguered duo arrived at Mike Medavoy's office in January 1995. He agreed to loan them $100,000 and represent *The Thin Red Line* and "The English Speaker" in a three-year deal, with an option on *The White Hotel*. However, Geisler and Roberdeau told Medavoy nothing about Gerry Rubin, the investor who still held an interest, instead signing a contract explicitly stating that the rights were theirs exclusively.

For his part, Medavoy was happy to have Malick back in his orbit. He finally saw an opportunity to use Malick's talent to their mutual benefit. After leaving Orion and serving a stint as the head of TriStar Pictures, Medavoy had now established Phoenix Pictures with partner Arnold Messing. As CEO, Medavoy had the power to green-light all but the most expensive movies. It was a smaller fiefdom than he was used to, and, with his departure from TriStar smarting, he had a point to prove. A film by the director of *Badlands* and *Days of Heaven*, whose reputation had grown substantially in his absence, would be a feather in the cap of the new studio—as well as a statement of principles, establishing Phoenix Pictures as an important company that nurtured artistic vision.

Medavoy recruited another old friend of Malick's, the ex-head of the AFI, George Stevens Jr., as an executive producer. It was a canny move. First, it nudged Geisler and Roberdeau further to the side. Second, Malick's dilatory approach might be sped up out of respect for his old friend. Malick insisted he was only writing, but Medavoy and Stevens knew Malick wanted to direct.

Sony turned down the project, but Medavoy took it to Bill Mechanic at Fox. Mechanic had gone to Fox after running the home entertainment division of Disney, where he'd overseen a string of hit movies like *Die Hard with a Vengeance* (1995), *Independence Day* (1996), and *Titanic* (1997). He agreed to the package on the proviso that Malick deliver five big-name actors from a list of bankable stars. The recruiting of Sean Penn, Woody Harrelson, and Nick Nolte, as well as the provision of smaller roles for John Cusack and George Clooney, the latter had volunteered to carry camera equipment, fulfilled that stipulation, and the film was green-lit.

Trusted collaborators were recruited. Jack Fisk had become a film director in his own right since *Days of Heaven*. He was in Ireland when he heard that Malick was making a new movie. He sent a note: "I am ready to start

The Thin Red Line (1995–1998)

again."[6] Likewise, editor and confidante Billy Weber was on board. Casting director Dianne Crittenden received a paperback copy of James Jones's novel through the mail and began casting.

In March 1995, in Mike Medavoy's mansion in Coldwater Canyon, a group of Hollywood actors gathered. At the table sat Kevin Costner, whose career, after a series of remarkable hits culminating in *The Bodyguard* (1992), was about to suffer the flop of *Waterworld* (1995). Will Patton, Ethan Hawke, Dermot Mulroney, Peter Berg, and Lukas Haas all read parts. Martin Sheen read the screen directions. Medavoy listened in, as did Geisler and Roberdeau. Hearing his words brought to life, Malick sensed where he wanted changes. Some speeches were clunky and overlong, sounding unnatural. He scribbled notes. Other table reads were held, and in June, Malick stayed at Medavoy's house for a week while workshopping the script.[7]

Malick found himself with an embarrassment of riches when it came to casting. He needn't worry about missing out on John Travolta this time. Travolta was in the film, having reunited with Malick over lunch. Other A-list stars lined up: Brad Pitt was eager; Johnny Depp wrote an agreement on a napkin to take union scale; and Sean Penn—who had met Malick when he was fourteen years old while hanging out with Emilio Estevez—sought Malick out in Texas, gunning for a role.

Leonardo DiCaprio was finishing the mammoth shoot on James Cameron's *Titanic* (1997) when he met Malick to discuss the role of Private Bead, but ultimately he was too tired to throw himself into another long shoot away from home. Nick Stahl took the role, which shrank considerably. Some of the young actors were awed by their opportunity to work with a legend. Brendan Fraser was surprised to find Malick a fan of his prehistoric fish-out-of-water film *Encino Man* (1992), asking Fraser of the caveman character he played: "Where did that guy come from? He just came down from the moon or something. He was like Charlie Chaplin. He was like Buster Keaton."[8]

Having previously given breakout roles to Sissy Spacek, Sam Shepard, Martin Sheen, and Richard Gere, Malick looked to unknowns to fill major parts. The British actor Ben Chaplin initially auditioned for the role of Private Witt, but it was given to Jim Caviezel, suggested to Malick by Sean Penn. Edward Norton was considered. Chaplin was offered Private Bell at the last minute when Viggo Mortensen—then also relatively unknown—dropped out. Another newcomer, Adrien Brody, was cast in the role of Fife, the cowardly corporal who plays a significant role in the novel. Brody had an unconventional look: an aquiline profile and bulging, panicky eyes. Jim Caviezel

THE MAGIC HOURS

came from an extremely conservative Christian background and had never seen a Malick film.

While in Boston, Malick received a request via Jack McNeese, an old Harvard friend, to meet up with two young actors: Matt Damon and Ben Affleck. Malick was close to the Affleck family (McNeese was Affleck's godfather) and had known the boys long before they began their acting careers. They weren't seeking roles in his new film but instead sought his advice on a screenplay called *Good Will Hunting* (1997). Matt Damon told Tom Shone:

> We went to Boston to see him. And we had it in the script that my character and Minnie [Driver]'s left together at the end of the movie. Terry didn't read the script but we explained the whole story to him, and in the middle of the dinner, he said, "I think it would be better if she left and he went after her." And Ben and I looked at each other. It was one of those things where you go: of course that's better. He said it and he probably doesn't even remember that he said it. He started talking about Antonioni. "In Italian movies a guy just leaves town at the end and that's enough." And we said of course that's enough. That's where we come from. If you just leave, that's a big enough deal. It doesn't have to build up to anything more.[9]

Veteran actor Nick Nolte repeatedly met Malick for lunch over four weeks. Initially, Malick intended Colonel Tall to be a younger man—as he's described in the book—but Malick wanted to work with Nolte and considered writing him a separate role as a general. Together they researched the possibility of the new role, but in the end Malick decided: "I think you should play Colonel Tall." Nolte replied: "I think I should too."[10] Age was never an obstacle to casting, and Malick wove Nolte's age into the script, having Travolta's general patronizingly congratulate the colonel on his age: "Most men your age would've retired by now." Nolte had been researching James Jones for two years in preparation to play him in the adaptation of Kaylie Jones's autobiographical novel, *A Soldier's Daughter Never Cries*. Once cast in Malick's film, Nolte realized his schedule clashed with his previous commitment and phoned director James Ivory to see if their shoot could be pushed back. Ivory was furious as he had already locked the locations. He recast Nolte with Kris Kristofferson, and the film was released in 1998.

The Thin Red Line (1995–1998)

The Thin Red Line's $56 million budget made this a substantially more expensive and more ambitious project than Malick had ever handled before. It was also his first studio film, following the two independent productions.[11] Malick needed a team to handle the change in scale. Australian producer Grant Hill had just finished work on *Titanic*. He'd deal with the day-to-day budgeting and the logistics. Having shot with multiple cinematographers in his previous films, this time Malick used a single director of photography. He interviewed a number of cameramen before finally hiring John Toll, impressed by the epic feel and intense battle scenes he'd achieved in Mel Gibson's *Braveheart* (1995). As with Néstor Almendros, Malick found in John Toll a cinematographer sympathetic to his aesthetic ideas and willing to find technical solutions to achieve the look he wanted. Director and cameraman met in Austin and had long discussions about the look of the film, the movement of the cameras, and the kit to use. They poured over the research materials Jack Fisk had gathered, including the book of paintings, *Images of War: The Artist's Vision of World War II*, edited by Ken McCormick and Hamilton Darby.[12]

A third draft of the screenplay incorporated the casting decisions, adjusting them for age, as in the case of Nolte, or growing a character to match the actor, as for Penn's Sergeant Welsh. Hans Zimmer came onto the production to start composing music prior to filming. The German musician was one of the most sought-after composers in Hollywood, with credits ranging from *Rain Man* (1988) to *The Lion King* (1994). His score for the Quentin Tarantino–scripted Tony Scott film *True Romance* (1993) had riffed on the score of *Badlands*.

Malick scouted the actual location of the Battle of Guadalcanal, noting the heat and humidity but also the colorful jungle, the light, and the hills. Nothing much had changed since the events depicted in Jones's novel, but unfortunately that included the mercilessly high rates of malaria and the presence of unexploded ordnance. Transporting hundreds of crew members and extras, not to mention Hollywood actors, to the remote island for months was impossible. Having scouted a number of locations, including Costa Rica, Malick chose Queensland in Northern Australia. Australia had its own film industry and a ready supply of skilled technicians and actors.

Malick was in a good place. He was settled in Austin permanently. He liked to go for jogs while listening to his favorite composers on his new Discman and regularly played basketball at his old school. His separation from Michèle was ongoing, and, after two failed marriages, Alexandra Quintard

Wallace née Wyatt-Brown was turning out to be the love of his life. Since leaving St. Stephen's, Ecky, as everyone called her, had graduated from the University of Texas before completing her master's degree at the Episcopal Seminary of the Southwest, where she was ordained a minister. She married Glen Woody Farris in 1961, but the marriage was short-lived. Her second husband, John Wilkins Wallace, was a successful oil and gas man. She lived a wealthy and socially active lifestyle, raising a family of six children with her second husband. They owned a property on the Colorado River called the Medway Ranch, named after the plantations Ecky's grandfather had owned. Here, she established a stable and a riding school.

Malick also befriended Ecky's adult children, especially her son Will Wallace, who had given up his first career as a lawyer to pursue his dream of becoming an actor. Malick cast him in a small role as Private Hoke. He has one of the first lines in the film, as the soldier who, along with Witt, is AWOL on a Polynesian island. Ecky's daughter-in-law Merie Weismiller Wallace was hired as an on-set stills photographer.

As Malick and Michèle's divorce negotiations began, Malick also split from his producers, Geisler and Roberdeau. At the beginning of June, he sent them a memo banning them from the set and directing any communication to Phoenix Pictures. Having worked so hard on getting the film over the finishing line, they had no intention of going quietly. Once filming started, Geisler and Roberdeau gave an interview to the *New York Times* in which they played up their own roles and the legend of the eccentric director who needed cajoling back to Hollywood.[13] George Stevens Jr. sent the article to Grant Hill, who passed it on to Malick and Mike Medavoy. Briefing the press without the approval of the producing partners and studio was a serious move that risked damaging an ongoing production. If the tactic was meant to get them back in the room, it backfired, turning the cracks of distrust into an irreversible breach. Geisler and Roberdeau were now out.

The pair felt aggrieved, but *The Thin Red Line* only became a viable reality when it landed on the desk of Mike Medavoy. Medavoy brought it to Fox and assembled the cast and the creative team. Geisler and Roberdeau had been less than forthcoming to Medavoy about the exclusivity of their ownership of the property and were now launching a shadow publicity campaign. It's worth noting a certain ruthlessness to Malick's behavior. It's difficult to believe he was unaware of the shortcomings of his partners. He knew full well that Medavoy's involvement radically altered their position. Malick seemed gentle, soft-spoken, and incredibly polite, but he was utterly

The Thin Red Line (1995–1998)

determined to pursue his own vision. And it was clear that the producers were more trouble than they were worth.

Malick also exerted control over his press coverage. His contract ensured he was not obliged to participate in promotion. Additionally, the studio wasn't allowed to use any photographs of him in their publicity materials, bar one shot. The photograph was unposed, low resolution, and grainy. Malick is turning halfway to the camera and wearing a large cowboy hat and has a pair of headphones slung around his neck. He's smiling, looking past the camera rather than at it. The picture is inevitably bathed in the golden light of early evening. The magic hour. It was taken by his father, Emil Malick. For all the arguments, Terry still saw himself through his father's eyes.

By June 1997, a second unit was shooting Malick's list of nature shots, as Paul Ryan had for *Days of Heaven*. Initially, Malick told Jack Fisk the film would be small, but compared to his first two films, it was astronomically larger. Grant Hill built flexibility into the budget and schedule to allow for Malick's unorthodox methods. In his first two low-budget films, Malick felt hostility from his crew. This time, armored with a reputation for creating what were now considered two masterpieces, he had the support of his crew and cast, as well as the studio. The actors attended a boot camp led by the military consultant and Marine Vietnam veteran Mike Stokey for two weeks to learn military basics.

The first day of principal photography, Sean Penn and Jim Caviezel confronted each other in the brig of a ship off the coast of Guadalcanal. Jack Fisk had built the set on a tennis court in Queensland, northern Australia. Malick, a little uncertain after the decades away, asked for input from the crew and his actors. Having arrived with their parts learned, some of the actors found Malick's probing way of shooting scenes off-putting. Direction was often gnomic: "Deliver the line like you're looking at a mysterious totem pole." Another actor was told he was "a squid being thrown up on the beach from the abyss."[14] Nolte, a recovering alcoholic and cocaine addict, received a note containing a phrase from Alcoholics Anonymous founder Bill Wilson: "Self will run riot."[15] Nolte got it immediately. Others, not on Malick's wavelength, were baffled. More disconcerting was the lack of hierarchy, with no clear lead actor in the picture.

Adrien Brody's claim that he was cast as the lead is an exaggeration. "The pressure on that film was that I had to carry the movie with a cast of stars that I truly admired," he told James Mottram.[16] Although he certainly has more lines in the script than in the finished film and is a larger character in the novel, neither the novel nor the script has a lead as such. Welsh and Witt, Bell and Doll, Staros (changed from the Jewish Stein in the novel to incorporate actor Elias Koteas's Greek heritage) and Tall all have substantial storylines. Nolte recognized that "several of the guys were determined to make themselves the lead." Sensing a worsening atmosphere, Malick organized a cast meeting. He listened patiently as they complained about scenes that were interrupted while other scenes went on long after the lines were finished. Malick heard them out, and at the end of the meeting, he agreed with them and said, "Let's do it." Then he went back to directing exactly as he wished. Nolte thought the move "brilliant!"[17]

But Malick won over the trust and affection of many of the cast and crew by frequently taking responsibility for any mistakes. When Jim Caviezel couldn't get a scene right, he said: "Oh, Jim, I'm a bit rusty here, so please forgive me!" When a technical issue came up and some of the footage was unusable, Malick insisted to the appalled focus puller: "No, that's my fault." One of the actors with the least experience, John Dee Smith, remembers how his mistakes led to a scene having to be replayed a number of times: "I was embarrassed and apologized to Terry. I went back to my room. Adrien was mad at me too, and I ended up packing my stuff because I was only supposed to be there for two weeks. I then got a note slipped under my hotel room door by one of Malick's assistants. I was to have dinner with Terry."[18]

During the dinner, Malick talked to Smith about his life. Smith recalls: "How I came out of poverty and my parents were killed and onward until I went to college before being cast in *The Thin Red Line*. Terry told me of his own faith and of his life in Texas. I ended up staying on the set and he used me for scenes where he could draw from my personal experiences and use it as dialogue. So there you have me talking about sleeping in the chicken coop a 'whole lot of nights,' all true stories, and being beaten by a block. Terry prompted me through these scenes, saying stuff like 'Tell more stories about the South.'"[19]

When early on in the shoot Malick called, "Cut," he was disheartened to see the makeup and hair people rush in to touch up the actors. From that point on, he decided never to say "cut," preferring to play scenes out until the cameras ran out of film.[20] Frequently, the shots seen in the final movie turned out to be the moments toward the end of the camera roll. Malick had learned to treasure these accidents and sought to create the conditions for them to occur.

At thirty-seven, Sean Penn was significantly more experienced than the other actors around him, with the exception of Nolte. With neophyte

The Thin Red Line (1995–1998)

Caviezel, though the two went running together, a bond didn't form; Caviezel's Christian faith and conservative politics contrasted with Penn's liberalism. Caviezel told Malick that Penn was a rock: "One day you can go up and talk to him, and there's some days he doesn't know who you are. That's Sean Penn." Shooting the scene of Private Witt and Sergeant Welsh at the plantation house during which they confront their different perspectives, Malick instructed Caviezel to tell Penn what he thought of him. Penn in turn used his skepticism about Caviezel's faith: "You still believe in the beautiful light?"

Partway through production on *Days of Heaven*, Malick realized his cast wasn't giving him what he wanted. On *The Thin Red Line*, this possibility was built into the process. He found certain relationships working, other performances growing and becoming more compelling, and others falling by the wayside. Some actors were more willing to adapt to Malick's improvisational style. Billy Weber recalls that Malick "wasn't happy with what he had written or Adrien's performance . . . he felt better about Jim and so he started changing it as he was shooting."[21] In the novel, Private Witt, a peripheral figure who turns up after one hundred pages, is a stern Kentucky man with an inferiority complex, a bad temper, and a hatred for Sergeant Welsh. The Witt of the film, by contrast, is Terrence Malick. Like Captain Willard in *Apocalypse Now* (1979), he is a pair of eyes. But whereas Martin Sheen's look is that of the traumatized assassin, Witt has a transcendent gaze that confronts the war in front of him, open to the beauty of nature, the suffering he observes, and the compassion and camaraderie he feels for his company. He sees "another world," "the Glory." He is the one soldier who apparently sees the light Malick sees. He is agape in combat fatigues.

In capturing that light, Malick had an ally in cinematographer John Toll. Toll used available light as much as possible, occasionally employing muslin to bounce light into the actors' faces while avoiding lighting rigs. "Because this is a Terrence Malick film, a lot of people will just assume that we sat around waiting for magic hour, but we simply didn't have the luxury of doing that on this picture," he says. "We shot relentlessly every day, in every conceivable lighting condition, from seven in the morning until it got dark at about six pm. Yes, there are magic hour shots in the film but only because we had to shoot until it got dark."[22] During lunch breaks, Malick took a small crew and shot the landscape and birds. Scenes were filmed repeatedly at different times of day to give Malick options when editing. Despite the urge to capture nature, Malick wasn't above employing trickery when it suited his

THE MAGIC HOURS

purposes. Colonel Tall's early morning musing on the "rosy-fingered dawn" features a sky that has been digitally replaced because it turned out not to be rosy-fingered enough. An exchange between Sean Penn and Jim Caviezel late in the film features footage of Penn in Queensland with Caviezel replying from Guadalcanal. Leslie Jones began an assembly edit on location.[23]

The battle scenes posed a new challenge with four set pieces: a preliminary attack on the hill stalls and causes increasing tension between Colonel Tall and Captain Staros; then the secondary attack on the same position; then the assault on the pillboxes located by Private Bell, which was led by John Cusack's Captain Gaff; and finally the attack on the Japanese bivouac area. The 1996 draft of the script produces many moments that survive intact into the finished film—many taken faithfully from the novel. The deaths first of the scouts and then of Whyte (Jared Leto), the officer who ordered the advance; the death of Keck (Woody Harrelson) when he accidentally pulls the pin out of his hand grenade; and the confrontation between Tall and Staros are almost word for word the same as in the script and novel.

To help visualize the battles, bigger scenes were storyboarded (something Malick previously resisted), although it's debatable to what extent Malick consulted them. Each battle scene was shot with the camera at eye level with the soldiers, following them down into the grass and dirt as they crouched and huddled for their lives. Malick's old friend and World War II veteran Arthur Penn was astonished by the verisimilitude Malick achieved: the film "had the feeling that you would eat dirt rather than put your head out. We were frightened, we were just frightened. And Terry got some of that into the movie: I'm surprised because he was never in the war."[24] John Toll employed an Akela crane—one of the largest cranes available. The Akela can follow a subject almost two hundred feet in one movement. Toll used it to produce swooping shots to give a sense of the scale of the battle while still remaining close to the actors' level, flying through the grass alongside them. It's a dolly, not a crane, Toll told his operators. It was to move level with the ground in a long shallow arc. Maintaining the look of the waist-high grass proved difficult. Every time someone moved, a visible track remained. "It was like working in snow, where you've got to cover your tracks," Toll recalls. "There's only so much you can do before you destroy the look of the location."[25]

A *New York Times* report from the set showed Malick in action: "The battle commences. Men scramble, aim, fire and duck, clambering across out-croppings and the charred timbers. A pall of black smoke hangs over

126

The Thin Red Line (1995–1998)

everything. The noise is deafening." Dash Mihok, who plays Private Doll, loses his footing, and the take is interrupted: "Mr. Mihok, now at the crest, berates himself, believing he had ruined the scene. Mr. Malick listens and watches with some amusement. 'Dash wants to be Rambo,' he announces with a grin, and the actor cools down."[26]

Steadicam operators, like Brad Shields, followed actors in the midst of the smoke and explosions. The American actors didn't know how the Japanese actors were going to react or where they were going to come from, giving a genuine spontaneity to their reactions. Vast amounts of footage were shot, ensuring there was enough coverage of each major character during the battles. Inevitably, there were accidents. Ben Chaplin received a cut on his face in the battle in the Japanese bivouac, as is visible in the picture.

Despite the scale, Malick retained his own vision. During one large-scale scene at the army base, hundreds of extras, trucks, and airplanes all had to be coordinated for a shot of a truck carrying C Company to the camp. The cameras roll, and everyone is in place. The vintage planes are radioed in, and the truck is ready to go. John C. Reilly, who plays Sergeant Storm, recalls: "All of a sudden, Terry's like, 'Oh look, there's a Red-Tailed Hawk! Look! John, John, get the camera! Get the camera! There he is!' We're all like . . . 'Are we really filming a hawk right now? Are you kidding? There's airplanes taking off!' And we sat there for five or ten minutes while he got different angles of this bird flying through the sky."[27] Woody Harrelson says: "He'd come out in the morning and he'd really *look*—at the way the grass was blowing in the wind on the hill and the way the sunlight was slipping across the grass. And he'd say, 'Hmm . . . let's set the camera up *here*. Facing *that* way.' You couldn't always tell what he was after, no. But everybody had faith in him. . . . You just *believed*, brother!"[28]

Far from the noise of battle, documentary cameraman Reuben Aaronson, in collaboration with the anthropologist Christine Jourdan, was leading a separate unit on Guadalcanal. Jourdan's lifework was the study of the people of the Solomon Islands. She gave the crew access to the villages to film the daily life of the islanders, the children playing, the rituals of ordinary life. After more than 120 days of shooting in northern Australia, Malick and a small group of actors and crew moved to Guadalcanal to supplement Aaronson's work. They shot scenes of the two AWOL soldiers played by Caviezel and Will Wallace in a village built by Jack Fisk and a team of locals. They also photographed the scene where the soldiers of C Company first walk through the grasslands and encounter a native, to their bewilderment—an episode

THE MAGIC HOURS

based on a chance encounter the team had while scouting the location back in June. While shooting one scene, Ecky went for a walk on the beach and overheard a Melanesian choir singing. She quickly brought Malick over. This part of the film became one of the great additions to the novel, creating a layer of local life, enriching its vision of a world in which different cultures coexist. Hans Zimmer wove the music into the soundtrack.

In the press, stories—partly inspired by the silence of the director—circulated about the production. Pressure was added by the fact that Steven Spielberg's *Saving Private Ryan* was filming at the same time. John Toll's wife, Lois Burwell, headed the makeup department on the rival film and was excitedly conveying how Spielberg was revisualizing the Second World War, particularly the dramatic opening assault on Omaha Beach. It wasn't the only connection the two productions shared. Tom Sizemore auditioned for a role in Malick's film but ultimately was forced to choose Spielberg as Malick delayed his decision too long. Tom Hanks also chose the lead in *Saving Private Ryan* over a smaller role in Malick's film. Malick sent Spielberg a Japanese battle flag as a gift and received a flak jacket in return. The two productions were in different theaters of war, but just as *Sugarland Express* had come out at the same time as *Badlands*, so *Saving Private Ryan* and *The Thin Red Line* would emerge at the same time, going head-to-head during award season.

After the crew returned to the United States, shots were picked up off Catalina Island, near Los Angeles. John Travolta's brigadier general gives Nick Nolte's Colonel Tall his pep talk before the mission. Nolte's hair had grown to an unmilitary length, but he inhabited his role again. Australian actress Miranda Otto was one of the only women to appear in the film, as Ben Chaplin's wife. Exteriors in San Pedro were filmed as flashbacks.

Billy Weber and Leslie Jones had assembled a five-and-a-half-hour cut from the 1.2 million feet of film shot.[29] Malick watched it through once, and then the work began. The editors divided the film into sequences. There hadn't been a voice-over in the script, but Malick now wrote one, which Billy Bob Thornton recorded. Malick threw it out. He started to experiment with different actors and approaches. John Dee Smith, playing Private Train, ended up recording the lion's share of the narration. The recording sessions were tortuous as Malick insisted on recording the same line over and over again with slight variations. The voice-over includes a slew of literary allusions, from John Steinbeck's *Grapes of Wrath* ("Are we all just one big soul?") to Stephen Crane's *Red Badge of Courage* ("We're living in a box") and William Wordsworth's *The Prelude* ("Darkness and Light. Strife and Love. Are

The Thin Red Line (1995–1998)

they the workings of one mind, the features of the same face?"). Malick's "Sanshō the Bailiff" script is cannibalized: "Are you thoughtful and kind? Are you righteous? Does your confidence lie in this? Are you loved by all? So was I!"[30] These lines are spoken by Elias Koteas (Captain Staros) rather than by a Japanese actor. Ben Chaplin, Dash Mihok, Jim Caviezel, Sean Penn, Miranda Otto, and Nick Nolte all contributed voice-overs as their characters. They're internal monologues, whereas Smith's and Koteas's (in this instant) are disassociated from their characters. In the case of Smith, the philosophical questioning doesn't seem to match the character he plays: a young man who jabbers nervously to Sergeant Welsh about how scared he is. Rather, his is the voice of the soul of C Company, or, given Malick's affinity with Smith, a direct voicing of the filmmaker's concerns and thoughts. Many audiences and critics would assume his voice was Witt's, which given the fluidity of the film is not necessarily wrong.

Hans Zimmer produced over six hours of original music, supplemented with preexisting music Malick was using as a temp score, including *The Unanswered Question* by Charles Ives; music by Gabriel Fauré, Arsenije Jovanovic, and Arvo Pärt; and the Melanesian and additional compositions by John Powell. Francesco Lupica, whom Malick had contacted for "Q," recorded his Cosmic Beam. This steel girder created an unearthly grinding sound and weighed four tons. At the Fox studio, the technicians worried its vibrations might damage the building. It provided the foreboding bass tone that opens the film as the crocodile slides into the water.

As work continued on *The Thin Red Line*, Malick was also overseeing other projects with Ed Pressman and Sunflower Productions. Directed by Leslie Woodhead, *Endurance* was a documentary on Haile Gebreselassie, the Ethiopian Olympic athlete. Malick knew Woodhead's documentaries about the Mursi, an ethnic group of cattle herders based in the southwestern part of Ethiopia. Woodhead said the idea originated from Malick: "He has a tremendous passion for long-distance running, and he wanted to make a film on why so many come from East Africa. . . . He found my documentaries on East Africa, and got in touch with me and asked if I'd like to direct it. I hadn't done a cinema documentary before; I'm a TV person."[31] Woodhead's description of meeting Malick for the first time at a Hollywood mansion deserves to be quoted in full:

And here was the legend himself, tall, grizzled beard, extraordinary, unsettling eyes—a lot like an anthropologist, it occurred to me. He

THE MAGIC HOURS

introduced himself in a quiet southern accent, and my relationship with Terrence Malick began. Over the years, that relationship has been hypnotic, maddening, challenging, rewarding, frustrating, stimulating, bewildering, and a hundred other conflicting things. Within minutes, Malick was spinning metaphors to describe the way he wanted to work with me: I would be Neil Armstrong on the moon, and he would be back in Mission control; we would be Jazz musicians swapping improvisations; we would be fishermen casting our nets together. I struggled to find some firm ground amid the fog of imagery which was compounded by Malick's hesitant, free-form sentences which never seemed to end, and to try and locate what I was getting involved with. He enthused about the Greek epic poet Pindar who celebrated the Olympic spirit, and about the nobility of Leni Riefenstahl's "up-angle" shots of athletes in her film of the 1936 Berlin Olympics.[32]

He told Woodhead to avoid voice-overs and beautiful shots, which he referred to as "cornflakes"[33]: another example of the do-as-I-say-not-as-I-do approach to filmmaking, noted by Sabina Murray. As a producer, he didn't want a Terrence Malick film.

In July 1998, Steven Spielberg released *Saving Private Ryan*. It was an immediate commercial smash that sparked a reevaluation of the Second World War and its portrayal. Combat scenes now had to stand comparison with Spielberg's two gut-wrenching large-scale battle scenes that bookended the movie. Spielberg had desaturated the film and mounted an electric drill to the camera to create a juddering image that added documentary realism and visceral authenticity. Pressure built up on *The Thin Red Line* to match *Saving Private Ryan*. Although from the same generation, Spielberg and Malick were polar opposites in their relationship to the media and in their status. Spielberg promoted his film as a celebration of the Greatest Generation and, personally, as a gift to his father, a veteran of the Second World War. The film is an unabashed celebration of the citizen soldiery. Spielberg was a superstar director whose film releases were events in and of themselves. In contrast, Malick was a legend to cinephiles rather than the public. He gave no interviews and did no promotion, and there was no reference to his father's war service. Veterans were invited onto the set, and their suggestions and advice had been sought, but they weren't part of any publicity campaign.

The Thin Red Line (1995–1998)

To speed work up, Malick had Saar Klein, his editor on *Endurance*, come onto *The Thin Red Line*. The process involved experimentation. Malick watched the footage while listening to music on his headphones—mainly Green Day (he remained a Radiohead skeptic)—to see which reels could be understood without the dialogue. When he didn't understand what was happening, the dialogue stayed or a voice-over track was introduced. Many characters were reconfigured: entire speeches, scenes, or even characters were scrapped. For actors who judge their roles by the number of lines, this was a brutal experience as characters they assumed to be major parts became background artists, faces in the company. Others disappeared entirely. Mickey Rourke's role as a sniper was cut. His character was introduced too late in the film, Weber says. Arguably, the cut could have been made at the screenplay stage. None of the deleted scenes that appear on the Criterion release—including Mickey Rourke's and extended scenes with George Clooney—feel indispensable. Fascinatingly, though uncredited and with no lines in the film, Barry Pepper can be spied crouching by Sean Penn as Jared Leto receives his fatal order to advance. Pepper plays a substantial role in *Saving Private Ryan*, as a sniper, and is the only actor to appear in both films. Tim Blake Nelson, John C. Reilly, and Nick Stahl also saw their roles shaved significantly. Malick phoned John C. Reilly, saying: "John, I just wanted to give you a heads up. I felt that some parts of the picture were like ice floes that separated from the main, and so some of your scenes, well, John, they just floated off."[34]

Adrien Brody became Malick's most famous victim. *Vanity Fair*'s interview with him, *Brody in Motion*, features such questions as "Your role in *The Thin Red Line* was one of the most sought after in Hollywood. How did you edge the competition?" Rumor had Brody turning up to the premiere believing himself to be the lead and unaware that his role had been drastically reduced. He told James Mottram: "It was extremely unpleasant because I'd already begun the press for a film that I wasn't really in. Terry obviously changed the entire concept of the film. I had never experienced anything like that."[35]

Billy Weber argued for still another cut: take Clooney's character out of the film altogether. The excision seemed the obvious decision. First of all, as with Rourke's character, Clooney's Captain Bosche, Staros's replacement, arrives too late in the film as a new character, and his recognizable face comes as a jolt to the audience. Also, the cut from Sergeant Welsh at Witt's grave to Welsh and Charlie Company marching past the graveyard matched in terms of both character and concept: from an individual grave of one soldier in the

THE MAGIC HOURS

jungle to a behind-the-lines graveyard—from a personally felt grief still blood wet from battle to an official sentiment ossifying into a publicly acknowledged memorial. Weber even approached Clooney at an internal studio screening to ask if he minded being cut. Clooney loved the picture and didn't need the extra publicity, so he generously told Weber to do whatever they thought needed doing. Potentially, he was also embarrassed at appearing in such a small role. But Malick didn't want to lose the scene. A week later, Malick changed his mind and told Weber to take it out. Weber was aghast. The trailer, the poster, and the whole advertising campaign for the movie were already public, with George Clooney's name prominently plastered all over them (despite his tiny role). It was too late. The scene stayed.[36] It's also worth remembering that Fox's participation and financing stipulated five big names. Clooney was one of those names, and his excision could have been seen as a breach of that agreement. The agreement, however, said nothing about how long he had to be in the film.

The film premiered on December 22, 1998, in time to qualify for the Oscars. Kevin Costner, Jon Voight, Nick Nolte, Sean Penn, and a smattering of the cast attended. Despite the story of Adrien Brody attending the premiere, there are no photos of him on the red carpet, and it seems unlikely. Perhaps he'd been warned off. The story added to the legend of Malick—this time less benign in his blithe indifference to his actors' feelings—and was recounted years later by George Clooney at a *Hollywood Reporter* actors' roundtable, which included Christopher Plummer's forthright criticism of the director. Legend grew also of a five-hour cut. This, however, never existed. It was simply the usual assembly cut prepared by the editors, which included much of what was shot, coverage and alternate versions of scenes, but was never intended to be the finished film. The number of actors excised from the film grew with every retelling. Gary Oldman and Viggo Mortensen were involved with the casting process—Mortensen was set to play Bell—but were released before filming began. Mortensen received thanks in the credits, along with Lucas Haas and several other actors who had been involved earlier on and whose contributions added something to the script. Ecky also received a credit as a continuity adviser, having sat with Malick through many of the screenings and offered advice.

The film went on wide release on January 20, 1999. The critics greeted the film with varying degrees of praise and bafflement, best summed up by Jonathan Romney's review in the *Guardian*, which awarded the film five question marks: "It's undeniably touched by brilliance."[37] Roger Ebert at the

The Thin Red Line (1995–1998)

Chicago Sun Times found the film fascinating but confusing.[38] At the *Washington Post*, Michael O'Sullivan called it "the thinking person's *Saving Private Ryan*," writing: "It can be called an anti-war film, but its disdain for the very conventions of the medium make it an anti-anti-war film."[39] As with *Days of Heaven*, the beauty of the cinematography confounded critics, given the brutal reality of its subject. Richard Schickel summed it up in *Time* magazine, describing Malick's film as "a meadow with a minefield."[40]

Splitting the difference, the New York Film Critics awarded *Saving Private Ryan* Best Picture and Terrence Malick Best Director. In a rare public appearance, Malick appeared at the awards banquet held at the Windows on the World restaurant at the top of the World Trade Center in New York. A private elevator was provided. Spielberg and Scorsese sat at one table, and next to them, Malick and Ecky sat with novelist William Styron, whom Malick asked to present his award. The Pulitzer Prize–winning author of *Sophie's Choice* and *Darkness Visible*, Styron knew James Jones in Paris and provided Malick with a link to the author.[41]

In February, the film had its international premiere at the Berlin Film Festival, where it won the top prize: the Golden Bear. The press conference was rendered comical by a confused journalist addressing his first question to Mr. Malick despite Malick's obvious absence. On February 9, the nominations for the Seventy-First Academy Awards were announced, and *The Thin Red Line* garnered seven nominations, including Best Picture, Director, Screenplay, Score, and Cinematography. It won none in the end; the awards were split between John Madden's feel-good romp *Shakespeare in Love* and Spielberg's *Saving Private Ryan* after a ferocious Oscars campaign. Malick discouraged participation in such bun-fights. Roberto Benigni's Holocaust comedy *Life Is Beautiful* was the biggest surprise of the night. When the nominees for Best Director were named and the camera zoomed in on each face, Malick's introduction was followed by a photograph of a director's chair with his name on it. There had been talk of Malick attending, but in the end he chose to babysit for some friends. Malick was happy to attend the parties and catch up with old friends, but he was not going to do the red carpet or squirm in his seat while the camera sought him out.

The return of Terrence Malick was a miracle of sorts, confirming him as an artist of unique vision. Once more, he found himself compared to Spielberg, but Spielberg, in the interim, had become a titan of popular entertainment and was now aspiring to be taken seriously. Other contemporaries,

133

THE MAGIC HOURS

such as AFI classmates David Lynch and Paul Schrader, had entire careers in the time between *Days of Heaven* and *The Thin Red Line*.

On March 9, Stanley Kubrick died in his sleep with his final film, *Eyes Wide Shut*, unfinished. It had been twelve years since his previous film, *Full Metal Jacket* (1987). George Lucas returned to directing after twenty-two years with *Star Wars: Episode One—The Phantom Menace*, which hit theaters in spring. Francis Ford Coppola had been directing the turgid nonsense of *Jack* (1996) and soon retreated to his vineyard to curate his legacy and the many alternate cuts of his most successful films. Aside from Spielberg, the last men standing of Malick's generation were the New Yorkers Martin Scorsese and Woody Allen.

So what did *The Thin Red Line* reveal of Malick? Aside from the obvious proof that he could still direct a film, it showed he could direct a big studio picture on an epic scale. From the two-hander of *Badlands* to the trio/quartet of *Days of Heaven*, *The Thin Red Line* involved a large ensemble cast, genuine Hollywood stars, a big budget production, a studio, and several epic battle scenes. Yet in creating his movie for Fox, no one could claim that Malick had "sold out" or in some way compromised his vision. If anything, the criticism was directed at precisely the elements—the voice-overs, the close attention to nature—that were idiosyncratic and singular to his filmmaking. It was James Jones's book but inarguably Malick's film. The single female narrators of his first two films became the male choir of C for Charlie Company. Digital effects, Steadicams, and the Akela crane were folded into his process with relative ease. The movement of the story, following the soldiers up into the hills toward their goal, created a camera movement along the so-called z axis. The x axis indicates lateral camera movements (left and right); the y axis is the vertical up-and-down movement. The z axis is the line that extends before and behind the camera. Zooms, pushes and pulls, and dolly and tracking shots, such as the famous shot of Colonel Drax walking through the trenches in Stanley Kubrick's *Paths of Glory* (1957), all move along the z axis. Of course, directors utilize all sorts of movements along all axes in the process of making a film, but with *The Thin Red Line*, Malick's camera became a forward-seeking presence, a point of view that peers, approaches, and investigates, advancing with the soldiers. The editing also pushed toward the extremes of montage. The attack on the Japanese bivouac conveys the horror and disorientation of deadly violence, the collapsing of time, and unexpectedly, the thrill of war, the flood of adrenaline, the "special, bright, delicious, poignant taste" Jones describes.

The Thin Red Line (1995–1998)

The film operates on many different levels while at the same time having a visceral immediacy. Big philosophical questions are stated with a naive simplicity, but the film works as a straightforward "war movie," a document of a campaign. It sets up the geography of the action and the coordination of the attack: see, for example, the use of artillery against the machine-gun emplacement called in by the infantry. With Jack Fisk's aid, the period details look authentic and lived in. The performances of the ensemble are consistently excellent, with numerous standout vignettes such as Keck's death, Welsh's moment of heroism, and Tall and Staros's confrontation. The observation of the natural world mirrors *Badlands* and *Days of Heaven*. Once more, characters live outdoors, only fleetingly aware of the beauty around them. A soldier marveling at the leaf of the mimosa pudica, the sensitive plant, folding at his touch is an epiphany blown away by mortar fire. The movement of sunlight on a hill could be the presence of a divine light or an unlucky moment of clarity revealing the soldiers' position to the waiting machine guns. *The Thin Red Line* is now rightly regarded by many as a masterpiece: Malick's third in a row.

Before the film was released, Malick met with Austin-based journalist Helen Thorpe at a terrace restaurant in Los Angeles. Here's a description of the director in the flesh: "My homework had given me the sense of a ghostly eminence, so it was startling to encounter Malick as a corporeal being. He has a bearish figure, a cropped white beard, a bald dome, and a vertical, Spanish-looking nose. My general impression was that he is the most reserved warm person, or the warmest reserved person, that I can recall ever meeting." When pressed to give an on-the-record interview, Malick says: "I'm still very shy about this sort of thing, from a wish to lead as normal and simple a life as possible." He wanted to keep the publicity at arm's length but still needed the touch to reassure him it was there. Perhaps, with his recent experience of Peter Biskind's *Vanity Fair* article (which had come out that December, just before the film's release), he longed for a sympathetic hearing to put the record straight. Why agree to meet a journalist if he didn't want to influence their view of him? With Thorpe, it produced the intended effect—a sympathetic portrait:

> The evening we met in L.A., Malick had seemed comfortable, even
> serene. His calm manner wasn't what I had expected, given the
> pressure he must be under to live up to past accomplishments. On
> the other hand, perhaps Malick has found that the real L.A. isn't

THE MAGIC HOURS

quite as awful as the L.A. of his imagination. And in one sense, his return must be easier than his arrival was, as he is already schooled in the vagaries of fame and what it does to the ego. Finally, I came to see that Malick's silence is an integral part of who he is. If he ever came to feel he deserved the attention that reporters are always trying to bestow on him, he would no longer be himself.[42]

That December had also seen the finalization of his divorce from Michèle Morette. He and Ecky wasted no time in marrying. This was the third marriage for both of them, and Malick was joining a family—this time one with six adult children. Ecky represented his future and also shared deep connections to his past. She was social and outgoing, independent and clever, forceful and outspoken. She also shared Malick's deeply spiritual outlook on life, having been educated at a seminary—an educational path she was continuing—and was qualified to serve as a minister. They attended church together. Malick visited his own family back in Bartlesville and gave the Golden Bear statuette he had won in Berlin to his parents. The canoe Jim Caviezel had paddled in the opening scenes of the film now hung from the ceiling of his home in Austin as a memento. The critical success of the film validated his decision to return to filmmaking. The film had not gone over budget or schedule, but it had underperformed at the box office—given the star power on show—even as it became Malick's most commercially successful movie yet.[43] Now the question was, Would it be twenty more years before the next Terrence Malick film? Or was he back?

8

The New World (1999–2005)

On Thursday, April 26, 1607, three ships, the *Susan Constant*, the *Discovery*, and the *Godspeed*, made landfall at Chesapeake Bay on the Atlantic coast of Virginia. Commanded by Captain Newport, the ships held 104 men and boys. No women were aboard. One member of the expedition had died during the four-month Atlantic crossing.

The men, including a number of wealthy adventurers but few craftsmen or farmers, were poorly skilled. They located their triangular fort on the basis of military criteria, aimed at defending the community from attack by other European powers coming by sea rather than considering more immediate requirements like drinking water. Mosquitoes bit, causing malaria, and the water was brackish. Despite their efforts at farming, their survival depended on the charity of the Native people and the speedy arrival of supply ships.

Any description of a beginning is inevitably partial. The calendar, language, and place names depend on a European framework of understanding. The Powhatan people saw something else: the arrival of aliens—a group of men who looked, sounded, dressed, smelled, and behaved differently, bizarrely, frighteningly. But the Europeans and the Powhatans were both experiencing a reconfiguring of the world. A New World had been arrived at or had arrived. Violence and exploitation followed—genocide was at hand—but for a brief moment there was wonder, surprise, and possibility. This was the beginning of "America" and the subject of Terrence Malick's next film. But the journey was neither short nor easy.

By 1999, Malick's position in Hollywood was better established than ever. *The Thin Red Line* put the ghost of Michael Cimino–like excesses—which had attached to the New Hollywood alumni—to rest. With a successful film at his back and the cream of Hollywood acting talent lining up, Malick found studios eager to discuss his next project. Ditching his erstwhile producing partners Robert Geisler and John Roberdeau was retrospectively

THE MAGIC HOURS

justified when their investing partner Gerry Rubin sued them. The case involved Mike Medavoy and Phoenix as well as Malick himself, who all found themselves defendants accused of facilitating Geisler and Roberdeau's withholding of profits from Rubin. Malick settled, and Medavoy and Phoenix extricated themselves. But Geisler and Roberdeau's legal woes mounted. Court records revealed that Medavoy found the pair to be "charlatans" he wanted rid of as soon as possible. The pair continued their activities, optioning Senator John McCain's memoir *Faith of My Fathers* despite the battering their reputations had taken. The stress was too much, and Roberdeau collapsed in the lobby of their Manhattan residence, dying of a heart attack. He was forty-nine years old.

Malick's other partnerships were faring better. The developing projects nurtured via Sunflower Productions were finally blossoming. In 2000, the first film coproduced by Sunflower was released in China. *Happy Times* is a small melancholy comedy from Zhang Yimou, who went on to direct the martial arts spectaculars *Hero* (2002) and *House of the Flying Daggers* (2004). Yimou was also in talks to direct *The Beautiful Country*, which Malick had written with Sabina Murray, but Yimou ended up withdrawing, and *Smoke* (1995) director Wayne Wang took over, only to be replaced by Norwegian Hans Petter Moland.

After his involvement in *Endurance*, Malick received an executive producer credit for the similarly titled *The Endurance*, narrated by Liam Neeson and directed by George Butler, about the ill-fated Antarctic expedition led by Ernest Shackleton. Malick had no direct contact with the director and was one of seven executive producers on the film. The adaptation of Larry McMurtry's *Desert Rose* was once more revived, as were new projects categorized as original stories, such as "The Capital" and "The Runaway," as well as "Realm: a Biographical Story," cowritten by Jay Woodriff and telling the story of the collaboration between the astronomers Edwin Hubble and Milton Humason.[1] With his *Thin Red Line* producer Grant Hill, Malick was announced as a producer for an adaptation of *Brighton Rock* that had been mooted a few years earlier when Malick approached Australian director Craig Monahan, whose 1998 film *The Interview* he greatly admired. Monahan passed because he was intent on writing his own projects.[2]

Now Malick had his eyes on British filmmaker Asif Kapadia, having seen his debut film, *The Warrior* (2001). He cold-called to express his admiration for the film and asked if Kapadia was interested in directing a film with Malick producing. They met several times in Los Angeles and once in Texas.

138

The New World (1999–2005)

The idea was an adaptation of Graham Greene's novel of a teenage gangster, *Brighton Rock*. Kapadia was reluctant to take on a film that would be compared to the John Boulting classic starring Richard Attenborough. Malick was a fan of the book and of Greene in general. The scene in *Badlands* where Martin Sheen records a message to the authorities when faking his and Holly's death is directly inspired by a similar scene in *Brighton Rock*.[3] Kapadia found Malick friendly, far from his image as a remote legend. When in Los Angeles, they lunched at cheap Mexican restaurants, and Malick left long digressive messages on the young director's voicemail. Kapadia wanted to update the book, but Malick liked the period setting. Malick didn't want to direct it himself, believing that a British filmmaker was needed. In 2010, Rowan Joffé directed a version updated to the mod era, by which point Kapadia and Malick had dropped out of the project.

Malick was also in talks to adapt Alan Tennant's book *On the Wing*. Malick shared Tennant's passion for birding. The book chronicles how Tennant and George Vose, a World War II veteran pilot flying a beat-up Cessna Skyhawk, tracked the migration of peregrine falcons from the Arctic to South America. Sunflower set up a production deal, and Robert Redford expressed interest in playing the role of Vose and potentially directing the film.[4]

At the Venice Film Festival in September 2002, Sergei Bodrov's film *Bear's Kiss* premiered in competition, reportedly from a screenplay partly penned by Malick, although the extent of his involvement remains unclear. At the same festival, the documentary *Rosy-Fingered Dawn: A Film on Terrence Malick* was also premiered. The film was the work of a group of Italian critics and friends: Luciano Barcaroli, Carlo Hintermann, Gerardo Panichi, and Daniele Villa. They had met the film director at the Milanesiana festival in Milan, Italy, in 2001, where a restored print of *Badlands* was being shown. Malick was generous with his time but reluctant to involve himself in the actual making of, let alone an appearance in, the documentary.[5] His absence became a shaping presence. The filmmakers use a mix of colleagues, actors, and friends—Jack Fisk, Sissy Spacek, Elias Koteas, and Sean Penn—to create an oral history with handheld video footage of a road trip to visit the locations of earlier films. The documentary added to Malick's mythic status without revealing much, and it led to the oral history *Rehearsing the Unexpected* (2016).

As *The Beautiful Country* moved into production, another Malick script, *Undertow*, was green-lit. Joe Conway, an English teacher at St. Stephens, met Malick on the basketball court. Malick introduced himself

THE MAGIC HOURS

simply as a writer. Over the months, Malick became a regular player and asked whether Conway would be interested in writing a screenplay. Malick pointed him toward the University of Texas screenwriting course, which Sabina Murray was attending and which was part of the pitching process. Malick suggested a story based on a message that a teenager had left on a runaway hotline: "About his younger brother he had to leave behind, and how he was looking for grandparents. Then [Malick] started to elaborate. There wasn't a clear sense that he was telling the truth, and maybe this was all fictionalized."[6]

As with *The Beautiful Country*, Malick was a cowriter and producer. He approached David Gordon Green, a young Texan director whose debut feature film, *George Washington* (2000), Malick had screened before its release. "They sent me the script and I began communicating with the original writer; we went back and forth and eventually adapted it more to what I was interested in exploring," Green said.[7] When *Undertow* started shooting, Malick was on set. Green told Wendy Mitchell of IndieWire: "It's an interesting feeling to stroll over to the monitor and see Malick be exuberant and thrilled or critical of your work on the spot as it happens. And to ask questions as any producer would and challenge you as any smart producer would, and ultimately to encourage you as the gracious producers will."[8]

The Beautiful Country was also shooting at the same time. Harvey Keitel had originally been cast in one of the few non-Asian roles before being replaced by English actor Tim Roth. *The Thin Red Line* collaborator Nick Nolte also had a small but significant role: "Malick told me of a female student whom he had been teaching in a Harvard screenwriting class and he told me that she had come up with a really good theme and described a little bit of it to me."[9] The lead actress, Bai Ling, had first met Malick when he cast her in the stage version of "Sanshō the Bailiff." Echoing his strictures to Alexandra, he told her not to watch TV. She told Rebecca Carroll: "We became friends, and later he said, 'I'm writing something. I may have something for you.' It was *The Beautiful Country*—he wrote a role for me, a character called Ling. So I feel like it's all a gift. Sometimes I feel like he's the passenger sent from God or nature."[10]

When *The Beautiful Country* premiered at the Berlin Film Festival, Malick attended to support the cast and crew. Sabina Murray agreed to meet Malick in the foyer of the Ritz-Carlton before the screening, only to be surprised to find him sporting a red fez: the definition of someone hiding in plain sight.[11] The film garnered respectful reviews.

140

The New World (1999–2005)

For all the scripts, treatments, and production credits, Malick was eager to get back into the director's chair. At the beginning of 2004, *Variety* reported that Terrence Malick's "Che" was part of a roster of eight films being financed by a new media conglomerate called Rising Star, a body comprising VIP, a German fund, and Ascendant Pictures.[12] Benicio Del Toro, cast as the revolutionary hero Ernesto "Che" Guevara, was working closely with Malick on the script. A $40 million budget was set, with a four-month shoot scheduled to begin in July on location in South America. Laura Bickford, Steven Soderbergh, and Del Toro, the team who had recently produced *Traffic* (2000), were on board, as was Fernando Sulichin. Javier Bardem was cast alongside Ryan Gosling, Benjamin Bratt, and Franka Potente as Che's band of revolutionaries. Malick contacted the Mexican cinematographer Emmanuel Lubezki, commonly known by his nickname "Chivo," meaning "goat." They shared their ideas on the use of natural light and began to formulate a "dogma," a list of rules formalizing Malick's preferences.

Malick had firsthand experience of the period, having arrived in Bolivia the day after Guevara had been executed. He knew Cuba and had met Castro. He had interviewed Guevara's widow, Aleida March. The film would complete unfinished business: the long-deferred *New Yorker* article. International sales began for the film. Vincent Maraval at Wild Bunch secured international sales in the UK, France, and Italy. But then he received a phone call from Malick, telling Maraval he was out. According to Billy Weber, there were financial problems.[13] Also, the studio was getting nervous about the danger of Bolivia as a location. Maraval was unimpressed, telling *Variety*: "It is totally irresponsible to pull out now." With a threat of legal action, he argued for a year's delay, but the backers and the cast weren't going to wait. Maraval said: "He's an artist and I admire him too much to be angry."[14] The news wasn't softened by the fact that Malick already had another film lined up.

"The Mother of Us All"—now renamed *The New World*—predated *Badlands* as a script. Its locations—Virginia and Canada—were more accessible than Bolivia. According to Weber, Malick got the decision from New Line in the space of a day with the pitch "*Romeo and Juliet* meets *Gladiator*."[15] Budgeted at $40 million, it could shoot in July 2004, a matter of months away. The move from "Che" to *The New World* was consistent with Malick's strategy of parallel projects.

Preproduction moved ahead at speed. Casting ideas percolated. Captain John Smith is described in Malick's screenplay as "a boisterous man of great

THE MAGIC HOURS

strength, a warm-hearted rebel, a lover of play and song." Wearing the earring "of a Moorish woman to whom he once was a slave," Smith has been "a prisoner of the Turks, a beggar in Moscow, has fought the Tartars in Transylvania and been shipwrecked in three seas." Born in 1976, the Irish actor Colin Farrell first found fame in the popular television drama *Ballykissangel*. His breakthrough in Hollywood came via a handful of eye-catching roles in films like *Tigerland* (2000) and Steven Spielberg's *Minority Report* (2002), through which he graduated to leading man status. While they were filming *At Home at the End of the World* (2004) in Canada, his costar Sissy Spacek asked if he'd read a script a friend of hers had written. The script was *The New World*. Farrell met Malick for margaritas.[16]

Malick had his cinematographer: Chivo joked he'd shoot seventh unit if need be. A year earlier, Malick had recruited a producer. Sarah Green made her name assisting John Sayles, one of the finest independent American directors, working on *Matewan* (1987) and *Eight Men Out* (1988) as an assistant production manager before getting promoted to a full producer position for *City of Hope* (1991) and two more of his features. She also produced the work of David Mamet and Julie Taymor. As was his habit, Malick cold-called her after getting her contact information from the head of Sony Pictures Classics, Michael Barker. "Che" was first in line, but when it fell through, Green was ready to step into the gap for *The New World*.

As with his first three films, *The New World* was a period film but was set in the most historically remote epoch yet and therefore the most difficult to reproduce convincingly. Malick's script included years of research. Jack Fisk was eager to recreate Jamestown and the Powhatan villages, using old techniques for the building process as far as possible. Authenticity wasn't simply a question of believability. After years of misrepresentation, Malick felt a moral duty to portray the Native Americans accurately. The filmmakers consulted Native American leaders: Chief Robert "Two Eagles" Green of the Patawomeck and Chief Stephen R. Adkins of the Chickahominy Tribe. Initially skeptical—the presumption of the title particularly put off Chief Adkins—the chiefs were won over by the filmmakers' dedication to authenticity. A significant step came with the recruitment of actor, dancer, and choreographer Raoul Trujillo. Trujillo sent in his audition on videotape, fully costumed, made up, and committed to the physicality of the part. He received a phone call from Malick the next day, full of praise. On learning of Trujillo's background as a choreographer, Malick hired him to build a small troupe, a core of fighters and dancers to represent the Powhatan people. On reading

The New World (1999–2005)

the script, Trujillo brought up the issue of language, arguing that Kevin Costner in *Dances with Wolves* (1990) and Bruce Beresford in *Black Robe* (1991)—in which Trujillo appeared—had both used Native languages. Malick took the point to heart and hired linguist Blaire Rudes from the University of North Carolina to reproduce an approximation of the now extinct Virginian Algonquian language. Trujillo trained his core sixteen cast members together for six weeks before the shoot, creating a visual language of gesture and movement.[17]

Another controversial element was the casting of the female lead. Pocahontas's age is uncertain in the texts, but she was almost certainly a child closer to twelve than eighteen. The script describes her: "A girl of sixteen, whom we first discover underwater, diving for mussels and catching a sturgeon by the tail. She trims her hair with pearls as she sits by the shore. She gazes in rapture at the wind rushing through the trees. The Indians all defer to her." The search for the actor took six months. Q'orianka Kilcher had initially been auditioning for a role in the TV show *Into the West* when she came to the attention of the casting team. Just fourteen, she was too young, Malick and Green concluded, but they continued to call her back. Kilcher was born in Germany, daughter of an Indigenous Peruvian and an American human rights activist. A seasoned performer, she'd appeared in Ron Howard's *How the Grinch Stole Christmas* (2000) and was an accomplished dancer, having performed in Hawaii, where she spent her childhood. On her fourth audition, she met Malick.[18] He asked her to speak in an English accent, though when she got the role she learned Algonquian, working with the dialect coach Catherine Charlton not only to get the pronunciation correct but also to mispronounce the English.

Christian Bale had auditioned unsuccessfully for *The Thin Red Line*, and Malick hadn't forgotten him; he offered him the role of John Rolfe, the English colonist Pocahontas marries and has a child with. Veteran Canadian actor Christopher Plummer was cast as Captain Newport. Character actors Ben Mendelsohn, Eddie Marsan, David Thewlis, and Ben Chaplin all took on smaller roles as colonists. Established Native American actors August Schellenberg and Wes Studi were to play Chief Powhatan, Pocahontas's father, and her uncle Opechancanough, respectively.

Initially, the intention was to film in Canada, but while scouting the real locations in Virginia, Jack Fisk discovered large stretches of untouched land up the Chickahominy and James Rivers. The Canadian locations were difficult to reach and miles apart. Fisk suggested that the film stay close to the

THE MAGIC HOURS

original locations. The capper came with the discovery that three historically accurate period ships were available at the Jamestown Settlement, a living museum. On a visit there, art designer Dave Crank overheard a guide expressing a hope that the film wouldn't end up copying Disney's *Pocahontas* (1995). Malick said: "Well, without a little poetry, you wouldn't have had *The Iliad* and *The Odyssey*."[19] He wanted to aim for authenticity, but there was also room for poetry.

The decision made, Fisk and his team began building the settlers' fort, using only locally sourced materials and recreating traditional techniques: thatching and using mud for cement. Crops the Native people cultivated were planted, as were grasses. The Powhatan settlement Werowocomoco was likewise recreated in its entirety, giving the actors and director a 360-degree environment in which to film and adding a level of verisimilitude that helped many of the younger extras connect with their ancestors. One of Trujillo's core warriors, Jason Green, said: "Being with the Core Warriors, seeing how they interact, made me feel like there was part of my life missing."[20] Trujillo says: "The dances and a culture were pretty much obliterated within the first twenty-five years of Jamestown and the colony."[21] Oral traditions and documents only went so far. The rest was perforce reinvented.

All the departments carried out research, consulting academics, historians, archaeologists, and representatives of the tribes. Jacqueline West handmade the costumes using hide, feathers, and seashells for the Powhatans and traditional materials for the colonists. Hair was shaved on one side of the head to keep the bowstring from getting tangled, and makeup designs used ash and clay and looked lived in. David Crank took over an old psychiatric hospital as a workshop and crafted props from locally sourced materials.

Filming began on August 1, 2004. Chivo and Malick had their "dogma" written out. Shooting had to use available natural light; underexposure was forbidden. The latitude in the image was to be maintained. The use of maximum resolution, deep focus, and backlighting was encouraged, and lens flare was to be avoided. Lenses were hard with short focal length and no filters beyond a polarizer. Zooming was forbidden; pans and tilts discouraged. Moves along the z axis were favored. All of Malick's films from that point on evolved a signature look of literally going forward. Just as Kubrick has his lateral tracking shots and symmetry, so Malick had his z axis moves, taking the audience forward and into the world, probing, peering, inquiring, exploring with a restless, intrusive eye. Widmer says: "It's always sucking you in; pulling you in."[22]

The New World (1999–2005)

As *The Thin Red Line* charts C Company's advance through enemy territory, so *The New World* follows the colonist penetrating the world of the Native peoples, though now the reciprocal and reverse movement of Pocahontas toward the Europeans and, ultimately, Europe complicated the dynamics. As with the use of the magic hour in *Days of Heaven*, the choice of the z axis movement was an aesthetic influenced by the story.

Chivo had just finished filming *Lemony Snicket's Series of Unfortunate Events* (2004). Having struggled with the demands of a big-budget Hollywood blockbuster, he savored the freedom Malick offered. The film was shot almost entirely on 35 mm with anamorphic lenses. Camera operator Jörg Widmer was astonished at the prospect of shooting the film with only three relatively short lenses: "I said, 'We'll never get through this movie with only three lenses. You need a long lens,' and Terry said, 'No, a wide shot is as good as the close-up.' So why not? Or if you want to, then you go closer, but physically."[23] Widmer operated the Steadicam—another element of the dogma: "From nine in the morning to eight in the evening, it was Steadicam, Steadicam, Steadicam."[24] According to the agreement, static tripod shots were only carried out "in the midst of our haste." Article E of the dogma stated: "Accept the exception to the dogma." Contradictions arose—backlighting had a tendency to create lens flare, for instance—but the dogma was a formulation of the style Malick had developed on *Badlands*, with Almendros on *Days of Heaven*, and with Toll on *The Thin Red Line*. His methodology—despite its novelty for his crew and production partners—was in fact remarkably consistent with how he'd always filmed. It was just written down now.

Malick made notes in the evening. "Terry is a thinker of the night," Widmer says. "The next morning he comes on set with new ideas." A second unit had a list of "Tao shots," the nature footage of wildlife, trees, and rivers, led for a time by Andrew Dominik, the director of *Chopper* (2000) and later *The Assassination of Jesse James by the Coward Robert Ford* (2007). During the week, the script was shot with full cast and crew, and on the weekend, Malick and his leads continued shooting with a reduced crew, capturing improvised material. The script grew as Malick typed in his trailer. If conditions were wet, Malick shot in the rain. Farrell remembers Malick picking up the camera during an electrical storm and rushing outside to capture the lightning, despite carrying what amounted to a lightning rod on his shoulder. Mosquitoes were a constant irritant. Days were long and filming continuous as Malick and Chivo burned through film. Sarah Green recalls: "I don't think I've heard Terry yell cut. You just hear the flap, flap, flap of the film in the camera."[25] In Chivo and Widmer, Malick found enthusiastic partners. Widmer comments: "Terry's really impatient on set because he wants to use the time he was given to shoot this movie, instead of waiting. The times between the takes are shorter than the takes. If you have a forty-five minute roll, you get to change the film, the max you have is two minutes, and then off you go again."[26] The original idea was to shoot from early to midmorning, then break until four and shoot through to ten at night, but union laws wouldn't allow it. Malick shot his interiors during the middle of the day and utilized light streaming through sections of removed roof.

This practice can be seen in a "Making of . . ." documentary for the DVD release, directed by Austin Lynch, Jack Fisk's nephew and David Lynch's son. Malick doesn't appear, though he's usually just off camera. Chivo captures scenes, directing the action in front of him and enthusing. At one point, he calls out gleefully: "Terry, this is the best shot in the movie!" showing the exuberance and good humor of the team. When Malick had used one million feet of film, Kodak sent him a bottle of champagne.

Malick had his core crew members, but among the cast, his methods still proved divisive. Christian Bale enjoyed the relaxed atmosphere on set, bemused to find himself filmed without warning. Colin Farrell was game to join in and take charge of the camera to shoot material. He spent time with Kilcher and her family to avoid the awkwardness of the intimate scenes. Kilcher showed a remarkable maturity. In one scene with Bale, she felt unwell and fell over. Laughing, Bale picked her up and carried her over the mud. The moment was spontaneous, and the shot made the final cut. "Terry's like a wizard but doesn't know that he's a wizard," Raoul Trujillo says.[27] New scenes were introduced shortly before filming, and frequently the camera strayed away from the actors. Malick talked through takes, instructing the actors as if shooting a silent movie. The battle scenes were coordinated, but there was still room for improvisation. During the death scene of Rupwew (Michael Greyeyes), a baby turtle was incorporated. Older actors—like August Schellenberg, Wes Studi and Christopher Plummer—were less impressed, but their real disapproval came later.

Malick was enjoying himself. With half the budget of *The Thin Red Line* and a smaller cast and crew, he was relaxed and particularly at ease with the camaraderie of Trujillo's troupe. He relished Farrell's foul-mouthed sense of humor, which reminded him of his Irish uncles. He pushed himself hard, working long days, happiest when he left the larger crew idle and went off with Widmer and Chivo and the actors to film in the meadows. "More film,"

The New World (1999–2005)

would come the shout from the fields.[28] To David Crank, the process seemed to be as important as the end result. "He wants to answer questions," Crank says. "And in the course of it, he's got a movie at the end. Picasso was painting because he had questions. And you had a painting at the end. But it really was driven by questions and not just by making a product."[29]

Many scenes never made the cut. One featured Ben Chaplin and Terry Jernigan as a pair of unfortunate colonists accompanying Smith in his exploration up the river. Alone and frightened, they're lured into the woods by two women from the tribe. The camera pulls back, and hacking sounds and the men's screams can be heard. Later, when Captain Smith is brought as a prisoner into Werowocomoco, a freshly severed hand is being passed around. It is all that is left of Chaplin's character. Some roles get cut, and others get *cut*. It's an intimation of the violence the "Naturals" are capable of—a counter to the patronizing stereotype of the "noble savage"; the village seen by Private Witt as a paradise at the beginning of *The Thin Red Line* is revealed later to be a place of disease, violence, and death rather than a simplistic idyll. However, the majority of the violence was perpetrated by the colonists. A scene of a massacre that destroys Werowocomoco, featuring severed limbs and gallons of blood, was filmed but cut. This was a source of disappointment for the Native Americans working on the picture, who hoped it might testify more graphically to the violence of the colonists.

In October, filming wrapped in Virginia and moved to England to capture another New World: Europe seen by Pocahontas as she travels as a representative of her people to meet King James. Pocahontas landed at Charlestown Harbour in Cornwall. Sixty miles to the north, Clovelly Beach in Devon stood in for Newfoundland, where a short scene showed Captain Smith in his further explorations. Wes Studi's bewildered Opechancanough wanders through the Hampton Court topiary gardens in a moment of baffled contemplation. The underwater scenes of the Powhatans and the introduction of Pocahontas diving in the river were shot in a tank in Richmond. As with Richard Gere's death shot in *Days of Heaven*, rudimentary film trickery was used to achieve a transcendental effect. Hatfield House, built in 1611 by Robert Cecil, 1st Earl of Salisbury and chief minister to King James, is a popular filming location, having been used for anything from *Greystoke* (1984) to *Paddington 2* (2017). The Marble Hall was used as King James's throne room. This scene featured Welsh actor Jonathan Pryce as the king and Alexandra Wallace Malick as the queen. This compliment to Ecky was another manifestation of Malick's habit of placing family members, names, pets, and occasionally himself in his films. Just as he had named his first film "A Jill Jakes Production," so Ecky received credit as a constant support and facilitator. As Jack Fisk attests, "Terry never talks of his films but rather our films. He never uses the credit 'A Terrence Malick film.'"[30]

The last day of shooting took place on November 4 in England. The shoot had taken three months, and New Line aimed for a 2005 release. Considering Malick's modus operandi, this was an optimistic schedule. Richard Chew—one of the editors of *Star Wars* (1977)—started while the shoot was ongoing, with Mark Yoshikawa assisting. Saar Klein joined the team with his partner Hank Corwin, who had edited another monster: Oliver Stone's *JFK* (1991), which exceeded *The New World* in footage. The editors divided the film into sections. Chew worked on the arrival of the English, with Yoshikawa concentrating on the trip up the river and the encounter with the Powhatans. Klein took on the battle, and Corwin worked on the section featuring Pocahontas's marriage to John Rolfe. During the editing process, Malick, to the chagrin of the other editors, consulted a young man who had camped by the location and impressed Malick with his knowledge of local flora and fungi. Bypassing expertise was another way of capturing the unexpected and spontaneous, but collaborators, working long hours, were exasperated.[31]

Nicolas Gonda was an intern working as a postproduction assistant. His responsibilities included driving Malick from where he was staying in Beverly Hills to the editing suites at Burbank. Malick was punctual to a fault, to the point that Gonda was anticipating the pickup time only to find Malick already waiting. In his top pocket, Malick kept cards on which he wrote throughout the day, and then he typed the notes up in the evening. "Sometimes those fleeting thoughts could be strands of an extraordinary discovery," Gonda says. "Over the years, the assembly line for ideation was so worked out that the thought Terry has staring out the window at Coldwater Canyon may then serve him by noon that day, when he's sitting with Hank Corwin in the editing room."[32] Malick would also show up before the editors arrived, making sure the editing rooms were a conducive space to work in. For Gonda, it was like an athlete pacing the track the morning of the big race.

With the sound mix, Malick wanted the natural environment—the birdsong and the sounds of the frogs, the wind in the forest and on the grass—to be an immersive part of the picture. He listed twenty birdsongs to include, and the sound editors contacted Ken Campbell and Kimball Garrett from the Los Angeles Natural History Museum's Department of Ornithology to secure their expert opinion on what bird dialects could be heard in 1607 Virginia. A

The New World (1999–2005)

bird previously thought to be extinct was rediscovered in 2002: the ivory-billed woodpecker. It is the last sound just before the final credits. Another extinct bird, the Carolina parakeet, was brought back to life via CGI for the briefest of shots. There had been some digital work in *The Thin Red Line*, and this was further evidence that Malick was no technophobe when it came to creating an effect he needed. He might already have been considering more ambitious use for CGI in his next project.

Less happy was composer James Horner, who discovered that most of his music wasn't going to be in the film. Instead, Malick liked his own temp track choices. Richard Wagner's *Das Rheingold* opened and closed the film, and the love affair between Captain Smith and Pocahontas played out to Mozart's Twenty-Third Piano Concerto, with Francesco Lupica's Cosmic Beam music once more sounding. In a radio interview for "On the Score" conducted by Daniel Schweiger, Horner complained that the deadline for the cut kept getting pushed back. Horner played Malick his themes on the piano with the scenes, but Malick, according to Horner, "didn't have any experience with real film music," an astonishing statement considering how highly regarded all of Malick's films are in terms of their soundtracks—especially Ennio Morricone's work for *Days of Heaven*. Horner tried educating Malick in film soundtracks by having him watch films like *One Flew Over the Cuckoo's Nest*, but Malick resisted. In his account, Horner took the matter into his own hands on seeing that "the good editors left"; he had sequences cut by his own music editors and the score added. But Malick returned the film to its former state. "Everybody told him it was unwatchable. Everybody! Everybody!" Horner claims. When Malick began to add Wagner and Mozart, Horner left the project, having recorded his score, which was released on CD. "I never felt so let down by a filmmaker in my life. . . . It was the most disappointing experience I've ever had with a man because not only did he throw out my score, he loved my score, he didn't have a clue what to do with it," Horner says. "I'm bitter because he did not make the movie he promised everybody he would make. Everybody felt betrayed, from the film company down to the editors. Everybody felt betrayed, and this was the man who took the story that could have been one of the great love stories and was one of the great love stories in history, and turned it into crap, and it's because he doesn't believe in those things. He doesn't understand them. And most importantly, he has not an emotion in his body. He's emotionless."[33] Horner's vitriol is extreme, and many of his observations are demonstrably untrue. Mark Yoshikawa stayed throughout the process and edited the alternate cuts.

THE MAGIC HOURS

Others are partial: the Wagner and Mozart are bold anachronistic choices, whereas Horner's own score is fairly bland, with too many echoes of his earlier work, especially his Oscar-winning score for James Cameron's *Titanic* (1997).

The reason for Horner's disappointment is likely that the conflict-averse Malick expressed his approval of the score when in reality he wasn't convinced. His strategy was to hear everyone out and then go his own way, as he had in his conference with the actors during *The Thin Red Line*. It was a magic trick, like the one he had used to distract Marlon Brando all those years ago. As Saar Klein puts it, "Terry is the most collaborative and the least collaborative director at the same time."[34]

A November 2005 release date was pushed to December 5, with the studio already requesting a fifteen-minute cut for the theatrical release. At the premiere, Yoshikawa took notes for further cuts, amused to be congratulated and told the film was perfect—"Don't touch a frame"—while knowing he'd be back in the editing suite the next morning to take out a quarter of an hour. Malick attended a screening to benefit AFI, though he skipped the red carpet. At the Beverly Wilshire after-party, Hans Zimmer told Malick: "Terry, all the angst you go through making your movies, it's worth it—for us."[35] Approached by reporters, Malick was polite but insisted: "I'm so shy about this. I'd rather you just enjoy the party." Malick later met Werner Herzog at a dinner hosted by Hans Zimmer. The two directors bonded over a mutual love of *The Lion King* (1994) and could be heard arguing about their favorite song from the film.[36]

The film received a limited Christmas Day release to qualify for the Oscars. In the following weeks, Yoshikawa made the requested cuts, and on January 20, 2006, a new version, down from 150 minutes to 135 minutes, hit the theaters. The critics were divided. Many believed it to be a masterpiece. Roger Ebert gave the film his maximum rating: "No one here has read a history book from the future."[37] Malick is a "visionary." But others complained that the film was slow, lacking narrative drive. For the BBC, Paul Arendt observed that the voice-over "often leaves his actors stranded, the politics are simplistic, and poor old Pokey has a tough time trying to represent the spirit of nature by pouting winsomely and flashing her Bambi thighs. But these are hard-eyed criticisms, and *The New World* is a film to which you have to surrender to enjoy."[38] Scott Foundas wrote that the movie is "less interested in expanding the boundaries of narrative cinema than in forsaking them."[39] It's a telling use of "boundaries." Surely the artist should be

150

The New World (1999–2005)

breaking through boundaries, and indeed forsaking them, rather than simply moving them.

While detractors accused the film of tedium, pretentiousness, and an increasingly recognizable visual style, even some of the praise sounded a defensive note. It's a film you need to meet halfway, its supporters insisted. Many refused. The film's perceived lack of humor also made it ripe for the sharpening of derision. In *Salon,* Stephanie Zacharek wrote that Malick "never met a tree he didn't like."[40] "That sound you're about to hear is the cracking of spines as Terrence Malick enthusiasts like me bend over backward trying to cut *The New World* a break," Mike Clark wrote in *USA Today.*[41] Battle lines were drawn. On one side, the Malickians were all in for the challenge his films offered. On the other, the anti-Malick critics pointed out that there was no *there* there: it was the empty Christmas tree Pauline Kael had mocked.

Malick kept out of the spotlight, but he was pained by the feedback, and Zacharek's zinger particularly stung. As a producer, he was acutely aware of the box office. For a historical epic, the budget of $30 million was not huge. Ridley Scott's *Gladiator* (2000) and *Kingdom of Heaven* (2005) both had budgets north of $100 million. *The New World* fared disappointingly domestically but played substantially better internationally. It was by no means a catastrophe, either critically or commercially, but it did not deliver on the "*Romeo and Juliet* meets *Gladiator*" pitch or match the performance of *The Thin Red Line.*

Some of the more damaging public criticism came not from the critical community but from members of the film's cast. In January 2006, Wes Studi let his own be heard. These statements couldn't be dismissed as an actor irritated by the size of his role being whittled down. Studi had believed the film would reproduce the Algonquin language but found that much of the dialogue had been cut. "There is a lot of dialogue missing in this theatrical release, that perhaps will be on the DVD, which is another 30 minutes or so; that is what Terrence is working on right now. A lot of effort was put into the re-creation of this language, as well as (deep sigh) around the Indian community, it was touted as having a lot to do with that language and the use of it."[42] Of Malick, he says: "He shoots some really great grass."

The most visible case occurred years after the film's release, in 2012. During an actors' roundtable organized by *Newsweek,* host David Ansen asked Christopher Plummer what it was like to work with Terrence Malick. Plummer chuckled: "He is quite an extraordinary guy, and I love some of his movies very much. But the problem with Terry, which I soon found, is he needs a writer desperately because he insists on doing everything. As we all know, he insists on writing, and overwriting, and overwriting, until it sounds terribly pretentious. You have to work terribly hard to make it sound real. And then he edits his films in such a way where he cuts everybody out of the story."[43] George Clooney, also present, interceded with the story of Adrien Brody being cut from *The Thin Red Line*, though he was quick to correct the legend that Brody had found out at the premiere. According to Clooney, Brody discovered that his role was no longer the lead at a junket when journalists (who had just seen the film) asked him what part he played.

Although the stories from *The Thin Red Line* were known to insiders, the actors hadn't gone on record. Adrien Brody was still relatively new to the business and only criticized Malick some years later, once established in his own right. Plummer's complaint had an air of actor's vanity to it: "I was put in all sorts of different spots, my character was suddenly not in the scene I thought I was in, in the editing room. It completely unbalances everything. This very emotional scene that I had suddenly was background noise. I could hear myself saying it, this long, wonderful, moving speech that I thought I was so fantastic in. It's now background sort of score, way mild in the distance, while something else is going on. And Colin Farrell just said, 'Oh you know, we're just going to be a couple fucking ospreys.'"[44]

The story gets a sympathetic hearing from his fellow actors, who chime in with a general resentment over their powerlessness in the face of directors. At the end of his career though, Plummer can afford to say what others might hesitate to reveal: "I had to write Terry a letter. I gave him shit. I'll never work with him again, of course. He won't have me. I told him, 'You are so boring. You get in these ruts. You've got to get yourself a writer.' My career with Mr. Malick is over."[45]

Raoul Trujillo argues that the film was as good as a white man could make it in the early 2000s. "I think it's an amazing film for what it is. That was in the days when people were still probably reluctant to buck the system too much. It's usually always the lead guy as a white guy, because that's going to be the story people want to see. You'd have to buck the system and Terrence is not a bucker. He plays by rules, but then in his own kingdom, he has his own set of rules."[46] In the bigger picture, the story of Pocahontas is a story of rape. It's not a love story, Trujillo argues. Studi agreed that the story needed a Native American presence behind as well as in front of the camera: "What it

The New World (1999–2005)

would take is for me to edit it. But I don't think they'll ever let me into an editing booth."[47]

As Studi indicated, the theatrical cut was followed by a 172-minute extended cut. The extended version feels more experiential and impressionistic. The voice-over becomes more complicated, with Colin Farrell's lines sometimes talking over spoken dialogue and even another voice-over, representing his own torn loyalties and identities: John Smith, the historical self-chronicler, the romanticist, and John Smith, the psychological individual. Malick also added title cards, taking as inspiration the chapter headings of Robert Louis Stevenson's *Treasure Island*, directly quoting it with the final card: "At Last . . ." In Japan, Mike Todd's Smell-O-Vision was making a limited comeback with the release of Malick's film.[48] This was an initiative the filmmakers only discovered later and soon snuffed out.

With the various cuts available via a Criterion edition, the reputation of the film has grown significantly. It holds a place analogous to Stanley Kubrick's *Barry Lyndon* (1975), a challenging film whose pace and slowness should be appreciated as a quality rather than a defect, eschewing Hollywood convention in search of an authentic feel of time. At the roundtable and despite his criticisms of Malick, Christopher Plummer said the film "doesn't look like Twentieth Century photography; it looks like Sixteenth Century photography." Plummer's and Studi's criticism didn't damage Malick's ability to find actors willing to risk appearing in his films. Michael Fassbender, one of the participants of the roundtable, later took a leading role in *Song to Song*.

Malick found it difficult to shake off one criticism that came from closer to home. Driving with Jack Fisk, Malick played a CD of James Horner's soundtrack for *The New World*. Fisk loved it, but Malick responded that his father, Emil, the music aficionado, thought it was trash.[49] His father's criticism cut deep and hurt as much as it had always hurt. Perhaps it also influenced his decision to use it sparingly.

Beyond the day-of-release reviews, Malick's work was now garnering serious academic consideration. Here, one of the few biographical details to leak through—his background in philosophy, and in particular his early interest in Heidegger—took on a disproportionate weight and made Malick the darling of numerous film-philosophy studies. Other elements of his early experience—his journalism or his fascination with political power (Che Guevara, Fidel Castro, Papa Doc Chevalier)—were subordinated or utterly ignored. The embrace of Malick, though, was conditional on the kind of philosophical treatment his films were amenable to. *The Thin Red Line* received its own anthology in the Philosophers on Film series, while *The New World* didn't fit into the Heidegger paradigm, with some dismissing it as too Kierkegaardian—an assessment that itself reveals a surprisingly dogmatic narrowness to a philosophical approach.[50] Although this attention elevated Malick in the eyes of some, it compounded the notion that he was an intellectual filmmaker whose work required a reading list, or at least a grounding in existentialist philosophy. Films to think about and ponder rather than experience and feel. This was almost the opposite of what he was seeking.

In reality, Malick's films were much broader in their appeal than such positioning supposed. *The New World* was a love story—continuing the nineteenth-century invention that Smith and Pocahontas were romantically involved—and as such risked its historical authenticity for the poetry. Like all of Malick's love stories, it was to end in disappointment and dissolution: Kit and Holly are separated; Abby's husband and her lover both die; Private Bell is betrayed by his wife; and Pocahontas is betrayed by Captain Smith—even John Rolfe has to accept that he has Pocahontas's admiration rather than her heart. The natural world was once more directly addressed—worshipped by Pocahontas as a mother and exploited by the colonists as a fickle resource that provides them with abundance and then famine. There are fewer action scenes than in *The Thin Red Line*: Captain Smith's capture by the Algonquin and an attack on the fort are well executed but relatively brief. Instead, the viewer is presented with the New World as an immersive experience: the film is as much an environment as a story, a film to "be" in more than to watch. Listen to the birdsong; move along the river; part the long grass and head into the trees; and then return to European "civilization" and see it with fresh eyes, a lens rinsed. That is the invitation the film holds out: a glimpse of a vividly realized Eden, and the poignancy of feeling it drift away. Critics were right that Malick's attention was drawn to the birds and the trees, but they were wrong to set that in opposition to human interest. It was comprehensive, not exclusive. Malick saw people as part of nature, whether they heeded it or not. The loss of the Eden is underlined by one of the unnoticed digital effects of the film: the aforementioned recreation of the extinct Carolina parakeet. The world is fragile, temporary: soon we'll all be gone, the way Pocahantas is suddenly dead.

The New World marked another significant step in Malick's career: it was the first time he enjoyed making a film. This increased his appetite for work. With *The Thin Red Line*, Malick discovered a team of collaborators rather than a hostile crew. *The Thin Red Line* proved that Malick could make a movie

The New World (1999–2005)

within typical studio constraints; *The New World* proved he could escape those constraints. Chivo Lubezki, Jörg Widmer, Sarah Green, Mark Yoshikawa, Saar Klein, and Hank Corwin joined longtime members of the production team Jack Fisk and Billy Weber as part of a circle of committed coworkers. Young filmmakers like A. J. Edwards and Nicolas Gonda were also coming on board, and Malick warmed to his role as mentor, passing on his own hard-won wisdom and never missing a chance to suggest a book to read.[51] This was the foundation of a creative community that Malick characterized as a jazz band. The circle found themselves immersed in Malick's world, talking philosophy, politics, science, and art. He demanded long hours and intense commitment both during filming and in postproduction (which increasingly overlapped), but the rewards were artistically and intellectually satisfying. One participant told me: "It sounds hokey, but we genuinely believed when we went into work in the morning that we were trying to reinvent the language of cinema."

The cohesion of the team and Malick's increased ability to impose his "dogma" made the look of a Malick film readily identifiable. Striking images in meticulous focus, with the camera moving along the *z* axis, probing, exploring; the actors never at rest, movement like a dance; the montage of scenes; the paucity of conventional scenes and dialogue; the voice-overs; the music choices taken from Malick's own collection—these all formed a distinctive aesthetic, familiar to both audiences and critics. Malick's first three films are distinct from one another, in genre and scope, despite similarities in the cinematography, music, and voice-over. From *The New World* on, there will be progression and evolution, but the movement will be in one direction—along the *z* axis of his vision—as a recognizable aesthetic emerges.

In the wider film community, Malick was now a better-known figure. Behind the scenes, he played key roles in the production of other people's films. The younger generation of directors like Harmony Korine, David Fincher, Asif Kapadia, Andrea Arnold, Lynn Ramsey, Christopher Nolan, Paul Thomas Anderson, Sofia Coppola, Richard Linklater, and David Gordon Green, having grown up watching *Badlands* and *Days of Heaven*, saw him as an ally and colleague. Malick had never lost contact with his contemporaries either. He might send Martin Scorsese a script to read, urge Mel Gibson to consider Jim Caviezel for the role of Jesus in *The Passion of the Christ* (2004), or hire Raoul Trujillo for his next film, *Apocalypto* (2006).

This new relaxed relationship with his role in the film world even led to a rare public appearance in October 2007 at the Rome Film Festival. He took

THE MAGIC HOURS

a lot of persuading, and the rules were stringent: no recording, no photographs, and no questions from the public were allowed. A world premiere of "Victor's Notebook," a short film directed by Felipe Herba in 1973 and starring Malick, was also canceled at his request. He preferred to speak about his favorite Italian films rather than his own work. He chose Mario Monicelli's *I Soliti Ignoti* (1958), Pietro Germi's *Seduced and Abandoned* (1964), and Federico Fellini's *The White Sheik* (1952). Speaking about *I Soliti Ignoti*—the English title of which is *Big Deal on Madonna Street*—Malick said: "This was the first Totò film to reach the United States. I am a big fan of Totò—his face irradiates a special love, gladness, and happiness, just like Roberto Benigni. Benigni is the true heir of artists like Totò and Charlie Chaplin."[52] Malick also commented on *Badlands* and *The New World* briefly, before leaving the stage to go to a screening of Sean Penn's *Into the Wild* (2007), which was showing at the festival and which, in its focus on a young man's attempt to escape society and find himself in nature, boasts its own Malickian influence.

In his personal life, Malick was enjoying life with Ecky. They shared hobbies and interests, both enjoying nature, animals, culture, travel, and Texas. They also shared their Episcopalian faith and attended church together as Ecky continued her studies and church work. She was a presence on the film set and gave Malick support during the long editing process. Their lives were entwined with old friends, including those from St. Stephen's with whom they went on holiday, and Ecky reported back to the *Spartan* alumni magazine with jokey references to her ox, "the Russian Bear." But she also had her own interests and activities separate from her husband's.

When Malick needed to, he found space, booking into airport hotels where he could write without distraction, just as he had once done in Paris and Death Valley. Here he was finishing the script for his next picture, one that had been gestating for some time. With a sense of security and stability in his life, perhaps it was finally time to go home.

9

The Tree of Life (2005-2011)

Whenever Terrence Malick goes through Waco, Texas, someone else drives him so he can cover his eyes. He doesn't want to see the changes. He wants to protect the past from the present, remember it as it was. But he also wants to guard it from fact. Remember not how it was but how he thinks it was. Malick and his family lived in Waco for just three years, from 1952 to 1955. It was at 3814 MacArthur Drive that he last lived with his family. Here was his childhood: a house of books and music, culture and science. This was where his mother was devoted to him; where his father filled the house with music and tension; where he played with his younger brothers: tag in the fields and stickball in the streets, riding bicycles and climbing trees. Here, his Irish uncles visited for days and stayed for months. Here, the suburbs met the countryside; Lake Waco was a ten-minute walk away, five if you ran. No light pollution in those days. At night, the stars, the sprinkle of the Milky Way, glittered brightly above. The large oak tree towered in the backyard, taller than it would ever be, relative to him. Here was an Eden ready to be lost. Here, his brother Larry was still alive; his brother Chris was happy. When he thought of Larry, he thought of 3814 MacArthur Drive.

Everything began in Waco. Everything was wonderful, then everything went wrong. The growing pains: the arguments with his father, Emil, and his first knowledge of bad things happening to good people. A tornado swept through town, killing 114 people.

And this is where he had to leave—an adventure, surely, but also an expulsion. From here, he was sent a hundred miles away to St. Stephen's Episcopal School, Austin, and into the wide world. A pilgrim, an exile, a prince cast abroad, with a yearning sense of loss.

In *The New World*, Malick returned to the beginning of "America," trying to capture a national lost innocence: before colonialism, before the violence, the murder, the spoliation, the genocide. Now he was drawn to another beginning, both more modest and more ambitious: his own childhood, his own entrance into the universe, and, as such, the beginning of the universe itself. "Project Q" had been abandoned in the early 1980s because there was no story, just a cosmological vision. But Malick's childhood in Waco began to dominate his writing, his relationship with his mother and his father, and his memories of his brothers, particularly Larry, the lost boy. Footage collected from various sites around the globe still existed—some stored in a friend's icebox—and the script was a growing monster, mixing long passages of prose with dialogue, photographs and images, and reams of research. It looked nothing like a shooting script, but this was what Malick returned to and began to hone into something that looked more like a conventional script.

Producer Bill Pohlad, whose credits include *Brokeback Mountain* (2005) and *Into the Wild* (2007) and who had worked for a time on "Che," was now recruited. Colin Farrell was provisionally attached as the lead. In August 2005, the *Hollywood Reporter* wrote that Malick was to shoot "Tree of Life" partly in India, with the film funded by the Mumbai-based Percept Pictures. As late as May 2006, there were reports that Mel Gibson was also in the cast, though more as a favor to Malick.[1] Farrell and Gibson soon dropped out, and the India plans evaporated. Heath Ledger replaced Farrell.[2] Pohlad knew Ledger from *Brokeback Mountain*, and they had dinner with Malick to talk over the film. Ledger was uncertain he could pull off the role as the father, having only recently become a father himself.[3] Grant Hill, who produced *The Thin Red Line* so efficiently and, in the interim, produced *The Matrix* (1999), joined Pohlad and Sarah Green as a producer. Mark Yoshikawa returned as one of five editors to handle a monumental amount of footage, with the promise that he'd be the last editor on the job. Chivo also read the script early, eager to continue his explorations with Malick.

Brad Pitt's production company Plan B was in talks with Malick about *Voyage of Time*—a documentary planned as a supplement to the dramatic feature—but was intrigued when Malick talked about *The Tree of Life*. Dede Gardner, Pitt's producing partner, was keen. Malick was bringing several projects toward fruition in parallel. He was producing "The Marfa Lights" with Ed Pressman's Sunflower Productions. Carlos Carrera was set to direct the Texan family drama, loosely based on *La Petite Fadette*, a novel by nineteenth-century French author George Sand.[4] Composer James Newton Howard was contacted via his agent Sam Schwarz—who represented James Horner and Ennio Morricone—to work on another new film, based on a script titled "Grace Abounding to the Chief of Sinners." It continued Malick's

The Tree of Life (2005–2011)

fascination with Jerry Lee Lewis, paralleling his life with that of Jerry Falwell, the TV evangelist. Malick visited Howard's studio in LA every week to talk over the script and the music he required. Inspired by Black preacher T. D. Jakes, Malick read parts of the script in his voice. He gave Howard notes, moving him toward minimalism: "And then one day, he didn't come," Howard says. "That was the end of that. So obviously, I did not ring his bell."[5]

In truth, Malick was moving forward on another film.

The Tree of Life was Malick's most ambitious and autobiographical project yet. On the script registered with the Writers Guild of America on June 25, 2007, a preface reads: "The 'I' who speaks in the story is not the author. Rather, he hopes that you might see yourself in this 'I' and understand this story as your own." Despite this protestation, Malick was coming home. The beginning of the universe and the beginning of himself were combined: a coming-of-age drama and a family portrait. At its heart was the relationship between Malick's on-screen surrogate Jack O'Brien (JOB for biblical scholars) and his family, including his mother and brothers but mostly his father: Mr. O'Brien. Overshadowing the story and the core emotional motivation for the larger philosophical questions was the death of his brother Larry Malick in 1968. In fact, the film is framed around the anniversary of his death, when the now adult Jack ponders the beginning of the universe and recalls his childhood, specifically the years spent in Waco. The script called for four distinct sections: a history of the universe involving elaborate visual effects; a natural history section charting the evolution of life on Earth; the representation of a 1950s childhood in Waco; and a contemporary section with Sean Penn. How these sections would interlock and be ordered was an open question. The pitch to studios was "*2001: A Space Odyssey* meets *To Kill a Mockingbird.*"

Along with the script, Malick had folders of research. The story was "the spine," as Nicolas Gonda says, "but then he pulls out a briefcase with little Manila files for different segments of the film, each of which is bursting at the seams with reference material, inspiration, pages of dialogue." For a dream sequence in Italy, he'd already meticulously scouted locations, not just choosing sites but noting the best angles to shoot at during certain times of day, certain times of year. Practicalities were also considered: the location of the parking lot, the available caterers. Even children's books he'd owned when he was eight had notes in the margin.[6]

On January 22, 2008, Bill Pohlad was driving to the Chateau Marmont in Los Angeles to meet Brad Pitt for further discussions about Plan B's

THE MAGIC HOURS

involvement when the news that Heath Ledger had been found dead in his apartment in New York came on the radio. Pohlad recalls: "I went to the meeting and met Brad there, just the two of us. And, obviously, we're both shocked and a bit overwhelmed by that news."[7] It was decided that Brad Pitt, who was already involved as a producer, would take over the role of the father. This proved a pivotal vote of confidence in the project and elevated the film's status. Pitt had risen from bit parts in TV soap *Dallas* and *Thelma and Louise* (1991) to become one of the most iconic stars of his age, with credits like *Seven Years in Tibet* (1997), *Ocean's Eleven* (2001), and *Legends of the Fall* (1994). He made a point of parlaying his mainstream appeal into more challenging work like Terry Gilliam's *Twelve Monkeys* (1995) and David Fincher's *Fight Club* (1999). He founded his production company Plan B in 2001 with his then wife Jennifer Aniston. On their divorce, he became sole owner of the company. That relationship and his subsequent relationship with Angelina Jolie also made Pitt a prime target for paparazzi.

For Mrs. O'Brien, relative unknown Jessica Chastain was cast. A native of Sacramento, California, Chastain studied at Juilliard before returning to the West Coast, where she landed a series of guest roles in television shows like *ER*. The actor became increasingly prominent in the theater, appearing in *Salomé* and *Othello*, in which she starred opposite Jon Ortiz and Philip Seymour Hoffman, but in 2007, she had still to break through to a wider public.

For the three siblings, A. J. Edwards and Nicolas Gonda visited hundreds of schools, videoing thousands of potential candidates. Malick was inspired by François Truffaut's casting of Jean-Pierre Léaud in *Les Quatre Cents Coups* (1959), but the preproduction process was so long that the first boys to be cast aged out of the roles. Hunter McCracken was cast as Jack, Laramie Eppler as RL, and Tye Sheridan as Steve, the youngest O'Brien boy. Of the three of them, only Sheridan had acting experience and that only at school-play level. In fact, Eppler never intended to go for a role, only accompanying a friend to the audition. Spotted in the waiting room and asked to read, Eppler was cast.[8]

Malick wanted to stay close to home in Austin, but the city was changing too rapidly to pass for the early 1950s, and an alternative location was found an hour to the south. Smithville, in Bastrop County, is the small town where *Hope Floats* (1998) had been filmed; its other claim to fame was the baking of the world's largest gingerbread man in 2006. Its main street is dominated by vintage clothing and thrift stores with the occasional bar and diner. The producers obtained filming permits for the entirety of Burleson Street, where the

160

The Tree of Life (2005–2011)

action of the film would take place. Karen Heck's home was hired by the production team and used as Brad Pitt's office. Malick liked the light that reflected onto her ceiling from the swimming pool in the yard, so it was also filmed.[9] Paul Viktorin's house was chosen to be the O'Brien family home. Jack Fisk knocked through another window and dressed the house in the style of the 1950s, tearing out the kitchen and installing one more appropriate to the time. A huge live oak was trucked in from a ranch and planted in the yard to be the eponymous tree.[10]

Just as Fisk had reproduced Jamestown and Werowocomoco for *The New World*, allowing Malick and his camera crew a 360-degree location to shoot in, so Burleson was dressed to look like the 1950s: Vintage cars were hired and parked on the street, and a community of extras were recruited to fill the background with daily life. Children played rope, mailmen went on their rounds, neighbors walked their dogs in front of the houses: all activity that could be glimpsed in the background or through the windows as the domestic scenes played out.

February 27, 2008, was the first day of shooting. The location was Olive Street, outside a large pink house that was used for interiors and its lawn. The crew members always referred to Brad Pitt as Mr. O'Brien over their walkie-talkies so as not to excite the crowds that had gathered to catch a glimpse of the star. Many of the scenes filmed that productive first day made it into the final cut of the film: Mr. and Mrs. O'Brien on a blanket on the lawn; O'Brien caressing his wife's belly; the birth scene; the baby's foot, which would later be used as a poster for the film; mother and child on the blanket; young Jack meeting baby RL; the planting of the tree; car lights passing over the O'Briens. When night fell, Malick and his camera team tested a lighting rig designed to mimic fireflies. Tired but satisfied, Malick took a moment to look up at the night sky and point out the constellation of Orion.[11]

For three weeks before the shoot, the actors playing the O'Brien boys had come to Smithville and lived with Jessica Chastain, getting to know one another; going bowling, go-karting, and swimming; and developing a bond. Malick told them they were to play versions of themselves, rather than characters. They each had their own wardrobes provided by Jacqueline West, which they chose from each morning. Between shots, Malick played ball with the boys, impressed by Laramie Eppler's fastball. Pitt was surprised at Malick's love of sports: "This guy was an incredible athlete, it turns out. And he's quite competitive. He's so soft spoken and so sweet and attentive to everyone on set, but get a ball in his hand and man, he's vicious."[12] Pitt shucked off

THE MAGIC HOURS

his film-star status: "We had a scene where I was supposed to be getting on their case, and they're laughing. They weren't taking it seriously because they were having fun, with a movie guy. So I had to take the eldest two off the set and say: 'This is serious. This is what we're here for, and don't come back until you're ready.' After that, they stopped looking at me as the guy they'd seen in movies."[13]

As both producer and star, Pitt found Malick's style of directing surprising at first. Malick introduced what he called "torpedoes," unscripted elements meant to disrupt scenes. For instance, without telling Chastain or Pitt, he introduced Tye Sheridan into a parental fight between Mr. and Mrs. O'Brien so they had to argue around and over him. Likewise, the family dog, Dexter, was sent in to shake things up. Malick talked during takes, suggesting ideas to the actors and encouraging the crew. Much of the live audio was unusable as a result. In post, one of the editors would go through the cut, taking out Malick's words so he could watch the footage without being annoyed by the sound of his own voice. Moments of weather, a bird's flight, the landing of a butterfly on Jessica Chastain's hand were captured as unique moments of accidental beauty, leading to Pitt describing Malick as an "imperfectionist."[14]

However, this spontaneity occurred in the context of a major film production. The trucking in of the tree, for example, was a complicated logistical feat requiring the downing of power lines. Life, full of accident and chance, was captured on film, but Malick was as ruthless as any director in manipulating the real world to create that vision. He wasn't above dunking Richard Gere's head in a fish tank for *Days of Heaven*, creating a perfect sky with digital replacement in *The Thin Red Line*, or adding two extinct Carolina parakeets in *The New World*. Likewise, the titular Tree of Life had to be dug up and transported on a huge flatbed truck that stopped traffic for miles around.

The excitement nevertheless came from the spontaneous moments: the look of contempt on Jack's face when his father flirts with a waitress or the toddler's expression of anger at the arrival of his brother. Cain and Abel right there, Malick thought. This was not acting; it was being. Malick typed new pages of script in the hotel every night and gave notes at the beginning of each day. As with *The New World*, he was enjoying himself, leaving the acrimonious and hostile atmosphere of *Badlands* and *Days of Heaven* far in the past. Jack Fisk says: "It was just fun going to work."[15] The group of loyal and faithful workers behind and in front of the camera continued to grow.

The Tree of Life (2005–2011)

Promoted from production assistant, Nicolas Gonda joined Bill Pohlad and Sarah Green as a producer. Assistant cameraman Erik Brown and Steadicam operator Jörg Widmer joined Chivo and Malick in their pursuit of natural light and the maximum resolution of the image. The characters were always backlit, and the sun was kept in shot, even when in reverse angles of a conversation. Filming was nonstop during the day, after a brief morning meeting. Different interiors were shot at different times of day to follow the sun and make the most of the natural light.

On *The New World*, Malick had told Chivo: "I will never use any shot that will humiliate you or make you feel bad. You can come to the editing any time you want, and you can take anything you want out of the movie."[16] This emboldened Chivo, and with Widmer, he pushed the limits of the cameras to come up with new perspectives. Widmer noticed the play of the shadows in the streets as the children ran. He filmed the effect, and the shot made the final cut. The LED lights used to simulate fireflies blinking in the dusk were never convincing. When one evening actual fireflies started flashing in the lawn, Widmer and his focus puller managed to capture them.[17] Some experiments didn't work out. To gain a child's point of view, Malick gave the camera to the child actors to film, but it was quickly obvious that the children couldn't operate the machinery. Another idea was to wire Jessica Chastain and lift her off the ground. Malick wasn't keen on the shot to begin with, but aided by Chastain's training in dance, it endeared itself to him and made the final cut.

Experienced Irish actress Fiona Shaw played Mrs. O'Brien's mother—inspired by and named after Malick's grandmother Kettie Thompson née O'Brien. She was surprised to find such a pacific figure: "You realize that the force to produce these fantastic films is very deep within him because his manner is gentle." The sixty-four-year-old director was still an imposing figure: "He's tall, he has a beard and he's very smiley. I don't think there's a great mystery about him. He just wants to be getting on with what he does and not necessarily to be discussed as a person." Before starting, Malick asked her to write scenes for her character, which he never used: "Which I also admired. He seems to boil the film down almost like a stew. He boils off anything he doesn't need."[18] Malick asked actors where they preferred to be—the kitchen or the garden—and filmed the scene in their chosen location. Continuity was a low priority. He shot the same scene at different times of day and in different locations.

Ecky liaised with locals in Smithville. There was even talk of buying property and founding an arts center. Others heard tell of an orphanage.

THE MAGIC HOURS

Ecky's contribution earned her an official credit of "Goodwill Ambassador." The life of the Malicks bled into the film in other ways. Their dogs appeared in scenes. For one church scene, Kelly Koonce, the episcopal priest of the Good Shepherd in Tarrytown where the Malicks regularly attended services, played the priest who gives a sermon from the book of Job.[19] Nicolas Gonda took the role of Jack's teacher.[20] Fisk and his team employed local craftspeople, and the police department agreed to close streets with little notice. It was a small crew, and Fisk only had fifteen cars to place in the background. Without lighting equipment, or trailers for the stars, the cast and crew were agile and mobile, with Malick, chasing the light, often changing his mind on where and what to film in the morning as opportunities arose.

The "Eternity" scenes on the beach—where the characters (both young and old versions of themselves) meet at the end of the film—were filmed at Matagorda Bay along the Gulf Coast between March and April. The scene with the drowned boy was shot at Barton Springs, a large and popular public pool near downtown Austin. Sean Penn, as adult Jack, was filmed in Houston amid the glass and steel architecture, its hard modernity contrasting with Smithville and the past. Here nature was hemmed in, trees were reduced to corporate shrubbery, and conversations were fragmentary. Ecky's son Will Wallace appeared as Jack's colleague, confiding in him about a relationship he was in the process of ending: "The story's told." The atmosphere of postmodern sterility—though with its own beauty—anticipates *Knight of Cups*. It was the first time in his career that Malick had put contemporary America on-screen. Another location was Reimer's Ranch, a few minutes' drive from Malick's home in Austin. Here, the young souls were preparing for birth, learning their lines from tiny books before being led to the world and life. These overtly poetical or mythical scenes were an innovation for Malick, inserting a layer of fantasy to the documentary footage and the impressionistic memories of childhood.

By the beginning of summer, the filming in Smithville was over, and the street returned to its former appearance. Jack Fisk's team restored Paul Viktorin's kitchen. A flat replicating the front of the Burleson Street house was transported to the Utah salt flats, where Jessica Chastain was filmed walking toward the sun, creating one of the most striking images of the picture. As a result of Brad Pitt's scheduling, these scenes were shot in the worst heat of the summer. The call came before sunrise and then again at dusk to avoid the worst heat of the day. Jack Fisk and his team built another house and

The Tree of Life (2005–2011)

submerged it in a deep swimming pool in Austin to film a form of prelife sequence, as a child swims out the open door and into life.

As with all of Malick's previous films, extensive second unit filming was in progress throughout the shoot. The script called for two major sequences outside of the narrative. The first was the creation scene, which was the core of the initial idea of the "Q" project. The footage shot in 1978–1979 was revisited, but the difference in film stock meant that little was usable. A rare fish swam toward the light, out of the footage shot in 1979, and into the final cut of *The Tree of Life*. Malick was in contact with wildlife photographers and filmmakers for years, attending natural history film festivals such as the Jackson Hole Film Festival to find the best camera operators and directors in the business. He spoke to Nigel Ashcroft about filming the crocodiles for *The Thin Red Line*. That didn't work out, but in 2007, Malick called again.

Flying to Austin, Ashcroft was surprised to be picked up at the airport by the director, driving his Honda. They talked in his office in Austin, and the conversations led to margaritas and then dinner as they went through the creation sequence for *The Tree of Life*. Over the next few days, they viewed DVDs of nature documentaries, noting shots that matched Malick's vision. Ashcroft says: "He loves a particular style, and it's not full in-the-face animal. It's shapes and light and movement . . . and that's much more appealing to him. He loves—as you can see from every shot of this film—the sun in the background. . . . He doesn't like long lens shots, which when shooting wildlife is quite tricky. He loves everything to be close on a wide lens. He loves everything to be in full focus, which is tricky with wildlife, and we had to do some macro shooting. There were lots of things which were almost physically impossible."[21] Ashcroft received a typed copy of the dogma Chivo was working from. The usual rules held: the camera was handheld but "without a handheld look." Camera moves had to be on the z axis, in highest definition and deepest focus. Malick had extensively researched and scouted locations for years. He had visited Iceland five or six times and knew the waterfall Ashcroft was shooting and the angle he wished to get it from. Malick wanted to be there in person but was tied up with the main unit and couldn't make it out.

For the cosmic section of the creation, Malick contacted experts in several fields, including Donna Cox from the National Center for Supercomputing Applications and Austin-based astronomer Volker Bromm, whose article about the early universe Malick had read in *Sky and Telescope*. They wished to visualize Pop III stars—stars composed of primordial gases—going

THE MAGIC HOURS

supernova and the subsequent nebulae forming into new stars, as well as a sequence moving through the Milky Way. The advisers concentrated on getting it right from the scientific point of view, and then Malick gave notes on the images they created, making some parts darker to suggest more mystery. Malick reached out to Michael Benson, the author of *Far Out: A Space-Time Chronicle* (2009). He wanted to incorporate Benson's work into the Genesis sequence; there were dozens of phone calls. Malick flew to London to meet Benson and go over the footage: "We had just finished two Jupiter test sequences, with one entirely based on existing Jupiter images, and in the other Double Negative had created the planet using purely digital tools. The purely CGI planet looked artificial; it couldn't compete with Jupiter as photographed by the Cassini spacecraft."[22] Benson criticized Hollywood space sequences for having a "roller-coaster effect." Malick agreed. Benson was impressed by Malick's low-key persona, with no hovering assistants or cell phone interruptions: "He doesn't check his watch, he knows how to listen, and we focused on the problem of how to represent such things as the birth of the universe and the evolution of life in scientifically accurate and visually compelling ways."[23]

Malick also called on an old friend from his first days in Hollywood. Doug Trumbull made his name as one of the leading pioneers of visual effects on *2001: A Space Odyssey* (1968). They'd first met while Trumbull was directing *Silent Running* (1972), hanging out at the cafés of Marina del Rey in Venice Beach. Trumbull worked briefly on "Project Q." Years later, they reconnected via James Horner—at that point a mutual friend—and over lunch discovered a mutual interest in astronomy. For the space sequence of *The Tree of Life*, Malick called Trumbull, who suggested that Malick return to physical effects and use fluids—like paint or milk—to recreate astrophysical phenomena. A laboratory nicknamed the Skunk Works—the name inspired by Lockheed's World War II research facility (as a tribute to Emil's war work)—was set up in Austin, and after filming finished for the week on Friday in Smithville, Malick met with Dan Glass and Trumbull and experimented. It was a small group in a warehouse in downtown Austin, looking for spontaneity, alert for the happy accident. There were frustrations. When a good shot was fluffed, Malick stalked outside to pace around until his temper was under control. He was probably reciting a canticle from Saint Anthony, a crew member joked.

Dan Glass had worked with Grant Hill on *The Matrix* films and was introduced to Malick in the summer of 2006 only weeks after *The New World*

The Tree of Life (2005–2011)

was completed. They met in a café in LA to talk about the new film. There were three sections requiring visual effects: the macroscale of the cosmos; the microscale of bacteria and cells; and the natural history section including the dinosaurs. The scientific advisers and Double Negative created many of the astrophysical shots along with Benson. The microbial sections became the province of a small team called One of Us, also based in London and augmented by the work of father-and-son team Chris and Peter Parks, who worked in their own studio. Mike Fink took on the difficult task of creating the dinosaurs. Malick wanted the camera to discover the dinosaurs incidentally. They shouldn't be well lit.

Although the film projected on 35 mm, Malick insisted that these sequences be shot in IMAX for higher resolution. Plates were filmed in California's redwood forest, Iceland, Hawaii, and the Atacama Desert in Chile. Shots from the Hubble telescope and NASA were also borrowed to create shots. Malick also wished to add Thomas Wilfred's Lumia, the moving fragment of light that opened and closed the film. The experimental musician (who died in 1968) invented an instrument to create abstract light projections linked to music. Malick chose Opus 161, the penultimate work of the inventor and musician.

Millions of feet had been filmed and a lengthy postproduction period scheduled: this time a major studio was not part of the equation. Rather than working concurrently as they had on *The New World*, the editors on *The Tree of Life* worked in a relay system, with each editor taking a four-month period. Billy Weber began the edit, then was joined by Daniel Rezende. Mark Yoshikawa and Jay Rabinowitz then took over. Hank Corwin joined for a period. Then Yoshikawa finished off the film as promised, working in total for a year and a half. The editing was as experimental as ever, but the uncertainties were greater. One major question persisted: How to incorporate the creation footage with the childhood section? Was it necessary to segregate them, or could the creation sequence be intercut with the story of the family? Otherwise, might it not seem an overlong prologue to the main story? The script interspersed images from the natural world throughout the 1950s segment, although the structure of the film was still much as it would remain in the final cut. In practice, the introduction of dinosaurs during the Texas sequence ended up feeling silly. Yoshikawa explains: "We decided to keep the sequence in its five big sections that you could recognize only after you solved the entire puzzle, if you put all the bits together." These five sections were organized into three movements. The first movement included "Grief,"

THE MAGIC HOURS

introducing RL's death; "The City," featuring Sean Penn; and "Creation," portraying the origins of the universe.

The second movement showed the beginning of life and was entitled "Birth of Souls," and in the "Childhood" section took up the majority of the film's running time.

The third movement was called "Eternity," and took the film to the end of time and life before returning briefly to Sean Penn and the city. Malick was intent on other beats as well in Jack's spiritual biography. The section where Jack discovers badness in the world was referred to as "Buddha Sights," a reference to the Four Sights through which the Buddha witnesses suffering and death in the world for the first time and which provoke the feeling of Saṃvega, a sense of urgency and need to escape the world of recursive suffering. Along with the Christian influences in the film, there are elements of Judaism and Buddhism as well. The Tree of Life as a sacred symbol crosses cultures and epochs, from the Mesopotamian epic of Gilgamesh through Assyrian, Manichean, Judaic, Christian, and Islamic iterations.

Within the most conventional section—the Waco-set O'Brien section "Childhood"—the narrative is still not entirely conventional. A scene where the brothers pretend to walk drunkenly and then meet a stranger with a limp who looks at them disapprovingly is actually two different scenes shot in different towns, with the characters in different costumes, and one of the brothers has changed. The scene works like memory, as imperfect as memory is—especially the memory of a childhood recreated by the adult mind. Most audiences won't notice the discrepancies, perhaps detecting a subliminal unease, a lack of certainty. Memory actually works by recreating rather than retrieving. There are other inconsistencies. Mr. O'Brien asks Jack to pass him his cigarette lighter, but we never see Mr. O'Brien smoke for the rest of the film. Friends and collaborators were called in to view cuts. One source of confusion was the relationship between Sean Penn's character and Hunter McCracken's: it was unclear they were supposed to be the same person at different stages in life. It was also a problem when it came to creating the first trailer. This was resolved by adding a shot of McCracken with an unsubtle voice-over line spoken by Penn: "I see myself as a child."

For the music, French composer Alexandre Desplat was hired during preproduction. Desplat was inspired by Georges Delerue and Maurice Jarre, for whom Malick had interned during his time at AFI in the late 1960s. Without having seen any footage, Desplat wrote music on Malick's instructions, which was then played for the actors as well as for specific scenes and moods.

168

The Tree of Life (2005–2011)

Malick stayed in close communication, requesting changes—"more like Mozart, lighter"—and offering encouragement. Sometimes the producers and Malick listened to new music at night after filming and then used ideas suggested by the music for the next day's shoot. Malick intended to use specific pieces of classical music, such as Hector Berlioz's *Requiem* for the concluding portion of the picture and some of the Bach pieces, but Bedřich Smetana's *Mà Vlast* and François Couperin's *Pièces de clavecin* (played as a duet between Mr. O'Brien and RL) were late additions suggested by the scenes themselves.

During this period, a student visiting the United States from New Zealand answered a help wanted ad in an Austin newspaper and found himself being interviewed by Terrence Malick to provide additional music for the film. Hanan Townshend went on to score a number of Malick's films.

On December 28, 2008, six months into the editing process, Malick was struck by a family tragedy that starkly mirrored the heart of his new film. His brother Chris died at the age of sixty. Chris was Malick's youngest brother. After graduating high school, Chris studied psychology at the University of Oklahoma. He enrolled in graduate school as a PhD student. But his life was marked by misfortune and tragedy. In the fall of 1973, Chris was driving his small car with his wife, Deborah, when he ran into a wrecker truck that was crossing the highway. The car burst into flames, and the driver of the truck managed to break the window and drag Christopher free. Deborah, however, died in the fire. Chris was rushed to the hospital and treated for severe burns. It was a devastating blow. Later, Chris married Ann Shearer, and they had two sons, David and Michael. As Larry had, Chris shared his father's love of music, becoming a talented pianist. Like his father, he worked in the oil business. In 1982, he started the Washita Production Company, specializing in buying existing natural gas production facilities. Problems with alcohol addiction led him to become a founding member of the Twelve and Twelve Incorporated, a halfway house for alcoholic men, which grew into a residential treatment and recovery facility, the largest in Oklahoma.

Rumor had it that Chris had taken his own life, after a diagnosis of a serious illness. Whatever the truth, his death came as a terrible blow to his family, as well as Malick and their aging parents. Terrence Malick had been the eldest of three sons: now he was an only child. He'd spent the last year exploring, reliving his childhood and his relationships with his younger siblings. *The Tree of Life* was an elegy to his lost brother Larry, and now Chris was gone too. It was a hammer blow of incomprehensible grief. The film is dedicated to LRM and CBM, Lawrence Raymond Malick and Christopher Barry Malick, his two brothers, but in keeping with Malick's sense of privacy, the dedication is buried at the end of the credits, long after most of the audience will have left the theater. The poignancy of reliving the story of their shared experience over and over again as the cut came together was overwhelming. Now there was this added pain, this fresh grief that so horribly mirrored the old grief, which first motivated the film. The stakes for getting it right were higher: no longer a look into the past but an attempt to understand renewed grief in the present. The questions the film asked felt weightier, more immediate. But those working around him knew very little about the circumstances, and the work continued.

The quote at the beginning of the film was taken from the book of Job. The Old Testament tale tells the story of the good man who—baffled by his misfortune—wonders how he deserves such pain and suffering at the hands of a God he has faithfully served and believed benign and just. When Mrs. O'Brien is consoled by her mother, she is told, "God sends flies to wounds he ought to heal." The film asks, Why do the good suffer? Where do grief and pain come from? What is the meaning of life when life is so fleeting and death arrives arbitrarily? The boy in the Barton Ponds swimming pool dies suddenly, unexpectedly, without any reason. Jack observes: "You let him die." After his funeral, the brothers play in the graveyard. Likewise, RL is already dead when we see him as a child. His image as he plays guitar on the step turns into a ghost as the sunlight comes out, rendering the screen door translucent. Breath and a handprint on the glass of a window provide a reminder of the transience of life: he will be gone, and nothing will remain but pain, absence, and memory.

Malick was close to his family. For years, Chris had served as a go-between, buffering Malick from the world and acting as a messaging service for his elder brother. Emil and Irene were still an important part of Malick's life, providing him with support at different stages in his career. His relationship with his mother was protective. Because of its profanity, he didn't want her to read the script of *The Thin Red Line*. On winning the Golden Bear at the Berlin Film Festival, he gifted the award to his parents. His father called the local paper to keep them informed of his famous son's triumphs. Malick had a reciprocal respect for his father, despite their differences. Emil's was the only photograph of Malick that he allowed to be published. At the end of *The Tree of Life*, Emil can be heard on the soundtrack, playing the piano.

The Tree of Life (2005–2011)

Although an extended postproduction period had been factored in, release dates still needed to be delayed. Throughout the editing, collaborators saw different cuts. Lubezki recalls seeing a six-hour version; there was enough footage that "you could almost make a whole movie about Sean."[24] Bill Pohlad, though, says that the footage of Penn's adult Jack was just an expansion of what is seen in the film rather than a separate storyline.[25] Likewise, Brad Pitt told reporters: "I've seen this film when it was four hours and then three and a half hours and then down to two and a half and then back to three and a half and down to its present incarnation of two and a quarter hours."[26]

The editors, at Malick's behest, created many of these different cuts while experimenting with the structure of the film. Keith Fraase came on as an assistant editor: "The original version of the movie was two hours and forty-five minutes. And we thought we'd finished mixing."[27] But after an interval, the team was called back to rework the film. There had been a different order to the sections. It began with the grief section, then the Genesis, and from there to the contemporary city section with Sean Penn as adult Jack. That section was longer and included more experimental visions that Jack was experiencing. Then the film proceeded to the childhood section in Waco. The Genesis section was the most polarizing, with some viewers arguing that it was the best thing in the film and others not understanding why it was there at all. They considered eliminating it entirely. But without the Genesis section, the film seemed flatter. Intertitles were put in and then taken out. Various quotes from the book of Job were put up before one was decided on. A. J. Edwards began work on an extended version of the film, in which Malick included many of the scenes cut for length. It has more information about the extended family around the O'Briens, Mrs. O'Brien's brothers, the Irish uncles, Mr. O'Brien's father, all linked closely to Malick's own life. Forty minutes longer, the extended cut deserves to be viewed as a different film.

Malick was in the editing suite every day from early in the morning until late at night. The editors rotated in and out during the day and over the weeks, tasked with different sections of the film. They came to understand Malick's own language when it came to editing. A "bomb" was a shot added to a cut to see if it provoked any thought; a "bevel" was a shot inserted between two other shots to create a connection. Malick worked on his correspondence first thing in the morning and made any necessary phone calls before going from room to room, checking on progress. Part of the day was spent on his electric typewriter. He didn't write on computers, and it would be years before he got a smartphone. He worked on other scripts as well as

THE MAGIC HOURS

writing pages of voice-over. Jessica Chastain did over twenty sessions of voice-over work, reading hundreds of pages. Malick experimented with different pieces of music and voice-over in different places. The experience proved emotionally draining. When the mournful music of Zbigniew Preisner's "Lacrimosa" was added to a key moment in the Genesis sequence, Malick wept.

During breaks, the editors and Malick would play the basketball game horse in a local parking garage where a hoop was available. "Terry had a really pure jump shot," Shane Hazen, an editor working on the cut, remembers. "Terry would go on a streak where he couldn't miss."[28] As with any editing room, there were disagreements, but Malick was open to criticism and sought out the reactions of the editors, as well as of friends and colleagues. He resisted watching whole cuts, preferring to concentrate on individual scenes. He only watched the complete film when it was close to being locked.[29]

By 2010, Malick was close enough to a finished version to allow a cut to be shown to Thierry Frémaux and the Cannes selection committee. Despite Frémaux's enthusiasm, Malick decided the film still wasn't ready. According to journalist Ann Thompson, six people got the opportunity to view the film at the Telluride Festival in September 2010.[30] A series of screenings were set up for potential distributors, with Fox Searchlight ultimately buying the rights. Throughout 2010, rumors began to leak about the nature of the film. Dinosaurs were mentioned, as were 1950s Texas, Brad Pitt, and Sean Penn. Jessica Chastain expressed frustration to have made a film with Brad Pitt and years later for it to still be unseen.[31] There was controversy when Icon set a release date in the UK in May 2011 that would precede the planned Cannes premiere and thereby disqualify the film from a Cannes slot. Ultimately, Icon backed down and canceled the UK release, allowing the Cannes premiere to go ahead.

A synopsis and first poster were released in early November 2010. The synopsis began: "From the Desk of Terrence Malick . . ." before recounting a quite detailed version of the film that reads more like a director's statement than the usual press release. In the story of Jack and his three brothers, "all seems marvelous to the child. He sees as his mother does with the eyes of his soul. She represents the way of love and mercy, where the father tries to teach his son the world's way of putting oneself first." The film tells of the spiritual quest of "adult Jack, a lost soul in a modern world, seeking to discover amid the changing scenes of time that which does not change: the eternal scheme of which we are a part." When one understands the creation of the universe,

172

The Tree of Life (2005–2011)

"each thing appears a miracle—precious, incomparable." Having come to terms with his family, Jack discovers "life's single most important lesson, of unselfish love."[32] By December, the first trailers were released along with the poster featuring the image of a baby's foot.

The world premiere took place during the Sixty-Fourth Cannes Film Festival in May 2011. Brad Pitt, Jessica Chastain, Bill Pohlad, Sarah Greene, Grant Hill, and Dede Gardner attended the press conference. (Sean Penn missed the initial press round as he was returning from Haiti but made the red carpet.) Malick was the subject of many questions, and his status as a recluse infuriated some journalists, who asked why he wasn't there, rejecting the initial excuse of shyness. Moderator Henri Béhar asked reverently, as if hoping for an insight into the life of a mystic: "Does he laugh? Does he never laugh? Does he talk? Does he never talk? Is he stern? Is he jovial? Does he eat? Does he like food?"[33] In fact, Terrence Malick was in Cannes: he just wasn't doing press. He met with the festival organizers and ate dinner with Angelina Jolie and Brad Pitt, as well as film critic Michel Ciment, who had interviewed him for *Positif* many years previously. *Positif* was a loyal supporter of Malick, whereas rival publication *Cahiers* had a more complicated relationship with the American auteur. Malick also ate with Rupert Murdoch, the controversial media mogul whose company was distributing the film. Some eagle-eyed fans recognized him, but he refused requests for autographs, saying he preferred to shake hands.[34] At the last minute, Rick Hess—one of Malick's closest confidants and a key figure in bringing together the financing of the film—arranged for Malick to appear at the end of the gala screening. The operation involved a boat and some hastily arranged backstage access, but it delighted and surprised the cast and crew as the audience applauded the end of the film.

If the gala premiere was greeted with an ovation, the press screening concluded to both applause and boos. Peter Bradshaw wrote: "Terrence Malick's mad and magnificent film [was] a rebuke to realism, a disavowal of irony and comedy, a meditation on memory, and a gasp of horror and awe at the mysterious inevitability of loving, and losing those we love."[35] Roger Ebert gave the film his full approval, calling it "a film of vast ambition and deep humility."[36] Positive reviews conceded the film's difficulty in finding an audience, as Todd McCarthy wrote in the *Hollywood Reporter*: "It is hardly a movie for the masses and will polarize even buffs."[37] Geoff McNabb described how this reflected on Malick himself and once more magnified the image of the filmmaker: "You have to admire Terrence Malick's cussedness and perversity. No other major American filmmaker, not even Stanley Kubrick at his most willful, has ever made a film quite as idiosyncratic as *The Tree of Life*."[38]

However, Lee Marshall for *Screen Daily* found the film too preachy and on the nose, leaving him missing the earlier films, "when the Texan auteur also knew how to spin a good yarn."[39] Malick skeptic Stephanie Zacharek in *Movieline* complained about the voice-overs.[40] Jason Zingale wondered if the film's laborious editing process was evidence that the film wasn't complete.[41] Ignatiy Vishnevetsky argued that "Malick's neither a great philosopher nor a great poet, and he probably has a firm enough grasp of both subjects to know that, yet his images are marked by what seems to be an uncontrollable impulse to philosophize and write poetry."[42]

The ad hominem nature of much of the criticism of *The Tree of Life* indicates that many were projecting their own version of Malick onto the blank of the director's absence. After all, is Ignatiy Vishnevetsky a definitive judge of who is a great philosopher and a great poet? Is Malick really claiming to be? Are voice-overs only for storytelling? Is telling a good yarn the height of cinema's ambition? There's also a discomfort with the clearly religious questions. The accusation of "preachiness" seems particularly misplaced given that the film is a crisis of faith rather than its triumph. One of the clearest assertions—"nuns taught us there are two ways through life"—is contradicted by the nuance and complexity of the rest of the film.

The Tree of Life represents a huge achievement. The film is exhilarating in its audacity and ambition, its intimacy, and its grandeur. The familiarity of certain Malickian techniques hides how they were evolving. The voice-overs, for instance, were for the first time voicing the filmmaker's own thoughts and questions, his spiritual autobiography—a rapprochement with God, but also a questioning, arguing conflict with him. As Jack says at the beginning of the film: "Brother. Mother. It was they who led me to your door." The education his mother provided and the grief caused by the loss of his brother brought him to a renewed relationship with God. This comes after a period of alienation: "How did I lose you? Wandered. Forgot you." This line will make up a substantial part of *Knight of Cups*. As with *Days of Heaven*, the stunning imagery proved too stunning for some. There was a randomness to some of the reactions. Why are dinosaurs more ridiculous than sharks? Once more, Malick addressed big, complicated questions with a beguiling directness and simplicity. *The Thin Red Line* asked, "What is this war?" *The Tree of Life* asked, "Why do we suffer?" There is a radicalism to such deeply simple questions

The Tree of Life (2005–2011)

reminiscent of William Blake's question in "The Lamb," "Dost thou know who made thee?" which is only a little simpler than its echo in "The Tyger," "Did he who made the Lamb make thee?" Nothing is settled for Malick: meaning must be pursued, discovered, sought, achieved. It is not given. We arrive in a world of manifest injustice and unfathomable beauty and complexity, and Malick is caught between the wonder of it all and the desperate yearning of inquiry. Why did you kill my brothers? the film asks God. Why do you let them die? There is an unspoken corollary to that: And why did you let me—with all my faults—live? And in an act of sublime hubris, Malick attempts to posit a godlike perspective that embraces the history of the universe and time and places that personal intimate grief, which is the shadow cast by love, into a context of meaning. God appears in a conventional Christian context, but also there are the "Buddha sights" of experience, the "Tao shots" of nature, the astrophysics of stella creation, and the microbiology of life, along with the self-conscious mythmaking of fairy tales and poetry. As Paul Tillich taught Malick at Harvard, the existence or not of a divine being is a corollary of the miracle of being, in and of itself. Do we believe in the world? The universe? Do we believe in life *before* death?

As with *The New World*, the film represented an experience to be lived through rather than a story to be told. This isn't the story of a childhood: it is the experience of it. The knee-high camera and the gradually broadening scope of our detailed focus and attention admit and create the wider world. The images and the music—the "Lacrimosa"—evoke powerful emotions that transcend our ability to appraise. They demand we surrender to the moment: we must be born anew with the film. See things as if for the first time. As Blake recognized, to our postlapsarian eyes, this will look naive and cutesy. The Lamb will always make the Tyger want to puke. Some snort; others are profoundly moved. Few are indifferent.

Though some were aware that the film was broadly autobiographical, not many realized just how personal it was in its detail: how closely the film resembled Malick's own life and how fresh the grief was. There is a reciprocal openness to the film. It asks us to embrace it, but its arms are wide open too.

On the Croissette, Malick's film dominated the conversation, and the presence of stars Brad Pitt, Angelina Jolie, and Sean Penn provided substantial media coverage. On May 22, jury president Robert De Niro rose and declared *The Tree of Life* the winner of the Palme d'Or. It had been a strong year: Michel Hazanavicius's *The Artist* went on to win the Oscar for Best Picture, and Nuri Bilge Ceylan's *Once Upon a Time in Anatolia*, the Dardenne brothers' *The Kid with a Bike*, and Lars von Trier's *Melancholia* all received strong critical reactions. The victory didn't break Malick's resolve to shun the spotlight. Winners of the major prizes are usually given a heads-up to return to Cannes to pick up their prizes in person, but Malick was already in Austin. Producers Bill Pohlad and Dede Gardner received the trophy in his stead amid the flashes of the photographers.

With the bolster of the award, *The Tree of Life* received a wide release. Malick wrote a letter to the projectionists, lamenting that "proper theater projection is fast becoming a forgotten art" but calling on them, "the last remaining artisans of movie exhibition," to help bring *The Tree of Life* to the screen. It lists a series of technical specifications, which show a detailed knowledge of the technicalities of projection, before signing off with "a fraternal salute, Terrence Malick, Director."[43]

Despite this care, one news story from Italy spoke to the film's unconventional narrative. The Cinema Lumière in Bologna showed the film with the first two reels in the wrong order before someone noticed and complained.[44] Also, some criticism arrived from closer to home. In an interview with *Le Figaro*, Sean Penn expressed his reservations about *The Tree of Life*, though his comments were largely positive: "I didn't at all find on the screen the emotion of the script, which is the most magnificent one that I've ever read. A clearer and more conventional narrative would have helped the film without, in my opinion, lessening its beauty and its impact. Frankly, I'm still trying to figure out what I'm doing there and what I was supposed to add in that context! What's more, Terry himself never managed to explain it to me clearly."[45] This first part was quoted in the *New Yorker*, though truncated. The complete version concludes: "But it's a film that I recommend, provided you go without preconceived ideas. It is up to everyone to find a personal, emotional or spiritual connection. Those who succeed in doing so generally come out of it very touched."[46]

At the San Sebastian Festival, the film picked up the FIPRESCI award given by the International Federation of Film Critics. Malick responded to the award in a letter stating: "I'm honored that you should take such a kind view of 'Tree of Life' and wish that I could thank you and your colleagues in person. At present, however, we're rushing toward a mix on the picture we shot last fall in Oklahoma and to finish shooting on a new one, a natural history film. I hope that you'll understand. It is uplifting to discover such generous hearts out there, encouraging me and those who work with me, and I hope that someday in the near future we'll gave [*sic*] the occasion to meet in

The Tree of Life (2005–2011)

person."[47] There's a joy and relief to Malick's letter. He was approaching his sixty-eighth birthday that November, but he had more energy and direction than ever before. Malick had caught a second wind, and he was fully intent on making up for lost time. Few would have guessed that Malick was about to enter the most productive period of his career.

One special audience member had seen a preview of the film in June in an ordinary theater in Bartlesville, Oklahoma. Relatives and friends gathered along with some special guests. Irene Malick sat in a wheelchair. Ecky briefly introduced the film and noted that this was Irene's first viewing.[48] Emil did not attend, nor did Malick himself. Irene's reactions are unrecorded, but they must have been complex. Her son was at the height of his achievements, but she was seeing the family she had now lost recreated before her. Larry and Chris were both dead. How must she have felt? The film directly addresses her. There is bitterness, and there are recriminations. This—as Biskind had once written—was a family of secrets and guilt, with subjects it never spoke of. And Malick was talking openly and honestly, opening the windows, letting in the sunshine, and airing the house.

December 19 of that same year, 2011, Irene Thompson Malick passed away. She was ninety-nine years old.

10

To the Wonder (2010-2011)

When the Palme d'Or was announced for *The Tree of Life*, Terrence Malick was in Austin at work. The three-year gap between the wrapping principal photography on *The Tree of Life* (August 2008) and the film's premiere (May 2011) might have been the longest of a career that already boasted prolonged periods of postproduction, but in that time his follow-up film had been conceived, shot, and partly assembled. The editing team celebrated the victory and then resumed work on the new film.

If *The Thin Red Line* had proved that Malick could still make films, *The New World* and *The Tree of Life* proved that filmmaking could be experimental and fun. Long gone were the tortured shoots and the acrimonious battles of *Badlands* and *Days of Heaven*. The pressure to find financing and a distributor would always prove a challenge for such an uncommercial filmmaker, but Malick had gathered his own network of backers and producers—led by Rick Hess, Bill Pohlad, Sarah Green, and Nicolas Gonda—devoted to realizing his vision and willing to create a space for the director's unorthodox methods. Money was raised, partly from the sale of foreign distribution rights and the rest from a series of small investors, which meant that Malick had to answer to no single figure and risk was evenly spread. After all, even Malick's most commercially successful films never reaped large profits. The opacity of Hollywood accounting makes it difficult to say much with certainty, but though *The Thin Red Line* and *The Tree of Life* made profits, neither film was a hit, and *The New World* was a certified flop, though it would make its money back eventually.[1]

Though commercial concerns didn't dictate Malick's thinking, Gonda insists that the director was never cavalier: "As his producer I can tell you, he never went over budget. Even if we ended up having to raise more money, there was never a point where Terry would look at me and say, 'That's not my problem.' If he knew money was an issue on any given day, he would be as

To the Wonder (2010–2011)

present in that dialogue as any producer I've ever worked with. And the same goes for time."[2]

Likewise, his creative collaborators shared his vision. In Chivo and Jörg Widmer, he had a team devoted to experimenting, and they were so attuned that they often finished each other's sentences, sharing a private language. "Rabbit holes" were spaces out of the sun to film during the day. "Quail hunting" was looking for the spontaneous moment. The "Tao shot" was an observation taken from nature, a bird's flight or an interesting play of light. "Torpedoing" was sending a surprise element into a scene—a dog or another actor—to shake things up. "Burbank"—Chivo's phrase—was anything too Hollywood: a camera angle, a style of acting, a request for a trailer. Malick was the opposite of Burbank.

But Burbank now provided Malick with A-list actors like Christian Bale, Brad Pitt, and Sean Penn, with others waiting their turn. The money wasn't great, and there was always the risk of the cutting room floor, but just to work with Malick was to claim personal knowledge of the legendary figure and a unique acting experience. Any actor considering a directing career might learn something along the way. Tim Blake Nelson, Ryan Gosling, and Natalie Portman all went on to direct their own films after working with Malick. Sean Penn's *Into the Wild* (2007) is clearly influenced by his experience with Malick. Many collaborators were picked up from the airport by Malick himself and taken to lunch, though the restaurant might not have been particularly swish. Producer Sophokles Tasioulis complained about being taken to the same Las Palomas restaurant for lunch: "I said, 'Terry, what do you do when Cate Blanchett or Brad Pitt come? Do you take them here?' He said, 'Yes.' He doesn't care; it's not important for him. And he has zero sense of being a star. Zero."[3]

Young editors, like Keith Fraase, who started as an intern on *The Tree of Life* before moving on to *The Voyage of Time*, began to take over from the veterans. Of the lifelong collaborators, Jack Fisk remained for the time being, with others helping out but no longer working directly. Instead, Malick now enjoyed the role of the mentor, "Papa Terry," as he was sometimes called, providing valuable experience to a pool of young technicians and filmmakers willing to work for him. He was godfather to their children and a guide in their careers, interested in their lives and their growth. He was demanding. Lives were consumed. Early morning starts and late nights were the order of the day, seven days a week. The mixture of discipline and artistic freedom would have been familiar to any of his fellow Spartans from their time at St. Stephen's.

THE MAGIC HOURS

Texan director A. J. Edwards started as an intern on *The New World* and operated the camera on the "Making Of" documentary before becoming increasingly involved for *The Tree of Life* and *To the Wonder* and providing additional editing for *Knight of Cups* and *Song to Song*. In 2014, he directed his own film *The Better Angels*, a portrayal of the childhood years of Abraham Lincoln starring Jason Clarke, Wes Bentley, Diane Kruger, and Brit Marling. With its use of voice-over, period detail, and pristine black-and-white photography, the film wore its Malickian influences heavily. Malick was a producer of the film, and many of the crew and production team were Malick alumni, including composer Hanan Townshend and producer Nicolas Gonda. During interviews, Edwards gave Malick credit for providing invaluable support, as well as suggesting the title, but the urge to escape the shadow of influence also grew strong.

This influence was everywhere, and the adjective Malickian entered the critical lexicon to denote a certain poetic attitude as well as a quality of cinematography, shifting meaning as it did so. Whereas the magic hour and the use of elliptical voice-overs had been considered the signature motifs of Malick's work, Malickian now expanded to create a subgenre of American independent cinema. Illustrative of this is Jacob T. Swinney's video titled "Not Directed by Terrence Malick." In the short trailer, works as diverse as Zach Snyder's *Man of Steel* (2013) and David Lowery's *Ain't Them Bodies Saints* (2013), Andrew Dominik's *The Assassination of Jesse James by the Coward Robert Ford* (2007), and Jason Reitman's *Up in the Air* (2009) were intercut to form an inarguably recognizable Malickian aesthetic.[4]

With familiarity came the danger of cliché. Ads for insurance companies and credit cards were also directed by Malick fans, and they too emulated their hero: the heliocentric, precisely focused imagery, the probing along the z axis, the voice-overs, and the music. From a lost legend and inspiration of the New Hollywood, Malick was now a vital influence on contemporary American cinema. *The Tree of Life* was not the kind of box office a Brad Pitt vehicle might expect, but rather an art-house succès d'estime. Brad Pitt's reputation as an actor willing to subvert his movie-star status—did the scene where he taught his sons to fight parody *Fight Club*?—and work with challenging directors was burnished and his moxie as a producer proved. Jessica Chastain welcomed a perfect storm as a number of movies finally emerged and catapulted her into international celebrity. Of the children playing the O'Brien boys, only the youngest, Tye Sheridan, continued his career in films, starring in David Gordon Green's

To the Wonder (2010–2011)

Joe (2013) with Nicolas Cage and leading Spielberg's *Ready Player One* (2019).

Announced at the 2010 Berlin Film Festival, Malick's next project had a cast already in place—Christian Bale, Javier Bardem, Rachel McAdams, and Olga Kurylenko—as well as a production team: Nicolas Gonda, Sarah Green, and Bill Pohlad.[5] Reportedly a love story, the project was thought to have the working title "The Burial," though Sarah Green denied that the film ever had that title. Among Malick's team, the film was referred to as "Project D." During the final stages of editing *The Tree of Life*, scouting, a schedule, a budget, and the cast all began to fall into place. Green and Gonda hired a crew ready to shoot a film by Malick's rules: light, improvisatory, able to turn on a dime without the safety net provided by a locked script and shot list. A jazz band, a guerrilla unit. Chivo received the call. Malick told him the story and explained how he wanted the movie shot.[6] He received a treatment. It was more than the actors got. Rumors of a script (and the question of its existence) became a running joke.[7] Outlines, pages, and discussions with Malick about the methodology dictated how scenes were performed. Hundreds of pages of research were hefted about in a briefcase: poetry and pragmatism folded together. The film would be smaller and more intimate than his recent work. Moving away from the history of the universe, the new project delved into the crannies of the human heart, the viscera of a relationship, and the bedrooms where love disintegrates; the setting shifted from a cosmic cathedral to a dilapidated, roadside chapel.

For the first time, Malick set his story entirely in the present. Neil, an American in Paris, falls in love with Marina, a Ukrainian immigrant. She has a child, Tatiana, from a previous relationship. The three move from Europe to Oklahoma, where their relationship flounders and Neil finds himself attracted to an old flame. As we've seen, the story was tantalizingly autobiographical, mirroring Malick's relationship and marriage with Michèle Morette, followed by their separation and the beginning of his relationship with Ecky. Michèle had played a vital role in Malick's life for over a decade. They tried to be a family, first in Paris and then in Texas, with Malick initially enjoying his role as a stepfather to her daughter, Alexandra. There was happiness for a while. And then there wasn't.

Michèle was also instrumental in Malick's return to filmmaking. After their divorce, they stayed in touch, and in 2008 came the devastating news that Michèle was seriously ill. The nature of the diagnosis is unclear, but soon after, Michèle died in Paris. She was sixty-one years old.

THE MAGIC HOURS

Another premature death. Another loss. The churn of mortality taking its toll.

"The Burial"—like *The Tree of Life*—would portray Malick's past through the lens of grief. As such, it isn't a dissection of a failed relationship so much as a postmortem of an irretrievable love. Marina shares Michèle's initial, and the monastery of Mont-Saint-Michel, the secret heart of the film, shares her name (Michèle/Michel) and is also nicknamed the Merveille, the marvel or the wonder. *To the Wonder* is obliquely dedicated to Michèle, a love poem and an elegy. Paradoxically, this most private director was exploring his deepest and most personal feelings through his films. Maybe the hidden nature of his life gave him license to explore it, safe in the knowledge that few knew the reality. Collaborators commented that the film was loosely biographical, but no one knew how biographical, and Malick didn't encourage speculation. Questioning him too closely, as Gonda puts it, was "like touching the wings of a butterfly." The film replayed the trauma of a failing love: a confession of inadequacy and betrayal. Malick's wife Ecky is also represented in fictionalized form, as the other woman in the love triangle, Jane. As with his previous films, she acted as a strong supportive backstage presence as well.

Some details changed. The setting shifted from Texas to his earlier childhood town of Bartlesville, Oklahoma, allowing Malick to be close to his parents. He was their only surviving child. Jack Fisk scouted locations and contacted the local community. Chivo asked for a house "that lights itself."[8] Fisk found two properties: one where the light was good in the morning and the other for the afternoon. On August 17, 2010, the *Tulsa World* reported an open casting call for "an upcoming family-oriented Hollywood romantic drama."[9] The male lead, Neil, was recast as Christian Bale was no longer available, having had to withdraw to fulfill his contractual obligations as Batman for Christopher Nolan. Ben Affleck finished filming *The Town* (2010) and was prepping *Argo* (2012) as his next project. He intended to take a break, but the opportunity to work with Malick was too tempting. Malick had already served as a mentor to Affleck, meeting and giving him and Matt Damon notes on *Good Will Hunting*. Malick told Affleck he was "more and more interested in silences," aiming for a Gary Cooper quality in Neil. But when Affleck showed Malick a compilation of Cooper clips, Malick was horrified: "Oh, no no no! He's just rattling on! Gary Cooper, he just stares off."[10] Affleck's name helped the project raise money, despite the absence of a script, and international sales effectively covered the budget, leaving the US distribution open for when the film was finished.[11]

To the Wonder (2010–2011)

In Paris, the Ukrainian actress Olga Kurylenko auditioned for the role of Marina. Having made a videotape, she was called to Austin to workshop for a day with Malick. "He talked to me and just looked at my eyes. It was very meditative. It's almost like he tried to see if I could guess what he's thinking by telepathy, to communicate without being too verbal. We're similar. I think he wouldn't work with people that are not similar to him, that don't understand." Kurylenko read Tolstoy's *Anna Karenina* and Dostoyevsky's *The Idiot* and *The Brothers Karamazov*. "Those books were our script," Kurylenko says. Malick emphasized the young Aglaya Yepanchin, and the tragic Nastasya Filippovna. "He has an encyclopedic knowledge of Russian literature."[12] For his role, Affleck gamely worked his way through Heidegger, hoping to glean some insights into his own character. Rachel McAdams was added to the cast as Jane, the fictionalized version of Ecky. Malick drove her around Bartlesville, pointing out houses and schools and telling her: "Perhaps, your character grew up there. . . went to school here." At one point, he took her to a field of buffalo, and they sat for a while looking at the beasts as they moved around them and across the prairie.[13]

Spanish actor Javier Bardem was cast to play Father Quintana, a priest who ministers to the disadvantaged in the slums while undergoing a crisis of faith. (His name came from another of Malick's young recruits, Julio Quintana, the cinematographer for *The Tree of Life* "Making Of" documentary.) Bardem also received a reading list and watched a documentary about Mother Teresa of Calcutta. Robert Bresson's 1951 film *Diary of a Country Priest* was another reference point. "It was a great experience," Bardem says. "[Terry] has a great sense of humor, and he has a great sense of humanity."[14] Child actor Tatiana Chiline was cast as Tatiana, Marina's daughter. Chiline and her mother were picked up at the airport by Malick and Ecky. Malick was on the phone with Julia Roberts, who was asking if there was a role for her in the movie.[15] Throughout the shoot, Malick spoke to Chiline and her mother in French, as he did with Kurylenko. He wrote Marina's voice-over in French. A little-discussed aspect of the film is its incorporation of different languages. Much of the film is in French and Spanish, with a smattering of Italian and Russian, and some American Sign Language. The Babel-like variety (does Saint-Michel's spire also hint at the Babelesque?) emphasizes the difficulty of communication but also the multiplicity of perspectives and cultures.

An eight-week shoot began in Bartlesville in September. Every morning, Malick presented his actors with a thought for the day he'd typed during the night or early in the morning. "The function of those memos are so

THE MAGIC HOURS

instrumental in his process of making movies," Gonda says.[16] Jack Fisk offered Malick and his team a menu of possible locations. With a minimal crew and no lighting equipment, filming moved fast, and Widmer and Chivo shot constantly. Chivo says: "We can truly use every second and have the option of reshooting a scene if we don't like a take or if the actors felt uncomfortable or want to try something else."[17] Actors and crew stayed in the same hotel, which had the atmosphere of a cruise ship. Malick had his suite in the hotel, and every night the film crew gathered on the rooftop bar for drinks to unwind. A scene at that bar appears in the film, as does a scene in which Marina's friend encourages her to throw her bag into the bushes by the hotel's entrance.

Already an experienced actor whose talent was somewhat obscured by his celebrity, Affleck was nevertheless baffled by Malick's process. It was "half-crazy in that we didn't really have dialogue, so I didn't really know what was happening." Malick was an artist, and his actors were paints: "He was accumulating colors that he would use to paint with later in the editing room. My character doesn't really do that much. It was kind of a wash for me in terms of learning something as an actor."[18] As with many, Affleck was put off when the camera roamed from him mid-scene. A more verbal, cerebral actor, he needed dialogue and motivation, but Neil was a stand-in for Malick: a point of view. Malick enjoyed teasing Affleck throughout the shoot and encouraged Kurylenko to surprise him, as she did when her character attacks Neil with a chicken. "That was a lot of fun," Kurylenko says. "We're laughing all that time, jumping around like rabbits, chasing each other around the house, being silly. Terry laughs like a child. As adults we lose that, but he kept it. He gets amazed like a child, like he's never lost that side. I loved making him laugh because it's very real."[19]

Kurylenko's performance is a dance compared to Neil's trudge away from the camera. Neil doesn't seem to understand her or—it's suggested—fulfill her. For the first time, there's sexual frankness in a Malick film. There's nudity and tactile eroticism—fingertips are the favored erogenous zones—a new territory for Malick. His previous love stories were relatively chaste; it's possible Holly and Kit never even consummate their love affair, given the awkwardness of the aftermath. Abby's affair with Bill and her marriage with the farmer take place off-screen, and, given Q'orianka Kilcher's age in *The New World*, sex is only suggested.

But here sex and nudity are portrayed, though it's meaningful that the two more protracted sex scenes are between Neil and Jane and between

To the Wonder (2010–2011)

Marina and the handyman with whom she has an affair. Neil's sexuality—as it's expressed to Marina—is about peeking, looking. Marina's is exhibitionist and uninhibited. Neil's delighted but also embarrassed by Marina, whose spontaneity and exuberance jars with the train carriage and the supermarkets, laundromats, and yards of suburban America.

From a biographical point of view, it's particularly striking how Marina's complaints about Neil mirror those Michèle made to Peter Biskind for his *Vanity Fair* article in 1998. We see Marina creeping around the house, investigating this man she lives with. Neil hides things from her, which recalls Biskind's observation of Malick's secretiveness. Likewise, Marina complains to a friend that he goes off without telling her: a complaint Michèle made. Neil is untrustworthy, faithless: he looks at other women, watching a girl at the swimming pool, and Marina sees him look.

In fact, Neil's American discomfort with Marina's European energy echoes in Affleck's performance. Just as Neil falls for a European he can't contain, so Affleck, the Hollywood actor, finds himself in a European art film like Jack Palance in *Le Mépris* (1963). As an audience, we're primed to empathize with Affleck's protagonist. He is, after all, a leading man. We look to him for the moral core of the film and for the action, but we're consistently denied. Neil has an occasionally affectionate relationship with Tatiana, though she takes little interest in his astronomical factoids and he loses patience with her. He is emotionally reticent, and the film magnifies that by cutting his dialogue to a minimum. He listens, bemused at times, barely suppressing irritation. We see his back more than his face. This is also mirrored in his job monitoring the pollution levels in the water and the soil, but he could—like Emil Malick—be working for the oil companies causing the pollution. There is not enough information in the film—as it exists—for us to understand. When he's confronted by residents whose health has been affected, it's unclear whether his silence conveys sympathy, culpability, or both. He takes snippets of children's hair as well as samples of water and earth. Whatever affects the environment affects us too.

This lack of clarity is not an accident. Malick shot scenes with substantially more dialogue, mostly improvised. He had written a subplot involving Neil's work in relation to corporate malfeasance and a company's pollution of the poorer neighborhoods. The story echoed the case brought to light by Erin Brockovich in California, which inspired Steven Soderbergh's eponymous film. When Rachel McAdams's boyfriend at the time, Welsh actor Michael Sheen, visited the set, Malick hired him to film for a couple of days. His role

THE MAGIC HOURS

fed directly into this subplot, and once the subplot went, so did his scenes. Likewise, Rachel Weisz filmed scenes as Neil's sister, and then Jessica Chastain appeared as his cousin. These were essentially alternative versions of the same character. Once the focus of the film became Marina, their roles and scenes were similarly dispatched, though Jane mentions Neil's sister in the film.

After their European romance, Marina and Neil's relationship is all downhill. Marina's mental health is questioned as Tatiana asks why her mother is unhappy, hinting at an underlying depression. Her free spirit is fringed with mania. Whereas Neil is emotionally constipated, Marina is over-powered by her emotions. She acts out, threatens suicide, and runs into the street shouting to the neighbors that Neil is trying to kill her. "Sorry," he apologizes weakly to the neighbors, corralling her inside and feeling the deadliest middle-class American emotion: embarrassment. They live with everything in boxes, as if they've just moved in. They put furniture together, but there's no sense of an actual home. They soon destroy the furniture in a violent row and then—in a moment rarely seen in films—have to clean up the messy aftermath.

Whereas Affleck was uncomfortable with improvisation, Kurylenko took to it, even diving into garbage containers. Her trust in Malick was complete. "Terry is not my director," Kurylenko says. "He's my friend. So, from that point, he's in a position to advise me. For me, there was no trespassing. I just met him and we became friends. And this person is a friend and will remain friends for the rest of my life." Malick was inspired to shoot more material of her, trying to bring out what he called her "feral nature."[20]

Much of the unscripted material was created with no clear idea where it would fit in the finished film. A misty dusk was a case in point. Even as the light failed, Kurylenko moved through the dripping landscape, followed by Chivo's camera. In a moment of inspiration, he shone a bright yellow light into her face as she turned around. This would provide the film with an enigmatic conclusion and the most important hidden plot point: Marina—like Michèle—dies.

Meanwhile, Javier Bardem's Father Quintana visited the slums and prisons and talked with drug addicts and convicts. These conversations were filmed by documentarian and photojournalist Eugene Richards. Bardem had initially been dubious about the lack of script, but he took to his role, surprised that though they were aware he was only an actor, people opened up and confessed their stories to him. A woman admitted it was nice to find anyone who listened. The stories collected were striking and moving: a grieving

To the Wonder (2010–2011)

mother, a repentant ex-member of the Ku Klux Klan, a prison inmate. Although some appeared in the body of the main film, Bardem and Richards both felt that the experience deserved a longer treatment, and so after several years they got permission to edit the footage into a forty-three-minute film titled *Thy Kingdom Come*. It premiered at the South by Southwest Film Festival in March 2018.

The opening scenes of *To the Wonder* were the last to be shot. In Paris and at Mont-Saint-Michel in the spring of 2011, Malick took his actors and a small crew—with Widmer taking over from Chivo, who was unable to travel—to capture the early stages of the love affair, including the trip to the Mont Saint-Michel—or La Merveille, as the monastery is better known—which provides the film with the "Wonder" of the title. It was a sad gray day with low clouds and cold. It made for an interesting wintry, melancholic beginning to the love affair, as the water came in and the lovers played on the quicksand. In Paris, the small crew had no permits, so they stole footage on the hoof, largely avoiding the attention of the paparazzi and gendarmes. Affleck himself did some filming with a small digital camera and was at his most relaxed and happiest as Neil. By mid-May, filming wrapped in time for Malick to drop in on Cannes, where *The Tree of Life* was about to premiere.

After *The Tree of Life* won the Palme d'Or, the media once more speculated about the absent Malick. Legends about the director were rehearsed. The *Los Angeles Times* revealed that Malick was a fan of the Ben Stiller comedy *Zoolander* (2001).[21] That this was considered news revealed that the black hole of Malick's presence or absence in the media landscape still bent light around it and sucked in many a film journalist. Malick—like many film directors—enjoyed films that were completely different from his own. Andrew Dominik's *The Assassination of Jesse James by the Coward Robert Ford* (2007), for instance, was too close to Malick's own style for him to view objectively, though he was asked for advice by the director and gave notes. Malick suggested that the film lose its voice-over. As with his screenwriters, his notes attempted to make the film less like his. He found it difficult to sit through a film. He visited multiplexes, bought tickets for all the films, and watched ten minutes of one before moving on to the next screening room and watching ten minutes of a different film, sampling the movies in bite-size chunks.

As the team of editors worked on *To the Wonder*, each received specific parts of the film or footage of specific characters to edit, with Mark Yoshikawa once more overseeing the final cut. As the actors read novels for inspiration,

THE MAGIC HOURS

the editors also got books and watch lists. François Truffaut's *Jules et Jim*, Gustav Flaubert's *Madame Bovary*, and Malick's perennial favorite, Walker Percy's *The Moviegoer*, were all proffered, along with the New Wave cinema of Jean-Luc Godard. One particular quote was taken from Margaret A. Doody's introduction to Samuel Richardson's epistolary novel *Pamela*, in which she states her admiration for the "formless, the radiant zigzag becoming" of the book.[22] Footage from *The Tree of Life* was incorporated. Bavarian director Werner Herzog visited the editing suite to see a cut. Asked about the title, Malick told him they had decided on *To the Wonder* only the day before. Herzog shook his head. "That's a terrible title," he said. "You should call it *The Land of Silence and Darkness*." Malick was confused. "But that's the title of one of your films, Werner," he said. The Bavarian director nodded and smiled, happy to have been of help. *The Land of Silence and Darkness* had shown at the New York Film Festival in 1973, the same festival where *Badlands* premiered.

At the Venice Film Festival, *To the Wonder* received its world premiere. This time the critical reaction was decidedly more negative. For *Time Out*, Dave Calhoun wrote: "Endless skies, sunsets seen through trees, hands running through corn fields and spray from garden hoses all begin to feel like parody."[23] *The Daily Telegraph*'s Robbie Collins supported the film but felt the need to warn his readers: "You have to accept Malick on his own terms."[24] *Variety*'s Justin Chang likewise recognized the dangers of overfamiliarity with the Malickian while appreciating that the filmmaker was also trying to innovate: "If shots of characters running through overgrown fields (at one point encountering a random herd of bison) feel de rigueur by this point, the modern conveniences shown here, such as a Skype chat on Marina's laptop, would seem to point Malick's sensibility in a promising new direction."[25] The battleground was solidifying into an attritional stalemate. The die-hard Malickians on one side whispered, "Philistines," while the swelling ranks of skeptics yelled, "Pretentious fools."

Malick himself didn't attend the screening at Venice, even incognito, though Ecky, his ambassador of goodwill, did, along with producer Sarah Green, Olga Kurylenko, Carlo Hintermann, Nicolas Gonda, and Italian actress Romina Mondello, who had a small role in the film as Marina's insufferably pretentious Italian friend. Rachel Weisz, Barry Pepper, Michael Sheen, and Michael Shannon had all finished on the cutting room floor, though this was no longer the surprise it had once been. It was crowded down there.

To the Wonder (2010–2011)

To the Wonder frustrates conventional expectations. It's direct and oblique, confessional and reticent, nakedly obvious and willfully opaque. Crucial information is alluded to without any apparent connection to the plot as a whole. For example, Marina has a medical examination that she fears might result in a hysterectomy, but the doctor is reassuring. This situation isn't anticipated by earlier scenes and receives no further mention. However, it's evidence that beyond Marina's psychological interiority, there's a physical interiority too. The hysterectomy hints at our own (and Neil's) misogynistic reaction to Marina as a "hysterical" woman. A male doctor and Neil discuss Marina's sexual history and reproductive status. It's also an intimation of mortality. Your body will ultimately kill you. And Marina will die. Was this examination a failure to pick up an early warning sign? Is she being misdiagnosed? Is this the most important scene of Marina's life? And yet it flashes by along with breakups and breakdowns, trips to the supermarket, the diner, and the launderette.

None of this is obvious or even apparent. Films usually package meaning into structures of well-defined, interconnected scenes, which lead to precisely placed denouements. Malick's radical dramaturgy is at once striking and off-putting. He demands that we engage more deeply and yet denies us the usual handholds. And by usual handholds, I mean something as basic as dialogue. In a crucial moment, Marina confesses her infidelity to Neil, but the audience can only infer this. We hear practically no dialogue. We hear her voice-over saying, "Forgive." They're in a drive-through restaurant, and in the midst of the scene, the server asks if they need anything else (ironically the only audible dialogue), so presumably Neil has ordered something. Then they're driving away. Have they collected the food? Abandoned it and driven away? What? Neil pulls the car over suddenly and gets out. He smashes the side mirror with his hand, a violent act that terrifies Marina. Then he pulls her out of the car and drives away, leaving her by the side of the road. We don't hear a single word he says. It isn't apparent that he says anything, at least verbally. It's heavily implied that Marina only had an affair to cause the split-up and escape the spiral of a toxic love Neil is too weak to end: "Weak people never bring anything to an end themselves. They wait for others to do it." It's the relationship equivalent of suicide by cop. In this sense, culpability should be shared. Neil's jealousy and anger are misplaced.

Father Quintana initially feels like at best an irrelevance, at worst a convenient interloper to serve as a mouthpiece for Malick's own increasingly overt social and spiritual concerns. In fact, Quintana and Marina are the lead

THE MAGIC HOURS

characters, with parallel stories of disappointed love and an inability to grasp meaning in the world. Just as Marina tries to love but fails to communicate with Neil, so Quintana attempts to seek meaning in an absent God and tries to provide pastoral care when he feels that his heart is "cold and hard." His inability to offer effective counsel or comfort to his parishioners mirrors Neil's ineffectiveness at work, where he monitors the dangerous environment, unable to intervene. They both are custodians failing their charges. These failings lead to a questioning of the nature of faith and love.

Light is a central element throughout the film, as with *The Tree of Life*, with the sun as an objective correlative for God and love both. But the light is evasive, fractured, filtered, and impossible to reach, often setting.

Pieced together, the film provides a revealing portrayal of Malick falling in and out of love. Nowhere is this more (or less) apparent than in the final scenes of the film. They bear some close inspection. First, we see Neil for the first time in a recognizably completed home, fully furnished and lived in, probably for a number of years. With a phone in his hand, he walks out to the garden, where a sizable family awaits him, but he seems to be a man distracted, a man who has just received some terrible news. The phone call was from Marina. She has been diagnosed with cancer. This information is not relayed to the audience. Next, we see Marina apparently waking up on a misty hillside, like a character from an Emily Brontë novel. She moves through the trees, dancing in her dew-soaked dress. These were moments Chivo filmed when the light was failing, with no idea where they'd be placed in the film. In the context of the phone call, they represent Marina's death. She is alone. There are horses on the horizon and a dog at her feet, and as she moves, she turns toward a golden light that shines in her face. It is an unusual light, strikingly bright and unnatural: like nothing we've seen in the film so far. A shot of Mont Saint-Michel—the Wonder—closes the film. Beaches in Malick—*The Thin Red Line*, *The Tree of Life*—symbolize the passage from this life into the hereafter. She is gone.

With this reading, the film becomes a direct sequel to *The Tree of Life*. It's more poignant and moving, personal and emotionally charged. Just as Malick's childhood was seen through grief at the death of Larry (LR/RL) in the former film, so his marriage to Michèle/Marina is seen from the perspective of failure and, again, grief. The story is there but obfuscated. Audiences and critics couldn't be blamed for not grasping it. Was it discretion on Malick's part or a failure of nerve? Or did the film operate like a poem, needing to be reread a number of times before revealing its meaning, its secrets? I

To the Wonder (2010–2011)

confess that the first time I saw the film I was baffled, loving it in parts but struggling (or as Malick's critics might have it forcing myself) to like it. Whereas *The Tree of Life* was an embrace, *To the Wonder* held me at arm's length. It has since become one of my favorites, a film that truly rewards rewatches.

It is also a film that Malick has considered recutting to produce an extended version, as he has with *The New World* and *The Tree of Life*. At the time of writing, this new cut has yet to appear. It should be noted though that those unsatisfied by *To the Wonder* are unlikely to be placated by any new cut. Malick has attempted to form a new cinematic language, a radical endeavor that is necessarily oblivious to conventional storytelling. Although editing had always been a long experimental process for Malick, *To the Wonder* is his most elliptical film, and what is left out is increasingly more important than what is shown. Think back to the breakup scene, which has more dialogue from the fast-food server than from the two leads. Editors going into work in the morning were well aware that they were attempting to push something new in cinematic language—something that opened up a series of questions. What was possible in cinema? How far could a scene be cut down? How much could dialogue be dispensed with? Would a new language emerge that avoided clichés? These were the questions Malick wanted to answer, and for the first time in his career, he seemed to be in a rush.

11

The "Weightless Trilogy" and *The Voyage of Time* (2010–2016)

Throughout the editing of *To the Wonder* in 2010, new projects were being hatched. Producers Sarah Green and Nicolas Gonda began to calculate the logistics of the next two films: the first in Los Angeles—"a city where the locations have agents," as Gonda says—and the second closer to home in Austin, Texas.[1] *Variety* reported in November 2011 that Malick was planning on directing two films: *Knight of Cups*, starring Christian Bale, Cate Blanchett, and Isabel Lucas, and "Lawless," starring Ryan Gosling, Bale, Blanchett, Rooney Mara, and Haley Bennett.[2] The apparent success of *The Tree of Life* and the speed with which Malick had put together *To the Wonder* contributed to the confidence of investors. Malick's ability to cast top Hollywood talent also helped, but talent came with tight schedules. To make the schedules work, the decision was made to film the two movies back-to-back.

At the Fun Fun Fun Fest, Gosling and Malick were pictured filming during the band Yacht's set, and a Tumblr page quickly began to fill with shots of the actors and director. In the age of smartphones, being anonymous was increasingly difficult. The production of "Lawless" was intertwined with *Knight of Cups*, which began in May 2012. The name was changed—first to "Limitless," then to "Weightless"—when it was realized that John Hillcoat's film, starring Shia LaBeouf and Tom Hardy, had the same title. Hillcoat acknowledged Malick in the credits of the film, which premiered at Cannes in 2012. "Weightless" came from a quotation from Virginia Woolf's *The Waves*. A character has a personal epiphany after a solar eclipse: "How can I proceed now, I said, without a self, weightless and visionless, through a world weightless, without illusion?"[3]

The "Weightless Trilogy" and *The Voyage of Time* (2010–2016)

Robert Sinnerbrink has argued that "The Weightless Trilogy" is a fitting name to describe the three dramatic films following on from and developing the technical experiments of *The Tree of Life*.[4] Editor Keith Fraase argues that the real trilogy is actually *The Tree of Life*, *To the Wonder*, and *Knight of Cups*, all of which have direct biographical links. *Song to Song* is instead a musical inspired by his Jerry Lee Lewis project. However, it's also possible to argue that the four-film sequence actually makes up a quartet of biographically inspired films. *The Voyage of Time* films provide a supplementary part of *The Tree of Life*, sharing the common origin in "Project Q" from the 1970s.

As we have seen, *The Tree of Life* deals with Malick's childhood in Waco from the perspective of grief for his brother. *To the Wonder* provides a self-lacerating account of his relationship with Michèle Morette, once more seen through the grief of Michèle's premature death. *Knight of Cups* covers the period in Malick's life when he was starting out in Hollywood as a screen-writer. This was also the period immediately after the suicide of his brother Larry. The self-destructiveness of his youngest brother, Chris (here, Barry, taking Chris's middle name), and the problematic relationship with his father are also explored in the context of a period of hedonism and loss, inspired partly by his own experiences and partly by those of his acquaintances, including *Days of Heaven* producer Bert Schneider. As with *To the Wonder*, *Knight of Cups* is updated, this time from the 1970s to the present day. The film talks directly to Alain Resnais's *Last Year at Marienbad* (1961) and Luis Buñuel in its dreamlike structure. The worlds of Michelangelo Antonioni and Federico Fellini with their parties and orgies are also evoked. Antonioni's *Blow Up* (1966) seems a direct inspiration here—the models, the tennis balls, the orgies, the wandering dissolute roué of well-dressed melancholy, along with epiphanic moments of bliss. It is also the closest Malick would come to filming Walker Percy's novel *The Moviegoer*.

Song to Song is the least autobiographical of the sequence, but it recalls the world of popular music Malick knew via Jacob Brackman and Carly Simon in the 1960s and 1970s. Malick's disillusionment with Hollywood is mirrored by the journey of BV (Ryan Gosling), the promising artist who ultimately abandons the industry.

The link is also evident in the themes and the characters running throughout the films. Jack from *The Tree of Life*, Neil from *To the Wonder*, and now Rick (Christian Bale) from *Knight of Cups* are all almost wordless watchers, passive observers speaking mostly in voice-overs, almost never as part of a dialogue. Rick is an alienated, stumbling pilgrim dogged by familial

THE MAGIC HOURS

grief in an extension of *The Tree of Life*. Rick—like Jack/Malick—has lost a brother to suicide. His remaining brother, Barry (Wes Bentley), is unstable and has a self-destructive streak of violence; he appears with wrists "taped up like a tennis player" after a suicide attempt. He lives in a loft in an industrial warehouse with a mattress: a television is (un)balanced on a chair. Whereas Rick has an almost pathological absence of affect, Barry—like Marina—is full of raw emotion but mocks his father's histrionics at their brother's funeral. At the family home, he smashes a chair on the tabletop. Their father, Joseph (Brian Dennehy), feels guilt over his son's death, but in a way that seems inherently self-dramatizing. A vision has him unsuccessfully washing his hands of blood.

Much of what we see has this theatrical aspect: a literal psychodrama. In a departure from the relative realism of *To the Wonder*, *Knight of Cups* slides through a series of quasi-surreal episodes. Rick's father sits in a dead office in a deserted building and then a moment later recites woes onstage to a handful of spectators. The family argues on rooftops and in restaurants, the dialogue often unheard. Rick and his brother drift through Skid Row, in central LA, with the frictionless motion of ghosts. Malick has reached his father's age: he is in fact older than his father was in that period. Thus, his father expresses Malick's current predicament: "You think when you reach a certain age things will start making sense, and you find out that you are just as lost as you were before. I suppose that's what damnation is. The pieces of your life never to come together, just splashed out there." Mother (Cherry Jones), no longer the venerated matriarch of *The Tree of Life*, appears briefly but is disconnected from the main drama, walking away from conflict, lost, baffled, and apart.

The theatricality is a reflection of Rick's career as a successful screenwriter, which in turn mirrors Malick's own start in the business in the late 1960s and early 1970s. Like Malick, Rick is paid for films that never get made. Episodes titled after tarot cards are defined by a series of romantic partners, all of whom are unreally beautiful with varying degrees of visible character. Della (Imogen Poots), a girlfriend, says Rick doesn't want love but "a love experience." It could equally be said he doesn't want a woman but a "woman experience." The critique is included in the film when Antonio Banderas's Mastrantonio-like party host talks of women: "They are like flavors. Sometimes you want raspberry, then after a while you want some strawberry." He could be the dissipated version of Marcello, who finishes Fellini's *La Dolce Vita* (1960) with an affable but defeated shrug.

194

The "Weightless Trilogy" and *The Voyage of Time* (2010–2016)

Rick's ex-wife Nancy (Cate Blanchett) is a doctor. While Rick sports with supermodels, she works with people with leprosy in one of Malick's darker jokes. With her seriousness, commitment, and independence, she recalls Jill Jakes, Malick's first wife. She describes the breakdown of their relationship, placing the blame firmly on Rick's/Malick's immaturity. "You used to get angry at me over little things," she says. "You wanted me to help you through the dangers of a young man's life." Helen (Freida Pinto), a model who is introduced to the sound of Eastern music, performs yoga, veering toward orientalism. She's inspired by Reita Faria, the Miss Universe Malick interviewed and had dinner with in the 1960s. Pinto says that she knew that the film was autobiographical but didn't know which parts were true and which weren't: "He's very cagey."[5] Elizabeth (Natalie Portman) is a married woman with whom Rick has an affair and by whom he is deeply affected, especially when she tells him of her pregnancy, her uncertainty whether he or her husband was the father, and the resultant abortion. A stripper named Karen (Teresa Palmer) is a force of nature, and Isabel (Isabel Lucas) is an image of beauty so ghostly in her vagueness she flits in and out of the film, part muse, part Beatrice from Dante's *The Divine Comedy*: a dream girl. Relationships come and go with no clarity as to their depth, their longevity, or the reason for their dissolution. No chronology is established. The film reels, intoxicated. Rick crawls on the glittery floor at a party, climbs into a cage in a strip club, and blisses out at a Vegas concert. He wanders the desert, where he is introduced—and where Malick used to go to be alone and write scripts. The location also recalls Antonioni's *Zabriskie Point* (1970).

Malick's team of close collaborators—Widmer, Fisk, Chivo, Gonda, and Green—returned. In one scene, Widmer appears on camera as a fashion photographer who takes an instant dislike to Rick. According to Chivo, a five-hundred-page screenplay existed, but no one saw it. (The number five hundred comes up frequently with these reputed screenplays.) Actors were given reading material—Walter Percy's *The Moviegoer* again—and some background about their own characters but had no idea how their roles fitted in with the overall story. Was there an overall story? Filmmaking followed the dogma but became looser, freer. The shoot took place in Los Angeles, Santa Monica, and Las Vegas. The cast filled out with recognizable faces, including the comic actor Nick Offerman and the *Rick and Morty* creator Dan Harmon. Offerman was in for a day: "I was an agent, and Christian Bale's over-sharing in a lobby, and then [Malick] said, 'Okay, maybe now you're a ghost.' We sort of continued to improvise and play off the same

THE MAGIC HOURS

material we had been doing. Then I went into a sound van, and recorded all of my material, because he said, 'Maybe I'll just have him hear your voice as he's in this lobby.' . . . It's really fun. He has a real train of thought filmmaking, but it's very creative."[6] Malick told Banderas:

> I'm shooting a lot of things, and I don't know what I'm going to edit because I have a movie where, if I put together the whole entire thing, it might be as long as a week. But, I invite you to play. Feel free. You have this monologue. You can start the monologue in the middle, if you want. I'm going to shoot it in different locations, in this party that we have over here. We're gonna shoot it in the pool, in the hall, in this dancing scene, in the garden. So, you just relax and enjoy acting. If you even have any idea, please just throw it out.[7]

The day lasted twelve hours. Recognizable faces, including Ryan O'Neal and Jason Clarke, can be seen fleetingly during the party scene.

Cate Blanchett described the experience as a "cross between cinema, philosophy, poetry, and a quasi-religious experience. It's almost like he's inventing a new form . . . he kept saying that he wanted to 'catch life on a wing.'"[8] Once more Fisk offered his menu, and Chivo and his team shot continuously: "We shoot so fast that we could shoot a movie in one week."[9] The production team broke Los Angeles up into different locations, precleared "goldfish bowls": downtown, Pasadena, Santa Monica, and Venice Beach. Moving from one location to the next became footage as Rick drives his vintage black Lincoln Continental through a Los Angeles typified by its freeways and cars. Between setups, Bale shot on a GoPro.

Occasionally, Bale became frustrated with his character's lack of dialogue. He observed, listened, and reacted, a dreamer unable to intervene in his own dream. Once, he broke down and ranted through a scene. Malick let him go on, asked if he had it all out of his system, and then continued on as before. Outdoing the director's wish for spontaneity, Bale dived from a dangerous pier and into the sea below, to the evident horror of Natalie Portman and the watching producers. "He literally leapt into the style of filmmaking," Gonda ruefully recalls.[10] The moment stayed in the film. After all, it's apt that the prince who lost the pearl go diving to find it.

When filming wrapped, Malick returned to Austin to begin filming the second of his new films: *Song to Song*, starring Ryan Gosling, Michael

The "Weightless Trilogy" and *The Voyage of Time* (2010–2016)

Fassbender, and Rooney Mara. Gosling had already participated in some shooting the year before at the City Limits music festival with Christian Bale, though this footage was rendered useless when Bale dropped out. Gosling came on board forewarned that there was no script. However, Malick's ideas about a music film had been percolating for some time. His connection with music industry figures like songwriter Paul Jabara, Jacob Brackman, and Carly Simon was part of the inspiration; he also had the unfilmed Jerry Lee Lewis story. Malick still believed his script "Grace Abounding to the Chief of Sinners" was a viable project.

Mara plays Faye, an aspiring songwriter who makes money as a dog sitter and Realtor's assistant. She is in the midst of an affair with Cook (Fassbender), a music producer she worked for. BV (Gosling) is a songwriter and protégé of Cook. He meets and falls in love with Faye, who keeps her relationship with Cook secret even as she also falls for BV. The first week of shooting, Mara and Gosling went from luxury apartment to luxury apartment, improvising their dialogue and romance, growing frustrated and bored with their roles and puzzled by Malick's process. A talented musician himself, Gosling could pick up a guitar or a keyboard and start noodling. Whereas François Truffaut's *Jules et Jim* (1962) influenced *To the Wonder*, Jean-Luc Godard's *Bout de Souffle* (1960) was on Malick's mind for *Song to Song*. In particular, the long conversation between Jean Seberg and Jean-Paul Belmondo at the core of that film inspired Mara and Gosling's scenes, as the pair—often in penthouses hovering airily above the city—try to work each other out and gradually fall in love.

Malick pushed the guerrilla style of filmmaking even further. The cast and crew traveled around in a van, hitting different locations on the fly and playing out scenes. Gosling and Mara filmed each other as they crossed from one location to another. Gosling reports: "You just have to be ready for when it happens. We did kind of hit a wall at a certain point and Terry said, 'Let's just go to Mexico.' So the next day, we picked up and went to Mexico."[11] The two-day shoot in Yucatán added different colors to the film, giving the characters an elsewhere, where Cook understands his jealousy and BV and Faye fall in love. Gosling intended to direct his own film *Lost River* (2014). Working with Malick provided an education. Every day, Malick gave his actor a camera to operate and instructions on what to shoot: "He doesn't place a lot of importance on the rituals that most people in the industry kind of depend upon: continuity, linear storytelling, traditional coverage, a script, hair, make-up, wardrobe, location."[12] Malick termed such elements "cinderblocks"

THE MAGIC HOURS

that weighed one down and obstructed free expression. Gosling was surprised at how funny Malick was: "He's one of the funniest people I've worked with."[13]

For her part, Rooney Mara learned the guitar. Irish-German actor Michael Fassbender played Cook, the Mephistophelean music promoter. He read John Milton's *Paradise Lost*, comparing his character to Satan, a snakelike writher. However, his character develops beyond that of the clichéd Svengali figure. His relationship with a waitress, Rhonda (Natalie Portman, in her second Malick film), offers him something more. They marry, and Cook also gifts her mother (Holly Hunter) a house, as part of a Faustian bargain. Inevitably, it ends tragically when—unable to deal with the drugs and excess of Cook's lifestyle (the motives and facts are unclear)—Rhonda overdoses. Once more, a premature death brings Malick down to earth.

Another *Knight of Cups* alum, Cate Blanchett, returns as an older woman with whom BV gets involved on the rebound from Faye. Their relationship is sabotaged by BV's mother, who wears her hair similarly to Blanchett. Was this Malick's wry undermining of his own mother worship? For her part, Faye also has an affair with an older woman, Zoey, played by French actress Bérénice Marlohe, replaying the lesbian romance of her breakout film *Carol* (2015), in which she has a love affair with Cate Blanchett's older woman.

BV and Cook's physical camaraderie has fraternal love and rivalry but also homoerotic tension. Cook and BV are in a creative and competitive partnership, with Cook as the charismatic and hedonistic businessman and BV as the soulful artist trying to stay true to his vision. Faye is both. She looks innocent, a Jean Seberg–like gamin, but she likes her sex violent and actively betrays BV. Her mutability is signaled by her constant changes of wig color (a nod to Brigitte Bardot in Godard's *Le Mépris*) and looks (from country to pixie, grunge, and fashion model). Fassbender, like Kurylenko in *To the Wonder*, embraces the wilder, more physical side of his character, at one point doing a monkey impression. Gosling provides a lighter touch, with a bemused, detached humor, until he is floored by Cook and Faye's betrayal and his father's impending death. Mara—not being a musician—never quite looks the part, holding her guitar as a prop rather than an instrument. Onstage, she is out of place, but it's in keeping with her deceptive character. Is she an impostor? As Rick was a film writer without any evidence of his actual work, so Faye is a songwriter without songs. Is this the central hollowness that sounds through both films? These are stories of creative people who have forgotten how to create.

The "Weightless Trilogy" and *The Voyage of Time* (2010–2016)

As *Knight of Cups* used real-life actors, writers, and showrunners to populate scenes, so rock stars such as Johnny Lydon, Iggy Pop, and Patti Smith pop up throughout *Song to Song*, and there are appearances from groups like the Red Hot Chili Peppers, who have a roughhouse scrap backstage with Cook. Mara was reluctant to go onstage with Patti Smith, but Smith placed a chair and invited Mara to sit while she played a song to her. Later, Smith gives Faye relationship advice based on her own life. In a particularly moving moment, she talks about the death of her husband, the MC5 guitarist Fred Smith. Swedish singer-songwriter Lykke Li plays BV's ex. The Black Lips, an Atlanta garage band, perform with Val Kilmer, who plays as an outlandish front man who sabotages the performance, chainsaws amps, and throws uranium dust into the audience: "I bought it from my mom." B-roll footage shows Malick in the wings, handing Kilmer props and giving him instructions as the band works through its set. The festival audience is split between yelling obscenities and enjoying the chaos of the show. Kilmer, whose biggest role was Jim Morrison in Oliver Stone's *The Doors* (1991), revels in his own creative vandalism. He impishly introduces Mara as Miley Cyrus.

Other music acts are glimpsed. Florence Welch shows up; Big Freedia twerks. Austin musicians Black Joe Lewis and the Honeybears have a recording session with an unhelpful Cook. Austin musician Dana Falconberry plays Faye's sister. Other bands like Arcade Fire and Fleet Foxes were filmed but didn't make the final cut. The camera moves into the mosh pit as one band performs, and the bodies of young men smash into one another in wild abandon. Everything is about sex, and sex is about power. Music dominates the soundtrack, featuring songs from the artists in the film as well as the rock and roll of Elmore James's "Rollin' and Tumblin'" and music by Gustav Mahler and Arvo Pärt.

In November, the forty-day shoot wrapped, and postproduction began on both *Knight of Cups* and *Song to Song*. The task ahead was gigantic. For *Knight of Cups*, Mark Yoshikawa, Keith Fraase, and A. J. Edwards, who all worked on *To the Wonder*, were joined by Geoffrey Richman. Fraase was the only editor to work on all three films of the "Weightless Trilogy," providing consistency. With Rehman Ali, he also edited *Voyage of Time*. For *Song to Song*, he was joined by Hank Corwin and Rehman Ali. The teams worked concurrently under Malick's supervision. However, without the safety net of a script, forming the footage into a coherent narrative proved dizzying. The camera movements and dogma that had broken with conventional filmmaking were themselves becoming a convention. Moments played against each

THE MAGIC HOURS

other, and a rhythm was sought between the performances—"rolling and tumbling" from song to song—and the weightless lives of the main characters.

One of the oddities of both *Knight of Cups* and *Song to Song* (which while occupying the "Weightless Trilogy" could also be viewed as a diptych of modern artistic yearning in contemporary America) is the lack of representation of drug use. Just as Mr. O'Brien in *The Tree of Life* is a smoker who never smokes a cigarette, so Rick in *Knight of Cups* and BV and Faye in *Song to Song* don't visibly take any coke, ecstasy, speed, acid, or heroin, though they are obviously inebriated some of the time. Cook is the exception, with his magic mushrooms dipped in honey. It's a curious reticence. Malick told some about one bad drug experience in the 1960s, but others heard from contemporaries of a more liberal prolonged drug use throughout the 1970s. At Harvard, Malick had been friends with Paul Lee, who was one of the founding editors of the *Psychedelic Review*. Throughout his Hollywood years, he attended parties in which drug use was commonplace, so even if he himself didn't partake, drugs were an inescapable reality: overt use and inebriated people the norm.

Malick split his days between editing suites while mornings were spent writing, talking to his friends on the phone, and working on other ideas. Balls were in the air or, like the tennis ball in the swimming pool of *Knight of Cups*, pushed endlessly beyond reach by the very act of reaching. *To the Wonder* was set for release in the spring, and *The Voyage of Time* was beginning to coalesce into two versions.

As 2013 started and Malick entered his seventieth year, an important chapter in his life closed. Emil Malick died on February 9, at Jane Phillips Hospital. He was ninety-six years old. A Requiem Mass was held at St. Luke's Episcopal Church, where Emil had been choirmaster for many years. Malick's parents were gone. His brothers were gone. Malick was left with his friends, his nieces and nephews, Ecky's children, and most importantly Ecky.

The newly prolific Terrence Malick was no longer the unassailable legend. In reality, his philosophy of filmmaking was remarkably consistent from *Lanton Mills* on. It evolved through a discernible trajectory, valuing spontaneity over perfection; surprise over continuity; music over language; poetry over prose; voice-over over dialogue. Filming engineered that spontaneity, and editing explored possibilities that were available in the footage. Whereas John Ford and Alfred Hitchcock edited in the camera, shooting only what they needed and thereby protecting their visions from studio-paid editors,

The "Weightless Trilogy" and *The Voyage of Time* (2010–2016)

Malick, as his own editor, wanted as many options as possible. Actors were paint in a paint box, he believed, and if he didn't need yellow, out the performance would go. It was brutal, but it was the only way Malick worked. Editing was always the longest part of the process. Actors provided reams of voice-over. Music was taken from a large playlist that Malick had compiled, though in the case of *Song to Song*, a great deal of contemporary music poured in. Malick loved taking in a whole new music scene, devouring it with refreshed enthusiasm. Moods took precedence over characters. The women in *Knight of Cups* were one-dimensional, but what did one-dimensional even mean? How many dimensions was Rick? Wasn't he simply Neil in Hollywood, better dressed? BV, Faye, and Cook were all similarly glimpsed rather than examined. Wasn't part of the problem that the films were—to invert Pirandello—plays looking for characters? Even people looking for characters?

More worryingly, the cooler reception of *To the Wonder* made potential investors leery. One financier sued Sycamore Pictures, Malick's company, which had been created in 2010. The lawsuit claimed that Malick and Sycamore had strung along investors, promising three *Voyage of Time* films: "Malick and Sycamore sold the Pictures as the crowning accomplishment of Malick's film-making brilliance. Malick himself described the production of the VOT Films as 'one of my greatest dreams, a dream I have been pursuing for my entire career.' But in reality, Malick never devoted the time necessary to create the three VOT Films and, instead, dedicated his energies to four *other* films in the last five years."[14] The promised films were two 45-minute films, one with poetic and the other with scientific narration, and a 90–150-minute feature film. The money and Malick's attention were—the company argued—taken up by other projects: *The Tree of Life* and the "Weightless Trilogy." "Although Sycamore and Malick forgot about making the 'most important' movies of Malick's career, they always made sure to take SSPL's [Seven Seas Partnership Limited] money," the complaint states snippily. Malick and Sycamore denied the accusations and countersued Seven Seas, arguing that they were seeking to renege on their financial commitments because they lacked funds. The lawsuit gifted the world an *Onion*-esque headline from the *Guardian*: "Terrence Malick Taken to Court for Forgetting to Make Film."[15]

Voyage of Time was in production intermittently throughout this period. In fact, the shooting and editing ran parallel to *The Tree of Life* right up until *Song to Song*. Emma Thompson recorded a narration.[16] However, Malick's

THE MAGIC HOURS

reluctance to share anything outside his immediate circle of collaborators meant he refused to update his financiers. There's also the possibility that if *To the Wonder* had been a hit, patience might have won out. The suits were dropped a year later when Malick returned the money Seven Seas had invested.

Along with *The Tree of Life*, *The Voyage of Time* was an offshoot of "Project Q," which had been touted as a family history of Malick's Persian ancestors, with a prehistoric prologue. A "sleeping god" was envisioned resting in the depths of the ocean and dreaming of the beginning of the universe. But this mutated, and *Voyage of Time* sought to explore the material separately from the biographical elements. But the same team—the Skunk Works squad with Dan Glass and Douglas Trumbull working on the astronomy sections and Paul Atkins shooting the wildlife and natural phenomena—was employed.

Emma Thompson's narration was a favor to Malick: a way for him to try out some ideas, and ultimately Cate Blanchett was cast to narrate the feature. In the interim, another English actress had recorded a temp for the edit, and Malick adored it so much he kept delaying Blanchett's sessions, though finally he gave in. The identity of this earlier actress was kept hidden. Brad Pitt, a producer on the film, lent his voice to the IMAX Experience cut. Malick also produced a version without narration, which he is said to have preferred. The two narrations were strikingly different. Blanchett's was more poetic, more recognizably Malickian, maintaining the tone and feel of *The Tree of Life*'s Genesis section: a series of probing questions, this time to a mother, a personification of nature—the "Mother of Us All," as *The New World* had originally been titled. Despite accusations of preachiness, it's worth noting that Malick is comfortable switching his deity's pronouns. Whatever he's preaching is not tied down to one orthodoxy.

For IMAX, Brad Pitt is a father talking to his child. The title card reads as a letter to a child. It is worth quoting because it reveals, even here in one of his most abstract films, an intimacy to Malick's voice. *The Voyage of Time* is again an autobiographical film, reaching into the childhood in Waco and Bartlesville and forward to those like him, with the same curiosity: "Dear Child, I remember when I was young, how, at night, I'd go out on the lower road, look up at the stars and wonder—where we came from and how things got set up, anyway—and where it all goes. It seemed there was something infinite in the trees, the stones. In everything. Everyone. Something which lasts. Beyond change. Beyond time. As you watch these passing scenes, how does it seem to you? Do you wonder too?"

The "Weightless Trilogy" and *The Voyage of Time* (2010–2016)

It's a wistful note to begin the journey on. Malick isn't addressing the viewer but the boy on "the lower road" who is looking up to the sky—perhaps the boy who took his forty-two-page project on the planets to school to show everyone.

Documentary producer Sophokles Tasioulis was approached indirectly to help with financing the film. He flew to Austin to meet Malick, Gonda, and Green. Tasioulis recalls: "Terry knew a lot about how to make nature documentaries. He knew all the hard labor, the patience, it takes."[17] Malick told Tasioulis about the long gestation of the project and explained how he'd been adding to it, researching, and filming. Tasioulis was shown the work in progress. Malick preferred not to be there. "Terry offered both sides," Tasioulis says. "All his material was vetted by scientists, every single frame, and he was in constant contact with the academic community and MIT. You name it. But of course, his approach was very different. If we do this, we need to find a way for this to live in the cinema."[18] The footage had an impressive cinematic quality, but Tasioulis also saw a danger that they could end up with "a ninety-minute moving postcard." Tasioulis began selling the film to foreign distributors, as well as getting funding for a shorter IMAX version. The use of IMAX cameras had an obvious impact on budget but also on filming, as anything moving too close to the lens distorted.

In the finished feature, a series of vignettes began the film and dropped in at various stages. Small low-resolution Japanese Harinezumi cameras had been sent to a number of photographers throughout the world, a resurrection of Malick's original plan to give cameras to patients released from psychiatric hospitals and his practice in his fictional features of having actors operate the cameras themselves. Dispatched in April 2012, the cameras arrived with a shot list and technical instructions: "variety and movement in camerawork (not always static wide shots) getting as personal as possible (being involved in the subjects/actions, not just observing from afar)." The list of material included faces, lovers, babies, school, worship of all kinds, elderly people, and fights and quarrels. The note also suggested giving the cameras to nonprofessionals: "that is—children, friends, elderly people, workers, family members, prisoners, police, prostitutes, industrial workers, or people who ordinarily don't use the camera—but who, from inexperience, might bring a special perspective to their work. It would be best for them to do this with you not far away."[19]

French filmmaker Jacques Perrin gave Malick access to his unused underwater footage. Perrin's footage actually belonged to Disney, but Malick

THE MAGIC HOURS

instructed his producers to mention two words to Disney: "Pearl Harbor." It turned out that during the publicity campaign for Michael Bay's blockbuster *Pearl Harbor* (2001), a track from Hans Zimmer's *The Thin Red Line* soundtrack was used without Malick's permission. Malick declined to sue and was now calling in the favor. Perrin's footage was made available. Some microbial footage and a shot of a chicken embryo standing in for a dinosaur from the "Q" sessions were cleaned up and included in the final cut.

More footage was obtained from NASA and the Solar Dynamics Observatory, and this was mixed with effects created in the Skunk Works lab, using flares, liquids and gases, flashlights and dry ice, models and glass paperweights. Scientific advisers Lynn Margulis and Andrew Knoll provided expert advice and suggestions. Ennio Morricone was considered for the soundtrack, but Hanan Townshend was recruited once more, and Malick encouraged him to begin the recording as the musicians tuned up. One such recording became the opening piece of the film.

Between finishing *To the Wonder* and shooting *Knight of Cups*, Malick took cinematographer Jörg Widmer and a small crew and cast of actors to New Mexico to film scenes from the prehistoric period of early man. Matthew Mungle and his team of makeup artists transformed the actors with wig and facial prosthetics, as well as modesty coverings for the ostensibly nude hominids. The makeup took two hours to apply, and the team began at 4:00 a.m. every day, shooting until evening with only short breaks. From Las Cruces, New Mexico, the team shot every day, moving north as they did so through a two-week period until they were in Colorado.

Paul Atkins, who worked on the Genesis section of *The Tree of Life*, continued his work on *Voyage of Time*—and also contributed second unit material for *Knight of Cups*. Atkins filmed in Chile, Iceland, Palau, Monterey Bay, Hawaii, the California redwoods, and the Atchafalaya Swamp in Texas. Operating the IMAX camera and adhering to Malick's demands could make the shoot dangerous. While shooting the eruption of Kīlauea, a volcano in Hawaii, the crew found that the soles of their boots were melting. With Malick's avoidance of a standoffish documentary style and his need for the z axis forward camera movement, cranes and heavy counterweights had to be transported to the most inhospitable locations. Malick provided Atkins with a shot list when he couldn't accompany the shoot, although Atkins was given carte blanche to capture Malick's "Tao shots": "He loved jellyfish for being 'one with their world' as they pulsed in harmony to the rhythms of sunlight and ocean currents."[20]

204

The "Weightless Trilogy" and *The Voyage of Time* (2010–2016)

For all the beauty in the film, Malick's awareness of nature "red in tooth and claw" is also there: the predation of cell life, the violence of the dinosaurs, or a sea lion taking chunks out of a mola. Likewise, the human vignettes include scenes of poverty and deprivation, slums, religious flagellation, and police violence. A mass slaughter of cattle as part of a Tana Toraja funeral ceremony in Indonesia, caught by the Harinezumi cameras, is particularly gruesome. As with *The Thin Red Line*, there's always blood on the grass, a crocodile in the lagoon.

In 2014, a four-minute trailer was screened at Cannes for potential buyers. One hundred and fifty buyers attended. Their phones were taken away on entry. Malick introduced the screening of the teaser (which he refused to watch). Once the full cut was ready, the distributors had an opportunity to see it and share their notes. Tasioulis says: "Terry sat down and listened very carefully and did what he thought of as compromising. From the outside, it looks like he moved a fraction of an inch, but for Terry he felt he had respected all they had said."[21] Many of the notes from the distributors concerned Cate Blanchett's voice-over, which didn't make the film any easier to understand. The voice-overs were a long process. When he supervised the Japanese dubbed version, Tasioulis was bemused by the fact that it took only three hours to lock, whereas the English language version took several weeks and over thirty sessions to record.

The voice-overs had become the single most recognizable element of Malick's films. He'd considered dropping them for *Knight of Cups*, only to fall in love with recordings of a passage from Plato read by Charles Laughton and John Gielgud's reading of *Pilgrim's Progress*. Sir Ben Kingsley provided additional voice-over. For Keith Fraase, it was a key to his process: "Asking Terry not to use voice-over is like asking Jackson Pollock not to splatter paint."[22] Interestingly, Olga Kurylenko suspected that Malick just falls in love with some voices. "He just wanted to hear me say things," she says.[23]

On February 15, 2015, *Knight of Cups* premiered at the Berlin Film Festival. Anticipation was muted, and the film failed to convince the skeptics. Malick attended the festival incognito, using the opportunity to meet his producers about *Voyage of Time*. Sophokles Tasioulis noted that, when meeting in Berlin and Cannes, Malick knew and spoke with all the old programmers, producers, and movers. The BBC's Nicolas Barber headlined his review "Malick's Worst Film," noting: "The result is ludicrous self-parody—somewhere between a Calvin Klein aftershave advertisement and a coffee-table book about the modernist mansions of the rich and famous."[24] The *New*

205

Yorker split the difference, with one critic Anthony Lane complaining: "Terrence Malick gets to the wonder, and he does it in style, but how much of ordinary life does he pass over, or ignore, in his longing to get there?" Richard Brody states: "Perhaps no film in the history of cinema follows the movement of memory as faithfully, as passionately, or as profoundly as Terrence Malick's new film, 'Knight of Cups.' It's an instant classic in several genres—the confessional, the inside-Hollywood story, the Dante-sque midlife-crisis drama, the religious quest, the romantic struggle, the sexual reverie."[25] Some identified sexism in the film, with Rick surrounded by anonymous beautiful women, all of whom conform to the modish ideals of beauty. The women are all different roles in regard to the man rather than different people in themselves. Generously, this could be seen as part of the film's own critique of narcissism. People become tools to be used, but even as Rick visits Christopher (played by writer Peter Matthiessen) to hear about Zen, it is Rick who has come for the wisdom while Natalie Portman wanders off. Christopher's advice is to Rick: a wife is mentioned as a distraction. Meditation, enlightenment—these are strictly for the boys. In an essay for the *New England Review*, Kristi McKim writes: "I regard this film's missteps as clues to the possibilities that I want fiercely to be all of ours."[26]

Both *To the Wonder* and *Knight of Cups* were out-and-out flops, and work on *Song to Song* continued but with no sign of any concession to popular taste. Malick might have defiantly sung the lyrics of "Rollin' and Tumblin'," a song that runs through the film: "If you don't like my peaches, don't shake my tree." The danger was that people might well stop shaking his tree.

Voyage of Time received its premiere in competition at the Venice Film Festival. Supporter Richard Brody of the *New Yorker* immediately anticipated the backlash: "It's a sort of vast and visually overwhelming nature documentary, albeit with brief acted sequences, and, as such, it's an easy film to parody and to mock—say, as the Terrence Malick Science-Wonder Visual Encyclopedia, or 'The Tree of Life' with the funny bits cut out. But that's true of any intensely serious work of art."[27] But mock they did. Robert Koehler wrote: "Time was, when he was actually doing good work, Terrence Malick seemed to appear with a new movie once a decade, if that. Now that he's making drivel, Malick can't stop himself from churning them out, which, a theory goes, is why they're drivel."[28] There were still some fence-sitters. "*Voyage of Time* is a grand and stately attempt," Jessica Kiang wrote in the *Playlist*. "But its grandeur, beauty and elegance don't make the project any less quixotic; Malick tilting at metaphysical, geophysical and astrophysical windmills."[29]

The "Weightless Trilogy" and *The Voyage of Time* (2010–2016)

The glee of the negative reviews is dispiriting, but that's not to say there weren't valid criticisms to be made. From mystery, Malick had become utterly knowable. As Kiang's headline put it: "Terrence Malick Has Made His Movie Again." My own reaction on seeing *Voyage* was similarly negative. I wrote a one-star review, addressing Malick: "Your gaze is directed wholly at the glory and you've forgotten to tie your shoelaces."[30] Cate Blanchett's voice-over—Kiang compares it to tiramisu—is too familiar: the voice of Galadriel and car ads. The forty-five-minute Brad Pitt narrated version was released on IMAX under the title *Voyage of Time: The IMAX Experience*. Gone are the contemporary video inserts of human distress and violence. According to *LA Times* critic Justin Chang, the film is "a glorious cosmic reverie, a feast for the eyes and a balm for the soul in these angry, contentious times."[31]

In 2017, *Song to Song* premiered at the South-by-Southwest Festival in Malick's hometown of Austin. The festivals had been getting progressively smaller: Cannes, Venice, Berlin, and now Austin. Perhaps hoping to boost interest in the film, Malick appeared for a Q&A with Michael Fassbender. Malick's friend, film director Richard Linklater, moderated. Malick spoke about his insecurity making films in a modern setting: "I remember feeling timid about it because it's hard to project yourself into the present. I think making a contemporary film you think about what images haven't been used in advertising, but what you come to see is there is as many images today as there were in the past."[32] Malick is hesitant in his replies, thoughtful and soft spoken with a recognizable Texan twang. He's relaxed, and the audience divided their questions between him and Michael Fassbender, who was a rising movie star.

The reviews were the worst of Malick's career. Wendy Ide in the *Observer* summed up the critical response: "a beautiful nothing."[33] "An absolute shocker," Kevin Maher reported in the *Times*: the only consolation was that Malick couldn't get any worse.[34] Surprisingly, Stephanie Zacharek offered the faintest of praise: "*Song to Song* is slightly less pretentious than Malick's last film, the 2015 sigh of ennui *Knight of Cups*, though it features just as many miniature actresses."[35] The fiercest criticism came from his old AFI classmate Paul Schrader, who wrote in a Facebook post: "If you could photograph the unwanted urine which dribbles from an old man's penis you would have a film titled *Song to Song*."[36] Even champion Matt Zoller Seitz was lukewarm in his appreciation, noting that *Song to Song* is "the first Malick film I've watched where the dots never came together to form a legible image."[37] Along with loyal Malickian Richard Brody, David Jenkins at IndieWire was one of the

THE MAGIC HOURS

few to give a wholeheartedly positive response: "Haters be damned, this is one of the best."[38] Jenkins placed *Song to Song* in the context of the span of films from *The Tree of Life* through the "Weightless Trilogy" to *The Voyage of Time*: a remarkable stretch of experimental American cinema.

The Malick legend was fading: his media silence was no longer worthy of comment, and the films, no longer rare events. Malick's personal appearances—which would have caused stir a few years earlier—hardly warranted reporting. In the audience in Austin, there was more eagerness to talk to Michael Fassbender. Malick appeared publicly at two "In Conversation" events following screenings of *Voyage of Time*. Here, he offered a rare inkling of the director's sensitivity to criticism. These conversations, held at the Smithsonian Institute in Washington, DC, included scientist and bestselling popular science writer Brian Greene, the author of *The Elegant Universe* (1999) and *A Hidden Reality* (2011). Malick waited in the greenroom until the film was over, explaining his reluctance to watch his films: "You're like a bowler. The ball's left your hand and you're trying to put body English on all the shots and trying to steer it a different way. And it's kind of agony." For the first time, Malick gave a public indication of doubt in the direction he had taken. "I keep insisting, only very lately, I've been working without a script, and I've lately repented of the idea," he said. "There's a lot of strain to working without a script, because you can lose track of where you are. As a movie director, you always feel, with a script, you're trying to drive a square peg in a round hole, and if there's no script, there's no round hole."[39]

The reviews showed that attitudes had ossified to the extent that the films were not being received as works of art but as the latest episodes in what we think of Terrence Malick. I was also guilty of this. A Malick release became an invitation to mock, and some criticisms were as automatic as flinches: the story was nonexistent, many critics opined, but *Song to Song* had, if anything, too convoluted a storyline and refused to proceed in a conventional storytelling manner. A ménage à trois is established among BV, Faye, and Cook, only for each member to go off and have other affairs. The voice-overs were whispery and philosophical, it was claimed, but the voice-overs were confessional, intimate, and often boldly straightforward: "I went through a period where sex had to be violent." As the first line of the film, it's a striking divergence from the whispered prayers of *The Tree of Life*.

Critics reduced Malick to clichés: the magic hour (which, with the sun frequently visible in the frame, he now rarely used), voice-overs, the too-beautiful cinematography, the pretentious themes, the nature photography,

The "Weightless Trilogy" and *The Voyage of Time* (2010–2016)

the overly religious or philosophical musings. But these criticisms reveal as much about the cultural prejudice of the moment as about Malick's cinema. *Song to Song* features birds and caterpillars, but birds and caterpillars exist. There's also the supermarket meat aisle and the oil drill where BV goes to work, next to a preternaturally (genetically modified?) green field. The relationships are as much about careers as any sense of intimacy. BV, Faye, and Cook enjoy themselves. They're selfish, conceited, and aware of the vacuity in the luxury while still enjoying the luxury, the private jets, the backstage passes, the sushi served on a naked young woman's body. The friend's ashes become a prop in a drinking game.

The layers of autobiography have already been mentioned in terms of the music scene of the 1960s and 1970s, which Malick was a part of: he had, after all, modeled for an album sleeve. But there are other layers. First there's Austin, Malick's adopted home, which plays a central role in the film: its festivals, bars, and restaurants but also its rivers, highways, and underpasses. About a two hours' drive away, the Enchanted Rock mountain features as the place where Faye and BV fall in love, the magical moment that they return to as the purest moment of their love and which closes the film, a memory often mistaken as a possible future, a reconciliation. Another layer is BV and his brothers, played by Tom Sturridge and Austin Amelio. BV is from a working-class background; his parents are separated. His father is ailing. His mother is the subject of a mother obsession (commenting perhaps wryly on Malick's own adoring portrait of Mrs. O'Brien in *The Tree of Life*).

Chris and Larry Malick were accomplished musicians, and with Larry's suicide and Chris's problems with alcoholism, Malick witnessed the downsides of a musician's lifestyle, the pressures and excesses, the listless hanging around and superficial camaraderie. Malick often likened filmmaking to music, and his favorite metaphor for the work of a film crew was a traveling band creating art in a collaborative atmosphere, but also an atmosphere rife with conflict and betrayal. Traces of his stalled version of the Jerry Lee Lewis story also reappear in the form of Val Kilmer's kicking-out-the-footlights cameo as Duane. The story of Rhonda, the woman Cook marries and drives to suicide, adds a layer of emotional weight: it is a riff on the "Star Is Born" legend, except here the waitress has no particular talent and she loses her life while the Svengali survives to corrupt another day. The grief of her mother, portrayed by Holly Hunter, is a startlingly raw emotion in the midst of the weightless narratives. As is BV's grief at seeing his father near death.

THE MAGIC HOURS

Malick's films were never greeted with universal acclaim, as Pauline Kael's review of *Badlands* attests. *Badlands'* and *Days of Heaven's* elevation to the status of classics was a long and slow process. *The Thin Red Line*, *The New World*, and *The Tree of Life* were also on their own upward trajectories via Criterion reissues and, in the case of the latter two, extended cuts. Whether the same will happen to the "Weightless Trilogy" is uncertain at the time of writing, though there is a growing move to reappraise the films more positively.

Although labeling them as a trilogy is debatable, watching them in a shared context reveals a consistency, a coherence that seemed lacking at the time of their release. They represent a clear filmmaker's vision exploring exciting new territory. Malick was experimenting radically with filmmaking and storytelling, abandoning traditional structures, pushing technological advances, and developing his own cinematic language. He was willing to sacrifice narrative clarity, chronology, and continuity as he sought answers far from conventional drama. He attempted to understand his own memories and formation in the context of a contemporary world, abandoning the nostalgia and the authentic detail of the period films. *To the Wonder* moves like an iPhone movie, a failing love in a pre-Trump United States of poisoned soil and alienation. Look at how much contemporary art appears in *Knight of Cups*—galleries, exhibits, video installations, fashion photography, architecture, light shows—placing its inarticulate screenwriter in the midst of often strikingly beautiful spectacle, both manufactured and natural: a spectacle that (by the way) is superseding cinema. Likewise, *Song to Song* takes on a contemporary music scene, contrasting its creative energy with its commercial trappings and exploitation, its romantic myths and toxic indulgences.

Malick's personal life became the source of inspiration even as the world at large and many collaborators remained unaware. His marriage to Michèle Morette in *To the Wonder* and the death of his brothers in *Knight of Cups* are the emotional core of both films. Watching a parent grow old and approach death is featured in both *Knight of Cups* and *Song to Song*. Malick's anxiety about his own career and the clash between art and commerce are explored in *Knight of Cups* and *Song to Song*. The trilogy suffered in its critical reception in being more akin to the European cinema of the 1960s than the contemporary American scene. Alain Resnais, Michelangelo Antonioni, Jean-Luc Godard, and François Truffaut were sources of inspiration, and their soundtracks, particularly those written by Georges Delerue, provided temp scores to edit by.

The "Weightless Trilogy" and *The Voyage of Time* (2010–2016)

The narrative of Malick's decline became overly familiar, and a joyful vindictiveness entered the discourse. Robert Koehler's article "What the Hell Happened with Terrence Malick?" was the most forthright harrumph.[40] Once you dismiss the voice-overs, you don't listen to what they're actually saying: the questions they're asking. And that poisonous word "pretentious" masquerades as considered judgment when it is in fact an ad hominem, bad-faith slur, impossible to counter.

Not that Malick didn't have his champions, but some of the praise could be as off-putting as the criticism, and the emphasis on Malick's brief stint as a philosopher became something of a cottage industry in itself—so much so that the "Weightless Trilogy" was discussed in terms of Kierkegaard and Heidegger rather than the dominant theme, which was, in a word, fucking. Malick might be fascinated by the wonders of nature, the trick of the light and the glories of creation, but in all three of these films, the strongest impulse is the yearning for beautiful bodies, the ticklish feel of fingertips traced on skin, the way a glance can stop your heart. At sixty-seven, he was both a cinematic poet of awe and "the horny kid in your graduate directing class," as David Ehrlich put it for *Slate*.[41] *To the Wonder* is a love letter of a doomed obsession between two incompatible people. *Knight of Cups* is a similarly affectionate—and nonjudgmental—remembering of promiscuity. *Song to Song* is polyamorous queer cinema. Faye is bisexual. BV wears makeup and women's clothing, as well as trying on Cook's jacket and wrestling with him. His breakup with Cook is as emotionally charged as his breakup with Faye. It shows how little attention was being paid to the actual films that this theme has been almost completely overlooked.

And despite his image as the remote hermit sage of cinema, Malick was aware of his declining reputation, aware enough that he felt that it was time to change course. The new film would be a scripted drama and a return to a period setting. But despite this apparent retreat, it would prove to be one of the most topical films he had made so far.

12

A Hidden Life and *The Way of the Wind* (2015-2023)

Franz Jägerstätter, born in 1907 in the small village of Sankt Radegund, Austria, was the illegitimate son of a chambermaid and a farmer. A healthy young lad and fond of fighting, he was also a reader, intelligent and curious about the world. Despite his love of books, he left school at fourteen to start work, and he was only eight when his father died in the First World War and he was adopted by his stepfather. In his twenties, he got a young woman called Theresia Auer pregnant. The two didn't marry—some said because of his mother's objections—though he cared for and supported his daughter. In 1930, Franz left Sankt Radegund for Eisenerz, an Austrian mining town where he worked for two years. He returned on a motorcycle—the first in the village. He became increasingly religious. In 1936, he married Franziska Schwaninger, known as Fani. Fani shared his faith, and for their honeymoon, they went on a pilgrimage to the Vatican. Fani gave birth to three daughters: Rosalia, Maria, and Aloisia. Franz was now a pillar of the community: a sacristan, preparing the church before Mass and locking it afterward. Many wanted him to stand as mayor of the village, but politics was not for him. He had his own way of looking at the world, informed by his Christian beliefs. In the plebiscite to approve Hitler's Anschluss—the annexing of Austria into the German Reich in 1938—Franz's was the only dissenting vote in the village.

Although trained for military service, as a sacristan Franz obtained a series of deferrals, but in 1940, he was finally conscripted. He refused to take the Hitler Oath, but despite this, he was allowed to return home as a farmer for the harvest. In 1943, he was called up once more. He again refused to swear the obligatory oath, declaring himself a conscientious objector and volunteering to work as a medic. He was arrested and sent to Tegel Prison, north of Berlin. There, he was visited by his priest from Sankt Radegund,

A Hidden Life and *The Way of the Wind* (2015–2023)

who begged him to relent. He refused, was charged with "undermining military morale," and was sentenced to death in July. In August, he was transported to the Brandenburg-Görden Prison and guillotined. He was thirty-six years old.

His sacrifice changed little, or nothing. It didn't alter the course of the war or inspire others to stand up to the Nazi regime. It wasn't part of a larger resistance movement, and after the war, he wasn't hailed as a hero. His wife was widowed and refused a pension; his daughters grew up without a father. In the village, Franz was deemed an obstinate man who had forsaken his duty to his country and his family. His case rested in obscurity until, in 1964, Gordon Zahn, an American sociologist, wrote a biography titled *In Solitary Witness*. Seven years later, Austrian television produced a docudrama on Franz's life called *The Refusal*, but it wasn't until 1997 that his death sentence was legally nullified by the German authorities. In 2007, a plaque was laid in Sankt Radegund, commemorating his life. Pope Benedict XIII declared Franz a martyr before his ultimate beatification the same year, putting him on the path to a possible sainthood. The belated recognition of Franz contrasted to the behavior of the Austrian Catholic Church during his lifetime, which flew swastikas from church flagpoles on Adolph Hitler's birthday.[1]

Terrence Malick first heard about Jägerstätter from his Harvard friend John Womack, a historian. In 2009, another friend, Martin Sheen, whose return to Catholicism had been precipitated by Malick, provided the narration to a short documentary titled *Franz Jägerstätter: A Man of Conscience*.[2] Having secured the rights to letters exchanged between Franz and Franziska,[3] Malick began working on a script. Jörg Widmer recalls: "He wrote the script for *A Hidden Life* and showed us it for years. He was always interested in unheard-of heroes. These people are so courageous, and nobody talks about them."[4]

An independent producer, Elisabeth Bentley, had also been looking into the possibility of making a film on the subject and had been shopping the idea around since 2007. By 2015, the two were working together. Malick was keen to return to a more linear story. Partly this was due to the reception of his recent works. Raising money was difficult as profits looked unlikely. Investors were more likely to be admirers of Malick's work who wanted to see the films themselves—patrons almost.

Changes took place in personnel. For the first time in his career, Malick was making a film without his friend and production designer Jack Fisk. Fisk had found himself as little more than a location manager on the last three films, and although "Radegund," as a period film, was more in his wheelhouse, he decided he didn't want to spend months away from his family in Europe.[5] Chivo also tapped out. The cinematographer had shot *Gravity* (2013), *Birdman* (2014), and *The Revenant* (2015), winning Oscars for each film. The latter carried over the dogma Chivo developed in collaboration with Malick, shooting in natural light and creating an immersive 360-degree reality.

Malick registered the script for *A Hidden Life* with the Writers Guild on July 6, 2016. It begins with a quotation from Søren Kierkegaard: "A tyrant dies, his rule is over. A martyr dies, his rule begins." The new title, *A Hidden Life*, was taken from the last lines of George Eliot's *Middlemarch*. The full quote reads: "For the growing good of the world is partly dependent on unhistoric acts; and that things are not so ill with you and me as they might have been, is half owing to the number who lived faithfully a hidden life, and rest in unvisited tombs."[6]

The statement has a biographical resonance. Hadn't Malick himself "lived faithfully a hidden life"? Haven't his films largely been about unhistoric actions that take place in the midst of the flow of historical periods of turmoil? Kit and Holly disappear into notoriety in *Badlands*. Likewise, the love triangle of *Days of Heaven* vanishes without trace into the river and the First World War. *The Thin Red Line* is full of individual acts absent from the historical record, such as Welsh's reluctant heroism and Witt's final sacrifice, a grave to be devoured by the jungle.

Malick was writing and filming against the background of the rise in populist nationalism across the world, typified in the United States by the candidacy of Donald Trump for president. Although the campaign was widely seen at the time as a quixotic and doomed venture, the substantial support the reality TV star's hate-flecked rhetoric was garnering did not go unnoticed. Malick's own Christianity was informed by the progressive tradition of the coeducational, desegregated St. Stephen's and his Episcopalian upbringing. The embrace of Trump by conservative church organizations, regardless of the many contradictions, was disheartening to those, like Malick, who took their faith seriously and saw it as diametrically opposed to the bigotry, corruption, and selfishness typified by Trump and many of his supporters. Malick was uncomfortable with discussions of his films as Christian, or even religious. For him the status of Christian was too difficult to attain, involving a radical generosity, and certainly not something to claim like the membership of some exclusive club or tribal identity. But now was

A Hidden Life and *The Way of the Wind* (2015–2023)

the time to examine the notion of what a good person should do when their country is turning in a bad direction, even if the prospect of a Trump presidency seemed, at this stage, highly unlikely.

The casting process for the film had begun in 2015. Austrian actor Valerie Pachner auditioned with Grant Hill and casting director Anja Dihrberg-Siebler. She knew nothing about the project other than its World War II setting. Given one of Fani's letters, she improvised a scene in English. A few weeks later, she received a phone call from Malick to say she had the role: "Now we only need to find you a husband," he said.[7] That search lasted six months. August Diehl had made a name for himself both in Germany and in American films, starring as Angelina Jolie's husband in *Salt* (2010) and as a gestapo officer in Quentin Tarantino's *Inglourious Basterds* (2009). He received a phone call from Malick the day after he had been cast. The call caught him in the rain as the director asked about his family life and his background: "I stood under a door entrance, trying to hide from the rain, and had a forty-five minute conversation with Terrence Malick, and it was already like a little bit of a Terrence Malick feeling, looking at the rain."[8] The cast received scripts and the Jägerstätters' letters to read. On her own initiative, Pachner spent six weeks on a farm, working and becoming comfortable with animals.[9] With its European cast, the film was less starry than Malick's recent pictures, but there were still some high-profile names, such as Jürgen Prochnow, Swiss actor Bruno Ganz, and Swedish actor Michael Nyqvist (the latter two sadly died before the film's release). Maria Simon, Karin Neuhäuser, Franz Rogowski, and Matthias Schoenaerts filled out the cast in small roles.

The topography of the real Sankt Radegund proved too flat and uninteresting, with power lines and modern architecture making the period filming prohibitively expensive. Ironically, the farmland surrounding the village looks more like Oklahoma than the Austrian farming village of popular imagination. Malick was drawn to northern Italy and the village of Sappada in the Veneto region. Here, the Dolomites offer towering backdrops, and the ramshackle wooden farm buildings were preserved. A number of villages created a composite of Sankt Radegund, as several locations created the Jägerstätter farm. Some interiors were shot in the actual Jägerstätter house in Sankt Radegund.

The cast and crew gathered in Italy a week before shooting began. There were rumors that the financing of the film might fall through at the last minute: a harsh reminder of how weakened Malick's position had become and how much was riding on this film. If there had been a question for Malick of

THE MAGIC HOURS

compromising to seek commercial success, the actual story of the film proved an inspiration to resist and stay true to his own vision of the world. Despite the worries, Malick was in good humor as he met his cast for the first time. Pachner found him a gentle and warm presence. "He's always questioning you, and he doesn't want to give answers," Diehl says. Franz Rogowski summed up the experience:

> The great thing about Terry is that he needs five minutes, or maybe even just five seconds, to know who you are. Nobody really knows how he does it, but it's pretty astonishing the way he talks to you on the first day and he seems like he wants you and who you are—but *precisely* who you are. You don't have to become something to be good; just the way you are is great. Then he uses this color that you bring and he paints the painting with the color you are. That's very rare. Normally it works more like: "Okay, you are red, and that's great, but what we need is purple for now, so let's work hard so you can be as purple-ish as possible," and you'll always feel a little bit like you're pretending.[10]

Before starting, Malick called a meeting of the cast and crew and explained to them: "Don't worry about continuity, don't worry about costumes, don't worry about dialogue." He waved his hand high in the air. "At the very top, the first thing that counts is the light." He lowered his hand: "And after that for a long time, nothing." He stopped his hand halfway down. "And then comes the light again. And then, after that, maybe the actors." The use of natural light was now second nature. "God is our gaffer," he told the crew.[11]

The actors spent a few days getting used to the farm equipment, milking cows and cutting grass with a scythe. The crew was small, with none of the usual footprint of a Hollywood production. With Widmer as cinematographer, the dogma of natural light continued. If anything, Malick pushed his preferences further. The lenses were even shorter, providing a deep focus. Widmer says: "You can connect so many things in one frame, and then you can tell the story in the foreground and in the background at the same time."[12] The audience decides what to focus on. Although Malick used digital cameras for parts of *To the Wonder*, *Knight of Cups*, and *Song of Songs*, this was his first film shot entirely digitally, allowing for even more footage to be shot without the budgetary consideration of film stock and developing costs and without interruptions to reload the camera. The duration of takes increased.

A Hidden Life and *The Way of the Wind* (2015–2023)

Actors played out the scene as written and then continued in their roles, occasionally reacting to Malick's whispered instructions. Rogowski gave an account of the atmosphere on set:

> Terry was inspiring in being so close to the people he works with. That includes all of the departments. It seems like he's very connected with everyone and very intimate. Sometimes while the camera's rolling he would approach you and whisper something in your ear, then leave the frame, and you would repeat what he just told you. Then you see a ray of light in a window and you just go there. You just follow the light. In *A Hidden Life* there's this scene where I'm sitting at a window in prison and talking about a potential future. That whole scene was based on improv, or based on just listening to the moment. I think that's what made it so special for me to work with him—besides the fact that I feel like we really like each other. I don't know how real that impression is, though, since everybody I know who worked with him feels like they're the chosen one.[13]

When shooting interiors, he directed the actors to "Vermeer themselves," to find the light and turn at an angle so it would address their faces and bodies in interesting ways. He wanted constant movement, like a dance. August Diehl found himself pacing backward and forward, toward and away from the camera. The lenses distorted any lateral movement, which meant that profiles were avoided and any movement had to be on the z axis.

Though back to working with a script, Malick used the techniques he had honed over the years. The same scene was shot in several different locations and at several times of day, something he'd call "cubism," referring both to the art movement and the Rubik's Cube puzzle, or "kaleidoscoping" a scene. This allowed him to assemble scenes in the edit with a broad variety of material. A conversation doesn't necessarily take place within a confined unit of time and place; it can stretch over days or weeks. These conversations go through *The Tree of Life* and *A Hidden Life*, taken up and revisited in different places and at different times.

Occasionally, stillness was reserved for what he called his Caspar David Friedrich shots, typified in the painter's most famous painting from 1818, *Wanderer above the Sea of Fog*, which shows a man from behind as he stands on a rocky peak regarding the panorama before him. So here, characters are shot from behind, the landscape before them. Despite the rules, Malick was open to the actors trying out their own ideas. The key was to find something authentic, Pachner says: "It felt like Terry just wanted to film life as it was happening. He didn't want to create something. There was one scene where I was pregnant, and I had, of course, a fake belly. Terry didn't like it because it was fake, and, in fact, it's not in the movie."[14]

Diehl was amazed at how energetic Malick—now well into his seventies—could be, setting off on scouting trips to find a tree early in the morning when the bees were waking up in the trunk, or a high alpine position to shoot a skyline. The sun was sought, but cloudless skies were shunned. The relentlessness of staying in character for long takes was exhausting, and even when he took a nap, Diehl woke up to find Malick and Widmer filming him.

Days were long and shooting incessant. Between setups, Malick and Widmer used the time to go and film something else, amassing as much footage as possible of the beauty around them, the changing weather and light effects, the rivers and waterfalls, the foliage and fauna. Some of the German crew might have grumbled about Malick's unorthodox methods just as his American crew had on *Badlands* all those years ago, but on the whole it was a happy set. Livestock roamed, and children (playing the Jägerstätter children at different ages) played in the long grass. Locals were enrolled as villagers, and once more Ecky was on set to provide goodwill. Malick was attentive to her and courteous, fetching her a chair when she looked tired. The spouses of many directors provide them with emotional support, but few consistently receive the acknowledgment of an official credit the way Ecky consistently did. In the evenings, the whole cast and crew frequently ate around the same table. Malick gave the actors new scenes or a poem or piece of philosophy to read and absorb for the next day. As with the Virginia woodlands for *The New World* and Smithville for *The Tree of Life*, Malick had created an idyll. He was with Holly and Kit in the woods and with Bill, Linda, and Abby by the river. Witt went AWOL to reach such a place.

The shoot lasted for six weeks in Italy before moving to Berlin, following the story chronologically. In the prison, the atmosphere was grim, and the cells were dark. Diehl recalls: "There's one rule: there is heaven and hell. Heaven means being in the light. You can't do anything in the darkness. You can cross it, but you have to go to the light and to do the scene there." Malick called cut and told Diehl to move into the light. "I got like a little bit angry and said, 'Well, I am sorry. But sometimes I'm also trying to forget the camera. I cannot act and create your picture at the same time.' He was

A Hidden Life and *The Way of the Wind* (2015–2023)

very calm. He listened to me. And he said with a very calm voice: 'Yes, you can.' And in this moment, I knew he was right. It's true."[15] Though not on the call sheet, Pachner also attended the filming in Berlin and Zittau, a beautiful city in Saxony that provided some locations, including the train station where Fani and Franz have an emotional farewell. Malick shot some of Pachner in the prison as part of Franz's dreams, but these scenes never made it into the film.

By September 2016, filming was complete. Once again, a substantial period was spent on adding voice-overs, editing, and mixing the film. The actors returned to the studios to voice their parts "at least forty times," according to Diehl. Pachner started work on the voice-overs while they were filming in Berlin and continued throughout the following years, also traveling to Austin to reunite with Malick and record under his direction. "It was important for me that Fani sound like a farmer and not just an actress who was perfectly reading her lines," Pachner says. "It had to be intimate but not too whispery. It had to have strength."[16] The actors mostly read from the letters, monologues that Malick wrote, and psalms.

In November, Donald Trump won the presidential election, and Malick continued with his film about a man who finds himself increasingly alienated by the political turn his country has taken. As Franz writes to his wife: "Oh my wife, what has become of our country?" The line now took on a different meaning.

Having worked briefly with Malick on "Grace Abounding to the Chief of Sinners," James Newton Howard was hired to write the score. Howard was a classically trained musician who had begun working as a session player for pop and rock acts such as Ringo Starr and Harry Nilsson in the 1970s. He collaborated as an arranger with Elton John at the peak of his popularity and wrote his first piece of film music for David Lynch's wrongly maligned *Dune* (1984). Since then, Howard had cemented a reputation as a prolific and award-winning composer for such filmmakers as M. Night Shyamalan, Peter Jackson, and Christopher Nolan. He began writing the music for *A Hidden Life* early on in the production and had a good relationship with Malick, with whom he spoke several times a day: "He has this commitment to his art and this uniquely tenacious way of approaching it that I've never seen anything close to before in my experience."[17] Malick was reluctant to show Howard any footage, preferring to choose where to place the music himself. He explained that the Jägerstätters were living in a Shangri-la but that there was already an "inherent sadness." He told Howard: "Part of what love is, is their sadness. It's

THE MAGIC HOURS

a risk. And there's also sadness in beauty." To capture that, Howard wrote a theme:

> I took a chance and I presented these arpeggios, this rolling left hand with a violin solo and a couple of strings, and I sent it off. Terry really liked it. But I always had the feeling that he didn't want to like it, because it was so evocative. And maybe it was too specific emotionally. And I think one of the things Terry looked for was not to gild the lily. So was it too romantic? Was it too sad? But I'm proud of that score, because I really feel that it's the first big melody score that he had allowed from a composer for some time."[18]

The long postproduction period was not entirely taken up by the one film. As had often been the case in his career, Malick already had other projects simmering. Of these, an old project had come to the fore, tentatively titled "The Last Planet." It continued the overtly religious theme of *A Hidden Life* but with the ambitious largeness of *The Tree of Life*. It took on the topic of the life of Jesus Christ. In popular film, portraits of Christ had been on the decline. Films with religious themes were no longer a popular cinematic genre with the odd, frequently controversial exception. Mel Gibson's *The Passion of the Christ* (2004), which starred Jim Caviezel, proved a surprise box office success while at the same time provoking accusations of anti-Semitism. Martin Scorsese had completed a trilogy of faith-based movies. *The Last Temptation of Christ* had caused furor in 1988 with its sequence featuring Willem Dafoe's Jesus dreaming of a domestic life with Mary Magdalene. *Kundun* displeased the Chinese government in 1997 and was released with muted enthusiasm by the studio. Scorsese's adaptation of Shūsaku Endō's 1966 novel *Silence* completed his "trilogy of faith" and told the story of a Jesuit missionary whose belief is put to the test in a violently hostile Japan. Malick saw the film and wrote Scorsese a letter: "One comes away wondering what our task in life is. What is it that Christ asks of us? And what new shapes will He assume in these dark times, like those of old? He might appear, as you show, even in those who oppose the faith or betray it, like Judas or Pilate. His love seems to be wider for it."[19] The extract from the letter stands as the most public avowal of Malick's Christianity, if any avowal were required. This was still the hands-on socially engaged Christianity of St. Stephen's ("What is it that Christ asks of us?"), but the idea of new, unfamiliar shapes to Christianity (Could Christ be Judas or a Pilate?) also involved a radical approach to any settled sense of

A Hidden Life and *The Way of the Wind* (2015–2023)

orthodoxy. "Our confusion is not anarchic," as Malick wrote of his reaction to Heidegger many years earlier. The confusion is the point. The questions that run through his films are not rhetorical but heartfelt, essential, genuinely seeking some insight.

By some reports, the script had been written before the filming of *The Thin Red Line*. In fact, locations were scouted around the world. Some key personnel were in annual communication with Malick for twenty years. Not this year, maybe next, a producer in Turkey was told, repeatedly. But by 2016, it was apparent that the time had finally come.

As *A Hidden Life* coalesced into its finished form and "The Last Planet" began, Malick also found time to film some quick commercials, using them as an opportunity to try out ideas, keep abreast of advances in the technology, and earn some welcome cash. A short film for a new Google phone, the Pixel 3, released on YouTube in October 2018, is credited to "director Terrence Malick and his co-workers." A blown soap bubble starts a montage of experiences showcasing the camera's capacity to capture color and movement. The music is provided by M83 and their song "Raconte-moi une histoire." A child recounts a story with an echo of Linda Manz's voice-over in *Days of Heaven*: "I heard about this frog. It's a very tiny frog, but it's also very special. If you touch it, your world can change forever. Blue becomes red, and red becomes blue—nothing's ever quite the same." This was not the first commercial work Malick had undertaken. In 2017, he shot a commercial for Mon Guerlain perfume called "Notes of a Woman," starring Angelina Jolie in a series of airy, well-lit rooms—actually the villa in the South of France where she occasionally lived with Brad Pitt. It was a wry reply to all those critics denouncing his films as perfume ads. He leaned into it. Who says Malick has no sense of humor?

Malick also directed his first virtual reality (VR) film, the seven-minute *Together*, billed as an "experience about the power of human connection. The piece fuses dance and technology, putting the viewer in the middle of an emotional narrative about breaking down barriers and bringing people closer." It features movement artists Jon Boogz and Lil Buck, who play two men separated by an invisible barrier. They combine dance and mime to the music of Simon Franglen, with images projected onto sheets around them in a studio space. Cinematographer Rodrigo Prieto is also credited. The film showed at the Tribeca Film Festival in 2018 in the Immersive section devoted to VR. IndieWire's Chris O'Falt was let down by the experience, citing Malick's inexperience with the format: "As a VR rookie, Malick becomes an

THE MAGIC HOURS

undergrad film major making his first short as he feels his way through the basics of visual language . . . you can feel Malick trying to figure out how to move the camera, or if it's possible to cut and reframe. As a result, Malick's ephemeral visual style only comes from the two-dimensional images projected on the backdrop."[20]

That fall, the Venice Film Festival premiered the extended cut of *The Tree of Life*, which had been commissioned by Criterion. The film is longer by more than forty minutes, deepening the childhood section. Jack's extended family, his sexual awakening, his knowledge of the neighborhood, and his transferal to St. Stephen's are all recounted, making the film even more closely biographical than the theatrical version. Chivo had also color-corrected the entirety of the film again. The 2011 cinematic release was Malick's preferred cut, but he told Criterion technical director Lee Klein: "No one asked Bob Dylan to play a song the same way every night. Why should I have to make one film?"[21] He even considered using the branching technology of DVDs to create an option to play certain scenes in random order. The finished film isn't just the usual added scenes of an extended cut; it represents a reconsideration that shifts the emphasis away from Jack's own experience and more toward his father's. We see Mr. O'Brien ruminate on his own father's sad and disappointed life, which closely resembles that of Malick's grandfather Abimelech, and his own sense of guilt. He is a more complex and contradictory character, cheating on his taxes and gambling, even as he maintains a strict hold over his household, his little fiefdom. He is contrasted with Mrs. O'Brien's brother, a more free-spirited favored uncle, who comes to stay for days and—as Irene's brothers would—stay for months. Your mom and dad don't just fuck you up, to quote Philip Larkin: "They were fucked up in their turn."[22] The empathy in the film is, if anything, deeper, more widespread. And the tornado that hit Waco is also featured, a terrifying intrusion of deadly nature.

The new version offered the tantalizing prospect that other recent films might see alternate versions released. At the time of writing, a new cut of *To the Wonder* has been posited as possible, but there have been no announcements.

Malick's producing work also continued. Mostly this involved executive producing projects to give them visibility and encourage filmmakers. In 2015, Malick and Natalie Portman served as executive producers on *The Seventh Fire*, a documentary directed by Jack Riccobono about the drug problem in a Native American community in Minnesota. The same year, he also got a

222

A Hidden Life and The Way of the Wind (2015–2023)

production credit on *Almost Holy*, Steve Hooper's documentary about Gennadiy Mokhnenko, a priest in Mariupol, Ukraine, whose unorthodox approach to street kids and the drug problem is sympathetically if somewhat uncritically presented. With both films, Malick came in at a later stage to offer help and guidance. Malick proved an inspiration to Laura Dunn, whose film *The Unforeseen* he had already produced alongside Robert Redford in 2007, by suggesting she read the work of Wendell Berry, the environmentalist and writer who became the subject of her documentary *Look & See: A Portrait of Wendell Berry*, released in 2016, codirected and produced with Jef Sewell. The same year saw the release of *The Vessel*, directed by Julio Quintana (the namesake of Javier Bardem's priest in *To the Wonder*) and starring Martin Sheen. Quintana had started with Malick as an intern on *The Tree of Life*, before graduating to the second unit on *To the Wonder*. Other Malick alumni also contributed, such as editor A. J. Edwards and composer Hanan Townshend.

Most of these films had a personal connection to Malick. A former protégé or colleague needed advice and help. As a first-time filmmaker, Malick had received support from established pros like Arthur Penn and Irvin Kershner, and now he was returning the favor. But the tenor of the films and their political concerns—the environmentalism, their criticism of unregulated capitalism, the problems of poverty and substance abuse—aligned with Malick's own concerns. There are also crossovers. Dunn's films about exploitation and pollution are reflected in the subplot of Ben Affleck's work in *To the Wonder*. Likewise, the image of the socially active priest mirrors that of Father Quintana in the same film.

In 2017, Malick got a phone call from Liza Womack. She was the daughter of one of his best friends from Harvard, John Womack Jr. She visited Malick when he was in Paris in the 1980s, and he had introduced her to counts and countesses, showing her a good time.[23] Unfortunately, the phone call was caused by a family tragedy. Liza's son, Gustav Åhr, had died of a drug overdose at the age of twenty-one. Gustav was better known to the world as Lil Peep, a tattooed rapper and internet sensation. A number of people were eager to make a documentary, but Liza was grieving and unable to cope, horrified that her son's memory might be exploited. She was also desperate to find some meaning. If a documentary was going to be made, she wanted Malick in charge. He brought in Sebastian Jones, with whom he had worked on *Knight of Cups*, *Voyage of Time*, and *Song to Song*, to codirect alongside music video director Ramez Silyan. The film focuses on Gustav, his

223

THE MAGIC HOURS

upbringing, and—at Malick's prompting—his relationship with his grandfather who was a surrogate father to the performer. John reads out a series of his letters to his grandson even as we watch Gustav begin to lose control of his own destiny. It is a raw, honest film: unsentimental and yet moving, nonjudgmental and yet tragic. The film—*Everybody's Everything*—echoes *Song to Song* in its chaotic musical journey and its exploration of the romantic myth of the artist, but here drug use is ever present, and the discovery of Gustav's corpse in the back of the tour bus is a sickening moment of reality. Without taking anything away from the directors, the film feels the most closely attended to by Malick. This is because of another consistent aspect of Terrence Malick's life: the strength and reciprocity of his friendships. Even as he was struggling to finish his own film, when called upon by a friend in need, he took upon himself the responsibility of the film. The film is a memorial to Gustav and an act of love toward John and Liza Womack.

In April 2019, the seventy-second edition of the Cannes Film Festival announced its lineup. Veterans Pedro Almodóvar, Marco Bellocchio, and Ken Loach mixed with exciting younger talents Céline Sciamma and Bong Joon-ho. Among the veterans was Terrence Malick's new film *A Hidden Life*, playing in the main competition. After the commercial flops of his last three films and the critical lambasting they had received, the premiere on May 19 was an event looked forward to with some trepidation. There was now to be a script, rumor had it. Or a storyline at least. But if once his films had felt like the hottest ticket in town, an event in themselves, now it wasn't clear that he had much else to say.

As the final quotation from George Eliot closed the film, the applause was loud and sustained, and the press appreciated a return to form. August Diehl and Valerie Pachner walked the red carpet and attended the press conference. Malick's own presence wasn't expected, but he was in attendance. Dressed in formal attire, he slipped into the screening so he could congratulate his actors. Matt Zoller Seitz ranks the film as "one of his finest films, and one of his most demanding."[24] For Walter Chau, it is "sublime."[25]

The film begins with contemporary footage of Hitler from Leni Riefenstahl's *Triumph of the Will* (1940). (Originally, the script began with the famous news footage of an unknown protestor facing the column of tanks on Tiananmen Square.) The Nazi propaganda imagery shows the pageantry evoking the kind of rural life that Franz and Fani Jägerstätter live in Sankt Radegund, located in the same province from which Hitler originally hailed. Their family life is depicted in a drifting series of vignettes. In *Days of Heaven*,

A Hidden Life and The Way of the Wind (2015–2023)

work was exploitative and hard; here it is still hard, but the Jägerstätters are farmers working on their own land. Their work is who they are; it's hard and dirty, but it's also occasionally play. They are part of a community whose members are interconnected and mutually dependent, helping with the harvest and meeting in the pub and the church.

When we cut to Franz marching in a Wehrmacht uniform, the effect is jolting. He's undergoing his compulsory military training but is allowed to return to the farm, where his antipathy toward the Nazi regime solidifies. We see documentary footage, some of it very grim, of the suffering caused by the regime. A freezing child, corpses in the snow. It's as shocking as the documentary footage of real death and human suffering that is interspliced in *Voyage of Time*. Franz isn't a member of a political party. He is a white, heteronormative man and a committed Catholic. His church has acquiesced to the regime, and the church hierarchy counsels compliance. There is some whispered sympathy, but the mayor is a convinced National Socialist, and most of the villagers perceive Franz's stance as baffling, before they become overtly hostile to it and to his family.

As Franz becomes more committed to his refusal to swear the oath of loyalty, every visit of the village postman feels like a step closer to an inevitable destiny. The delay takes so long that the tension becomes unbearable as we see his love of his children and Fani and understand the grief and pain his ethical choice will cause them. A complex portrait of Jägerstätter and his decision begins to emerge. Is there narcissism in such a sacrifice? Or the idiocy of the holy fool? When prison comes with its bullying guards and dehumanizing privations, it's almost a relief compared to the torture of waiting. Franz's lawyer offers him a deal to make him free, leading Franz to answer, "I'm already free." The story of Franz's final transformation into a martyr is paralleled with Fani's transformation into a widow. The emotional rawness of these scenes belies the accusation that Malick somehow doesn't care about people.

Franz's understanding of his freedom in the prison is like Mrs. O'Brien's assertion in *The Tree of Life* that her son was always in God's hands or Witt's sight of the "glory" in a wartime brig. It is the apprehension of a truth that transcends appearances and ordinary categories. It is a hard-won revelation that comes through the suffering life inevitably provides—suffering Malick himself felt with the loss of his brothers.

On a technical level, *A Hidden Life* represents a change in direction rather than the reversal hinted at in the idea of a "return to form." The

THE MAGIC HOURS

narrative might have derived from a script, and its true story framework and period setting impose a certain discipline, but the film plays out in a way that is entirely Malick's: shots rather than scenes, deep focus, and an immersive sense of an environment. The voice-overs are once more different: a series of letters communicating between husband and wife rather than internal musings. As a student, Malick had studied Martin Heidegger's sense of being in the world—the famous "Dasein" quoted several times in these pages—but *A Hidden Life*, in common with many of his films, portrays characters the world wouldn't let be: those who were torn from their idyllic homes or simply had to fall into the world of adulthood, experience, and compromise. These were not outlaws or soldiers, explorers or artists, but a family who—as stated by Fani in the film—"lived above the clouds." But you cannot live aloof to suffering, nor should you. Heidegger himself had been in the world by also being in the National Socialist Party. It's possible to read the film as a repudiation of Malick's earliest philosophical hero, who had conformed with, celebrated, and benefited from the regime that executed Jägerstätter. There's talking about being in the world, but there needs also to be an ethical engagement with being in that world. Valorizing the "authentic" can lead to a false dichotomy, an elevation of one reality as the Real, as in the Real Volk, the True Americans. The "authentic" becomes another flavor of ice cream, as Tonio in *Knight of Cups* might say. The rural life and nature—even great cinematography of nature—can become a fetish substituting authenticity against the implied falseness of our modern urban lives, but no more real for all that.

With this in mind, Malick questions his own work as an artist. What does it serve? What does it do?

In the film, Ohlendorf, played by Johan Leysen, is painting the murals in the church where Franz is sacristan. He explains his own role as an artist and the limits of art and in so doing allows Malick to comment on the film itself: "I help people look up from those pews and dream. They look up and they imagine that if they lived back in Christ's time, they wouldn't have done what the others did." Every film is a what-if thought experiment, a virtual reality to test ethical choices. But it can also encourage a Zeus-like aloofness and a complacent self-delusion. Ohlendorf comments with striking cynicism: "They [the audience] would have murdered those whom they adore." Our approval of a moral hero like Jägerstätter, who stands isolated and alone in contrast to his community, denies an obvious arithmetic: we can't all be the lone voice against the bigots, or there wouldn't be any bigotry.

A Hidden Life and The Way of the Wind (2015–2023)

On a Wednesday afternoon in December, a small group of invited guests gathered in the screening room of the Vatican film library. Elisabeth Bentley and Terrence Malick stood up to introduce the special screening of *A Hidden Life*. It was a story, he said, that "challenges our souls, our consciences and our fears and puts into play our tendency to forget the past so as not to take responsibility."[26] Understanding the past, confronting it, was about taking responsibility, engaging in the world, as it is, as it was, and as it might yet be.

This should have been Malick's opportunity to show he could appeal to a larger audience. At almost three hours and with no stars, the film was unlikely to draw a mass audience, but it had been shot for $8 million, and international distribution had largely paid for the budget already. However, when it began its release in late January 2020, news of COVID-19 had begun to have a chilling effect on cinema attendance, and by March cinemas around the world were closing their doors. Although the film would be released to streaming services, it is impossible to discover to what extent *A Hidden Life* found its audience. Its critical reputation as Malick's "comeback" film has solidified but is by no means—when has it ever been?—a consensus. One interesting win over was David Thomson, who had praised *Badlands* in his *New Biographical Dictionary of Film* as "the most assured first film by an American since *Citizen Kane*," only to sum up his career as a decline that "is one of the most alarming tales in the death of film."[27] Now, he was asserting that *A Hidden Life* was the best film of 2019, "a straight masterpiece."[28]

Malick had continued his method of going straight into a new project, and it was fortunate that the principal photography of his new film had been completed before the arrival of COVID-19. "The Last Planet" had now become "The Way of the Wind," a reference to the biblical passage Ecclesiastes 11:5: "As thou knowest not what is the way of the wind, nor how the bones do grow in the womb of her that is with child; even so thou knowest not the work of God who doeth all." An ambitious film, it featured a series of scenes from the life of Jesus. Leo Tolstoy's 1892 synthesis and translation of the Gospels—*The Gospel in Brief*—was among Malick's recommendations to collaborators, along with *The Memoirs of Saint Peter: A New Translation of the Gospel of St. Mark*, by Michael Pakaluk.[29] Both books give a down-to-earth account of Jesus as a contemporary historical figure. Pakaluk's translation maintains the text's original use of the present tense, giving it a breathless oral immediacy, while Tolstoy attempts to make Jesus a campaigner of sorts, a humanist. Hungarian actor Géza Röhrig, who had garnered international recognition in the horrific Holocaust drama *The Son of Saul* (2015), was cast in the lead role. Having appeared briefly in *A Hidden Life*, Belgian actor Matthias Schoenaerts was playing Peter, and the celebrated British actor Mark Rylance—who had appeared in Steven Spielberg's *Bridge of Spies* (2015) and *The BFG* (2016)—was cast as different versions of Satan.[30] Turkish actor Numan Acar turned up on location in Turkey to learn that he was one of a group of actors who had been cast as apostles, but the actors themselves had to discover which ones they were. This uncertainty was not for everyone—they were not given a script—and some left. Line producer Ali Akdeniz told Acar he'd first done a recce for the film over twenty years earlier and had been in contact with Malick ever since.[31] There were ten days of preparation as the actors bonded and Malick began to formulate his idea of the cast, and then the journey began. Acar says: "We did almost the entire journey together. Turkey, Italy, Morocco, Malta. We bonded like a rock band. Everybody who came in, nobody wanted to leave. It was so welcoming. And we're in these insane locations. I remember a moment in Malta. You can see these olive trees, which are more than two thousand years old. It's almost like we're making a documentary."[32]

Heading toward his eighties, Terrence Malick was still outside, being in the world, going on location, moving around with his rock group. "I really felt like he's a twenty-two-year-old student making his first student movie," Acar says. "He's so excited about everything, about the locations and some mountains you cannot access so easily, but he was like a young goat jumping on the stones and jumping everywhere. Finding the place to shoot and it was really rock and roll. We're doing a crazy guerrilla student movie with this man. He never got exhausted. If I reach his age, I want to have this passion."[33]

In Iceland, Malick stood facing the wind blowing off the glacier. He clambered up hills in North Africa and explored the beauty of Italy once more. There were no generators, no lighting crew, no trailers—there weren't even chairs. Location manager Markus Bensch knew that he shot facing east in the morning and west in the evening and shot interiors at noon. Equipment could be placed to the north or south. "When you do a Malick film, everyone comes out a better person on the other end," Bensch says.[34] With his crew and his actors, he was still pursuing the spontaneous, sending in his torpedoes to disrupt the scene, finding his rabbit holes and his Tao shots, typing on his electric typewriter in his hotel room at night, and whispering instructions to the actors even as they played their scenes. Takes could last as long as ninety minutes. Widmer got a cramp and passed the camera to an

A Hidden Life and *The Way of the Wind* (2015–2023)

assistant, and the take continued without a break. The lenses were wider than ever, the technology more advanced, and yet what he sought now was what he had sought from the very beginning: a moment of truth; of being in the world; of life.

Veteran Greek composer Eleni Karaindrou—famed for her work on the films of Theo Angelopoulos—was commissioned. James Newton Howard contributed additional music: "I ended up writing something he loved, a very simple theme: two notes and very diaphanous, translucent with gauzy orchestration. It just felt like it was hovering in the air. And of course, with Terry's directing style, he'll pan out over the ocean, and you see the water rippling, and anything sounds good over Terry's incredible beauty. It sounded like a wave to him. I ended up working on it for more than four months. So we did a lot of different versions. He had no problem: he could continue to pursue what he wanted to get. He's a T. rex in sheep's clothing. But every time people talk about Terry, they start smiling."[35]

In 2021, Malick shot an advertisement for Ford, with Alexis Zabé as cinematographer and Don Cheadle as narrator. A year later, Malick and Dutch artist and photographer Viviane Sassen collaborated on a short film called *Towards a Dream*, sponsored by high-end fashion house Louis Vuitton. A group of children use a luggage trunk to explore the US and particularly the wildernesses around New Mexico and Texas. The extent of Malick's involvement is unclear, though his style—the slightly closer close-ups, the z axis movement—is readily recognizable.

At the time of writing—May 2024—editing on *The Way of the Wind* was ongoing. The COVID-19 pandemic had a delaying effect, with editing having to proceed remotely via Zoom. There were rumors of ill health, and Ecky and Malick, both approaching their eighties at the time, had to be particularly careful in shielding themselves from possible infection. Malick's postproductions were always lengthy, and this was no exception. He wanted to get it exactly right. This was a film about Jesus, after all, not some gangster picture, he told his editors.

There's also a chance that Malick has already embarked on a new project: lining up a cast, finalizing locations, delving into old folders stuffed with notes. Who knows if a version of Walker Percy's *The Moviegoer* or "The English Speaker" or "Grace Abounding to the Chief of Sinners" might finally reach our screens? The director of *Gummo* (1997)—which starred Malick actor Linda Manz—and *Spring Breakers* (2012), Harmony Korine, told *GQ* he was considering returning to mainstream filmmaking to film a script

THE MAGIC HOURS

Malick wrote: "Terrence Malick wrote a script that he wants me to direct. It's a really, really beautiful script. And that's maybe one of the only things that I could imagine pulling me back into like actual, traditional moviemaking."[36] A series of interactive artworks titled *Works of Nature* is also due to show at the ACMI in Australia, executive produced by Malick with narration by Cate Blanchett, poetry by Daisy Lafarge, and music by Jonny Greenwood, Meredith Monk, Jon Hopkins, the late Jóhann Jóhannsson, and Howard Skempton. An evolution of *Evolver*, which premiered at Tribeca in 2022, it is the work of the London-based art collective Marshmallow Laser Feast and featured at the Cannes Film Festival in 2024.

On reaching his eightieth birthday, Malick received congratulations from Francis Ford Coppola via Instagram:

> Belated birthday to the great Terry Malick! (aside from all else, the funniest person I've ever met.)
>
> I know that humor is a sure sign of intelligence. Terry and I once travelled as tourists, and I remember I never could stop laughing. So much so, that I later asked Terry if he'd come to the Philippines to appear in Apocalypse Now as the "rivets salesman" from Joseph Conrad's Heart of Darkness, and he said he would. But my source of funding was cut off, and I had to stop shooting. Nevertheless, his own body of work is monumental![37]

Aside from the revelation that the publicity-shy Malick once agreed to appear in what promised to be a large studio picture, the post also showed an aspect of Malick that is spoken about by many who work with him but not widely known: his sense of humor—"the funniest person I've ever met." Malick's life might have been hidden from the public, but, as hopefully this book has testified, it hasn't been small. He is in all senses a large and complex man, comprising the artist and philosopher, the son and brother, the lover and husband: a seeker of the sublime who nevertheless possesses a keen sense of the ridiculous.

Return to Ohlendorf, the artist of *A Hidden Life*. He's a figure like Tarkovsky's artist hero in *Andrei Rublev* (1973), a film that showed in the same edition of the New York Film Festival that *Badlands* closed. In *A Hidden Life*, Ohlendorf has this to say: "What we do, is just create—sympathy. We create—we create admirers. We don't create followers. Christ's life is a demand. You don't want to be reminded of it. So we don't have to see what happens to the

A Hidden Life and *The Way of the Wind* (2015–2023)

truth. A darker time is coming—when men will be more clever. They won't fight the truth, they'll just ignore it. I paint their comfortable Christ, with a halo over his head. How can I show what I haven't lived? Someday I might have the courage to venture, not yet. Someday I'll—I'll paint the true Christ."

Terrence Malick might not think it, and certainly would not claim it, but he has always had the courage to venture, whether into the hinterlands of German philosophy, the jungles of Bolivia, or for that matter the hurly-burly of Hollyweird. In doing so, he has pushed cinema in new directions and invented new possibilities for the language of film. The idea of a comeback is ludicrous because it assumes that there is one place someone should be. It is a commercial consideration, not an artistic one. As Franz says from prison when offered a deal that would compromise his values in exchange for his freedom, "I'm already free." Malick could say the same.

Throughout his life, Malick has sought truth, pursued his inquiries, followed his vision, and asked simple yet unanswered questions, even at the danger of sounding naive or unfashionably earnest. But throughout his investigations, there are manifold opportunities for empathy, for awe. The hidden lives he reveals (including his own) are clothed in a light that comes with its very own magic. As he told Yvonne Baby in his last interview: "For an hour, or for two days, or longer, these films can enable small changes of heart, changes that mean the same thing: to live better and to love more. And even an old movie in poor and beaten condition can give us that. What else is there to ask for?"[38]

Acknowledgments

The idea of a book was first suggested by Pat McGilligan, whom I was interviewing for my podcast *Writers on Film*. His help and encouragement were fundamental. My editor was Ashley Runyon. I would like to thank all at the University Press of Kentucky, especially Margaret Kelly. Carlo Hintermann and Paul Maher Jr. were two writers who proved invaluable, having already ventured across the waters. Paul Cronin read the manuscript multiple times and gave me detailed advice and support. Other readers include Kaleem Aftab, Andy English, Lidia Garbin, Adrian Martin, Uwe Meyer, and Reno Lauro. Thanks also go to those who were willing to talk with me and generously gave me their time and insights: Brooke Adams, Numan Akar, Michael Benson, Tony Bill, Tatiana Chiellini, David Crank, August Diehl, Rick Drew, Jim Erikson, Jack Fisk, Keith Fraase, Nicolas Gonda, Shane Hazen, Karen Heck, Curtis Hessler, Carlo Hintermann, James Newton Howard, Olga Kurylenko, Mike Medavoy, Sabine Murray, Valerie Pachner, George Stevens Jr., Sophokles Tasioulis, Billy Weber, Paul Viktorin, Jörg Widmer, Paul Williams, John Womack, Michelle Olmstead, Hugues Fournier, and Nat Segaloff. I've also been supported and encouraged by my friends in the wider film-writing community: Raphael Abrams, Jo-Ann Titmarsh, Wendy Ide, Lee Marshall, Leigh Singer, Jonathan Romney, Nicholas Barber, James Mottram, Jason Solomons, Patrick Heidmann, Dave Calhoun, Damon Wise, Stephanie Banbury, Marta Bałaga, Leo Goi, Hugo Emmerzael, David Whitney, Ed Potton, Luke Hicks, David Rooney, and Stephen DeLay. It is always a pleasure to talk to people about Malick, as James Newton Howard told me: "Every time people talk about Terry, they start smiling."

Many libraries and librarians have proved an invaluable resource—libraries are the writer's secret weapon. Among them were Grace Dumelle at Newberry Library in Chicago; Debbie Neece and Denise Goff, Bartlesville Public Library; Sonia Schoenfield, Cook Memorial Library; Jessica Holden,

Acknowledgments

Joseph P. Healey Library; Cristina Meisner and Emily Wittenberg, AFI; Hannah Kubacak, Waco McLennan County Library; and Laura Youngstrum, Reddick Public Library District, Ottawa, Illinois. Michelle Olmstead and St. Stephen's were very helpful.

My British family—my mom, Rosaleen Bleasdale, and Francis and Catherine and their partners, Sharon and Neil, my nephews Joseph and Ben—as well as my Italian family, Angiolina, Nico, Mauro, Federico, Riccardo, Daniela, Aaron, Isacco, Aida, Alma, Beatrice, Filippo, and Ambra.

Finally, I must express my love and gratitude to the three women who made this book possible and to whom this book is dedicated: Lidia Garbin, Alice Bleasdale, and Rosaleen Joanne Bleasdale.

Notes

1. Beginnings (1943-1955)

1. Much of this information was garnered from Wikipedia, though it should be noted that recent discoveries of the James Webb Telescope are challenging the current dating and conceptual framework of the big bang.

2. Arianne Ishaya, "Assyrian-Americans: A Study in Ethnic Reconstruction and Dissolution in the Diaspora," Nineveh Online, accessed April 3, 2022, https://www.nineveh.com/ASSYRIAN-AMERICANS.html.

3. Ibid.

4. US Census Bureau, 1910 United States Federal Census, New Jersey, accessed July 11, 2022, https://www.ancestry.com/discoveryui-content/view/16772510:7884?tid=&pid=&queryId=93ad70ca46dedcd08e002f46b55c8bfa&_phsrc=NgS75&_phstart=successSource.

5. David Gaunt, *Massacres, Resistance, Protectors: Muslim-Christian Relations in Eastern Anatolia during World War I* (PiscatawayGorgias, 2006), 81–120.

6. Ibid.

7. Ishaya, "Assyrian-Americans."

8. "The Tree of Life" unpublished first draft, registered with the Writers Guild of America, June 25, 2005, script, 81 (hereafter cited as Script).

9. This scene appears in the extended edition of the film.

10. Massachusetts Institute of Technology, *MIT Yearbook* (Cambridge: Massachusetts Institute of Technology, 1936), 359.

11. Ibid., 10.

12. Mike Murphy, "Prominent Director Has Local Roots," *Daily Times* (Ottawa, Ill), January 14, 1999, 1.

13. Ibid.

14. *Washington Countion* (Dewey, OK), July 1, 1949.

15. Script, 30.

16. Script, 30.

17. Script, 39.

18. "Waco Tornado—May 11, 1953," National Weather Service, accessed July 11, 2022, https://www.weather.gov/fwd/wacotormay1953.

Notes to Pages 12–19

19. "School Notes," *Waco Tribune-Herald*, November 30, 1952, 54.

20. Script, 39.

21. "Five Awards in Picture Competition Announced," *Waco Tribune-Herald*, October 17, 1954, 31.

22. Susan Albert, quoted in Paul Maher Jr., *All Things Shining: an Oral History of the Films of Terrence Malick* (Self-Published, 2021), 96.

2. Schooling (1955-1968)

1. Jim Romberg, author's interview, March 2022.

2. Eric Benson, "The Not So Secret Life of Terrence Malick," *Texas Monthly*, April 2017, https://www.texasmonthly.com/arts-entertainment/the-not-so-secret-life-of-terrence-malick/.

3. Yvonne Baby, *Le Monde*, May 17, 1979, trans. Hugue Fournier in One Big Soul, Facebook Page, https://m.facebook.com/notes/395924798463893/?paipv=0&eav=Afa O1lRDlUm4v4YmSVykykE6YmAZe5uwKm98wYcBh41X3bgk87SCa8oByfeWp Hwt_1Y.

4. Bill Krohn, email to Adrian Martin, December 2005.

5. Romberg, interview.

6. Ibid.

7. "Spartans Begin 1957 Play Today," *Austin American*, September 20, 1957, 21.

8. Romberg, interview.

9. Terry Malick, "The Role of the Negro in Faulkner," *St. Stephen's Review*, May 1961, 17–19.

10. James Baldwin, "Faulkner and Desegregation," *Partisan Review*, 1956.

11. "Social and Local Personal Notes," *Evening News* (Harrisburg, PA), March 17, 1942, 8.

12. Romberg, interview.

13. "Ecky Wyatt-Brown Malick reported, 'Patrica Morrison '63, Terry Malick '61 and I are all living together in the dilapidated and now flooded Charlie Hotel in West Hollywood . . . what started as a short sprint to Napa (Bunny Run Vineyard of Rue Winterbotham Ziegler '63, and a tour of Grace Cathedral by Florence Owens Dodington '61) became a marathon in Los Angeles in March. Having Patricia on board has been a Godsend; she is my assistant and I am her laundress. Terry, being both footman and ox, developed back problems and thereby appealed to his old proctor Sam Todd '58, for relief. Sam reluctantly consented, waving his magic scepter and turning the laundress into the ox.'" "Alumni News," *Spartan Magazine*, Summer 2014, 30.

14. Craig Malisow, "Don't Ask, Don't Tell," *Houston Press*, May 21, 2009, https://www.bishop-accountability.org/news2009/05_06/2009_05_21_Malisow_Dont Ask.htm.

15. Romberg, interview.

16. Ibid.

17. Yvonne Baby, *Le Monde*.

18. Maher, *All Things Shining*, 96.

Notes to Pages 19–28

19. Romberg, interview.

20. "Terrence Malick Valedictorian of School in Texas," *Bartlesville (OK) Examiner Express*, May 7, 1961, 5.

21. Maher, *All Things Shining*, 101.

22. Sam Todd, quoted in Maher, *All Things Shining*, 101.

23. Billy Weber, author's interview, June 2022.

24. Jacob Brackman, quoted in Maher, *All Things Shining*, 102.

25. Melanie Y. Fu, "Terrence F. Malick '65: A Nontraditional Start to Filmmaking," *Crimson*, May 25, 2015, https://www.thecrimson.com/article/2015/5/25/terrence-malick-1965-profile/.

26. Carlo Hintermann et al., *Terrence Malick: Rehearsing the Unexpected* (London: Faber, 2016), 1.

27. Stanley Cavell, *The Claim of Reason: Wittgenstein, Scepticism, Morality and Tragedy* (Oxford: Clarendon, 1979), 125.

28. Stanley Cavell, *The World Viewed: Reflections on the Ontology of Film*, enlarged ed. (Cambridge, MA: Harvard University Press, 1979), xxiv.

29. Stanley Cavell, *Little Did I Know: Excerpts from Memory* (Stanford, CA: Stanford University Press, 2010), 426.

30. "Award Scholarship for Harvard Rating," *Chicago Tribune*, May 24, 1963.

31. Andrew Multer, "The Critic on Stage," *Crimson*, September 18, 1978, https://www.thecrimson.com/article/1978/9/18/the-critic-on-stage-pihe-knew/.

32. Stephen Most, quoted in Maher, *All Things Shining*, 104.

33. Ben W. Heineman Jr., "The Exception and the Rule," *Crimson*, February 29, 1964, https://www.thecrimson.com/article/1964/2/29/the-exception-and-the-rule-pbrecht/.

34. William Weld, quoted in Helen Thorpe, "The Man Who Wasn't There," *Texas Monthly*, December 1998, https://www.texasmonthly.com/articles/the-man-who-wasnt-there-2/.

35. Curtis Hessler, quoted in Fu, "Terrence F Malick '65."

36. John Womack Jr., *Zapata and the Mexican Revolution* (New York: Knopf, 1968).

37. John Womack Jr., author's correspondence, March 2022.

38. "There is also one fine, very pious performance as Mephistopheles in friar's robes by Andreas Teuber, an Oxford student." Renata Adler, *New York Times*, February 7, 1968.

39. Curtis Hessler, author's interview, June 2023.

40. William Weld, quoted in Thorpe, "The Man Who Wasn't There."

41. Hessler, interview.

42. Jon Lee Anderson, *Che Guevara: A Revolutionary Life* (New York: Bantam, 1997), 738–39.

43. Weber, interview.

44. The piece, which was published in the *New Yorker*, April 13, 1968, is a moving observation of the vigil in New York on Palm Sunday after the death of Dr. King.

45. Hintermann et al., *Rehearsing the Unexpected*, 4.

46. Carly Simon, *Boys in the Trees: A Memoir* (New York: Constable, 2015), 174.

Notes to Pages 28–37

47. Maher, *All Things Shining*, 97.

48. William Starling, *Strings Attached: The Life and Music of John Williams* (London: Robson, 2012).

49. Shaun Considine, "Terrence Malick and Badlands: An All American Triumph," *After Dark Magazine*, June 1974.

50. Hubert Dreyfus, quoted in Maher, *All Things Shining*, 116. Dreyfuss went on to title one of his books with a Terrence Malick quote. Hubert Dreyfus and Sean Kelly, *All Things Shining: Reading the Western Classics to Find Meaning in a Secular Age* (New York: Free Press, 2011).

51. Beverly Walker, "Malick on *Badlands*," *Sight and Sound* 44, no. 2 (Spring 1975): 82–83.

52. Terrence Malick, trans., *Heidegger's "The Essence of Reason"* (Evanston, IL: Northwestern University Press, 1969), 15.

53. Malick, *Heidegger*, 16.

54. Terrence Malick, interview by Joseph Gelmis, 1974 (hereafter cited as Gelmis interview).

3. Hollywood (1969-1971)

1. Andreas Teuber, quoted in Paul Maher Jr., *All Things Shining: an Oral History of the Films of Terrence Malick* (Self-Published, 2021), 113–16.

2. Jacob Brackman, "Why Do We Love *The Graduate*?," *New Yorker*, July 19, 1968.

3. Michel Ciment, "Entrietien avec Terrence Malick," *Positif*, June 1975.

4. Shaun Considine, "Terrence Malick and *Badlands*: An All American Triumph," *After Dark Magazine*, June 1974.

5. Beverly Walker, "Malick on *Badlands*," *Sight and Sound* 44, no. 2 (Spring 1975): 82–83.

6. George Stevens Jr., author's interview, February 2022.

7. Ibid.

8. Nat Segaloff papers, Margaret Herrick Library, Academy of Motion Picture Arts and Sciences.

9. Ibid.

10. Bernard Drew, "*Badlands* Bears Fruit for Young Director," *Journal News*, (New York), March 26, 1974, 15.

11. Bob Thomas, "Filmmaker Made His Movie the Hard Way," Associated Press, May 12, 1974.

12. Caleb Deschanel, author's interview, September 2023.

13. Terrence Malick, interview by Joseph Gelmis, 1974.

14. George Stevens Jr., *My Place in the Sun: Life in the Golden Age of Hollywood and Washington* (Lexington: University Press of Kentucky, 2022), 269.

15. Deschanel, interview.

16. Ibid.

17. Theresa Schwartzman, "Can Malick Tell a Joke?," *Rohstoff Filmmagazin*, captured February 7, 2012, https://web.archive.org/web/20120207092312/http://www.rohstoff-filmmagazin.org/contributions/Terence_Malick_Schwartzman.html.

238

Notes to Pages 38–48

18. Susan Compo, *Warren Oates: A Wildlife* (Lexington: University Press of Kentucky, 2009), 200.

19. Schwartzman, "Can Malick Tell a Joke?"

20. "Slayer Wanted to Be Somebody," *Los Angeles Times*, January 31, 1958, 1.

21. Compo, *Warren Oates*, 201.

22. Alex Cox, author's correspondence, July 2022.

23. Tony Bill, author's interview, July 2022.

24. Ibid.

25. Mike Mcdavoy, author's interview, July 2022.

26. Ibid.

27. Curtis Hessler, author's interview, May 2023.

28. Walker, "Malick on *Badlands*," 82.

29. Kershner went on to direct *The Empire Strikes Back* (1982) and *Never Say Never Again* (1983).

30. A draft script dated November 17, 1970, is credited to Terry Malick, John Milius, and H. J. Fink.

31. Don Siegel asserts that he and Dean Reisner rewrote the Fink script without using much of the Malick and Milius version. He credits himself with shifting the location to New York, regardless of the fact that Malick's script is set in San Francisco and he and Kershner scouted locations there. See Don Siegel, *A Siegel Film: An Autobiography* (London: Faber & Faber, 1996), 357–76.

32. Jack Fisk, author's interview, January 2023.

33. Hessler, interview.

34. Peter Bart, "Silence of the Malick: What's His Line?," *Variety*, December 20, 1998, https://variety.com/1998/voices/columns/silence-of-the-malick-what-s-his-line-1117489630/.

35. Irvin Kershner, quoted in Carlo Hintermann et al., *Terrence Malick: Rehearsing the Unexpected* (London: Faber, 2016), 9–13.

36. Erik Bauer, "I Was Never Conscious of Any of My Screenplays Having Acts, It's All Bullshit: John Milius," Creative Screenwriting, February 11, 2015, https://www.creativescreenwriting.com/i-was-never-conscious-of-my-screenplays-having-any-acts-its-all-bullshit-john-milius/.

37. Nat Segaloff papers.

38. Stevens, author's correspondence, April 2023.

4. *Badlands* (1971–1973)

1. See James Melvin Reinhardt, *The Murderous Trail of Charles Starkweather* (Springfield, IL: Charles C. Thomas, 1960); William Allen, *Starkweather: The Story of a Mass Murderer* (Boston; Houghton Mifflin, 1976); Ninette Beaver, *Caril* (Philadelphia: Lippincott, 1974); Michael Newton, *Waste Land: The Savage Odyssey of Charles Starkweather and Caril Ann Fugate* (New York: Pocket Books, 1998).

2. Shaun Considine, "Terrence Malick and *Badlands*: An All-American Triumph," *After Dark*, June 1974 reprinted, in Paul Maher Jr., *All Things Shining: an Oral History of the Films of Terrence Malick* (Self-Published, 2021), 32–37.

239

Notes to Pages 49–61

3. Michel Ciment, *Positif* (1975), translated by Laura Leeck and reproduced in Lloyd Michaels, *Terrence Malick* (Chicago: University of Illinois Press, 2009), 110.

4. Tony Bill, author's interview, May 2022.

5. Beverly Walker, "Malick on *Badlands*," *Sight and Sound* 44, no. 2 (Spring 1975): 82.

6. *AFI Filmmaker's Newsletter*, June 1974, reprinted in Maher, *All Things Shining*, 23–30.

7. Edward Pressman, *Making of "Badlands*," documentary (New York: Criterion, 2013), Blu-ray Disc, 1080p HD.

8. Jeff McArthur, *Pro-Bono: The 18-Year Defense of Caril Ann Fugate* (Burbank, CA: Bandwagon Books, 2012), 349.

9. Jack Fisk, author's interview, January 2023.

10. Billy Weber, author's interview, June 2022.

11. Quoted in Carlo Hintermann et al., *Terrence Malick: Rehearsing the Unexpected* (London: Faber, 2016), *Rehearsing the Unexpected*, 29.

12. *Making of "Badlands."*

13. Paul Williams, author's interview, February 2022.

14. Interview, *Rosy-Fingered Dawn: a Film on Terrence Malick*, directed by Luciano Barcaroli et al. (FilmAnnex, 2002).

15. Fisk, interview.

16. Gelmis interview, 17.

17. Ibid.

18. Ibid., 21.

19. Fisk, interview.

20. Gelmis interview, 21.

21. Robin Probyn, author's correspondence, June 2023.

22. Ciment, *Positif.*

23. Susan Compo, *Warren Oates: A Wildlife* (Lexington: University Press of Kentucky, 2009), 258.

24. John Womack Jr., author's correspondence, March 2022.

25. Fisk, interview.

26. Quoted in Nathanial Penn, "*Badlands*: An Oral History," *GQ*, May 26, 2011, https://www.gq.com/story/badlands-oral-history.

27. Fisk, interview.

28. Doug Knapp, quoted in Penn, "*Badlands.*"

29. Penn, "*Badlands.*"

30. Williams, interview.

31. Peter Biskind, *Easy Riders, Raging Bulls: How the Sex-Drugs-and-Rock 'N Roll Generation Saved Hollywood* (London: Simon and Shuster, 1998), 249.

32. Biskind, *Easy Riders, Raging Bulls.*

33. Fisk, interview.

34. Ibid.

35. George Stevens Jr., author's interview, May 2022.

Notes to Pages 61–70

36. Virginia Keathley, "Charlotte Got in the Act Too," *Tennessean* (Nashville), August 30, 1974, 55–56.

37. It was called "The Third Truth" but was never made.

38. Billy Weber, author's interview, June 2022.

39. Roger Ebert, "Pocket Money," review of *Pocket Money*, *Chicago Sun Times*, February 15, 1972.

40. Ray Bennett, "Pocket Money Is Not Much," *Windsor Star* (Ontario, Canada), March 7, 1972, 31.

41. John M. McInery, "Pocket Money," *Scranton (PA) Tribune*, April 8, 1972, 21.

42. Hintermann et al., *Rehearsing the Unexpected*, 72.

43. Penn, "*Badlands*."

44. Considine, "Terrence Malick and *Badlands*."

45. Vincent Canby, "Malick's Impressive *Badlands* Screened at Festival," *New York Times*, October 15, 1972.

46. Michel Ciment, author's interview, May 2022.

47. Bob Thomas, "Film Maker Made His Movie the Hard Way," Associated Press, May 12, 1974.

48. *Women's Wear Daily*, 1974 quoted in Helen Thorpe, "The Man Who Wasn't There," *Texas Monthly*, December 1998.

49. Walker, "Malick on *Badlands*," 82.

50. Reinhardt, *Murderous Trail*, 43–44.

51. Ibid., 22–23.

52. Walker, "Malick on *Badlands*," 82.

53. Pauline Kael, "The Current Cinema: *Sugarland* and *Badlands*," *New Yorker*, March 18, 1974, 130.

54. Quoted in Susan Goodman, "She Lost It at the Movies: Premier Film Critic Pauline Kael Takes a Tough Look at Life On Screen and Off," *Modern Maturity*, March/April 1998, 48.

55. David Thomson, *The New Biographical Dictionary of Film*, 6th ed. (London: Abacus, 1975–2014), 659–60.

56. Malvina Stephenson, "White House Aide Rockwell Is Cool in Middle of Crisis," *Tulsa Daily World* (OK), April 14, 1974, 18.

57. Considine, "Terrence Malick and Badlands," 37.

5. *Days of Heaven* (1973-1978)

1. G. Richardson Cook, "The Filming of *Badlands*: An Interview with Terry Malick," *Filmmakers Newsletter* 7, no. 8 (June 1974): 30–32.

2. Terrence Malick, interview by Joseph Gelmis, 1974.

3. Bernard Drew, "*Badlands* Bears Fruit for Young Director," *Journal News* (New York), March 26, 1974, 15.

4. AFI Masterclass, January 21, 1973, quoted in Paul Maher Jr., *All Things Shining: An Oral History of the Films of Terrence Malick* (Self-Published, 2021), 79.

5. George Stevens Jr, author's interview, February 2022.

Notes to Pages 70–82

6. Tony Bill, author's interview, May 2022.

7. Zodiac Killer, letter, May 8, 1974, https://en.wikisource.org/wiki/Zodiac_Killer
_letter,_May_8th_1974.

8. Ned Merrill, "The Gravy Train/The Dion Brothers (1974, Jack Starrett)," Blogspot,
February 5, 2009, https://knifeinthehead.blogspot.com/2009/01/gravy-trainthe-dion
-brothers-1974-jack.html.

9. Carlo Hintermann et al., *Terrence Malick: Rehearsing the Unexpected* (London:
Faber, 2016), 92.

10. Billy Weber, author's interview, June 2022.

11. John Travolta, interview, *Entertainment Weekly*, 1999 quoted in Rodrigo Perez,
"Terrence Malick Wanted John Travolta & 15 Things You Didn't Know About 'Days of
Heaven,'" Indiewire, June 9, 2011, https://www.indiewire.com/features/general
/terrence-malick-wanted-john-travolta-15-things-you-didnt-know-about-days
-of-heaven-118135/.

12. Paul Williams, author's interview, February 2022.

13. Hintermann et al., *Rehearsing the Unexpected*, 104.

14. Harry Knowles, "Stallone Answers December 9th & 10th Questions in a Double Round—Plus Harry's Seen ROCKY BALBOA at BNAT!!!," Ain't It Cool News,
December 16, 2006, http://legacy.aintitcool.com/node/30932.

15. John J. Winters, *Sam Shepard: A Life* (Berkeley, CA: Counterpoint, 2017),
193–94.

16. Brooke Adams, author's interview, January 2023.

17. Hintermann et al., *Rehearsing the Unexpected*, 108.

18. Linda Manz, interview by Bobbie Wygant, aired October 31, 1978, on KXAS-
TV (Dallas–Fort Wort Channel 5), UNT Libraries Special Collections.

19. Rebecca Bengal, "Catching Up with the Original Punk Rock Girl of Film," *New
York Times*, May 5, 2014, https://archive.nytimes.com/tmagazine.blogs.nytimes.com
/2014/05/05/now-screening-catching-up-with-the-original-punk-rock-girl-of-film/.

20. Jack Fisk, author's interview, February 2022.

21. Ibid.

22. Eric Benson, "The Not So Secret Life of Terrence Malick," *Texas Monthly*, April
2017, https://www.texasmonthly.com/arts-entertainment/the-not-so-secret-life-of
-terrence-malick/.

23. Adams, interview.

24. Néstor Almendros, *Man with a Camera*, trans. Rachel Philips (New York: Far-
rar, Straus, Giroux, 1984), 169.

25. Ibid., 171.

26. Weber, interview.

27. Almendros, *Man with a Camera*, 176.

28. Rick Drew, author's interview, August 2022.

29. John Bailey, *Shooting Days of Heaven* (New York: Criterion Collection, 2007),
Blu-ray Disc, 1080p HD.

30. Almendros, *Man with a Camera*, 177.

31. Ibid., 183.

Notes to Pages 82–91

32. James McNeill Whistler, "Mr Whistler's Ten O'Clock" (public lecture, Prince's Hall, Piccadilly, February 20, 1885).

33. R. Drew, interview.

34. Adams, interview.

35. Ibid.

36. Néstor Almendros, "Photographing Days of Heaven," trans. Hal Trusell, *American Cinematographer*, June 1979, https://theasc.com/articles/photographing-days-of-heaven.

37. Adams, interview.

38. Tom Buckley, "Star Claims Film's Story Lost in Cutting Room," *Indianapolis Star*, November 20, 1978.

39. Sam Shepard, *Shooting Days of Heaven* (New York: Criterion Collection, 2007), Blu-ray Disc, 1080p HD.

40. Ibid.

41. Adams, interview.

42. R. Drew, interview.

43. Shepard, interview.

44. R. Drew, interview.

45. Fisk, interview.

46. R. Drew, interview.

47. Almendros, *Man with a Camera*, 180.

48. Hintermann et al., *Rehearsing the Unexpected*, 124–25.

49. Weber, interview.

50. Ibid.

51. Nick Pinkerton, "Calling Linda Manz," *Village Voice*, June 1, 2011, https://www.villagevoice.com/2011/06/01/calling-linda-manz/.

52. Weber, interview.

53. Ibid.

54. Richard Gere, *Shooting Days of Heaven* (New York: Criterion Collection, 2007), Blu-ray Disc, 1080p HD.

55. Hintermann et al., *Rehearsing the Unexpected*, 144.

56. Yvonne Baby, *Le Monde*, May 17, 1979, trans. Hugue Fournier in One Big Soul, Facebook Page, https://m.facebook.com/notes/395924798463893/?paipv=0&eav=Afa OllRDlUm4v4YmSVykykE6YmAZe5uwKm98wYcBh41X3bgk87SCa8oByfeWpH wt_1Y.

57. Gregg Kilday, "Shedding Light on a Dark Horse," *Los Angeles Times*, August 9, 1978.

58. Harold C. Schonberg, "Days of Heaven," *New York Times*, September 14, 1978.

59. Monica Eng, "Days of Heaven," *Chicago Tribune*, October 9, 1978.

60. Pauline Kael, *5001 Nights at the Movies: A Guide from A to Z* (New York: Henry Holt, 1985), 137.

61. Dave Kerr, "Days of Heaven," *Chicago Reader*, May 10, 1985.

62. Gene Siskel, "Days of Heaven," *Chicago Tribune*, October 9, 1978.

63. Frank Rich, "Days of Heaven," *Time*, September 18, 1978.

Notes to Pages 91–100

64. Roger Ebert, "Days of Heaven," Roger Ebert, December 7, 1997, https://web
.archive.org/web/20070925050429/http://rogerebert.suntimes.com/apps/pbcs.dll/article
?AID=%2F19971207%2FREVIEWS08%2F401010327%2F1023.

65. Hintermann et al., *Rehearsing the Unexpected*, 140.

66. Baby, *Le Monde*.

67. Ibid.

68. Weber, interview.

69. "TERRENCE MALICK—TMZ Captures A Hollywood Bigfoot!," TMZ, June
13, 2012, https://www.tmz.com/2012/06/13/terrence-malick-benicio-del-toro-video
-director/.

70. David Handelman, "The Absence of Malick: Why Did Movie Director Terrence
Malick Disappear after His First Two Brilliant Movies?," *California Magazine*, November 1985.

71. Peter Biskind, "The Runaway Genius," *Vanity Fair*, December 1998.

6. Paris-Texas (1979-1995)

1. Jeanine Basinger, *The Star Machine* (New York: Knopf, 2007), 298.

2. Peter Bart, "The Silence of Malick, What's His Line?," *Variety*, December 20,
1998.

3. David Thomson, "Is *Days of Heaven* the Most Beautiful Film Ever Made?,"
Guardian, September 1, 2011, https://www.theguardian.com/film/2011/sep/01/days
-of-heaven-beautiful-film.

4. Mike Kaplan, "Encounters with Mike Hodges," HuffPost, March 22, 2013, https://
www.huffpost.com/entry/encounters-with-mike-hodg_b_2932422.

5. Thomas Chong, *Cheech and Chong: The Unauthorized Biography* (London:
Simon & Schuster, 2008), 180.

6. Mike Medavoy, author's interview, July 2022.

7. Peter Biskind, "The Runaway Genius," *Vanity Fair*, December 1998.

8. Quoted in Paul Maher Jr., *All Things Shining: an Oral History of the Films of Terrence Malick* (Self-Published, 2021).

9. Billy Weber, author's interview, June 2022.

10. Quoted in Carlo Hintermann et al., *Terrence Malick: Rehearsing the Unexpected*
(London: Faber, 2016), 147.

11. Jay West, "Interview with Visual Effects Supervisor Richard Taylor re: 1979's
Classic *Star Trek: The Motion Picture* plus RARE Behind the Scenes Production Images
from His Collection!," Beyond the Marquee, June 28, 2013, http://beyondthemarquee
.com/21991.

12. Weber, interview.

13. Joe Gillis, "Waiting for Godot," *Los Angeles*, December 1995, https://www
.eskimo.com/~toates/malick/art5.html.

14. Jacob Brackman and Irvin Kershner both referred to this script.

15. Weber, interview.

16. Biskind, "Runaway Genius."

17. Ibid.

Notes to Pages 100–119

18. Ibid.

19. Martin Sheen and Emilio Estevez, *Along the Way: The Journey of a Father and Son* (London: Simon & Schuster, 2012), 292–93.

20. Ibid., 292.

21. Ibid., 293.

22. Ibid., 293.

23. Jim Romberg, author's interview, March 2022.

24. Andrew Maranz, "The Terrence Malick–Lil Peep Connection," *New Yorker*, December 9, 2019, https://www.newyorker.com/magazine/2019/12/16/the-terrence-malick-lil-peep-connection.

25. Pat H. Broeske, "Days of Typing," *Los Angeles Times*, December 13, 1987, 12.

26. Ibid.

27. Medavoy, author's interview, July 2022.

28. Biskind, "Runaway Genius."

29. Ibid.

30. Terrence Malick, interview by Joseph Gelmis, 1974, 14.

31. D. M. Thomas, "Celluloid Dream," *Guardian*, August 24, 2004, https://www.theguardian.com/film/2004/aug/28/books.featuresreviews.

32. Joan Didion, "The Thin Red Line," *Vogue*, July 1964, https://archive.vogue.com/article/1964/7/movies.

33. Two drafts of "The English Speaker" are circulating on the internet. One has no date and is subtitled "First Draft revised," and the other is subtitled "Fourth Draft June 6, 2002" and has been registered with the Writers Guild.

34. Biskind, "Runaway Genius."

35. D. M. Thomas, *Bleak Hotel: The Hollywood Saga of the White Hotel Quartet* (London: Quartet Books., 2008).

36. Mary Williams Walsh, "Re-enter the Reluctant Dragon, Terrence Malick," *Los Angeles Times*, March 21, 1993, 170.

37. Quoted in Maher, *All Things Shining*, 225.

38. Michael Fleming, "Producers Face Life without Prestige Pix," *Variety*, January 31, 2000, https://variety.com/2000/voices/columns/producers-face-life-without-prestige-pix-1117775967/.

39. Sabina Murray, author's interview, October 2022.

40. Ibid.

7. *The Thin Red Line* (1995-1998)

1. James Jones, *WWII: A Chronicle of Soldiering* (Chicago: University of Chicago Press, 1976), 36.

2. James Jones, *The Thin Red Line* (New York: Scribners, 1962), vii.

3. Jones, *Chronicle*, 36–38.

4. Ibid., 40.

5. Ibid., 14.

6. Jack Fisk, author's interview, January 2023.

7. Mike Medavoy, author's interview, July 2022.

245

Notes to Pages 119–129

8. Tim Grierson, "Brendan Fraser Knows the Hurt—That's Why He Stands By *The Whale*," *Los Angeles Times*, February 28, 2023, https://www.latimes.com/entertainment-arts/awards/story/2023-02-27/brendan-fraser-knows-the-pain-of-the-whale.

9. Tom Shone, "Malick Gave *Good Will Hunting* Its Ending," *These Violent Delights*, January 5, 2011, https://tomshone.blogspot.com/2011/01/how-good-will-hunting-got-its-ending.html.

10. Nick Nolte, interview by James Mottram, February 1999.

11. To be precise, *The Thin Red Line* was a three-way coproduction among Phoenix Pictures, Geisler Roberdeau Productions, and Fox 2000.

12. Ken McCormick and Hamilton Darby, eds., *Images of War: The Artist's Vision of World War II* (New York: Orion Books, 1990).

13. Mary Blume, "Terrence Malick Is Back, with an Epic," *New York Times*, September 13, 1997, https://www.nytimes.com/1997/09/13/style/IHT-terrence-malick-is-back-with-an-epic.html.

14. Bruce Handy, "His Own Sweet Time," *Time*, October 13, 1997, https://content.time.com/time/subscriber/article/0,33009,987179-4,00.html.

15. Nick Nolte, *Making of: Actors* (New York: Criterion Collection, 2010), Blu-ray Disc, 1080p HD.

16. James Mottram, "The Prime of Mr Adrien Brody," *Independent*, April 21, 2001.

17. Nick Nolte, quoted in Paul Maher Jr., *All Things Shining: an Oral History of the Films of Terrence Malick* (Self-Published, 2021), 248.

18. Paul Maher Jr., "Pacific Hell amid Days of Heaven: Terrence Malick's *The Thin Red Line*," PopMatters, October 1, 2010, https://www.popmatters.com/terrence-malick-thin-red-line-2496138266.html.

19. Maher, "Pacific Hell."

20. "Audio commentary," *The Thin Red Line (1998)* (New York: Criterion Collection, 2010), Blu-ray Disc, 1080p HD.

21. Billy Weber, author's interview, June 2022.

22. Stephen Pizzello, "*The Thin Red Line*: The War Within," *American Cinematographer*, April 2021, https://theasc.com/articles/the-thin-red-line-the-war-within.

23. Weber, interview.

24. Arthur Penn, quoted in Carlo Hintermann et al., *Terrence Malick: Rehearsing the Unexpected* (London: Faber, 2016), 157.

25. Pizzello, "*Thin Red Line*."

26. Clyde H. Farnsworth, "A Director Who Dropped Out Drops Back In," *New York Times*, October 5, 1997, https://www.nytimes.com/1997/10/05/movies/film-a-director-who-dropped-out-drops-back-in.html.

27. Maher, "Pacific Hell."

28. Woody Harrelson, quoted in Richard T. Kelly, *Sean Penn: His Life and Times* (London: Faber, 2005), 335.

29. This cut has sometimes been mistaken for a lost director's cut of the film. It was not.

30. Unpublished screenplay, "Sanshō the Bailiff," 13.

Notes to Pages 129–140

31. Lee Nichols, "Going the Distance," *Austin Chronicle*, June 4, 1999, https://www .austinchronicle.com/screens/1999-06-04/522132/.

32. Leslie Woodhead, "Don't Mention the D Word" (Forman Lecture, University of Manchester, 1999), https://www.lesliewoodhead.com/dont-mention-the-d-word/.

33. Ibid.

34. Kristopher Tapley, "John C. Reilly on 'Sisters Brothers,' Working for Terrence Malick and Owing His Career to Sean Penn," *Playback* podcast, *Variety*, September 20, 2018, https://variety.com/2018/film/podcasts/playback-podcast-john-c-reilly-the-sisters -brothers-1202943708/.

35. Mottram, "Prime of Mr Adrien Brody."

36. Weber, interview.

37. Jonathan Romney, "Treading the Line," *Guardian*, February 26, 1999.

38. Roger Ebert, "The Thin Red Line," *Chicago Sun Times*, January 8, 1999.

39. Michael O'Sullivan, "Red Line: Above and Beyond," *Washington Post*, January 8, 1999.

40. Richard Schickel, "Cinema Ho Ho Well No," review of *The Thin Red Line*, *Time*, December 28, 1998.

41. Godfrey Cheshire, author's interview, December 2022.

42. Helen Thorpe, "The Man Who Wasn't There," *Texas Monthly*, December 1998.

43. Box office numbers are notoriously opaque. While not doing anywhere near the business of *Saving Private Ryan*, Malick's film made a profit and, likely, had very long legs in the ancillary markets. "The Thin Red Line," Box Office Mojo, accessed January 12, 2023, https://www.boxofficemojo.com/release/rl1735689729/weekend/.

8. *The New World* (1999-2005)

1. Paul Maher Jr., *All Things Shining: an Oral History of the Films of Terrence Malick* (Self-Published, 2021), 288.

2. Adam Dawtrey, "Malick 'Rocks' On: Director Wears Producer Hat on Interme-dia Pic," *Variety*, March 16, 2001, https://variety.com/2001/film/awards/malick-rocks -on-1117799530/.

3. Asif Kapadia, author's interview, October 2022.

4. Cathy Dunkley and Dana Harris, "Redford Taxis to National Geographic's *Aloft*," *Variety*, July 9, 2003, https://variety.com/2003/film/markets-festivals/redford-taxis-to -nat-l-geo-s-aloft-1117889102/.

5. Carlo Hintermann, author's interview, July 2022.

6. Marjorie Baumgarten, "In the 'Undertow' with Director David Gordon Green and First-Time Screenwriter Joe Conway," *Austin Chronicle*, November 12, 2004, https://www.austinchronicle.com/screens/2004-11-12/237323/.

7. Stephen Garett, "Southern Discomfort," *Filmmaker Magazine*, Fall 2004, https://www.filmmakermagazine.com/archives/issues/fall2004/features/southern _discomfort.php.

8. Wendy Mitchell, "DVD RE-RUN INTERVIEW: David Gordon Green Talks About 'Undertow,' His 'Southern Tall Tale,'" IndieWire, April 25, 2005, https://www

Notes to Pages 140–150

.indiewire.com/2005/04/dvd-re-run-interview-david-gordon-green-talks-about -undertow-his-southern-tall-tale-78274/.

9. Chris Neumer, "Nick Nolte & *The Beautiful Country*," *Stumped Magazine*, July 2005, https://www.stumpedmagazine.com/interviews/nick-nolte/.

10. Bai Ling, interview by Rebecca Carroll, *Independent*, July 1, 2005, https:// independent-magazine.org/2005/07/01/qa-bai-ling/.

11. Sabina Murray, author's interview, October 2022.

12. Marc Graser, "Pics Pumped at Ascendant," *Variety*, January 18, 2004, https:// variety.com/2004/film/markets-festivals/pics-pumped-at-ascendant-1117898672/.

13. Billy Weber author's interview, June 2022.

14. Alison James, "'Che' Fray Drives Firm Wild," *Variety*, March 8, 2004, https:// variety.com/2004/film/news/che-fray-drives-firm-wild-1117901405/.

15. Weber, interview.

16. *Making "The New World"* (NewYork: Criterion, 2016), Blu-ray Disc, 1080p HD.

17. Raoul Trujillo, author's interview, October 2022.

18. Carlo Hintermann et al., *Terrence Malick: Rehearsing the Unexpected* (London: Faber, 2016), 265.

19. David Crank, author's interview, April 2023.

20. *Making "The New World."*

21. Trujillo, interview.

22. Jörg Widmer, author's interview, December 2022.

23. Ibid.

24. Ibid.

25. Sarah Green, *Making "The New World."*

26. Widmer, interview.

27. Trujillo, interview.

28. Jim Erikson, author's interview, April 2023.

29. Crank, interview.

30. Jack Fisk, author's interview, February 2022.

31. *The Making "The New World."*

32. Nicolas Gonda, author's interview, November 2022.

33. James Horner, interview by Daniel Schweiger, Film Music Radio, September 26, 2006.

34. *The Making of "The New World."*

35. Bill Higgins, "It's Malick's World," *Variety*, December 19, 2005, https://variety .com/2005/scene/awards/it-s-malick-s-world-1117934959/.

36. Werner Herzog, email, February 2023.

37. Roger Ebert, "The Pocahontas Story Stripped Bare," RogerEbert.com, January 19, 2006, https://www.rogerebert.com/reviews/the-new-world-2006.

38. Paul Arendt, "The New World," BBC, January 26, 2006, https://www.bbc.co.uk /films/2006/01/17/the_new_world_2006_review.shtml.

39. Scott Foundas, "Back to the Garden," *LA Weekly*, December 22, 2005, https:// www.laweekly.com/back-to-the-garden-2/.

Notes to Pages 151–161

40. Stephanie Zacharek, "The New World," Salon, December 21, 2005, https://www.salon.com/2005/12/23/new_world/.

41. Mike Clark, "This 'New World' Not Worth Braving," *USA Today*, December 22, 2005, https://usatoday30.usatoday.com/life/movies/reviews/2005-12-22-new-world-review_x.htm.

42. Dick Stevens "INTERVIEW: Does Wes Studi Like *The New World*?," Coming Soon, January 10, 2006, https://www.comingsoon.net/movies/news/508895-interview_does_wes_studi_like_the_new_world.

43. Daily Beast, "Plummer: I'll Never Work with Him Again," YouTube, January 23, 2012, https://www.youtube.com/watch?v=xw08GQw0hBI.

44. Ibid.

45. Ibid.

46. Trujillo, interview.

47. Dick Stevens "Interview: Does Wes Studi Like 'The New World'?"

48. Mark Shilling, "Venture Makes Scents of 'World,'" *Variety*, April 10, 2006, https://variety.com/2006/film/markets-festivals/venture-makes-scents-of-world-1117941355/.

49. Fisk, interview.

50. David Davies, *The Thin Red Line*, Philosophers on Film (London: Routledge, 2009).

51. Gonda, interview.

52. Terrence Malick, quoted in Bin Chen, "Terrence Malick Interview: Rome Film Festival," You May Find Yourself, January 27, 2011, https://www.youmightfindyourself.com/post/2970761213/terrence-malick-interview-rome-film-festival.

9. *The Tree of Life* (2005–2011)

1. Aakanksha Naval-Shetye, "Guess Who's Coming to Town!," *Times of India*, May 17, 2006, https://timesofindia.indiatimes.com/bombay-times/guess-whos-coming-to-town/articleshow/1534117.cms.

2. Nyay Bhushan, "Percept Finds 'Life' with Malick Feature," *Hollywood Reporter*, August 31, 2005, https://web.archive.org/web/20080503123221/http://www.hollywoodreporter.com/hr/search/article_display.jsp?vnu_content_id=1001051294.

3. Bill Pohlad, author's interview, September 2022.

4. Variety Staff, "Malick 'Lights' on Saga," *Variety*, June 27, 2006, https://variety.com/2006/more/news/malick-lights-on-saga-1200336997/.

5. James Newton Howard, author's interview, March 2023.

6. Nicolas Gonda, author's interview, November 2022.

7. Pohlad, interview.

8. Gonda, interview.

9. Karen Heck, author's interview, June 2022.

10. Paul Viktorin, author's interview, June 2022.

11. Paul Maher Jr., *All Things Shining: An Oral History of the Films of Terrence Malick* (Self-Published, 2021).

Notes to Pages 161–173

12. Steve Rose, "Brad Pitt Talks about Terrence Malick and *The Tree of Life*," *Guardian*, June 30, 2011, https://www.theguardian.com/film/2011/jun/30/brad-pitt-interview-terrence-malick.

13. Ibid.

14. Brad Pitt, Cannes Press Conference, May 2011.

15. Jack Fisk, author's introduction, January 2023.

16. "The Tree of Life," *American Cinematographer*, August 2011.

17. Jörg Widmer, author's interview, December 2023.

18. Maher, *All Things Shining*, 359.

19. Matthew Odam and Charles Ealy, "Actors, Producers Know Different Sides to Malick," *Austin American-Statesman*, June 3, 2011, D1–4.

20. Gonda, interview.

21. Nigel Ashcroft, *The Tree of Life* Q&A chaired by Paul Appleby, Watershed, July 2011, https://www.watershed.co.uk/audio-video/the-tree-of-life-qa/.

22. Michael Benson, author's interview, October 2022.

23. Ibid.

24. Bill Dezowitz, "Cinematographer Emmanuel Lubezki Climbs *The Tree of Life*," IndieWire, February 10, 2012, https://www.indiewire.com/2012/02/immersed-in-movies-cinematographer-emmanuel-lubezki-climbs-the-tree-of-life-182992/.

25. Pohlad, interview.

26. Steven Zeitchik, "Will the Real Terrence Malick Please Stand Up?," *Los Angeles Times*, May 22, 2011, https://www.latimes.com/entertainment/la-xpm-2011-may-22-la-ca-terrence-malick-20110522-story.html.

27. Keith Fraase, author's interview, February 2023.

28. Shane Hazen, author's interview, April 2023.

29. Fraase, interview.

30. Ann Thompson, "Waiting for Malick," IndieWire, September 13, 2010, https://www.indiewire.com/2010/09/waiting-for-malick-which-film-fest-will-debut-tree-of-life-238429/.

31. Kaleem Aftab, "Jessica Chastain," *Interview*, November 18, 2010, https://www.interviewmagazine.com/film/jessica-chastain.

32. Matt Goldberg, "First Poster and Synopsis for Terrence Malick's *The Tree of Life*," Collider, November 3, 2010, https://collider.com/the-tree-of-life-movie-poster-synopsis-terrence-malick/.

33. FirstAndLastLook, "*The Tree of Life* Full Press Conference—Cannes Film Festival 2011," YouTube, May 24, 2012, https://www.youtube.com/watch?v=op4bSIibBmU.

34. Zeitchik, "Will the Real Terrence Malick Please Stand Up?"

35. Peter Bradshaw, "Cannes 2011 Review: *The Tree of Life*," *Guardian*, May 16, 2011, https://www.theguardian.com/film/2011/may/16/cannes-2011-the-tree-of-life-review.

36. Roger Ebert, "The Blink of a Life, Enclosed by Time and Space," Roger Ebert, June 1, 2011, https://www.rogerebert.com/reviews/the-tree-of-life-2011.

Notes to Pages 173–178

37. Todd McCarthy, "*The Tree of Life*: Cannes Review," *Hollywood Reporter*, May 16, 2011, https://www.hollywoodreporter.com/news/general-news/tree-life-cannes-review-188564/.

38. Geoffrey Macnab, "First Night: *The Tree of Life*, Cannes International Film Festival," *Independent*, May 17, 2011, https://www.independent.co.uk/arts-entertainment/films/reviews/first-night-the-tree-of-life-cannes-international-film-festival-2285000.html.

39. Lee Marshall, "The Tree of Life," *Screen Daily*, May 16, 2011, https://www.screendaily.com/the-tree-of-life/5027636.article.

40. Stephanie Zacharek, "Cannes Review: *Tree of Life* Is All about Life, but Does Malick Care Much for People?," *Movieline*, May 2011, http://movieline.com/2011/05/cannes-review-tree-of-life-is-all-about-life-but-does-malick-care-much-for-people.

41. Jason Zingale, "The Tree of Life," Bullz-eyer, June 2011, http://www.bullz-eye.com/mguide/reviews_2011/the_tree_of_life.html.

42. Ignatiy Vishnevetsky, "*The Tree of Life*: A Malickiad," Mubi Notebook, May 27, 2011, https://mubi.com/notebook/posts/the-tree-of-life-a-malickiad.

43. Terrence Malick, "Notice to Projectionists regarding *The Tree of Life*," https://aphelis.net/actual-copy-terrence-malicks-notice-projectionists-tree-life/.

44. Fernando Pellerano, "Proiezioni sfasate di «Tree of life» Ma nessuno (o quasi) se ne accorge," *Corriere di Bologna*, June 7, 2011, https://corrieredibologna.corriere.it/bologna/notizie/cultura/2011/7-giugno-2011/proiezioni-sfasate-tree-of-life-ma-nessuno-o-quasi-se-ne-accorge--190813663595.shtml.

45. Richard Brody, "Sean Penn vs Terrence Malick," *New Yorker*, August 21, 2011, http://www.newyorker.com/online/blogs/movies/2011/08/sean-penn-vs-terrence-malick.html#ixzz1d9v3mJqJ.

46. Jim Emerson, "Did Sean Penn Really Pee on *The Tree of Life*?," Roger Ebert, August 22, 2011 https://www.rogerebert.com/scanners/did-sean-penn-really-pee-on-the-tree-of-life.

47. Kevin Jagernauth, "Sean Penn Has Issues but Recommends *Tree of Life*; Malick Says 'Burial' Is 'Rushing toward a Mix,'" Playlist, August 22, 2011, https://www.indiewire.com/news/general/sean-penn-has-issues-but-recommends-tree-of-life-malick-says-burial-is-rushing-toward-a-mix-116787/.

48. Jeff Martin, "Family 'Tree,'" *Millions*, June 9, 2011, https://themillions.com/2011/06/family-tree.

10. *To the Wonder* (2010–2011)

1. These are the figures gathered from Box Office Mojo. *The Thin Red Line* made $97 million worldwide from a budget of $50 million; *The Tree of Life* made $58 million worldwide from a budget of $32 million. Neither of these would make much of a profit given that the marketing is not included in the budget, but the ancillary money in the prestreaming days would likely have been substantial. However, I'm being generous in using worldwide numbers rather than taking into account the domestic-international

Notes to Pages 179–188

split. *The New World* made $49 million worldwide from a $30 million budget. Further back, the figures are even more unclear. *Days of Heaven*'s $3.5 million worldwide doesn't seem to account for much of the international market. It only had a budget of $3 million. *Badlands* had a $300,000 budget, but no box office numbers are extant.

2. Nicolas Gonda, author's interview, November 2022.

3. Sophokles Tasioulis, author's interview, November 2022.

4. Jacob T. Swinney, "Not Directed by Terrence Malick," VIMEO, November 2, 2015, https://vimeo.com/144447762.

5. Nikki Finke, "Terry Malick Romances Next Drama Film," Deadline, February 3, 2010, https://deadline.com/2010/02/terry-malick-romances-next-drama-film-24408/.

6. "To the Wonder," *American Cinematographer*, April 2013.

7. Olga Kurylenko, author's interview, April 2023.

8. Jim Hemphill, "Lyrical Images: Emmanuel Lubezki on Shooting *To the Wonder*," *American Society of Cinematographers Magazine*, April 2013, https://theasc.com/ac_magazine/April2013/TotheWonder/page2.html.

9. Michael Smith, "Tulsans Invited to Audition for Hollywood Film," *Tulsa World*, August 17, 2010, https://tulsaworld.com/entertainment/movies/tulsans-invited-to-audition-for-hollywood-film/article_830dd5fa-b195-5431-88ba-f53af2bdd0d6.html.

10. Chris Heath, "Ben Affleck: Filmmaker of the Year 2012," GQ, November 15, 2012, https://www.gq.com/story/ben-affleck-cover-story-gq-men-of-the-year-2012.

11. Gonda, interview.

12. Kurylenko, interview.

13. Catherine Shoard, "Rachel McAdams: 'With a Terrence Malick Film There Will Be No Shortage of Beauty and Surprise,'" *Guardian*, February 14, 2013, https://www.theguardian.com/film/2013/feb/14/rachel-mcadams-malick-to-the-wonder.

14. Leah Zak, "Exclusive: Javier Bardem Talks the Sorrow, Joy of Being 'Biutiful' & Working with Terrence Malick," IndieWire, December 12, 2010, https://www.indiewire.com/2010/12/exclusive-javier-bardem-talks-the-sorrow-joy-of-being-biutiful-working-with-terrence-malick-121239/.

15. Tatiana Chiline, author's interview, October 2022.

16. Gonda, interview.

17. Hemphill, "Lyrical Images."

18. Heath, "Ben Affleck."

19. Kurylenko, interview.

20. Ibid.

21. Steven Zeitchik, "Will the Real Terrence Malick Please Stand Up?," *Los Angeles Times*, May 22, 2011, https://www.latimes.com/entertainment/la-xpm-2011-may-22-la-ca-terrence-malick-20110522-story.html.

22. Margaret Doody, "Introduction" to *Pamela (or Virtue Rewarded)*, ed. Samuel Richardson (London: Penguin, 2003), quoted in Bilge Ebiri, "Behind the Scenes: Radiant Zigzag Becoming; How Terrence Malick and His Team Constructed *To the Won-*

Notes to Pages 188–198

der," *Vulture*, April 18, 2013, https://www.vulture.com/2013/04/how-terrence-malick-wrote-filmed-edited-to-the-wonder.html.

23. David Calhoun, "To the Wonder," *Time Out*, February 18, 2013, https://www.timeout.com/movies/to-the-wonder.

24. Robbie Collins, "To the Wonder," *Daily Telegraph*, September 3, 2012, https://www.telegraph.co.uk/culture/film/venice-film-festival/9517129/Venice-Film-Festival-2012-To-The-Wonder-review.html.

25. Justin Chang, "To the Wonder," *Variety*, September 2, 2012, https://variety.com/2012/film/reviews/to-the-wonder-1117948163/.

11. The "Weightless Trilogy" and *The Voyage of Time* (2010–2016)

1. Nicolas Gonda, author's interview, November 2022.

2. Diana Lodderhose, "Bale, Blanchett to Star in Two Terrence Malick Pics," *Variety*, November 1, 2011, https://variety.com/2011/film/news/bale-blanchett-to-star-in-two-terrence-malick-pics-1118045399/.

3. Virginia Woolf, *The Waves* (Loondon: Hogarth Press, 1931), 212.

4. Robert Sinnerbrink, *Terrence Malick: Film Maker and Philosopher* (London: Bloomsbury, 2019), 162.

5. Freida Pinto, author's interview, December 2023.

6. Steve Weintraub, "Nick Offerman Talks *We're the Millers*, Working with Terrence Malick, Filming in London for *Parks and Recreation*, Cast Departures, and More," *Collider*, August 8, 2013, https://collider.com/nick-offerman-were-the-millers-parks-and-recreation-interview/.

7. Adam Chitwood, "Antonio Banderas Talks Terrence Malick's Process; Says He Thinks He Made the Cut and Reveals All the Footage Edited Together Could Be a Week Long," *Collider*, April 17, 2014, https://collider.com/terrence-malick-knight-of-cups-antonio-banderas/.

8. Diana Drumm, "NYFF: Cate Blanchett Talks the 'Quasi-Religious Experience' of Working with Terrence Malick, Woody Allen & More," IndieWire, October 5, 2013, https://www.indiewire.com/2013/10/nyff-cate-blanchett-talks-the-quasi-religious-experience-of-working-with-terrence-malick-woody-allen-more-92938/.

9. Emmanuel Lubezki, interview by E. Oliver Whitney, ScreenCrush, March 4, 2016, https://screencrush.com/emmanuel-lubezki-interview/.

10. Nicolas Gonda, interview.

11. Billy Goodykoontz, "Ryan Gosling on Terrence Malick: 'It's a Whole New Way of Working,'" *Arizona Star*, March 22, 2017, https://eu.azcentral.com/story/entertainment/movies/billgoodykoontz/2017/03/22/ryan-gosling-song-to-song-interview-terrence-malik/99504548/.

12. Ibid.

13. Christopher Rosen, "Ryan Gosling Explains What It's Like to Make a Terrence Malick Movie," *Entertainment Weekly*, March 23, 2017, https://ew.com/movies/2017/03/23/ryan-gosling-terrence-malick/.

Notes to Pages 201–207

14. Seven Seas Partnership v. Sycamore Pictures, No. 13 CV 5054 (S.D.N.Y. 2013). https://deadline.com/wp-content/uploads/2013/07/sevenseas-filedcomplaint__130 721190347.pdf.

15. Ben Child, "Terrence Malick Taken to Court for 'Forgetting' to Make Film," *Guardian*, July 22, 2013, https://www.theguardian.com/film/2013/jul/22/terrence-malick -sued-forgetting-to-make-film.

16. Steve Weintraub, "Emma Thompson Talks *Saving Mr. Banks*, Her Preparation Process, Getting Input from Richard Sherman, Terrence Malick's *Voyage of Time*, More," *Collider*, December 20, 2013, https://collider.com/emma-thompson-saving-mr -banks-interview/.

17. Sophokles Tasioulis, author's interview, November 2022.

18. Ibid.

19. Paul Maher Jr., *All Things Shining: An Oral History of the Films of Terrence Malick* (Self-Published, 2021), 509.

20. Ibid., 531.

21. Tasioulis, interview.

22. Keith Fraase, author's interview, November 2022.

23. Olga Kurylenko, author's interview, April 2023.

24. Nick Barber, "Terrence Malick's Worst Film Ever," BBC Culture, February 10, 2015, https://www.bbc.com/culture/article/20150210-terrence-malicks-worst-film -ever.

25. Richard Brody, "Terrence Malick's *Knight of Cups* Challenges Hollywood to Do Better," *New Yorker*, March 7, 2016, https://www.newyorker.com/culture/richard -brody/terrence-malicks-knight-of-cups-challenges-hollywood-to-do-better.

26. Kristi McKim, "Moving Away and Circling Back: On *Knight of Cups*," *New England Review* 39, no. 2 (2018): 61–72, 72.

27. Richard Brody, "Terrence Malick's Metaphysical Journey into Nature," *New Yorker*, September 8, 2016.

28. Robert Koehler, "*Voyage of Time: Life's Journey* (Terrence Malick, Germany)— Special Presentations," *Cinemascope*, September 2016.

29. Jessica Kiang, "Terrence Malick Has Made His Movie Again with *Voyage of Time: Life's Journey*," *Playlist*, September 6, 2016.

30. John Bleasdale, "Venice 2016: *Voyage of Time* Review," Cine-Vue, September 8, 2016, https://cine-vue.com/2016/09/venice-2016-voyage-of-time-review.html.

31. Justin Chang, "Review: Terrence Malick's *Voyage of Time* Offers a Gorgeous IMAX History of the Universe," *LA Times*, October 6, 2016.

32. "Made in Austin: Look into Song to Song," South by Southwest, Austin, Texas, March 11, 2017.

33. Wendy Ide, "*Song to Song* Review—Sprawling, Sexy, Shallow," *Observer*, July 9, 2017, https://www.theguardian.com/film/2017/jul/09/song-to-song-review-sprawling -sexy-and-shallow-terrence-malick-ryan-gosling-rooney-mara-fassbender.

34. Kevin Maher, "Film Review: *Song to Song*," *Times*, July 7, 2017, https://www .thetimes.co.uk/article/film-review-song-to-song-hmgqck0t3.

Notes to Pages 207–218

35. Stephanie Zacharek, "Tiny Dancers Abound in *Song to Song*," *Time*, March 23, 2017, https://time.com/4710633/ong-to-song-terrence-malick/.

36. Paul Schrader, quoted in Michael Nordine, "Paul Schrader Writes an Anatomical Review of Terrence Malick's *Song to Song*, and It Doesn't Involve Thumbs," IndieWire, May 27, 2017, https://www.indiewire.com/features/general/paul-schrader-reviews -terrence-malick-song-to-song-1201833222/.

37. Matt Zoller Seitz, "Song to Song," Roger Ebert, March 17, 2017, https://www .rogerebert.com/reviews/song-to-song-2017.

38. David Jenkins, "Review: *Song to Song*," IndieWire, July 7, 2017, https://lwlies .com/festivals/song-to-song-first-look-review/.

39. In Conversation with Brian Greene, Washington National Space and Air Museum, March 15, 2017.

40. Robert Koehler, "What the Hell Happened with Terrence Malick?," *Cinéaste* 38, no. 4 (2013): 4–9, http://www.jstor.org/stable/43500877.

41. David Ehrlich, "Cinema's Poet of Awe? or That Horny Kid in Your Directing Class?," *Slate*, March 3, 2016, https://slate.com/culture/2016/03/terrence-malicks -knight-of-cups-starring-christian-bale-reviewed.html.

12. *A Hidden Life* and *The Way of the Wind* (2015-2023)

1. For more on Franz Jägerstätter, see Gordon Zahn, *In Solitary Witness: The Life and Death of Franz Jägerstätter*, rev. ed. (Springfield, IL: Templegate, 1986); Erna Putz, *Franz Jägerstätter—Martyr: A Shining Example in Dark Times*, trans. Catherine Laura Danner (Grünbach, Upper Austria: Buchverlag Franz Steinmaßl, 2007).

2. Jason A. Schmidt and Ron Schmidt, dirs., *Franz Jägerstätter: A Man of Conscience* (Los Angeles: Hope Media Productions, 2009).

3. Franz Jägerstätter and Erna Putz, eds., *Franz Jägerstätter: Letters and Writings from Prison* (Maryknoll, NY: Orbis Books, 2009).

4. Jörg Widmer, author's interview, December 2022.

5. Jack Fisk, author's interview, February 2022.

6. George Eliot, *Middlemarch* (n.p.: Blackwood, 1871–1872).

7. Valerie Pachner, author's interview, February 2023.

8. August Diehl, author's interview, January 2023.

9. Pachner, interview.

10. Mitchell Beaupre, "Franz Rogowski on the Physicality of Great Freedom, the Meaning of Love, and the Draw of Auteur Cinema," Film Stage, March 2, 2022, https:// thefilmstage.com/franz-rogowski-on-the-physicality-of-great-freedom-the-meaning -of-love-and-the-draw-of-auteur-cinema/.

11. Diehl, interview.

12. Jörg Widmer, author's interview.

13. Franz Rogowski, quoted in Beaupre, "Franz Rogowski."

14. Pachner, interview.

255

Notes to Pages 219–229

15. Diehl, interview.

16. Pachner, interview.

17. James Newton Howard, author's interview, April 2023.

18. Ibid.

19. Terrence Malick, quoted by Martin Scorsese in American Academy of Religion, "Conversation with Religion and the Arts Awardee Martin Scorsese," YouTube, April 9, 2018, https://www.youtube.com/watch?v=k03xprfBI2A.

20. Chris O'Falt, "Terrence Malick Tries His Hand at Virtual Reality, and Becomes a First-Year Film Student," IndieWire, May 2018, https://www.indiewire.com/features /craft/terrence-malick-vr-together-1201960457/.

21. Terrence Malick, quoted in Chris O'Falt, "Criterion's *The Tree of Life* Is Not a Director's Cut, but a New Movie from Terrence Malick," IndieWire, August 2018, https://www.indiewire.com/features/craft/criterion-tree-of-life-terrence-malick-new -movie-1201999468/.

22. Philip Larkin, "This Be the Verse," in *High Windows* (London: Faber, 1974).

23. Andrew Marantz, "The Terrence Malick–Lil Peep Connection," *New Yorker*, December 9, 2019, https://www.newyorker.com/magazine/2019/12/16/the-terrence -malick-lil-peep-connection.

24. Matt Zoller Seitz, "A Hidden Life," Roger Ebert, December 13, 2019, https:// www.rogerebert.com/reviews/a-hidden-life-movie-review-2019.

25. Walter Chau, "A Hidden Life," September 12, 2019, FilmFreakCentral, https:// www.filmfreakcentral.net/ffc/2019/09/telluride-2019-a-hidden-life.html.

26. Sr. Bernadette Mary Reis, "*A Hidden Life*: Screening in the Vatican," Vatican News, December 5, 2019, https://www.vaticannews.va/en/world/news/2019-12 /hidden-life-malick-jagerstatter-film.html.

27. David Thomson, *The New Biographical Dictionary of Film*, 6th ed. (London: Abacus, 1975–2014).

28. Jonathan Kirshner, "A Very Acute Watcher: A Conversation with David Thomson," Los Angeles Review of Books, March 23, 2021, https://lareviewofbooks.org /article/a-very-acute-watcher-a-conversation-with-david-thomson/.

29. Leo Tolstoy, *The Gospel in Brief*, ed. with an introduction by F. A. Flowers (1892; repr., Lincoln, NE: Bison Books, 1997); Michael Pakaluk, *The Memoirs of Saint Peter: A New Translation of the Gospel of St. Mark* (Washington, DC: Regency Gateway, 2019).

30. Catherine Shoard, "Mark Rylance to Play Four Versions of Satan for Terrence Malick," *Guardian*, September 9, 2019, https://www.theguardian.com/film/2019 /sep/09/mark-rylance-satan-terrence-malick-geza-rohrig-matthias-schoenaerts-the -last-planet.

31. Numan Acar, author's interview, December 2022.

32. Ibid.

33. Ibid.

34. Dodd Vickers, "Markus Bensch," *Locations on Two Podcast*, YouTube, November 8, 2020, https://youtu.be/jZAZCRq1qSU.

35. Howard, interview.

Notes to Pages 230–231

36. Zach Baron, "Harmony Korine's Hi-Tech Vision for the Future of Movies," *GQ*, August 23, 2023, https://www.gq.com/story/harmony-korine-lord-of-the-edge.

37. Francis Ford Coppola, "Happy Belated Birthday," Instagram, December 2, 2023, https://www.instagram.com/francisfordcoppola/p/C0XFT0lpOdy/.

38. Yvonne Baby, *Le Monde*, May 17, 1979, trans. Hugue Fournier in One Big Soul, Facebook Page, https://m.facebook.com/notes/395924798463893/?paipv=0&eav=Afa O1lRDlUm4v4YmSVykykE6YmAZc5uwKm98wYcBh41X3bgk87SCa8oByfeWpH wt_1Y.

Index

Acar, Numan, 228
Affleck, Ben, 106, 120, 182–87, 223
Alfred, William, 23
Almendros, Néstor, 79–82, 84–86, 90–92, 100, 145
Alpert, Richard, 22
American Film Institute (AFI), 33–39, 41, 44, 48, 52, 58, 67–69, 118, 134, 150, 168, 207
Antonioni, Michelangelo, 40, 106, 120, 193, 195, 210
Arendt, Hannah, 23–24
Arkin, Alan, 43, 49
Ashby, Hal, 40
Atkins, Paul, 202, 204

Baby, Yvonne, 92, 231
Badlands (1973), 1, 10–11, 17, 21, 23, 34, 38; making of and reception, 45–74, 76, 79–81, 85, 90–93, 96, 99, 103, 145, 156, 210, 218, 230
Baldwin, Dona, 53
Baldwin, James, 16
Baldwin, Janit, 58, 67
Bale, Christian, 6, 105, 106, 143, 146, 179, 181, 182, 192–97
Bardem, Javier, 22, 141, 181, 183, 186–87, 223
Bart, Peter, 43, 49, 95
Beatty, Warren, 34–35
Beautiful Country, The (2004), 115, 138–40
Bergman, Ingmar, 16, 35, 109
Bill, Tony, 38–39, 49, 64, 70, 233
Biskind, Peter, 60–61, 89, 94, 96, 100, 103–4, 109–11, 135, 177, 185

Blanchett, Cate, 179, 192, 195–96, 198, 202, 205–7, 230
Bluhdorn, Charles, 94, 96–99, 102
Brackman, Jacob, 22–25, 27–28, 31–33; coproducing *Badlands*, 50, 63; coproducing *Days of Heaven*, 72, 74, 76, 79, 81, 87, 97, 193, 197
Brando, Marlon, 43, 74, 150
Brecht, Bertolt, 22
Brody, Adrien, 119, 123, 131–32, 152
Buckley, Kevin, 25
Bujold, Geneviève, 77
Burton, Richard, 24, 32, 77

Calley, John, 39
Caron, Leslie, 34, 40
Cassavetes, John, 35, 48
Castro, Fidel, 74, 79, 141, 153
Cavell, Stanley Louis, 20–25, 33, 36
Caviezel, Jim, 119, 123–27, 129, 136, 155, 220
Chaplin, Ben, 119, 127, 129, 143, 147
Chastain, Jessica, 160–64, 172–73, 180, 186
Chomsky, Noam, 31
Ciment, Michel, 49, 64, 173
Clooney, George, 118, 131–32, 152
Cohen, Rob, 104–5
Conway, Joe, 115, 139–40
Coppola, Francis Ford, 33, 40, 74, 90, 92, 134, 230
Coppola, Sofia, 155
Corman, Roger, 52
Costa-Gavras (Konstantinos Gavras), 26
Cox, Alex, 39–40
Crittenden, Dianne, 53–54, 59, 76–78, 119

259

Index

Damon, Matt, 120, 182

Daniel, Frank, 34

Days of Heaven (1978), 1, 6, 8, 10; inspiration for, 15–18, 38; making of and reception, 70–99, 112, 125, 133, 145–49, 162, 210, 214, 224

Deadhead Miles (1973), 39, 43–44, 49–50

Dean, James, 33, 54, 57, 73

Debray, Régis, 26

Demme, Jonathan, 52

De Niro, Robert, 54, 76, 175

Deschanel, Caleb, 34–38

Diehl, August, 6, 215, 217–19, 224

Dirty Harry (1971), 41, 43, 48, 50, 71

Drew, Rick, 81, 85

Dreyfus, Hubert, 30

Duvalier, François, 26, 74

Eastwood, Clint, 41–43, 50

Ebert, Roger, 62, 91, 132, 150, 173

Edwards, A. J., 155, 160, 171, 180, 199, 223

Endurance (1998), 129, 131, 138

Endurance, The (2000), 138

Estevez, Emilio, 55, 58, 119

Estevez, Ramon, 55

Evolver (2022), 230

Fassbender, Michael, 153, 197–98, 207–8

Faria, Reita, 25, 195

Faulkner, William, 16–17

Fellini, Federico, 35, 106, 156, 193–94

Fisk, Jack: work on *Badlands*, 52–53, 55–59, 61–62; work on *Days of Heaven*, 78–79, 81, 88, 94; work on *The New World*, 139, 142–43, 148, 153, 155; work on *The Thin Red Line*, 118, 121, 123, 127, 135; work on *The Tree of Life*, 161–62, 164; work on *To the Wonder*, 179, 182, 184, 195–96, 213

Fonda, Jane, 40

Fonda, Peter, 54, 71

Ford, John, 35, 200

Fugate, Caril Ann, 45–47, 51–52, 66–67

Fujimoto, Tak, 56–57, 60–61

Gelmis, Joseph, 31, 70, 106

Gere, Richard, 76–77, 79–80, 82–84, 88, 90, 119, 147, 162

Gibson, Mel, 121, 155, 158, 220

Glass, Dan, 166, 202

Gleason, Michie, 99–100

Godard, Jean-Luc, 26, 34, 188, 197–98, 210

Gonda, Nicolas, 148, 155, 159, 160, 163–64, 178, 180–82, 184, 188; "Weightless Trilogy," 192, 195–96, 203

Gosling, Ryan, 106, 141, 179, 192–93, 196–98

Gottlieb, Carl, 42

Gravy Train, The (a.k.a. *The Dion Brothers*) (1974), 71

Green, David Gordon, 71, 140, 155

Grogan, Clem, 48

Guerin, Ann Dewey, 15, 17

Guevara, Ernesto "Che," 26–28, 34, 74, 141, 153

Gulager, Clu, 37

Harrelson, Woody, 118, 126–27

Heidegger, Martin, 20, 21, 23–25, 30–31, 48, 63, 105, 153, 183, 211, 221, 226

Hellman, Monte, 40

Herba, Felipe, 72, 156

Herzog, Werner, 68, 150, 188

Hessler, Curtis, 23–24, 43

Hidden Life, A (2019), 6, 22; making of and reception, 212–21, 224–27, 230

Hill, Grant, 122–23, 138, 158, 166, 173, 215

Hines, John Elbridge, 14

Hiss, Alger, 44

Hitchcock, Alfred, 35, 106, 200

Hodges, Mike, 96

Hoffman, Dustin, 73, 76

Hopper, Dennis, 73

Horner, James, 149–50, 153, 158, 166

Hudson, Rock, 39, 78

Husserl, Edmund, 21, 23, 30

Ivory, James, 120

Jägerstätter, Franz, 212–16, 224

Jakes, Jill Bowman, 34–36, 43, 48, 60–62, 64, 66, 79, 104, 149, 195

Jarre, Maurice, 35, 168

Jensen, Robert, 46–47

Index

Jervey, Lingard. *See* Malick, Terrence
Johnson, Don, 54
Jolie, Angelina, 160, 173, 175, 215, 221

Kael, Pauline, 44, 67–68, 90, 151, 210
Kapadia, Asif, 138–39, 155
Kazan, Elia, 33
Kennedy, Theodore, 36
Kershner, Irvin, 41–44, 63
Kierkegaard, Søren, 25, 211, 214
Kilcher, Q'orianka, 6, 18; casting of *The New World*, 167, 170, 208
Klein, Saar, 131, 148, 150, 155
Knight of Cups (2015), 1; as autobiography, 25, 41, 70, 105, 164, 174, 180; making of and reception, 192–94, 198–207, 210–11, 226
Kottke, Leo, 88–89
Korine, Harmony, 155, 229–30
Kubrick, Stanley, 37, 64, 70, 95–96, 134, 144, 153, 174
Kurylenko, Olga, 101, 182–84, 186, 188, 198, 205

Lanton Mills (1969), 13, 48–51, 54, 56, 61, 64, 83–84, 110, 120, 224
Larner, Stevan, 57, 61, 63
LaRue, Lash, 37
Leary, Timothy, 22
Ledger, Heath, 158, 160
Lee, Paul, 22, 23, 200
Lil Peep (Gustav Åhr), 223
Loach, Ken, 56, 224
Lowell, Robert, 23
Lucas, George, 40, 92, 134, 192
Lynch, Austin, 146
Lynch, David, 34, 44, 52, 89, 97, 134, 219

Malick, Abimelech, 2–5, 8, 98, 222
Malick, Christopher Barry, 10–11, 14, 170
Malick, Emil Avimalg, 5; death of, 200; family, 16–19, 21, 29, 50, 59, 66, 104, 110, 123, 153, 157, 170, 177, 185; marriage with Irene, 7–14
Malick, Freydon, 3, 4, 9
Malick, Lawrence Raymond, 9; closeness to Terrence Malick, 11–12, 14, 18;

death of, 28–29, 157, 159, 169, 170, 177, 190, 209
Malick, Terrence Frederick: at AFI, 31–45; early life, 1, 2, 4–10; Harvard, time at, 19–33, 200; journalism, time in, 25–28; Oxford, time at, 23–25; schooling, 14, 16–31. *See also entries for individual films*
Manz, Linda, 38, 77, 83, 86–87, 92–93, 221, 229
Mara, Rooney, 192, 197–98
Marvin, Lee, 49–50, 54, 62–63, 71
McAdams, Rachel, 6, 181, 183
McBride, Jim, 102–3
McQueen, Steve, 43, 62
Medavoy, Mike: *Great Balls of Fire*, 102–3, 108, 112–13; as Malick's agent, 40–42, 44, 50, 62, 70, 73, 96; *The Thin Red Line*, 118–19, 122, 138
Melcherd, Jim, 15, 17
Meyer, August, 46
Mihok, Dash, 127, 129
Milius, John, 41–43, 90
Morette, Michèle Marie, 100–104, 107–10, 113, 121–22, 136, 181–82, 185–86, 190, 193, 210
Morricone, Ennio, 88–91, 149, 158, 204
Most, Stephen, 22
Murray, Sabina, 114–15, 130, 138, 140

Newman, Paul, 49, 62–63, 71
New World, The (2005), 3, 105; making of and reception, 137–56, 157, 161–63, 166–67, 178, 180, 184, 202
Nicholson, Jack, 41, 72–73
Nolan, Christopher, 155, 182, 219
Nolte, Nick, 118, 120–24, 128–29, 132, 140
Norris, Patricia, 79, 81, 91

Oates, Warren, 37–40, 50, 52–53, 55, 58, 76

Pachner, Valerie, 6, 215–19, 224
Peckinpah, Sam, 37, 40
Penn, Arthur, 34–37, 44, 50, 52, 60, 126, 223

Index

Penn, Sean: in *The Thin Red Line*, 118–19, 121, 123–26, 129, 131–32, 139, 156; in *The Tree of Life*, 159, 164, 168, 171–73, 175–76, 179
Pinto, Freida, 25, 195
Plummer, Christopher, 132, 143, 146; criticism of Malick, 151–53
Polanski, Roman, 48, 51
Portman, Natalie, 179, 195–98, 206; coproducing *The Seventh Fire* with Malick, 222
Pressman, Edward, 50–51, 59–60, 67, 112–14, 129, 158
Probyn, Brian, 56–57

Quaid, Dennis, 76, 102
Quintard, Mary Shepherd, 17

Ray, Michèle, 26–27
Redford, Robert, 56, 223
Reger, Larry, 51
Reilly, John C., 127, 131
Reinhardt, James, 65
Resnais, Alain, 22, 193, 210
Roberdeau, John, 106–9, 111–14, 117–19, 122, 138
Röhrig, Géza, 227
Romberg, James, 42–43, 102
Rosenberg, Stuart, 49, 62
Rosenblatt, Rand, 22
Rubin, Gerry, 111, 113, 118, 137–38
Rusk, Dean, 29
Ryan, Paul, 81, 88, 91–92, 97–98, 106, 123
Rylance, Mark, 228
Ryle, Gilbert, 24–26

Sandhaus, Richard, 99
Sargis, Nanajohn, 3–5, 8, 53, 98
Sartre, Jean-Paul, 15
Saving Private Ryan (1998), 117, 128, 130–33
Schneider, Bert, 73–75, 81, 88, 91, 100, 103, 193
Schneider, Harold, 78, 81, 86, 88
Schrader, Paul, 34, 134, 207
Schultz, Jackie, 77, 86
Scorsese, Martin, 133, 134, 155, 220
Sebring, Jay, 48

Segal, George, 35
Segaloff, Nat, 34, 233
Segovia, Andrés, 28–29
Seitz, Matt Zoller, 207, 224
Shakespeare, William, 15
Shaw, Fiona, 9, 163
Shaw, Robert, 41
Shawn, Wallace, 27, 76
Shawn, William, 27, 36, 67
Sheen, Charlie, 55, 58
Sheen, Janet, 55
Sheen, Martin, 6; in *Badlands*, 54–56, 59, 60, 66; meeting with Malick in Paris, 82, 101, 107, 119, 139, 213
Shepard, Sam, 76, 79, 83–84, 88, 119
Simon, Carly, 27–28, 72, 193, 197
Sinatra, Frank, 39, 74
Song to Song (2017), 1, 10, 103, 153, 180, 193; making of and reception, 196–201, 206–11, 223–24
Spacek, Mary Elizabeth ("Sissy"), 10, 53–56, 58–59, 63, 65, 67, 82, 88, 119, 139, 142
Spielberg, Steven, 40, 44, 67, 68, 70, 92, 117, 128, 130, 133, 134, 142, 181, 228
Stahl, Nick, 119, 131
Stallone, Sylvester, 73, 76
Stanton, Harry Dean, 37–39
Starkweather, Charles, 38, 45, 47–48, 51–54, 65–67
Stevens, George, 32, 35
Stevens, George, Jr., 32–33, 36, 44, 61, 70, 118, 122
Strasberg, Lee, 53, 77
Stroller, Lou, 59–61
Studi, Wes, 143, 146, 151–53

Tarantino, Quentin, 34, 71, 121, 215
Tarkovsky, Andrei, 68
Tasioulis, Sophokles, 179, 203, 205
Tate, Sharon, 36–37, 48
Taylor, Elizabeth, 24, 32, 35
Taylor, Richard, 97–98, 100
Teuber, Andreas, 24, 32
Thin Red Line, The (1998), xi, 1, 6, 21, 95, 107–15; making of and reception, 116–36, 137–38, 145, 151–54, 158, 170, 204–5, 210, 214, 221

262

Index

Thompson, Emma, 201–2
Thompson, Irene, 5–11, 18, 29, 170, 177
Thompson, John, 5
Thompson, Josephine, 9
Thompson (O'Brien), Katherine "Kettie," 5, 7, 9–10, 163
Thomson, David, 68, 96, 227
Thoreau, Henry David, 20
Tillich, Paul, 21–22, 175
Tipton, George, 63
Tipton, Jennifer, 114
Todd, Samuel, 14, 17, 19
To the Wonder (2012), 1, 6, 22, 97; as autobiography, 100–104, 110; making of and reception, 178–91, 192–94, 197–204, 206, 210–11
Travolta, John, 73, 76–77, 90, 119–20, 128
Tree of Life, The (2011), xi–xii, 1; as autobiography, 6–13, 29, 38, 100, 103, 105, 111; extended cut of, 222; making and reception of, 157–77, 178–83, 187–88, 190–91, 200–204, 208–10
Truffaut, François, 16, 34, 40, 64, 79–80, 86, 90, 160, 188, 197, 210
Trujillo, Raoul, 142–44, 146, 152, 155
Tucker, James Lydell, 17–18, 22

Undertow (2004), 115, 139–40

Voyage of Time (2016), 105, 158, 179, 193, 199–208, 225

Wallace, Will, 122, 127, 164
Wajda, Andrzej, 109, 113–14
"Way of the Wind," 227–30
Weber, Billy, 62–63, 72, 80, 86–88, 97, 99, 119, 125, 128, 131–32, 141, 155, 167
Weinstein, Paula, 73, 102
Weld, William, 23
Wexler, Haskell, 86, 88, 91
Whitelaw, Sandy, 40–41
Whitney, David. *See* Malick, Terrence
Williams, John, 28
Williams, Paul, 50, 54, 56, 60–62, 74, 233
Wittgenstein, Ludwig, 20, 23, 25
Womack, John, Jr., 23, 24, 32, 58, 213, 233
Womack, Liza, 102, 223–24
Woodhead, Leslie, 129–30
Wurlitzer, Rudy, 40, 76
Wyatt-Brown, Alexandra "Ecky": assisting Malick with filmmaking, 147–48, 156, 163, 177, 181–83, 188, 200, 218, 229; marriage with Malick, 136; renewed romance with Malick, 115, 121–22; at St. Stephen's, 17

Yoshikawa, Mark, 148–50, 155, 158, 167, 187, 199

Zacharek, Stephanie, 151, 174, 207
Zimmerman, Vernon, 39, 49

Screen Classics

Screen Classics is a series of critical biographies, film histories, and analytical studies focusing on neglected filmmakers and important screen artists and subjects, from the era of silent cinema through the golden age of Hollywood to the international generation of today. Books in the Screen Classics series are intended for scholars and general readers alike. The contributing authors are established figures in their respective fields. This series also serves the purpose of advancing scholarship on film personalities and themes with ties to Kentucky.

Series Editor
Patrick McGilligan

Books in the Series

Olivia de Havilland: Lady Triumphant
  Victoria Amador
Mae Murray: The Girl with the Bee-Stung Lips
  Michael G. Ankerich
Harry Dean Stanton: Hollywood's Zen Rebel
  Joseph B. Atkins
Hedy Lamarr: The Most Beautiful Woman in Film
  Ruth Barton
Rex Ingram: Visionary Director of the Silent Screen
  Ruth Barton
Conversations with Classic Film Stars: Interviews from Hollywood's Golden Era
  James Bawden and Ron Miller
Conversations with Legendary Television Stars: Interviews from the First Fifty Years
  James Bawden and Ron Miller
They Made the Movies: Conversations with Great Filmmakers
  James Bawden and Ron Miller
You Ain't Heard Nothin' Yet: Interviews with Stars from Hollywood's Golden Era
  James Bawden and Ron Miller
Charles Boyer: The French Lover
  John Baxter
Von Sternberg
  John Baxter
Hitchcock's Partner in Suspense: The Life of Screenwriter Charles Bennett
  Charles Bennett, edited by John Charles Bennett
Hitchcock and the Censors
  John Billheimer
The Magic Hours: The Films and Hidden Life of Terrence Malick
  John Bleasdale
A Uniquely American Epic: Intimacy and Action, Tenderness and Violence in Sam Peckinpah's The Wild Bunch
  Edited by Michael Bliss
My Life in Focus: A Photographer's Journey with Elizabeth Taylor and the Hollywood Jet Set
  Gianni Bozzacchi with Joey Tayler
Hollywood Divided: The 1950 Screen Directors Guild Meeting and the Impact of the Blacklist
  Kevin Brianton

He's Got Rhythm: The Life and Career of Gene Kelly
Cynthia Brideson and Sara Brideson
Ziegfeld and His Follies: A Biography of Broadway's Greatest Producer
Cynthia Brideson and Sara Brideson
Eleanor Powell: Born to Dance
Paula Broussard and Lisa Royère
The Marxist and the Movies: A Biography of Paul Jarrico
Larry Ceplair
Dalton Trumbo: Blacklisted Hollywood Radical
Larry Ceplair and Christopher Trumbo
Warren Oates: A Wild Life
Susan Compo
Helen Morgan: The Original Torch Singer and Ziegfeld's Last Star
Christopher S. Connelly
Improvising Out Loud: My Life Teaching Hollywood How to Act
Jeff Corey with Emily Corey
Crane: Sex, Celebrity, and My Father's Unsolved Murder
Robert Crane and Christopher Fryer
Jack Nicholson: The Early Years
Robert Crane and Christopher Fryer
Anne Bancroft: A Life
Douglass K. Daniel
Being Hal Ashby: Life of a Hollywood Rebel
Nick Dawson
Bruce Dern: A Memoir
Bruce Dern with Christopher Fryer and Robert Crane
Intrepid Laughter: Preston Sturges and the Movies
Andrew Dickos
The Woman Who Dared: The Life and Times of Pearl White, Queen of the Serials
William M. Drew
Miriam Hopkins: Life and Films of a Hollywood Rebel
Allan R. Ellenberger
Vitagraph: America's First Great Motion Picture Studio
Andrew A. Erish
Jayne Mansfield: The Girl Couldn't Help It
Eve Golden
John Gilbert: The Last of the Silent Film Stars
Eve Golden
Strictly Dynamite: The Sensational Life of Lupe Velez
Eve Golden
Stuntwomen: The Untold Hollywood Story
Mollie Gregory
Jean Gabin: The Actor Who Was France
Joseph Harriss
Yves Montand: The Passionate Voice
Joseph Harriss
The Herridge Style: The Life and Work of a Television Revolutionary
Robert Herridge, edited and with an introduction by John Sorensen
Otto Preminger: The Man Who Would Be King, updated edition
Foster Hirsch
Saul Bass: Anatomy of Film Design
Jan-Christopher Horak
Lawrence Tierney: Hollywood's Real-Life Tough Guy
Burt Kearns

Hitchcock Lost and Found: The Forgotten Films
Alain Kerzoncuf and Charles Barr
Pola Negri: Hollywood's First Femme Fatale
Mariusz Kotowski
Ernest Lehman: The Sweet Smell of Success
Jon Krampner
Sidney J. Furie: Life and Films
Daniel Kremer
Albert Capellani: Pioneer of the Silent Screen
Christine Leteux
A Front Row Seat: An Intimate Look at Broadway, Hollywood, and the Age of Glamour
Nancy Olson Livingston
Ridley Scott: A Biography
Vincent LoBrutto
Mamoulian: Life on Stage and Screen
David Luhrssen
Maureen O'Hara: The Biography
Aubrey Malone
My Life as a Mankiewicz: An Insider's Journey through Hollywood
Tom Mankiewicz and Robert Crane
Hawks on Hawks
Joseph McBride
John Ford
Joseph McBride and Michael Wilmington
Showman of the Screen: Joseph E. Levine and His Revolutions in Film Promotion
A. T. McKenna
William Wyler: The Life and Films of Hollywood's Most Celebrated Director
Gabriel Miller
Raoul Walsh: The True Adventures of Hollywood's Legendary Director
Marilyn Ann Moss
Veit Harlan: The Life and Work of a Nazi Filmmaker
Frank Noack
Harry Langdon: King of Silent Comedy
Gabriella Oldham and Mabel Langdon
Mavericks: Interviews with the World's Iconoclast Filmmakers
Gerald Peary
Charles Walters: The Director Who Made Hollywood Dance
Brent Phillips
Some Like It Wilder: The Life and Controversial Films of Billy Wilder
Gene D. Phillips
Ann Dvorak: Hollywood's Forgotten Rebel
Christina Rice
Mean . . . Moody . . . Magnificent! Jane Russell and the Marketing of a Hollywood Legend
Christina Rice
Fay Wray and Robert Riskin: A Hollywood Memoir
Victoria Riskin
Lewis Milestone: Life and Films
Harlow Robinson
Michael Curtiz: A Life in Film
Alan K. Rode
Ryan's Daughter: The Making of an Irish Epic
Paul Benedict Rowan
Arthur Penn: American Director
Nat Segaloff

Film's First Family: The Untold Story of the Costellos
 Terry Chester Shulman
Claude Rains: An Actor's Voice
 David J. Skal with Jessica Rains
Barbara La Marr: The Girl Who Was Too Beautiful for Hollywood
 Sherri Snyder
Lionel Barrymore: Character and Endurance in Hollywood's Golden Age
 Kathleen Spaltro
Buzz: The Life and Art of Busby Berkeley
 Jeffrey Spivak
Victor Fleming: An American Movie Master
 Michael Sragow
Aline MacMahon: Hollywood, the Blacklist, and the Birth of Method Acting
 John Stangeland
My Place in the Sun: Life in the Golden Age of Hollywood and Washington
 George Stevens, Jr.
Hollywood Presents Jules Verne: The Father of Science Fiction on Screen
 Brian Taves
Thomas Ince: Hollywood's Independent Pioneer
 Brian Taves
Picturing Peter Bogdanovich: My Conversations with the New Hollywood Director
 Peter Tonguette
Jessica Lange: An Adventurer's Heart
 Anthony Uzarowski
Carl Theodor Dreyer and Ordet: *My Summer with the Danish Filmmaker*
 Jan Wahl
Wild Bill Wellman: Hollywood Rebel
 William Wellman Jr.
Harvard, Hollywood, Hitmen, and Holy Men: A Memoir
 Paul W. Williams
The Warner Brothers
 Chris Yogerst
Clarence Brown: Hollywood's Forgotten Master
 Gwenda Young
The Queen of Technicolor: Maria Montez in Hollywood
 Tom Zimmerman